LITHUANIAN-ENGLISH ENGLISH-LITHUANIAN Dictionary & Phrasebook

LITHUANIAN-ENGLISH
ENGLISH-LITHUANIAN
Dictionary & Phrasebook

Jurgita Baltrušaitytė

HIPPOCRENE BOOKS, INC.
New York

Seventh printing, 2015.

For information, address:
Hippocrene Books, Inc.
171 Madison Avenue
New York, NY 10016
www.hippocrenebooks.com

Library of Congress Cataloging-in-Publication Data

Baltrusaityte, Jurgita.
Lithuanian-English, English-Lithuanian dictionary & phrasebook / Jurgita Baltrusaityte.
p. cm.
ISBN-13: 978-0-7818-1009-8
ISBN-10: 0-7818-1009-4
1. Lithuanian language--Dictionaries--English. 2. English language--Dictionaries--Lithuanian. 3. English language--Conversation and phrase books--Lithuanian. I. Title: Lithuanian-English, English-Lithuanian dictionary and phrasebook. II. Title.

PG8679.B27 2004
491'.92321--dc22

2004042465

TABLE OF CONTENTS

ACKNOWLEDGMENTS

My deepest appreciation and gratitude is given to the following people whose assistance made this project possible:

Dr. Giedrius Subačius for his insight, expertise, and time spent on editing my writing.

My beloved parents, Judita Baltrušaitienė and Jurgis Baltrušaitis, for all that I am today and for their long-distance moral support, pray, trust, and belief in me.

Petronėlė Paškauskienė, for her kindness and valuable suggestions.

Teresė Bogutienė, Jonas Boguta, and Arūnas Deniušis for technical assistance and support.

INTRODUCTION

Lithuania

Lithuania, a beautiful heart-shaped country of amber, sandy beaches, lakes, forests, and lovely churches, is located by the Baltic Sea, in the geographic center of Europe.[1] Although small, Lithuania is twice the size of Belgium. It borders with Latvia, Byelorussia, Poland, and Russia (the Kaliningrad Region). As of 2003, Lithuania had 3,463,000 inhabitants about 83% of whom were ethnic Lithuanians. There are Protestants, Jews, Russian Orthodox, and Muslims who live in Lithuania; however, more than 79% of the population claim to be Roman Catholics.

Lithuanian and Latvian are the only existing Baltic languages. It is thought that the two languages were one until the 5th or the 7th century. Phonetically and morphologically, Lithuanian is very similar to Sanskrit.

The name of Lithuania was first mentioned in chronicles in 1009 A.D. The Grand Duchy of Lithuania was formed by Mindaugas, who was crowned Lithuania's first and only king in 1253. In the 15th century, under the rule of Vytautas the Great, Lithuanian lands extended from the Baltic to the Black Sea. It was one of the strongest and largest countries in Europe. In 1569, the Lublin Union was signed, and a Polish-Lithuanian state was established. This state existed until 1795 when Russia, Austria, and Prussia divided the country among themselves. Czarist Russia annexed the Lithuanian part of the state.

In 1918, Lithuania reemerged as the Independent Republic of Lithuania only to be occupied by the Soviet

[1]According to the French National Geographic Institute, the center of Europe lies at 54°51′N and 25°19′ E (i.e., about 20 kilometers north of Vilnius).

Union in 1940. In 1941, Lithuania was occupied by Germany and in 1944 by the Soviet Union once again. Lithuania lost about 30% of its population during the World War II and the years that followed. The loss was one of the heaviest in Europe. To illustrate, in 1941, about 35,000 people were deported to Siberia by the Soviets; in 1941–1944, the Nazi genocide of Lithuanian Jews took place (250,000 people); in 1943–1944, 10,000 people were deported to Germany for labor and 60,000 emigrated to the West; in 1945–1953, an estimated 250,000 people were deported to Siberia; and, in 1941–1951, about 50,000 participants of the Lithuanian resistance and 25,000 Soviet collaborators died in Lithuanian forests.

Lithuania was annexed by the Soviet Union until March 11 of 1990, when the Supreme Council of the Republic of Lithuania declared the restoration of Lithuania's Independence. Lithuania was the first country to break free from the Soviet Union. The other two Baltic countries, Estonia and Latvia, followed shortly after.

Today, Lithuania is a democratic country that is prepared to join both the European Union and NATO in 2004. Citizens of the United States of America, the United Kingdom, the European Union, and Australia do not need visas to enter Lithuania.

More information about Lithuania can be found on the web sites of the Lithuanian Tourism Department (www.tourism.lt) or Lithuanian Development Agency (www.lda.lt) as well as other internet sites.

THE LITHUANIAN ALPHABET

Letter	*Pronunciation*	*English Equivalent*
a	ah	f**a**ther (when long), h**u**ngry (when short)
ą	ah (nasal)	f**a**ther
b	beh	**b**ig
c	tseh	gri**ts**
č	cheh	**ch**ocolate
d	deh	**d**oor
e	eh (broad)	ch**a**t (when long), g**e**t (when short)
ę	eh (nasal)	ch**a**t (always long)
ė	eh (narrow)	m**e**n (always long)
f	ef	**f**un
g	geh	**g**ood
h	hah	**h**ome
i	i (short)	b**i**g
į	i (nasal)	k**ee**n
y	i (long)	k**ee**n
j	yot	**y**ogurt
k	kah	**k**ing
l	el	**l**oud
m	em	**m**ouse
n	en	**n**et
o	oh	c**au**ght (when long), **O**slo (when short)
p	peh	**p**oet
r	er	**r**ow (rolling)
s	es	*s*alt
š	esh	**sh**ot
t	teh	**t**ool
u	uh (short)	p**u**t, b**oo**k

ų	uh (nasal)	d**oo**med
ū	uh (long)	d**oo**med
v	veh	**v**egetable
z	zeh	**z**ero
ž	zheh	plea**s**ure

PLEASE NOTE: The Lithuanian-English dictionary follows the Lithuanian alphabet. Therefore, in the Lithuanian dictionary the letter Y precedes the letter J, etc. Furthermore, the Lithuanian consonants **č, š, ž** form their own subentries, while Lithuanian vowels do not follow a strict alphabetization system.

PRONUNCIATION GUIDE

The Vowels

The following vowels are always *long: ą, ę, ė, o, y, į, ū, ų,* and *i* and *u* are always *short. A* and *e* may be *long or short. O* is *short* only in words of foreign origin (e.g., ***O**slas* (Oslo), *chr**o**mas* (chrome)).

The Diphthongs

Diphthong	*Pronunciation*	*English Equivalent*
ai	y	*m**y**, sh**y***
au	ow	*h**ow***
ei	ay	*l**ay***
ie	ye	**ye**llow
ui	uey, ou	*chop-**suey**, L**ou**ie*
uo	ou	*Plym**ou**th*

Uo is pronounced like Italian *uo* in ***b**uo**no**.*

Mixed Diphthongs

a, e, i, u + l, m, n, r =	**al, el, il, ul,** **am, em, im, um,** **an, en, in, un,** **ar, er, ir, ur**

Mixed diphthongs are straightforward in their pronunciation.

The Consonants

The most important difference between English and Lithuanian consonants is that Lithuanian *p*, *t*, and *k* are not aspired (i.e., there is no puff of breath after them).

Another difference is that, in Lithuanian, there are soft (i.e., palatized) and hard (i.e., unpalatized) consonants. Consonants are always palatized before the diphthong *ie* and before front vowels *i, į, y, e, ę, ė*. Furthermore, if *i* precedes *a, ą, o, u, ų,* and *ū*, it indicates palatalization. That is, *i* is not pronounced as a separate sound in this position; it only softens the preceding consonant. For example, ***l*** is hard in ***lūpa*** (lip) but soft in ***liūtas*** (lion).

The following three digraphs occur in Lithuanian:

dz pronounced as *ds* in la***ds***
dž pronounced as *j* in ***j***azz (*džiazas*) or *g* in a**g**itated
ch pronounced as *Spanish j* in Don ***J***uan

Accent (stress)

Unlike in some other languages (e.g., French or Polish), in Lithuanian, there is no one rule for stressed syllabi, and stress appears to "jump" around quite inconsistently. For this reason, in declension patterns, in conjugation pattern, and in phrases at the end of this book, the syllable that is stressed will be underlined.

In colloquial Lithuanian a final stressed syllable is sometimes dropped. In this case, the colloquial stress moves by one syllable back to the front of a word.

Colloquial Lithuanian stress is sometimes used slightly differently from the standard Lithuanian that is presented in this book.

ABBREVIATIONS

acc.	accusative
adj.	adjective
adv.	adverb
arch.	archaic
col.	colloquial
conj.	conjunction
comp.	comparative
dat.	dative
f.	feminine
fin.	financial
gen.	genitive
instr.	instrumental
inter.	interjection
irr.	irregular
loc.	locative
m.	masculine
m./f.	masculine and feminine
med.	medical
n.	noun
n.d.	not declined
nom.	nominative
num.	numeral
part.	particle
pl.	plural
polit.	political
prep.	preposition
pron.	pronoun
sing.	singular
techn.	technical term
theat.	theatrical
v.	verb
vlg.	vulgar
voc.	vocative

A BRIEF GRAMMAR

Articles

There are no articles (i.e., substitutes for English *a, an, the*) in the Lithuanian language.

Nouns

There are two genders in Lithuanian nouns: masculine and feminine. A handful of nouns can be both feminine and masculine. All nouns that end in **-as** are masculine. Nouns have singular and plural forms. Some nouns have only a singular form (e.g., *medus* (honey, m.), *kraujas* (blood, m.), *cukrus* (sugar, m.)), and some have only a plural form (e.g., *žirklės* (scissors, f.), *kelnės* (trousers, f.)).

Many of the words that refer to people's professions or nationalities have the same root but different endings for feminine and masculine forms. For example, all feminine forms of nationalities end in **-ė** (e.g., *amerikie**tis*** (American, m.), *amerikiet**ė*** (American, f.), *kin**as*** (Chinese, m.) *kin**ė*** (Chinese, f.), *ind**as*** (Indian, m.), *ind**ė*** (Indian, f.).

With professions, there is no such uniformity. When the masculine ending for a profession is **-jas**, the equivalent feminine ending is **-ja**. For instance, *mokyto**jas*** (teacher, m.), *mokyto**ja*** (teacher, f.), *vairuoto**jas*** (driver, m.), *vairuoto**ja*** (driver, f.). Otherwise, the feminine ending is **-ė**. For example, *bankinink**as*** (banker, m.), *bankinink**ė*** (banker, f.), *profesor**ius*** (professor, m.), *profesor**ė*** (professor, f.), *sekretor**ius*** (secretary, m.), *sekretor**ė*** (secretary, f.), *batsiuv**ys*** (shoemaker, m.), *batsiuv**ė*** (shoemaker, f.).

There are seven declensional cases in Lithuanian:

1. Nominative — who? what?—*kas?*
2. Genitive — whose? of what?—*ko?*

3.	Dative	to whom?—*kam?*
4.	Accusative	whom? what?—*ką?*
5.	Instrumental	with whom? with what?—*(su) kuo?*
6.	Locative	where? in what?—*kur? kame?*
7.	Vocative	*used for addressing, calling*

The basic, nominative, form will always be given in the dictionary along with the noun's declension number in parenthesis. The following tables will assist you in determining what ending to use in what case.

The First Declension of Nouns

Nouns that belong to the first declension are masculine and have the following endings: ***-as***, ***-is***, ***-ys*** (e.g., *stalas* (table), *brolis* (brother), *arklys* (horse)). The stressed syllable is underlined for your convenience. The sounds that are in parentheses () are usually not pronounced in colloquial Lithuanian.

Singular

N.	stal**as**,	brol**is**,	arkl**ys**
G.	stal**o**,	brol**io**,	arkl**io**
D.	stal**ui**,	brol**iui**,	arkl**iui**
A.	stal**ą**,	brol**į**,	arkl**į**
I.	stal**u**,	brol**iu**,	arkl**iu**
L.	stal**e**,	brol**y(je)**,	arkl**y(je)**
V.	stal**e**!	brol**i**!	arkl**y**!

Plural

N.	stal**ai**,	brol**iai**,	arkl**iai**
G.	stal**ų**,	brol**ių**,	arkl**ių**
D.	stal**am(s)**,	brol**iam(s)**,	arkl**iam(s)**
A.	stal**us**,	brol**ius**,	arkl**ius**
I.	stal**ais**,	brol**iais**,	arkl**iais**
L.	stal**uose**,	brol**iuose**,	arkl**iuose**
V.	stal**ai**!	brol**iai**!	arkl**iai**!

The Second Declension of Nouns

Nouns that belong to the second declension are feminine and end in **-a**, **-ė**, and **-i** (e.g., *mama* (mother), *gėlė* (flower), *marti* (daughter-in-law)). The type of *marti* is very rare, only two nouns are present in standard Lithuanian (*marti*, *pati* (wife)).

Singular

N.	mama,	gėlė,	marti
G.	mamos,	gėlės,	marčios
D.	mamai,	gėlei,	marčiai
A.	mamą,	gėlę,	marčią
I.	mama,	gėle,	marčia
L.	mamoj(e),	gėlėj(e),	marčioj(e)
V.	mama!	gėle!	marti!

Please note that **t** changes into **č** when declining *marti*.

Plural

N.	mamos,	gėlės,	marčios
G.	mamų,	gėlių,	marčių
D.	mamom(s),	gėlėm(s),	marčiom(s)
A.	mamas,	gėles,	marčias
I.	mamom(is),	gėlėm(is),	marčiom(is)
L.	mamose,	gėlėse,	marčiose
V.	mamos!	gėlės!	marčios!

Third Declension of Nouns

Feminine (e.g., *akis* (eye)) and masculine (e.g., *dantis* (tooth)) nouns that end in **-is** in nominative and **-ies** in genitive belong to the third declension of nouns.

Singular

N.	akis,	dantis
G.	akies,	danties

D.	ak**iai**,	dan**čiui**
A.	ak**į**,	dan**tį**
I.	ak**im(i)**,	dant**im(i)**
L.	ak**y(je)**,	dant**y(je)**
V.	ak**ie**!	dan**tie**!

Please note that **t** changes into **č** in dative of *dantis*.

Plural

N.	ak**ys**,	dan**tys**
G.	ak**ių**,	dan**tų**
D.	ak**im(s)**,	dant**im(s)**
A.	ak**is**,	dan**tis**
I.	ak**im(is)**,	dant**im(is)**
L.	ak**yse**,	dant**yse**
V.	ak**ys**!	dan**tys**!

The Fourth Declension of Nouns

Nouns that end in **-us** and **-ius** belong to the fourth declension. They are all masculine (e.g., *žmogus* (human being, man), *sūnus* (son), *profesorius* (professor)).

Singular

N.	žmog**us**,	sūn**us**,	profesor**ius**
G.	žmog**aus**,	sūn**aus**,	profesor**iaus**
D.	žmog**ui**,	sūn**ui**,	profesor**iui**
A.	žmog**ų**,	sūn**ų**,	profesor**ių**
I.	žmog**um(i)**,	sūn**um(i)**,	profesor**ium(i)**
L.	žmog**uj(e)**,	sūn**uj(e)**,	profesor**iuj(e)**
V.	žmog**au**!	sūn**au**!	profesor**iau**!

Plural

N.	žmon**ės**,	sūn**ūs**,	profesor**iai**
G.	žmon**ių**,	sūn**ų**,	profesor**ių**
D.	žmon**ėm(s)**,	sūn**um(s)**,	profesor**iam(s)**

A.	žmones,	sūnus,	profesorius
I.	žmonėm(is),	sūnumis,	profesoriais
L.	žmonėse,	sūnuose,	profesoriuose
V.	žmonės!	sūnūs!	profesoriai!

Please note that plural for *žmogus* is declined differently. All other words that end in **-us** and **-ius** have the same endings as *sūnus* or *profesorius* when they are declined in plural.

The Fifth Declension of Nouns

This declension has a limited number of nouns some of which are irregular. Feminine nouns that end in **-uo** (*sesuo* (sister)) and **-ė** (*duktė* (daughter)) in nominative (*gen.* **-ers**) and masculine nouns that end in **-uo** (*vanduo* (water), *akmuo* (stone), *dubuo* (bowl), *šuo* (dog)) in nominative (*gen.* **-ens**) belong to the fifth declension.

Singular

N.	vanduo,	šuo (irregular),	sesuo,	duktė
G.	vandens,	šuns,	sesers,	dukters
D.	vandeniui,	šuniui,	seseriai,	dukteriai
A.	vandenį,	šunį,	seserį,	dukterį
I.	vandeniu,	šuniu,	seseria,	dukteria
L.	vandeny(je),	šuny(je),	sesery(je),	duktery(je)
V.	vandenie!	šunie!	seserie!	dukterie!

Plural

N.	vandenys,	šunys,	seserys,	dukterys
G.	vandenų,	šunų,	seserų,	dukterų
D.	vandenim(s),	šunim(s),	seserim(s),	dukterim(s)
A.	vandenis,	šunis,	seseris,	dukteris
I.	vandenim(is),	šunim(is),	seserim(is),	dukterim(is)
L.	vandenyse,	šunyse,	seseryse,	dukteryse
V.	vandenys!	šunys!	seserys!	dukterys!

Adjectives

Like nouns, Lithuanian adjectives have two genders: masculine and feminine. They are singular and plural.

All masculine adjectives end in **-s**.

There are three declensions of adjectives in Lithuanian.

First Declension of Adjectives

All adjectives that end in **-(i)as** (e.g. *mažas* (small, little); *žalias* (green)) in the masculine nominative singular belong to the first declension. The feminine form is formed by dropping the **-s** in the nominative singular.

Singular

	Masculine	*Feminine*
N.	maž**as**,	maž**a**
G.	maž**o**,	maž**os**
D.	maž**am**,	maž**ai**
A.	maž**ą**,	maž**ą**
I.	maž**u**,	maž**a**
L.	maž**am(e)**,	maž**oj(e)**

Plural

	Masculine	*Feminine*
N.	maž**i**,	maž**os**
G.	maž**ų**,	maž**ų**
D.	maž**iem(s)**,	maž**om(s)**
A.	maž**us**,	maž**as**
I.	maž**ais**,	maž**om(is)**
L.	maž**uose**,	maž**ose**

The final **-s** of the D. pl., the final **-e** of the L. sg., and the final **-is** of the I. pl. f. is frequently dropped in colloquial

Lithuanian. This tendency is observed for the second and third declension adjectives as well. Sounds that are dropped in colloquial Lithuanian are given in parentheses ().

The neuter form is formed by dropping the **-s** from the first and second declension N. sg. m. (e.g., *Kaip žalia!* (How green!), V. (e.g. *Čia gražu* (It is beautiful here). The neuter form is not declined, and it always goes separately without a following noun (as it is usual with masculine or feminine adjectives).

Second Declension of Adjectives

All adjectives that end in **-us** (e.g. *gražus* (beautiful)) in masculine and **-i** in feminine nominative singular belong to the second declension.

Singular

	Masculine	*Feminine*
N.	gražus, platus,	graži, plati
G.	gražaus, plataus,	gražios, plačios
D.	gražiam, plačiam,	gražiai, plačiai
A.	gražų, platų,	gražią, plačią
I.	gražiu, plačiu,	gražia, plačia
L.	gražiam(e), plačiam(e),	gražioj(e), plačioj(e)

Plural

	Masculine	*Feminine*
N.	gražūs, platūs,	gražios, plačios
G.	gražių, plačių	gražių, plačių
D.	gražiem(s), platiem(s),	gražiom(s), plačiom(s)
A.	gražius, plačius,	gražias, plačias
I.	gražiais, plačiais,	gražiom(is), plačiom(is)
L.	gražiuose, plačiuose,	gražiose, plačiose

Please note that **-ti-** and **-di-** are replaced by **-či-** and **-dži-** respectively before the vowels **a**, **o**, and **u**.

Third Declension of Adjectives

Adjectives that end in **-is** in masculine and **-ė** in feminine nominative singular belong to the third declension.

These adjectives are frequently derived from nouns (e.g., *plastmasė*→*plastmasinis* (plastic→plastic), *auksas*→*auksinis* (gold→golden), *medis*→*medinis* (wood→wooden)).

Singular

	Masculine	*Feminine*
N.	auksin**is**,	auksin**ė**
G.	auksin**io**,	auksin**ės**
D.	auksin**iam**,	auksin**ei**
A.	auksin**į**,	auksin**ę**
I.	auksin**iu**,	auksin**e**
L.	auksin**iam(e)**,	auksin**ėj(e)**

Plural

	Masculine	*Feminine*
N.	auksin**iai**,	auksin**ės**
G.	auksin**ių**,	auksin**ių**
D.	auksin**iam(s)**,	auksin**ėm(s)**
A.	auksin**ius**,	auksin**es**
I.	auksin**iais**,	auksin**ėm(is)**
L.	auksin**iuose**,	auksin**ėse**

Comparison of Adjectives

Like in English, there are three degrees of comparison in Lithuanian: the positive, the comparative, and the superlative.

The Positive Degree

The positive degree denotes a characteristic or quality (e.g., *mažas* (small), *gražus* (beautiful), *medinis* (wooden)).

The Comparative Degree

The comparative degree is formed by dropping the ending **-(i)as**, **-us** or **-is** of the masculine singular form and adding **-esnis** (m.) or **-esnė** (f.) (e.g., *mažesnis* (smaller)). Positive degree adjectives are declined above.

Adjectives in comparative degree are declined like first declension adjectives.

Singular

	Masculine	*Feminine*
N.	mažesn**is**,	mažesn**ė**
G.	mažesn**io**,	mažesn**ės**
D.	mažesn**iam**,	mažesn**ei**
A.	mažesn**į**,	mažesn**ę**
I.	mažesn**iu**,	mažesn**e**
L.	mažesn**iam(e)**,	mažesn**ėj(e)**

Plural

	Masculine	*Feminine*
N.	mažesn**i**,	mažesn**ės**
G.	mažesn**ių**,	mažesn**ių**
D.	mažesn**iem(s)**,	mažesn**ėm(s)**
A.	mažesn**ius**,	mažesn**es**
I.	mažesn**iais**,	mažesn**ėm(is)**
L.	mažesn**iuose**,	mažesn**ėse**

The comparative degree indicates a greater degree of some quality in one object than in another. For example, *Mano galva mažesnė negu tavo* (My head is smaller than yours), *Jo namas didesnis už mano* (His house is bigger than mine). English "than" is translated by Lithuanian *negu, nei,* and *už.*

The Superlative Degree

The superlative degree is formed by dropping the ending **-(i)as**, **-us**, or **-is** of the masculine singular form and adding **-iausias** (m.) or **-iausia** (f.). Please note that stem endings **-d-** and **-t-** are replaced by **-dž-** and **-č-** respectively. This degree is declined as first declension adjectives of positive degree.

The superlative degree indicates that an object has the highest possible degree of some quality. For example, *Mano suknelė gražiausia* (My dress is the most beautiful).

To indicate the same degree of some quality, use *toks pat* (m.) or *tokia pati* (f.) (e.g., *Aš toks pat aukštas kaip jis* (I am as tall as he)).

Comparison of Neuter Adjectives

Neuter adjectives have **-iau** and **-iausia** endings in comparative and superlative respectively. For example, *Čia gražiau* (It is more beautiful here), *Šiame kambaryje šalčiausia* (It is the coldest in this room).

Participles

There are participles in Lithuanian. Functionally they are similar to adjectives, that's why they are marked as adjectives in both dictionaries of this books (in Lithuanian grammars participles are defined as forms of verb). Words that end in *–uotas, –a; otas, -a; -(i)amas, -a; -ęs; -usi;* and some other (*civilizuotas, -a; garbanotas, -a; lemiamas, -a; nevedęs; nuliūdęs, -usi; ištekėjusi*) most often are marked as *adj.* but they are participles. This is made for the convenience sake as both adjectives and participles denote features attributed to things.

Adverbs

Adverbs are formed 1) from the first declension adjectives (**-as**, **-a**) by dropping the **-(i)as** and adding **-(i)ai** or 2) from the second declension adjectives (**-us**, **-i**) by dropping the **-us** and adding **-iai** (e.g. *gražus*→*gražiai* (beautiful→beautifully), *siauras*→*siaurai* (narrow→narrowly). Some frequent adverbs have no **-(i)ai** ending, e.g. *toli* (far), *beveik* (almost), *maždaug* (approximately).

Comparison of Adverbs

The comparative degree of adverbs ends in **-iau** (instead of **-ai** or **-iai** in positive degree). For adverbs that end in **-ai**, the superlative ending is **-iausiai**. For adverbs that do not end in **-ai**, the superlative ending is **-iausia**. For example, *gražiai*→*gražiau*→*gražiausiai* (beautifully→more beautifully→most beautifully), *arti*→*arčiau*→*arčiausiai* (near→nearer→nearest). Please note that **-d-** and **-t-** are replaced by **-dž-** and **-č-** before **-iau**.

Pronouns

The use of personal pronouns in Lithuanian is similar to that in English. One must remember, however, that "it" does not exist in Lithuanian as all nouns are either masculine or feminine. For example, one will refer to *stalas* (table) as *jis* (he) and to *kėdė* (chair) as *ji* (she).

Declension of Personal Pronouns

Singular

	I—aš	*You—tu*	*He—jis*	*She—ji*
N.	aš,	tu,	jis,	ji
G.	manęs,	tavęs,	jo,	jos

	I—aš	*You—tu*	*He—jis*	*She—ji*
D.	man,	tau,	jam,	jai
A.	mane,	tave,	jį,	ją
I.	manim(i),	tavim(i),	juo,	ja
L.	many(je),	tavy(je),	jam(e),	joj(e)

Plural

	We—mes	*You—jūs*	*They(m.)—jie*	*They(f.)—jos*
N.	mes,	jūs,	jie,	jos
G.	mūsų,	jūsų,	jų,	jų
D.	mum(s),	jum(s),	jiem(s),	jom(s)
A.	mus,	jus,	juos,	jas
I.	mumis,	jumis,	jais,	jom(is)
L.	mumyse,	jumyse,	juose,	jose

Please note that, like French *tu* or German *du*, Lithuanian *tu* (you) is a familiar form that is used with close friends, children, closest family members, and with God. *Jūs* (you) is used in all other situations. *Jūs* (you) is also used to address groups of people (i.e. more than one person).

Possessive Pronouns

My, mine—mano
Your, yours—tavo
His—jo
Her, hers—jos
Our, ours—mūsų
Your, yours—jūsų
Their, theirs (m.)—jų
Their, theirs (f.)—jų

Savo is a reflexive possessive pronoun that always refers to the subject of the sentence. For example, ***Ji** skaito **savo** knygą* (**She** is reading **her** book), ***Jis** mato **savo** mamą* (**He** sees **his** mother), but ***Ji** skaito **jo** knygą* (**She** is reading **his** book).

Verbs

There are three conjugations of verbs in Lithuanian. The conjugation is determined by the third person, present tense. First conjugation verbs end in **-a**, second conjugation verbs in **-i**, and third conjugation verbs in **-o**. A short Lithuanian word ***Alio!*** (Hello!) used when answering the phone may assist in remembering what ending belongs to which conjugation.

Present Tense

1st Conjugation: *kepti* (to bake), *puošti* (to decorate), *eiti* (to walk, to go; irregular), *būti* (to be; irregular). In colloquial Lithuanian, the final **-i** is often dropped, e.g. *kept*, *puošt*, *eit*, *būt*, etc.

Aš kep**u**, puoš**iu**, ein**u**, es**u**
Tu kep**i**, puoš**i**, ein**i**, es**i**
Jis, ji kep**a**, puoš**ia**, ein**a**, yr**a**
Mes kep**am(e)**, puoš**iam(e)**, ein**am(e)**, es**am(e)**
Jūs kep**at(e)**, puoš**iat(e)**, ein**at(e)**, es**at(e)**
Jie, jos kep**a**, puoš**ia**, ein**a**, yr**a**

2nd Conjugation: *mylėti* (to love)

Aš myl**iu**
Tu myl**i**
Jis, ji myl**i**
Mes myl**im(e)**
Jūs myl**it(e)**
Jie, jos myl**i**

3rd Conjugation: *matyti* (to see)

Aš mat**au**
Tu mat**ai**
Jis, ji mat**o**
Mes mat**om(e)**
Jūs mat**ot(e)**
Jie, jos mat**o**

Past Tense

1st Conjugation: *kepti* (to bake), *puošti* (to decorate), *eiti* (to walk, to go; irregular), *būti* (to be; irregular), *vesti* (to marry, to lead, to guide).

Aš kep**iau**, puoš**iau**, ėj**au**, buv**au**, ved**žiau**
Tu kep**ei**, puoš**ei**, ėj**ai**, buv**ai**, ved**ei**
Jis, ji kep**ė**, puoš**ė**, ėj**o**, buv**o**, ved**ė**
Mes kep**ėm(e)**, puoš**ėm(e)**, ėj**om(e)**, buv**om(e)**, ved**ėm(e)**
Jūs kep**ėt(e)**, puoš**ėt(e)**, ėj**ot(e)**, buv**ot(e)**, ved**ėt(e)**
Jie, jos kep**ė**, puoš**ė**, ėj**o**, buv**o**, ved**ė**

2nd Conjugation: *mylėti* (to love).

Aš mylė**jau**
Tu mylė**jai**
Jis, ji myl**ėjo**
Mes mylė**jom(e)**
Jūs mylė**jot(e)**
Jie, jos myl**ėjo**

3rd Conjugation: *matyti* (to see), *rašyti* (to write), *žinoti* (to know).

Aš ma**čiau**, ra**šiau**, žino**jau**
Tu mat**ei**, raš**ei**, žino**jai**
Jis, ji mat**ė**, raš**ė**, žino**jo**
Mes mat**ėm(e)**, raš**ėm(e)**, žino**jom(e)**
Jūs mat**ėt(e)**, raš**ėt(e)**, žino**jot(e)**
Jie, jos mat**ė**, raš**ė**, žino**jo**

Please note that **-t-** and **-d-** change into **-č-** and **-dž-** in first person. Also, for 2nd and 3rd conjugation verbs with **-ė-** and **-o-** in infinitive stem, the final **-ti** is dropped and **-j-** is inserted between the stem and the ending.

Frequentative Past Tense

Frequentative past tense denotes an action that used to happen (i.e., happened frequently and repeatedly). For example, *Kai buvau maža, **žaisdavau** su lėlėmis* (When I was little, **I used to play** with dolls).

Frequentative past tense is formed by dropping the infinitive ending **-ti** and adding **-dav-** in front of the past tense endings: singular 1) **-au**, 2) **-ai**, 3) **-o**; plural 1) **-om(e)**, 2) **-ot(e)**, 3) **-o**.

Verbs of all conjugations have identical endings. For example, *skaityti* (to read):

Aš skaity**davau**
Tu skaity**davai**
Jis, ji skaity**davo**
Mes skaity**davom(e)**
Jūs skaity**davot(e)**
Jie, jos skaity**davo**

Future Tense

Future tense is formed by dropping the infinitive ending **-ti** and adding the future ending according to the person: singular 1) **-(s)iu**, 2) **-(s)i**, 3) **-(s)**; plural 1) **-(s)im(e)**, 2) **-(s)it(e)**, 3) **-(s)**. Please note that the indicator of the future tense **-s-** sometimes disappear because of the following contractions:
s + s = s, **š + s = š,** **z + s = s,** **ž + s = š**

1st Conjugation: *kepti* (to bake), *puošti* (to decorate), *eiti* (to go, to walk; irregular), *būti* (to be; irregular).

Aš kep**siu**, puoš**iu**, ei**siu**, bū**siu**
Tu kep**si**, puoš**i**, ei**si**, bū**si**
Jis, ji kep**s**, puoš, ei**s**, bu**s**
Mes kep**sim(e)**, puoš**im(e)**, ei**sim(e)**, bū**sim(e)**
Jūs kep**sit(e)**, puoš**it(e)**, ei**sit(e)**, bū**sit(e)**
Jie, jos kep**s**, puoš, ei**s**, bu**s**

2nd Conjugation and 3rd Conjugation verbs have the same future tense endings as 1st Conjugation verbs.

Reflexive Verbs

Reflexive verbs indicate self-directed action. There are two groups of reflexive verbs in Lithuanian: *simple reflexive verbs* (i.e., the reflexive particle **-si-** or **-s** is added at the end) and *compound reflexive verbs* (i.e., **-si-** is inserted between the prefix and the verb proper). The latter group also includes all reflexive verbs in their negative form (e.g., *aš prausiuo**si*** (I am washing myself) is a simple reflexive verb, but *aš **nesi**prausiu* (I am not washing myself) is a compound reflexive verb).

Compound reflexive verb are conjugated as simple verbs in all tenses, only the **-si-** is inserted. For example, *sužeisti* (to hurt somebody), *susi**ž**eisti* (to hurt oneself):

Aš sužeid**žiu**, sus**i**žeid**žiu**
Tu sužei**di**, sus**i**žei**di**
Jis, ji sužeid**žia**, sus**i**žeid**žia**
Mes sužeid**žiam(e)**, sus**i**žeid**žiam(e)**
Jūs sužeid**žiat(e)**, sus**i**žeid**žiat(e)**
Jie, jos sužeid**žia**, sus**i**žeid**žia**

Simple reflexive verbs are more difficult to conjugate.

Present Tense

1st Conjugation: *prausti* (to wash), ***praustis*** (to wash oneself)

Aš praus**iu**, praus**iuosi**
Tu praus**i**, praus**iesi**
Jis, ji praus**ia**, prausiasi
Mes praus**iam(e)**, praus**iamės**

Jūs prausiat(e), prausiatės
Jie, jos prausia, prausiasi

2nd Conjugation: *tikėti* (to believe), ***tikėtis*** (to hope, to expect)

Aš tikiu, tikiuosi
Tu tiki, tikiesi
Jis, ji tiki, tikisi
Mes tikim(e), tikimės
Jūs tikit(e), tikitės
Jie, jos tiki, tikisi

3rd Conjugation: *mokyti* (to teach), ***mokytis*** (to learn, to study)

Aš mokau, mokausi
Tu mokai, mokaisi
Jis, ji moko, mokosi
Mes mokom(e), mokomės
Jūs mokot(e), mokotės
Jie, jos moko, mokosi

Past Tense and Past Frequentative Tense

In past tense and past frequentative tense, reflexive verbs are conjugated as nonreflexive verbs, only the **-si-** is added at the end (for simple) or between the main verb and prefix (for compound). For example, *aš mokiau* (I taught), *aš mokiau**si*** (I learned), *aš sužeidžiau* (I hurt (someone)), *aš su**si**žeidžiau* (I hurt myself), *aš mokydavau* (I used to teach), *aš mokydavau**si*** (I used to study), *aš sužeisdavau* (I used to hurt (someone)), *aš su**si**žeisdavau* (I used to hurt myself).

Future Tense

As in the past tense, in compound and negated reflexive verbs, **-si-** is inserted between the prefix (or the negative particle) and the verbal stem. For example, *aš su**si**žeisiu* (I will hurt myself).

Simple reflexive verbs are conjugated as follows (e.g., *mokytis* (to learn)):

Aš moky**siuos(i)**
Tu moky**sies(i)**
Jis, ji moky**sis**
Mes moky**simės**
Jūs moky**sitės**
Jie, jos moky**sis**

Imperative

There are three forms of imperative in Lithuanian with the suffix **-k-** (e.g., *mokyti* (to teach)):

2nd person, singular:

moky + k = mokyk! (teach!)

2nd person, plural:

moky + kit(e) = mokykit(e)! (teach!)

1st person, plural:

moky + kim(e) = mokykim(e)! (teach!)

Reflexive verbs follow the following patterns (e.g., *mokytis* (to learn, to study):

2nd person, singular:

moky + kis = mokykis! (study!)

2nd person, plural:

moky + kitės = mokykitės! (study!)

1st person, plural:

moky + kimės = mokykimės! (let's study!)

Please note that if the stem ends in **g** or **k**, these letters are dropped, and **k** is added. For instance, *bėgti* (to run) → bė**g** + k = bėk! (run!)

Word Order

The formal word order in Lithuanian is the following:

Subject + verb + object (direct or indirect) + adverb + infinitive + other parts of the sentence.

However, in both written and spoken Lithuanian, the word order is free. For example, the sentence *Today I saw a beautiful girl in the movies* may be written in any of the following ways:

Aš mačiau gražią mergaitę kine šiandien.
Šiandien aš mačiau gražią mergaitę kine.
Šiandien kine aš mačiau gražią mergaitę.
Gražią mergaitę mačiau aš kine šiandien.
Gražią mergaitę aš šiandien mačiau kine.
Kine šiandien aš mačiau gražią mergaitę.
Kine gražią mergaitę šiandien aš mačiau.

A word that is used at the end of a sentence frequently has a logical stress, making some minor stylistic difference among these sentences.

Questions

Like in English or French, the simplest way to formulate a question in Lithuanian is to raise your voice at the end of a declarative sentence. For example, *Tu vakar buvai darbe.* → *Tu vakar buvai darbe?* (Yesterday, you were at work. → Yesterday, you were at work?)

The particle **ar** in sentence initial position also indicates an interrogative sentence. For example, ***Ar*** *vakar tu buvai darbe?* (Were you at work yesterday?)

Interrogative Words

Kiek?	How much? How many?
Kaip?	How?
Kur?	Where?
Kodėl?	Why?
Kas?	Who? What?
Su kuo?	With whom?
Kada?	When?
Kuris?	Which one? (m.)
Kuri?	Which one? (f.)
Iš kur?	Where from?
Ką?	What? Whom?
Kam?	What for? For whom?
Koks?	Of what kind? (m.)
Kokia?	Of what kind? (f.)

Negation

The negative particle in Lithuanian is **ne**. **Ne** always precedes the word it negates and most often is written together with verbs, adjectives, and adverbs. **Ne** gives the word an opposite meaning. For example, *aš dirbu* → *aš **ne**dirbu* (I work → I do not work); *Šis namas **ne**gražus* (This house is not beautiful); *Ji **ne**gražiai dainuoja* (She sings not beautifully).

However, **ne** is written separately from nouns, adjectives, and verbs when it contradicts something. For example, *Jis **ne** vairuotojas, bet statybininkas* (He is not a driver but a construction worker); *Ji **ne** davė, o ėmė* (She did not give but took).

Ne is also written separately from pronouns and numerals. For instance, *ne aš* (not I), *ne jūs* (not you), *ne tavo* (not yours), *ne kiekvienas* (not everyone), *ne pirmas* (not first).

Ne and **yra** (i.e., 3rd person of *būti* (to be)) make a contraction **nėra** (is not/are not). For example, *Ji **nėra** gera studentė* (She is not a good student).

The direct object of a negated verb requires the genitive case. For example, *Aš turiu skėtį* (Acc.) (I have an umbrella), but *Aš **neturiu skėčio*** (Gen.) (I do not have an umbrella).

Unlike in English, in Lithuanian, there may be several negations in one sentence. For example, *Vakar aš niekur nėjau* (Yesterday, I didn't go anywhere (Literally: Yesterday, I nowhere didn't go); *Jis niekada nieko nežino* (He never knows anything (Literally: He never nothing doesn't know)).

Conjunctions

The most common Lithuanian conjunctions are the following:

ir	and
bei	and
nes	because (middle of a sentence)
kadangi	because (end of a sentence)
bet	but, however
o	but, and
tačiau	but, however
arba	or
jog	that
kad	that
todėl	therefore
nors	though
kai	when

Prepositions

ant (+Gen.)	on
apie (+Acc.)	about
aplink (+Acc.)	around
be (+Acc.)	without
dėl (+Gen.)	for, because of, due to

iki (+Gen.)	until
iš (+Gen.)	from
išskyrus (+Acc.)	except
į (+Acc.)	to
įstrižai (+Gen.)	diagonally across
lig, ligi (+Gen.)	until
link (+Gen.)	toward
nuo (+Gen.)	since, from
pas (+Acc.)	at (somebody's)
pasak (+Gen.)	according to
per (+Acc.)	across, through, during
po (+Gen.)	after
po (+Acc.)	in (with numerals)
po (+Instr.)	under, after
prie (+Gen.)	near, in the vicinity of
prieš (+Acc.)	before, against, in front of
priešais (+Acc.)	in front of
su (+Instr.)	with
šalia (+Gen.)	beside, next to, close to
tarp (+Gen.)	between
už (+Gen.)	behind
už (+Acc.)	for (what)
viduj (+Gen.)	within, inside of
virš (+Gen.)	above

LITHUANIAN-ENGLISH DICTIONARY

A, Ą

abi *pron. f.* both
abortas *m. (1)* abortion
abu *pron. m.* both
abrikosas *m. (1)* apricot
ačiū *inter.* thank you
adapteris *techn. m. (1)* adapter
adata *f. (2)* needle
administracija *f. (2)* administration
adresas *m. (1)* address
adresatas, -ė *m. (1), f. (2)* addressee
Adventas *m. (1)* Advent
advokatas, -ė *m. (1), f. (2)* attorney
afera *f. (2)* fraud
agentas, -ė *m. (1), f. (2)* agent
agentūra *f. (2)* agency
agurkas *m. (1)* cucumber
aikštė *f. (2)* square
airis, -ė *m. (1), f. (2)* Irish
aiškus, -i *adj. (2)* clear
akademija *f. (2)* academy
akiniai *m. pl. (1)* glasses, spectacles
akis *f. (3)* eye
aklas, -a *adj. (1)* blind
akmuo *m. (5)* stone
akseleratorius *m. (4)* accelerator
aktorius, -ė *m. (4), f. (2)* actor
akustika *f. (2)* acoustics
akvarelė *f. (2)* watercolor
akvariumas *m. (1)* aquarium
albumas *m. (1)* album
alėja *f. (2)* avenue
alergija *f. (2)* allergy
alergiškas, -a *adj. (1)* allergic
alfabetas *m. (1)* alphabet
alga *f. (2)* salary
alijošius *m. (4)* aloe
alio! hello! (when answering the phone)
aliuminis *m. (1)* aluminum
alkanas, -a *adj. (1)* hungry
alkis *m. (1)* hunger
alkti *v. (1)* want to eat, become hungry
alkoholikas, -ė *m. (1), f. (2)* alcoholic
alkoholis *m. (1)* alcohol
alpinistas, -ė *m. (1), f. (2)* mountain-climber
alpti *v. (1)* faint
altorius *m. (4)* altar
aludaris, -ė *m. (1)* brewer
aludė *f. (2)* pub, bar
alus *m. (4)* beer
ambasada *f. (2)* embassy
ambasadorius, -ė *m. (4), f. (2)* ambassador
amerikietis, -ė *m. (1), f. (2)* American
amerikietiškas, -a *adj. (1)* American
amuletas *m. (1)* amulet, good-luck charm
amžius *m. (4)* century, age
ana *pron. f.* that, that one
analitikas, -ė *m. (1), f. (2)* analyst
analizė *f. (2)* analysis
anarchija *f. (2)* anarchy
anas *pron. m.* that, that one
anekdotas *m. (1)* anecdote, joke
aneksija *f. (2)* annexation
angelas *m. (1)* angel
angina *med. f. (2)* tonsillitis
anglas, -ė *m. (1), f. (2)* English(wo)man
angliavandeniai *m. pl. (1)* carbohydrates
anglis *f. (3)* coal
anglistas, -ė *m. (1), f. (2)* English philologist
anksti *adv.* early
antibiotikas *m. (1)* antibiotic
antklodė *f. (2)* blanket
antradienis *m. (1)* Tuesday
anuliuoti *v. (1)* annul
apdovanojimas *m. (1)* award
apdrausti *v. (1)* insure
apetitas *m. (1)* appetite
apgamas *m. (1)* mole
apgaulė *f. (2)* deception, fraud

apgauti *v. (1)* deceive
apie *prep.* about
apykaklė *f. (2)* collar
apylanka *f. (2)* detour
apiplėšimas *m. (1)* robbery, burglary
apytikriai *adv.* approximately
apytikris, -ė *adj. (3)* approximate
apkabinti *v. (1)* hug, embrace
aplankas *m. (1)* (paper) file
aplink *prep.* around
aplinkybė *f. (2)* circumstance
aplodismentai *m. pl. (1)* applause
apmokestinti *v. (1)* impose tax (on)
apranga *f. (2)* clothing
aprašymas *m. (1)* description
apribojimas *m. (1)* restriction, limitation
aprūpinti *v. (1)* provide (for)
apsauga *f. (2)* security; protection
apsemti *v. (1)* flood
apsidairyti *v. (3)* look around
apsidrausti *v. (1)* insure oneself
apsikabinti *v. (1)* hug one another, embrace one another
apsikirpti *v. (1)* have a haircut
apsimesti *v. (1)* pretend
apskritai *adv.* generally, in general
apskritas, -a *adj. (1)* round
apskritimas *m. (1)* circle
apsukrus, -i *adj. (2)* street-smart, clever
aptarnavimas *m. (1)* service
Apvaizda *m./f. (2)* Providence
apvalus, -i *adj. (2)* round
arba *prep.* or
arbata *f. (2)* tea
arbatinukas *m. (1)* teapot
arbatpinigiai *m. pl. (1)* tip, gratuity
archeologas, -ė *m. (1), f. (2)* archeologist
archeologija *f. (2)* archeology
architektas, -ė *m. (1), f. (2)* architect
architektūra *f. (2)* architecture
archyvas *m. (1)* archive
arena *f. (2)* arena
areštas *m. (1)* arrest
areštuoti *v. (1)* arrest
arfa *f. (2)* harp
argumentas *m. (1)* argument
aristokratas, -ė *m. (1), f. (2)* aristocrat
arka *f. (2)* arch
arklidė *f. (2)* stable
arklys *m. (1)* horse
armija *f. (2)* army
arogancija *f. (2)* arrogance
aromatas *m. (1)* aroma
arterija *f. (2)* artery
arti *adv.* near, close
artimas, -a *adj. (1)* close, intimate
artojas, -a *m. (1), f. (2)* ploughman
asamblėja *f. (2)* assembly
asilas *m. (1)* donkey; stupid person
asmenavimas *m. (1)* conjugation
asmuo *m. (5)* person
asociacija *f. (2)* association
aspirantas, -ė *col. m. (1), f. (2)* graduate student
aspirinas *m. (1)* aspirin
astma *med. f. (2)* asthma
astronomas, -ė *m. (1), f. (2)* astronomer
astronomija *f. (2)* astronomy
aš *pron.* I
ašara *f. (2)* tear
ašigalis *m. (1)* (North/South) pole
aštrus, -i *adj. (2)* sharp; spicy
aštuoni, -ios *num.* eight
aštuonkojis *m. (1)* octopus
ataskaita *f. (2)* report; account
atbulai *adv.* reversely, the wrong way
atdaras, -a *adj. (1)* open
ateistas, -ė *m. (1), f. (2)* atheist
ateiti *v. (1; irr.)* come
ateitis *f. (3)* future
ateizmas *m. (1)* atheism
atėjimas *m. (1)* coming, arrival
ateljė *f. (2)* (artist's) studio
atgal *adv.* back, backwards
atgauti *v. (1)* get back
atgimimas *m. (1)* revival, rebirth
atidarytuvas *m. (1)* bottle-opener
atidengti *v. (1)* uncover, unveil
atidėti *v. (1)* set/ put aside
atiduoti *v. (1)* give back, return (something)
atimti *v. (1)* take (from) (by force)
atkaklus, -i *adj. (2)* persistent
atlaidai *m. pl. (1)* church festival
atleidimas *m. (1)* forgiveness; dismissal (from work)
atleisti *v. (1)* forgive; fire (from work)
atletas, -ė *m. (1), f. (2)* athlete
atletiškas, -a *adj. (1)* athletic
atliekos *f. pl. (2)* waste
atlyginimas *m. (1)* salary

atlikėjas, -a *m. (1), f. (2)* performer
atlikti *v. (1)* carry out, fulfill
atmintis *f. (3)* memory
atmosfera *f. (2)* atmosphere
atnaujinti *v. (1)* renew
atnešti *v. (1)* bring, fetch
atomas *m. (1)* atom
atominis, -ė *adj. (3)* nuclear, atomic
atostogauti *v. (1)* be on vacation
atostogos *f. pl. (2)* vacation
atpažinti *v. (1)* identify
atradimas *m. (1)* discovery
atrišti *v. (1)* untie, unleash
atsakingas, -a *adj. (1)* responsible
atsakomybė *f. (2)* responsibility
atsakovas, -ė *m. (1), f. (2)* defendant
atsarga *f. (2)* caution; reserve
atsargiai *adv.* carefully
atsargumas *m. (1)* caution, prudence
atsigauti *v. (1)* recover; come to one's senses
atsigulti *v. (1)* lie down
atsiliepti *v. (1)* answer; speak (of)
atsilyginti *v. (1)* pay; get even
atsiminimai *m. pl. (1)* memoirs
atsipalaiduoti *v. (1)* relax
atsiprašau sorry
atsiprašymas *m. (1)* apology
atsiprašyti *v. (3)* apologize
atsiraugėti *v. (1)* belch
atsiremti *v. (1)* lean (upon, against)
atsisakyti *v. (3)* refuse, decline
atsisėsti *v. (1)* sit down
atsiskaityti *v. (3)* settle accounts
atsistatydinti *v. (1)* resign
atsistoti *v. (1)* stand up
atsisukti *v. (1)* turn around
atsisveikinti *v. (1)* say good-bye
atsitikimas *m. (1)* event, incident
atsitiktinai *adv.* accidentally
atsitūpti *v. (1)* squat down
atsiųsti *v. (1)* send
atskiras, -a *adj. (1)* separate
atspausdinti *v. (1)* print
atspėti *v. (1)* guess
atstatyti *v. (3)* rebuild
atstovas, -ė *m. (1), f. (2)* representative
atstovauti *v. (1)* represent
atstovybė *f. (2)* embassy
atstumas *m. (1)* distance
atsuktuvas *m. (1)* screwdriver
atšalti *v. (1)* get colder
atšaukti *v. (1)* recall, cancel
atšilti *v. (1)* grow warmer
atvaizdas *m. (1)* image, reflection
atvejis *m. (1)* case
Atvelykis *m. (1)* Sunday after Easter
atvėsti *v. (1)* cool off
atvykimas *m. (1)* arrival
atvykti *v. (1)* arrive, come
atvirkščiai *adv.* the wrong way; on the contrary
atvirkščias, -a *adj. (1)* reverse
atvirukas *m. (1)* postcard
audeklas *m. (1)* cloth, fabric
audinys *m. (1)* cloth, fabric
auditorija *f. (2)* auditorium, lecture hall
audra *f. (2)* storm
augalas *m. (1)* plant
auginti *v. (1)* bring up, raise
auglys *med. m. (1)* tumor
auka *f. (2)* sacrifice; victim
auklė *f. (2)* nanny
auklėti *v. (1)* educate, train
auksakalys *m. (1)* goldsmith
auksas *m. (1)* gold
auksinis, -ė *adj. (3)* golden
aukščiau *adv.* higher, above
aukštai *adv.* high, above
aukštaitis, -ė *m. (1), f. (2)* highlander (inhabitant of Aukštaitija)
aukštas, -a *adj. (1)* tall
aukštyn *adv.* upwards
aukštis *m. (1)* height
ausinės *f. pl. (2)* headphones
ausis *f. (3)* ear
auskaras *m. (1)* earring
austi *v. (1)* weave
australas, -ė *m. (1), f. (2)* Australian
australiškas, -a *adj. (1)* Australian
austras, -ė *m. (1), f. (2)* Austrian
austrė *f. (2)* oyster
austriškas, -a *adj. (1)* Austrian
autobiografija *f. (2)* autobiography
autobusas *m. (1)* bus
autobuso stotelė bus stop
autobusų stotis bus station (depot)
automobilis *m. (1)* car, automobile
autonomija *f. (2)* autonomy
autoritetas *m. (1)* authority
autorius, -ė *m. (4), f. (2)* author
avalynė *f. (2)* footwear
avangardas *m. (1)* avant-garde

avansas *m. (1)* advance payment
avantiūristas, -ė *m. (1), f. (2)* adventurer
avarija *f. (2)* wreck, accident
avėti *v. (2)* wear (shoes, boots)
aviacija *f. (2)* aviation
aviena *f. (2)* lamb
avietė *f. (2)* raspberry
avilys *m. (1)* (bee)hive
avinas *m. (1)* ram
avis *f. (3)* sheep
aviža *f.sg. (2)* oat
avižinis, -ė *adj. (3)* oat
ąžuolas *m. (1)* oak
ąžuolinis, -ė *adj. (3)* oak

B

badas *m. (1)* hunger, starvation
badauti *v. (1)* starve
bagažas *m. (1)* luggage
baidarė *f. (2)* kayak, canoe
baigimas *m. (1)* graduation, finish
baigti *v. (1)* finish
bailys, -ė *m. (1), f. (2)* coward
baimė *f. (2)* fear
baisus, -i *adj. (2)* terrible, horrible
bajoras, -ė *m. (1), f. (2)* noble person
bajorija *f. (2)* nobility
baklažanas *m. (1)* eggplant
bakterija *f. (2)* bacterium
bala *f. (2)* puddle
balandis *m. (1)* pigeon; April
baldai *m. pl. (1)* furniture
balerina *f. (2)* ballet dancer
baletas *m. (1)* ballet
baleto artistas, -ė *m. (1), f. (2)* ballet dancer
balionas *m. (1)* balloon
balius *col. m. (4)* ball, party
balkonas *m. (1)* balcony
balnas *m. (1)* saddle
balsas *m. (1)* voice
balsavimas *m. (1)* voting
balsė *f. (2)* vowel (letter)
baltaodis, -ė *m. (1), f. (2)* white (person)
baltas, -a *adj. (1)* white
baltymai *m. pl. (1)* protein
baltymas *m. (1)* (egg/eye) white
baltiniai *m. pl. (1)* white shirt; linen
bananas *m. (1)* banana
banda *f. (2)* herd; loaf of white bread
bandymas *m. (1)* attempt, trial
banditas, -ė *m. (1), f. (2)* bandit
bandyti *v. (3)* attempt, put to test, try
banga *f. (2)* wave
bankas *m. (1)* bank
bankininkas, -ė *m. (1), f. (2)* banker
banknotas *m. (1)* banknote, bill
bankrotas *m. (1)* bankruptcy
bankrutuoti *v. (1)* become bankrupt, become insolvent
baras *m. (1)* bar, pub
baravykas *m. (1)* boletus (a kind of mushroom)
barikada *f. (2)* barricade
barjeras *m. (1)* barrier
barnis *m. (1)* quarrel
barokas *m. (1)* baroque
barščiai *m. pl. (1)* borsch (soup)
barti *v. (1)* scold
barzda *f. (2)* beard
basas, -a *adj. (1)* barefoot
baseinas *m. (1)* swimming pool
basutės *f. pl. (2)* sandals
batas *m. (1)* shoe
baterija *f. (2)* battery
batonas *m. (1)* long loaf of white bread
bauda *f. (2)* penalty, fine
baudžiauninkas, -ė *m. (1), f. (2)* serf
baudžiava *f. (2)* serfdom
bausmė *f. (2)* punishment
bausti *v. (1)* punish
bazė *f. (2)* base (military/ commercial)
bažnyčia *f. (2)* church
be *prep.* without
bebras *m. (1)* beaver
bedarbis, -ė *m. (1), f. (2)* unemployed
begėdis, -ė *m. (1), f. (2); adj. (3)* shameless person
bėgikas, -ė *m. (1), f. (2)* runner
beginklis, -ė *adj. (3)* unarmed
bėgioti *v. (1)* jog
bėglys, -ė *m. (1), f. (2)* fugitive, runaway
bėgti *v. (1)* run
bei *conj.* and
beje *part.* by the way
bejėgis, -ė *adj. (3)* helpless

beletristika *f. (2)* fiction
belgas, -ė *m. (1), f. (2)* Belgian
belgiškas, -a *adj. (1)* Belgian
bemuitis, -ė *adj. (3)* duty free
benamis, -ė *m. (1), f. (2); adj. (3)* homeless person
bendraamžis, -ė *m. (1), f. (2)* peer (of the same age)
bendraautoris, -ė *m. (1), f. (2)* co-author
bendrabutis *m. (1)* dormitory
bendradarbis, -ė *m. (1), f. (2)* coworker
bendras, -a *adj. (1)* common; general
bendrauti *v. (1)* communicate, associate
bendrija *f. (2)* community; association
bendrovė *f. (2)* company
bent *part.* at least
benzinas *m. (1)* gasoline, petrol
beprotis, -ė *m. (1), f. (2); adj. (3)* mad/ crazy person
berankovis, -ė *adj. (3)* sleeveless
beraštis, -ė *m. (1), f. (2); adj. (3)* illiterate (person)
berniukas *m. (1)* boy
beržas *m. (1)* birch
bespalvis, -ė *adj. (3)* colorless
bet *conj.* but, however
betonas *m. (1)* concrete
bevaikis, -ė *m. (1), f. (2); adj. (3)* childless (person)
beveik *part.* almost
beždžionė *f. (2)* monkey, ape
Biblija *f. (2)* Bible
biblioteka *f. (2)* library
bibliotekininkas, -ė *m. (1), f. (2)* librarian
bifšteksas *m. (1)* beefsteak
bijoti *v. (3)* fear, dread
byla *f. (2)* case, file
biliardas *m. (1)* pool
bilietas *m. (1)* ticket
bylinėtis *v. (1)* be at suit, litigate
biografas, -ė *m. (1), f. (2)* biographer
biografija *f. (2)* biography
biologas, -ė *m. (1), f. (2)* biologist
biologija *f. (2)* biology
birža *fin. f. (2)* exchange
birželis *m. (1)* June
bitė *f. (2)* bee
bitininkas, -ė *m. (1), f. (2)* beekeeper
biudžetas *m. (1)* budget
biuletenis *m. (1)* bulletin
biuras *m. (1)* bureau, office
biurokratas, -ė *m. (1), f. (2)* bureaucrat
biznierius, -ė *col. m. (4), f. (2)* business person
biznis *col. m. (1)* business
bizūnas *m. (1)* whip
blaivus, -i *adj. (2)* sober
blakė *f. (2)* bedbug
blakstiena *f. (2)* eyelash
blankas *m. (1)* form (document)
blauzda *f. (2)* shin, calf (of the leg)
blynas *m. (1)* pancake
blogai *adv.* badly
blogas, -a *adj. (1)* bad
blokada *f. (2)* blockade
blondinas, -ė *m. (1), f. (2)* blonde person
blukti *v. (1)* fade
blusa *f. (2)* flea
boba *col. f. (2)* (old, ugly) woman
bokalas *m. (1)* mug
boksas *m. (1)* boxing
boksininkas, -ė *m. (1), f. (2)* boxer
bokštas *m. (1)* tower
bomba *f. (2)* bomb
bordo *col. adj. (n.d.)* burgundy (color)
bortas *m. (1)* side/ board (of a ship)
boružė *f. (2)* lady-bug
bosas *m. (1)* bass; *col.* boss
botagas *m. (1)* whip
braidyti *v. (3)* wade
braižas *m. (1)* style of handwriting; touch (manner)
brandus, -i *adj. (2)* mature; ripe
brangakmenis *m. (1)* gem, jewel
brangenybė *f. (2)* treasure; jewel
brangiai *adv.* dearly; expensively
brangti *v. (1)* rise in price
brangus, -i *adj. (2)* dear; expensive
braškė *f. (2)* strawberry
bręsti *v. (1)* mature
brėžinys *m. (1)* sketch
briedis, -ė *m. (1), f. (2)* elk, moose
britas, -ė *m. (1), f. (2)* British
brolis *m. (1)* brother

brolienė *f. (2)* sister-in-law (brother's wife)
bronchitas *med. m. (1)* bronchitis
brunetas, -ė *m. (1), f. (2)* brunette
bruožas *m. (1)* trait, feature
bučinys *m. (1)* kiss
bučkis *col. m. (1)* kiss
bučiuotis *v. (1)* kiss
būdas *m. (1)* temper, disposition, character
budėti *v. (2)* be on duty
budistas, -ė *m. (1), f. (2)* Buddhist
budizmas *m. (1)* Buddhism
būdvardis *m. (1)* adjective
bufetas *m. (1)* buffet
būgnas *m. (1)* drum
buhalterija *f. (2)* accounting, bookkeeping
buhalteris, -ė *m. (1), f. (2)* accountant
būklė *f. (2)* state, condition
bulgaras, -ė *m. (1), f. (2)* Bulgarian
bulgariškas, -a *adj. (1)* Bulgarian
bulius *m. (4)* bull
bulvaras *m. (1)* boulevard
bulvė *f. (2)* potato
bulvinis, -ė *adj. (3)* potato
bunkeris *m. (1)* bunker
burė *f. (2)* sail
būrelis *m. (1)* circle, club
buriavimas *m. (1)* sailing
burokas *m. (1)* beet(-root)
būsena *f. (2)* state, condition
būsimas, -a *adj. (1)* future
būstas *m. (1)* lodging, home
butelis *m. (1)* bottle
būti *v. (1, irr.)* be
būtybė *f. (2)* creature
būtinai *adv.* certainly

C

caras *m. (1)* czar
cechas *m. (1)* shop (in a factory), department
celė *f. (2)* cell (prison); hermitage
cementas *m. (1)* cement
centas *m. (1)* cent
centimetras *m. (1)* centimeter
centralizacija *f. (2)* centralization
centras *m. (1)* center
centrinis, -ė *adj. (3)* central
cenzūra *f. (2)* censorship
cepelinas *m. (1)* zeppelin (Lithuanian dish)
ceremonija *f. (2)* ceremony
cerkvė *f. (2)* church (Russian Orthodox)
chalatas *m. (1)* robe, dressing gown
chalva *f. (2)* halvah
chaosas *m. (1)* chaos
charakteris *m. (1)* disposition, temper, character
chemija *f. (2)* chemistry
chirurgas, -ė *m. (1), f. (2)* surgeon
chirurgija *med. f. (2)* surgery (field of)
choras *m. (1)* choir, chorus
choristas, -ė *m. (1), f. (2)* member of a chorus
choreografija *f. (2)* choreography
chronologija *f. (2)* chronology
chuliganas, -ė *m. (1), f. (2)* hooligan
cigaras *m. (1)* cigar
cigaretė *f. (2)* cigarette
ciklas *m. (1)* cycle
ciniškas, -a *adj. (1)* cynical
cinizmas *m. (1)* cynicism
cirkas *m. (1)* circus
cirkuliacija *f. (2)* circulation
cista *med. f. (2)* cyst
citrina *f. (2)* lemon
cituoti *v. (1)* quote, cite
civilizacija *f. (2)* civilization
civilizuotas, -a *adj. (1)* civilized
cukrainė *f. (2)* confectionery
cukraligė *med. f. (2)* diabetes
cukrus *m. (4)* sugar

Č

čekis *m. (1)* check
čempionas, -ė *m. (1), f. (2)* champion
čerpė *f. (2)* roof tile
česnakas *m. (1)* garlic
čia *adv.* here
čiaudėti *v. (2)* sneeze
čiaudulys *m. (1)* sneeze
čiaupas *m. (1)* tap, faucet
čigonas, -ė *m. (1), f. (2)* gypsy
čiuožėjas, -a *m. (1), f. (2)* skater
čiuožykla *f. (2)* skating rink
čiupinėti *v. (1)* touch, feel
čiužinys *m. (1)* mattress

D

dabar *adv.* now, presently
daigas *m. (1)* sprout
daiktas *m. (1)* thing
daiktavardis *m. (1)* noun
dailė *f. (2)* art, fine arts
dailininkas, -ė *m. (1), f. (2)* painter (artist)
daina *f. (2)* song
dainininkas, -ė *m. (1), f. (2)* singer
dairytis *v. (3)* look around
daktaras, -ė *m. (1), f. (2)* doctor
dalia *f. (2)* fate, lot, luck
dalyba *mat. f. (2)* division
dalykas *m. (1)* thing (abstract); object
dalykiškas, -a *adj. (1)* business-like
dalis *f. (3)* part, share
dalyti *mat. v. (1)* divide, *mat.* give out
dalyvauti *v. (1)* participate, take part
dama *f. (2)* lady
danas, -ė *m. (1), f. (2)* Dane
danga *f. (2)* cover
dangoraižis *m. (1)* skyscraper, highrise
dangtis *m. (1)* lid, cover
dangus *m. (4)* sky, heaven
dantenos *med. f. pl. (2)* gums
dantis *m. (3)* tooth
dantys *m. pl. (3)* teeth
dantistas, -ė *m. (1), f. (2)* dentist
dantų pasta toothpaste
dar *part.* still, more, even
darbas *m. (1)* work, job
darbininkas, -ė *m. (1), f. (2)* worker
darbinis, -ė *adj. (3)* work
daryti *v. (3)* do, make
daržas *m. (1)* (vegetable/ flower) garden
daržovė *f. (2)* vegetable
data *f. (2)* date (day)
datuoti *v. (1)* date (chronologically)
daug *num.* many, much, a lot of
daugėti *v. (1)* increase
daugyba *mat. f. (2)* multiplication
daugiskaita *f. (2)* plural
dauguma *f. (2)* majority
daužyti *v. (3)* break, crush
dažai *m. pl. (1)* paint
dažyti *v. (3)* paint
dažnai *adv.* often, frequently
dažnas, -a *adj. (1)* often, frequent
debatai *m. pl. (1)* debate
debesis *m. (3)* cloud
dėdė *m. (2)* uncle
dėdienė *f. (2)* aunt (uncle's wife)
dedikuoti *v. (1)* dedicate
defektas *m. (1)* defect
deficitas *m. (1)* deficit
degalai *m. pl. (1)* fuel
degalinė *f. (2)* gas station
degti *v. (1)* burn
degtinė *f. (2)* vodka
degtukas *m. (1)* match
deimantas *m. (1)* diamond
deivė *f. (2)* goddess
deja *inter.* unfortunately, alas
dėkingas, -a *adj. (1)* grateful
deklaracija *f. (2)* declaration
dekoracija *theat. f. (2)* set, scenery
dėkoti *v. (1)* thank
dėkui *inter.* thanks
dėl *conj.* because of, due to
delegacija *f. (2)* delegation
delfinas *m. (1)* dolphin
delnas *m. (1)* palm (of a hand)
dėmė *f. (2)* spot, stain
dėmesys *m. (1)* attention
dėmėtas, -a *adj. (1)* stained
demokratas, -ė *polit. m. (1), f. (2)* democrat
demokratija *f. (2)* democracy
denis *m. (1)* deck (on a ship)
derėtis *v. (1)* bargain, negotiate
derybininkas, -ė *m. (1), f. (2)* negotiator
derybos *f. pl. (2)* negotiation
derinti *v. (1)* coordinate
derinys *m. (1)* combination
derlingas, -a *adj. (1)* fertile (soil)
derlius *m. (4)* harvest
derva *f. (2)* resin, tar
desertas *m. (1)* dessert
dėstyti *v. (3)* teach
dėstytojas, -a *m. (1), f. (2)* lecturer, instructor (in college)
dešimt *num.* ten
dešimtmetis *m. (1)* decade (ten years)
dešinė *f. (2)* right side
dešra *f. (2)* sausage
detalė *f. (2)* detail
detektyvas, -ė *m. (1), f. (2)* detective

dėti *v. (1)* lay/ put down
devyni, -ios *num.* nine
dezinfekuoti *v. (1)* disinfect
dėžė *f. (2)* box
dėžutė *f. (2)* box (small)
diabetas *med. m. (1)* diabetes
diabetikas, -ė *m. (1), f. (2)* diabetic
diagnozė *f. (2)* diagnosis
dialektas *m. (1)* dialect
dialogas *m. (1)* dialog
didelis, -ė *adj. (3)* big
dydis *m. (1)* size
didmeninis, -ė *adj. (3)* wholesale
didvyris, -ė *m. (1), f. (2)* hero
diena *f. (2)* day
dienoraštis *m. (1)* diary
dievaitis, -ė *m. (1), f. (2)* god(dess); idol
Dievas *m. (1)* God
dykuma *f. (2)* desert
dingti *v. (1)* disappear
diplomas *m. (1)* diploma
diplomatas, -ė *m. (1), f. (2)* diplomat
diplomatija *f. (2)* diplomacy
diplomatiškas, -a *adj. (1)* diplomatic
dirbti *v. (1)* work
direktorius, -ė *m. (4), f. (2)* director, principle
dirigentas, -ė *m. (1), f. (2)* conductor
dirva *f. (2)* soil, ground
diržas *m. (1)* belt
diskas *m. (1)* disk
diskriminacija *f. (2)* discrimination
diskriminuoti *v. (1)* discriminate
diskusija *f. (2)* discussion, debate
distancija *f. (2)* distance
dividendas *m. (1)* dividend
dizainas *m. (1)* design
dizaineris, -ė *m. (1), f. (2)* designer
dokumentas *m. (1)* document
doleris *m. (1)* dollar
domėtis *v. (2)* be interested
dominti *v. (1)* interest
doras, -a *adj. (1)* honest, proper
dorybė *f. (2)* virtue
dorovė *f. (2)* morals
dosnumas *m. (1)* generosity
dosnus, -i *adj. (2)* generous
dotacija *f. (2)* subsidy
dovana *f. (2)* present, gift
dozė *f. (2)* dose
drąsa *f. (2)* courage
drąsus, -i *adj. (2)* courageous, brave
draudimas *m. (1)* insurance; prohibition
draugas, -ė *m. (1), f. (2)* friend
drausmė *f. (2)* discipline
drausmingas, -a *adj. (1)* disciplined
drausti *v. (1)* forbid
drėgmė *f. (2)* humidity
drėgnas, -a *adj. (1)* damp, humid
dribsniai *m. pl. (1)* flakes
dryžuotas, -a *adj. (1)* striped
drobė *f. (2)* cloth, linen
drovėtis *v. (2)* be shy
drugelis *m. (1)* butterfly
druska *f. (2)* salt
du *num.* two
dugnas *m. (1)* bottom
dujos *f. pl. (2)* gas
dukra *f. (2)* daughter
dukterėčia *f. (2)* niece
duktė *f. (2)* daughter
dūmai *m. pl. (1)* smoke
dumblas *m. (1)* mud
duobė *f. (2)* pit, hole
duomenys *m. pl. (4)* data, facts
duona *f. (2)* bread
duoninė *f. (2)* bread store; bread container
duoti *v. (1)* give
durininkas, -ė *m. (1), f. (2)* doorman
durys *f. pl. (3)* door
durti *v. (1)* stab
dusulys *m. (1)* short breath
dusti *v. (1)* suffocate, choke
dušas *m. (1)* shower
dvasia *f. (2)* spirit
dvasingas, -a *adj. (1)* spiritual (possessing spiritual qualities)
dvasingumas *m. (1)* spirituality
dvėsti *v. (1)* die (for animals)
dvibalsis *m. (1)* diphthong
dviese *adv.* two (together)
dvynys, -ė *m. (1), f. (2)* twin
dviratininkas, -ė *m. (1), f. (2)* cyclist
dviratis *m. (1)* bicycle
džiaugsmas *m. (1)* joy, gladness
džiazas *m. (1)* jazz
džinsai *m. pl. (1)* jeans

džinsinis, -ė *adj. (3)* jeans
džiova *med. f. (2)* tuberculosis, consumption
džiunglės *f. pl. (2)* jungle
džiūti *v. (1)* dry
džiuvėsis *m. (1)* dried toast

E, Ę, Ė

efektas *m. (1)* effect
efektingas, -a *adj. (1)* effective
eglė *f. (2)* fir-tree, spruce-tree; Christmas tree
egzaminas *m. (1)* examination
egzekucija *f. (2)* execution
egzotika *f. (2)* exotic
eilėraštis *m. (1)* poem
eismas *m. (1)* traffic
eiti *v. (1, irr.)* go, walk
ekipažas *m. (1)* crew
ekologija *f. (2)* ecology
ekonomija *f. (2)* economy
ekonomika *f. (2)* economics
ekonomistas, -ė *m. (1), f. (2)* economist
ekranas *m. (1)* screen
ekskursija *f. (2)* excursion, field trip
eksperimentas *m. (1)* experiment
ekspertas, -ė *m. (1), f. (2)* expert
eksponatas *m. (1)* displayed piece (in a museum)
ekspozicija *f. (2)* exposition, display
ekstravagantiškas, -a *adj. (1)* extravagant
elegancija *f. (2)* elegance
elegantiškas, -a *adj. (1)* elegant
elektra *f. (2)* electricity
elektrikas, -ė *m. (1), f. (2)* electrician
elektroninis paštas e-mail
elektroninio pašto adresas e-mail address
elgesys *m. (1)* conduct, behavior
elgeta *m./f. (2)* beggar
elitas *m. (1)* elite
elitinis, -ė *adj. (3)* elite
elnias, -ė *m. (1), f. (2)* deer
elniena *f. (2)* venison
emblema *f. (2)* emblem
emigracija *f. (2)* emigration
emigrantas, -ė *m. (1), f. (2)* emigrant
emisija *f. (2)* emission
emocija *f. (2)* emotion
emocingas, -a *adj. (1)* emotional
energija *f. (2)* energy
energingas, -a *adj. (1)* energetic
engti *v. (1)* oppress
entuziastas, -ė *m. (1), f. (2)* enthusiast
entuziazmas *m. (1)* enthusiasm
epidemija *f. (2)* epidemic
epilepsija *med. f. (2)* epilepsy
epizodas *m. (1)* episode
era *f. (2)* era
erdvė *f. (2)* space
erelis *m. (1)* eagle
erkė *f. (2)* tick
erotika *f. (2)* erotic
erotiškas, -a *adj. (1)* erotic
eršketas *m. (1)* sturgeon
erzinti *v. (1)* tease; annoy
eskizas *m. (1)* sketch
esmė *f. (2)* essence
estas, -ė *m. (1), f. (2)* Estonian
estetas, -ė *m. (1), f. (2)* aesthete
ėsti *v. (1)* eat (speaking of animals)
estiškas, -a *adj. (1)* Estonian
etika *f. (2)* ethics
etiškas, -a *adj. (1)* ethical
etiketė *f. (2)* label
etnografas, -ė *m. (1), f. (2)* ethnographer
etnografija *f. (2)* ethnography
euras *m. (1)* euro
europietis, -ė *m. (1), f. (2)* European
europietiškas, -a *adj. (1)* European
Europos Sąjunga European Union
evakuacija *f. (2)* evacuation
evakuoti(s) *v. (1)* evacuate
evoliucija *f. (2)* evolution
ežeras *m. (1)* lake
ežys *m. (1)* hedgehog

F

fabrikas *m. (1)* factory
faksas *m. (1)* fax
faktas *m. (1)* fact
fakultetas *m. (1)* department (at university)
faksas *m. (1)* fax
fanatikas, -ė *m. (1), f. (2)* fanatic

fanatizmas *m. (1)* fanaticism
fantastika *f. (2)* science fiction
fantazija *f. (2)* fantasy, imagination
farmacija *f. (2)* pharmacy (field of)
farmacininkas, -ė *m. (1), f. (2)* pharmacist
faršas *m. (1)* ground meat
fasonas *m. (1)* style/ cut (of a dress)
fašistas, -ė *m. (1), f. (2)* fascist
fašizmas *m. (1)* fascism
favoritas, -ė *m. (1), f. (2)* favorite
fazė *f. (2)* phase, period
fėja *f. (2)* fairy
feministė, -as *f. (2), m. (1)* feminist
ferma *f. (2)* farm
fermeris, -ė *m. (1), f. (2)* farmer
festivalis *m. (1)* festival
figūra *f. (2)* figure
fiktyvus, -i *adj. (2)* fictitious
filialas *m. (1)* branch, subsidiary
filmas *m. (1)* film
filmuoti *v. (1)* shoot (a film)
filologas, -ė *m. (1), f. (2)* philologist
filosofas, -ė *m. (1), f. (2)* philosopher
finansai *m. pl. (1)* finance, finances
finansininkas, -ė *m. (1), f. (2)* financier
finansinis, -ė *adj. (3)* financial
fizika *f. (2)* physics
fizikas, -ė *m. (1), f. (2)* physicist
fizinis, -ė *adj. (3)* physical
flirtas *m. (1)* flirt
flirtuoti *v. (1)* flirt
folkloras *m. (1)* folklore
forma *f. (2)* form
formalus, -i *adj. (2)* formal
formuoti *v. (1)* form
fotoaparatas *m. (1)* (photo) camera
frakas *m. (1)* tuxedo
frakcija *polit. f. (2)* faction
frazė *f. (2)* phrase
frontas *m. (1)* front
funkcija *f. (2)* function
futbolas *m. (1)* football, soccer
futbolo rungtynės soccer match

G

gabalas *m. (1)* piece
gabus, -i *adj. (2)* gifted
gaidys *m. (1)* rooster
gailėtis *v. (2)* pity
gaisras *m. (1)* fire
gaisrininkas, -ė *m. (1), f. (2)* fire(wo)man
gaivinti *v. (1)* freshen, refresh
gal *part.* maybe
galas *m. (1)* end
galėti *v. (2)* be able
galia *f. (2)* power
galimybė *f. (2)* possibility
galingas, -a *adj. (1)* powerful
galūnė *f. (2)* ending; limb
galva *f. (2)* head
gamyba *f. (2)* production
gamykla *f. (2)* factory, plant
gaminys *m. (1)* product, article
gamta *f. (2)* nature
gana *adv.* enough
gandas *m. (1)* rumor
garantija *f. (2)* guarantee, warranty
garažas *m. (1)* garage
garbanotas, -a *adj. (1)* curly
garbė *f. (2)* honor
garbingas, -a *adj. (1)* honorable
gardus, -i *adj. (2)* delicious
garnyras *m. (1)* garnish
garsas *m. (1)* sound
garstyčios *f. pl. (2)* mustard
garsus, -i *adj. (2)* loud; famous
garvežys *m. (1)* locomotive
gatvė *f. (2)* street
gaublys *m. (1)* globe
gaudyti *v. (3)* catch
gauja *f. (2)* gang
gauti *v. (1)* receive
gavėjas, -a *m. (1), f. (2)* receiver
Gavėnia *f. (2)* Lent
gėda *f. (2)* shame
gedėti *v. (2)* grieve, mourn
gedulas *m. (1)* mourning
geismas *m. (1)* desire
geisti *v. (1)* desire
gelbėti *v. (1)* rescue
gėlė *f. (2)* flower
geležinkelio stotis railway station
geležinkelis *m. (1)* railway
geležis *f. (3)* iron
geltonas, -a *adj. (1)* yellow
genas *m. (1)* gene
genealogija *f. (2)* genealogy
genealus, -i *adj. (2)* (of) genius, brilliant
generacija *f. (2)* generation

genijus *m. (4)* genius
genys *m. (1)* woodpecker
geografija *f. (2)* geography
gerai *adv.* well; ok
geras, -a *adj. (1)* good; *col.* cool
gerėti *v. (1)* grow better
gerklė *f. (2)* throat
gerti *v. (1)* drink
gesti *v. (1)* spoil, deteriorate
getas *m. (1)* ghetto
gidas, -ė *m. (1), f. (2)* guide
gydyti *med. v. (3)* treat
gydytojas, -a *m. (1), f. (2)* doctor
giedoti *v. (1)* sing (of hymns)
giedras, -a *adj. (1)* clear, serene
gylis *m. (1)* depth
gimda *f. (2)* uterus, womb
gimdymas *m. (1)* child-birth
gimdyti *v. (3)* give birth
gimdyvė *f. (2)* woman in child-birth
gimimas *m. (1)* birth
gimimo diena birthday
giminė *m./f. (2)* relative
gimnazija *f. (2)* gymnasium (prestigious high school)
gimtasis, -oji *adj.* native
ginčas *m. (1)* argument, quarrel
ginčytis *v. (1)* argue, quarrel
gynėjas, -a *m. (1), f. (2)* defender
gynyba *f. (2)* defense
ginklas *m. (1)* weapon
ginkluotas, -a *adj. (1)* armed
gintaras *m. (1)* amber
gintarinis, -ė *adj. (3)* amber
ginti *v. (1)* defend
gipsas *m. (1)* plaster; *med.* cast
gira *f. (2)* a sour drink, kvass
girdėti *v. (2)* hear
giria *f. (2)* forest
girtas, -a *adj. (1)* drunk
girtuoklis, -ė *m. (1), f. (2)* drunkard
gysla *f. (2)* vein
gitara *f. (2)* guitar
gyti *v. (1)* recover, get better
gyvas, -a *adj. (1)* alive
gyvatė *f. (2)* snake
gyvenimas *m. (1)* life
gyventi *v. (1)* live
gyventojas, -a *m. (1), f. (2)* inhabitant
gyvybė *f. (2)* life
gyvulys *m. (1)* animal
globoti *v. (1)* patronize, take care (of)
gluosnis *m. (1)* willow
gobelenas *m. (1)* tapestry
godus, -i *adj. (2)* greedy
grafas *m. (1)* earl, count
grafienė *f. (2)* countess
grafika *f. (2)* graphics
graikas, -ė *m. (1), f. (2)* Greek
graikiškas, -a *adj. (1)* Greek
grakštus, -i *adj. (2)* graceful
gramatika *f. (2)* grammar
grandinė *f. (2)* chain
grandinėlė *f. (2)* chain (jewelry)
granitas *m. (1)* granite
grasinimas *m. (1)* threat
grasinti *v. (1)* threaten
graudus, -i *adj. (2)* sad, sorrowful
graužti *v. (1)* nibble; nag
grąža *f. (2)* change
grąžtas *m. (1)* drill
gražuolė *f. (2)* beautiful girl/woman
gražus, -i *adj. (2)* beautiful, handsome
greitas, -a *adj. (1)* quick, fast
greitoji pagalba *f. (2)* ambulance
greta *adv.* beside
gręžti *v. (1)* drill
griaudėti *v. (1)* thunder
griaustinis *m. (1)* thunder
griauti *v. (1)* demolish, destroy
grybas *m. (1)* mushroom
grybelis *med. m. (1)* fungus
griebti *v. (1)* snatch, grab
grietinė *f. (2)* sour cream
grietinėlė *f. (2)* cream
grietininis, -ė *adj. (3)* cream
griežtas, -a *adj. (1)* strict
grimas *theat. m. (1)* makeup
grynas, -a *adj. (1)* pure, clear
grindys *f. pl. (3)* floor
gripas *med. m. (1)* flu, influenza
griūti *v. (1)* fall (down)
grįžimas *m. (1)* return
grįžti *v. (1)* return
groti *v. (1)* play (a musical instrument)
grūdas *m. (1)* grain, corn
gruodis *m. (1)* December
gubernatorius, -ė *m. (1), f. (2)* governor
gudrus, -i *adj. (2)* street-smart, clever
gulbė *f. (2)* swan
guldyti *v. (3)* lie down (something/somebody)

gulėti *v. (2)* lie
gulti *v. (1)* lie (down)
guma *f. (2)* rubber
guminis, -ė *adj. (3)* rubber
gundyti *v. (3)* tempt
guosti *v. (1)* comfort
gvazdikėliai *m. pl. (1)* clove

H

halė *f. (2)* hall, covered market
haremas *m. (1)* harem
harmonija *f. (2)* harmony
hemarojus *med. m. (4)* hemorrhoids
herbas *m. (1)* state emblem; coat of arms
hercogas *m. (1)* duke
hercogienė *f. (2)* duchess
hidroelektrinė *f. (2)* hydro-electric power station
higiena *f. (2)* hygiene
higieniškas, -a *adj. (1)* hygienic
himnas *m. (1)* hymn, anthem
homeopatija *f. (2)* homeopathy
honoraras *m. (1)* royalties
humanistas, -ė *m. (1), f. (2)* humanist
humaniškas, -a *adj. (1)* humane
humanitaras, -ė *m. (1), f. (2)* humanitarian
humoras *m. (1)* humor
humoristas, -ė *m. (1), f. (2)* humorist
humoristinis, -ė *adj. (3)* humorous, comic

I, Į, Y

į *prep.* in(to), to (direction)
įberti *v. (1)* pour (into)
įdarbinti *v. (1)* give/ get somebody a job
įdegti *v. (1)* get a tan
idėja *f. (2)* idea
identifikacija *f. (2)* identification
identifikuoti *v. (1)* identify
ydingas, -a *adj. (1)* defective
idiotas, -ė *m. (1), f. (2)* idiot
įdomus, -i *adj. (2)* interesting
įdukra *f. (2)* adopted daughter, foster-daughter
įdukrinti *v. (1)* adopt (a girl)
įeiti *v. (1, irr.)* enter
įėjimas *m. (1)* entrance
ieškoti *v. (3)* search, look for
įgelti *v. (1)* sting
įgyvendinti *v. (1)* realize, put into practice
ignoruoti *v. (1)* ignore
įkainoti *v. (1)* estimate, evaluate
įkaitas, -ė *m. (1), f. (2)* hostage
įkalbėti *v. (1)* persuade
įkalinti *v. (1)* imprison
įkąsti *v. (1)* bite; sting
iki *prep.* until, as far as
ikrai *m. pl. (1)* caviar
įkurti *v. (1)* found
ilgainiui *adv.* in due course, in time
ilgas, -a *adj. (1)* long
įlipti *v. (1)* get/ climb into, embark
iliustracija *f. (2)* illustration
iliustruotas, -a *adj. (1)* illustrated
ilsėtis *v. (2)* rest
imigracija *f. (2)* immigration
imigrantas, -ė *m. (1), f. (2)* immigrant
imigruoti *v. (1)* immigrate
imitacija *f. (2)* imitation
įmoka *f. (2)* installment, payment
įmonė *f. (2)* enterprise
imperatorius, -ė *m. (4), f. (2)* emperor
importas *m. (1)* import
importinis, -ė *adj. (3)* imported
importuoti *v. (1)* import
imti *v. (1)* take
įnašas *m. (1)* contribution; *fin.* deposit
indas *m. (1)* dish, china
indas, -ė *m. (1), f. (2)* Indian
indiškas, -ė *adj. (1)* Indian
indėlis *m. (1)* deposit, investment
indėnas, -ė *m. (1), f. (2)* Native American
indėniškas, -a *adj. (1)* Native American
individas *m. (1)* individual
individualus, -i *adj. (2)* individual
infekcija *f. (2)* infection
infekcinis, -ė *adj. (3)* infectious
infliacija *f. (2)* inflation
informacija *f. (2)* information
informacinis, -ė *adj. (3)* informative
iniciatyva *f. (2)* initiative
iniciatyvus, -i *adj. (2)* initiative
injekcija *med. f. (2)* injection

inkaras *m. (1)* anchor
inkorporuoti *v. (1)* incorporate
inkstas *m. (1)* kidney
inspekcija *f. (2)* inspection
institutas *m. (1)* institute
instrukcija *f. (2)* directions, instructions
instrumentas *m. (1)* instrument
integracija *f. (2)* integration
intelektas *m. (1)* intellect
intelektualas, -ė *m. (1), f. (2)* intellectual
intelektualus, -i *adj. (2)* intellectual
inteligentas, -ė *m. (1), f. (2)* cultured/ educated person
interesantas, -ė *m. (1), f. (2)* visitor, caller
internatas *m. (1)* boarding school
internetas *m. (1)* internet
interviu *m. (n. d.)* interview
intymus, -i *adj. (2)* intimate
inventorius *m. (4)* inventory
investavimas *m. (1)* investment
investicija *f. (2)* investment
investuoti *v. (1)* invest
inžinierius, -ė *m. (4), f. (2)* engineer
ypač *adv.* especially
įpakavimas *m. (1)* packing, package
įpareigojimas *m. (1)* obligation
ypatybė *f. (2)* peculiarity, characteristic
įpėdinis, -ė *m. (1), f. (2)* heir
įplaukos *f. pl. (2)* income, receipts
įprastas, -a *adj. (1)* usual
įprotis *m. (1)* habit
ir *conj.* and
įrankis *m. (1)* tool, instrument
įregistruoti *v. (1)* register
įrėminti *v. (1)* frame
įrenginiai *m. pl. (1)* equipment
irgi *conj.* also
irklas *m. (1)* paddle
įrodymas *m. (1)* proof, evidence
ironija *f. (2)* irony
ironiškas, -a *adj. (1)* ironic
irzlus, -i *adj. (2)* irritable
įsakymas *m. (1)* order, command
įsikurti *v. (1)* settle, take one's residence
įsilaužėlis, -ė *m. (1), f. (2)* burglar
įsilaužti *v. (1)* break in
įsimylėti *v. (2)* fall in love
įsipareigojimas *m. (1)* obligation, engagement
įsipareigoti *v. (1)* pledge oneself
įsivaizduoti *v. (1)* imagine
islamas *m. (1)* Islam
ispanas, -ė *m. (1), f. (2)* Spaniard
ispaniškas, -a *adj. (1)* Spanish
įspėjimas *m. (1)* warning
įspėti *v. (1)* warn
įspūdingas, -a *adj. (1)* impressive
įstaiga *f. (2)* office
įstatymas *m. (1)* law, statute
isterija *med. f. (2)* hysteria
isteriškas, -a *adj. (1)* hysterical
istorija *f. (2)* history, story
įstoti *v. (1)* enter (school/ party)
įsūnis *m. (1)* adopted son
įsūnyti *v. (1)* adopt (a boy)
iš *prep.* from
išaiškinti *v. (1)* explain
išauklėti *v. (1)* educate, bring up
išdavikas, -ė *m. (1), f. (2)* traitor
išdidumas *m. (1)* pride, arrogance
išdidus, -i *adj. (2)* proud, arrogant
išduoti *v. (1)* betray, give away
išdžiūti *v. (1)* dry out
išeiti *v. (1, irr.)* leave; be published
išėjimas *m. (1)* exit
išgelbėti *v. (1)* rescue, save
išimti *v. (1)* take/ pull out
išjungti *v. (1)* turn off, switch off
iškaba *f. (2)* sign, signboard
iškamša *f. (2)* stuffed (animal/ bird)
iškeisti *v. (1)* exchange
iškilmės *f. pl. (2)* festivities
iškrauti *v. (1)* unload
iškrypėlis, -ė *m. (1), f. (2)* pervert
iškristi *v. (1)* fall out
išlaidos *f. pl. (2)* expenditures, expenses
išlaikymas *m. (1)* maintenance
išlaikytinis, -ė *m. (1), f. (2)* dependent
išlaisvinti *v. (1)* liberate
išleidimas *m. (1)* issue; emission
išlošti *v. (1)* win, gain
išmalda *f. (2)* alms, charity
išmatos *f. pl. (2)* excrement
išmatuoti *v. (1)* measure
išmesti *v. (1)* throw away
išmintis *f. (3)* wisdom, reason
išmintingas, -a *adj. (1)* wise
išmoka *f. (2)* payment
išmokyti *v. (3)* teach
išmokti *v. (1)* learn

išnaikinti *v. (1)* destroy, annihilate
išnaša *f. (2)* footnote
išnaudojimas *m. (1)* exploitation
išnaudoti *v. (1)* exploit
išniekinti *v. (1)* desecrate, dishonor
išnuomojamas, -a *adj. (1)* for rent
išnuomoti *v. (1)* lease
išorė *f. (2)* exterior, appearance
išpakuoti *v. (1)* unpack
išpažintis *f. (3)* confession
išpirka *f. (2)* ransom
išplauti *v. (1)* rinse out, wash
išplėsti *v. (1)* expand, extend
išpranašauti *v. (1)* foretell, predict
išprievartauti *v. (1)* rape
išprievartavimas *m. (1)* rape
išprotėti *v. (1)* go crazy/ mad
išradėjas, -a *m. (1), f. (2)* inventor
išrasti *v. (1)* invent
išsaugoti *v. (1)* preserve, conserve
išsikraustyti *v. (3)* move out
išsilavinimas *m. (1)* education; intelligence
išsimokėtinai *adv.* by installments
išsiskyręs, -usi *particip.* divorced
išsiskirti *v. (1)* divorce; break up
išskalbti *v. (1)* wash
išskristi *v. (1)* fly out
iššūkis *m. (1)* challenge
ištaisyti *v. (3)* correct
ištarti *v. (1)* pronounce
ištekėjusi *particip. f.* married (woman)
ištekėti *v. (1)* marry (when a woman marries a man)
ištinimas *m. (1)* swelling
ištinti *v. (1)* swell
ištirti *v. (1)* investigate, examine
ištisai *adv.* completely, entirely
ištrėmimas *m. (1)* deportation, exile
ištrinti *v. (1)* erase
ištuoka *f. (2)* divorce
ištvermė *f. (2)* endurance
išvada *f. (2)* conclusion
išvaduoti *v. (1)* liberate
išvalyti *v. (3)* clean
išvaryti *v. (3)* expel, drive out
išvarža *med. f. (2)* hernia
įtaka *f. (2)* influence
įtakingas, -a *adj. (1)* influential
italas, -ė *m. (1), f. (2)* Italian
itališkas, -a *adj. (1)* Italian
įtampa *f. (2)* tension
įtariamasis, -oji *m., f.; adj.* suspect
įtarimas *m. (1)* suspicion
įtarti *v. (1)* suspect
įtartinas, -a *adj. (1)* suspicious
įteikti *v. (1)* hand, deliver
įteisinti *v. (1)* legalize, legitimize
įterpti *v. (1)* insert
įtikinamas, -a *particip.* convincing
įtikinti *v. (1)* convince, persuade
įtikti *v. (1)* please
įvadas *m. (1)* introduction
įvairus, -i *adj. (2)* various, diverse
įvardis *m. (1)* pronoun
įvykdyti *v. (3)* fulfill, carry out
įvykis *m. (1)* event, accident
izoliacija *f. (2)* isolation
izoliuoti *v. (1)* isolate
iždas *m. (1)* treasury
iždininkas, -ė *m. (1), f. (2)* treasurer
įžeidimas *m. (1)* insult

J

jachta *f. (2)* yacht
jaguaras *m. (1)* jaguar
japonas, -ė *m. (1), f. (2)* Japanese
japoniškas, -a *adj. (1)* Japanese
jau *adv.* already, by now
jaudintis *v. (1)* be agitated/ excited, be worried
jaukus, -i *adj. (2)* cozy
jaunas, -a *adj. (1)* young
jaunikis *m. (1)* bridegroom
jaunystė *f. (2)* youth
jaunoji *f.* bride
jausmas *m. (1)* feeling, sense
jausti *v. (1)* feel
jautiena *f. (2)* beef
jautis *m. (1)* bull
jautrus, -i *adj. (2)* sensitive
JAV USA
jėga *f. (2)* strength, power
jėgainė *f. (2)* power-plant
jei(gu) *conj.* if
ji *pron. f.* she
jie *pron. m. pl.* they
jis *pron. m.* he
jodas *m. (1)* iodine
jodinėti *v. (1)* ride on horseback
jokia *pron. f.* no (. . . whatever), none
joks *pron. m.* no (. . . whatever), none
jos *pron. f. pl.* they

joti *v. (1)* go/ ride on horseback
jubiliatas, -ė *m. (1), f. (2)* birthday person
jubiliejus *m. (1)* anniversary, jubilee
judėti *v. (1)* move
juk *part.* after all
jungiklis *m. (1)* switch
jungti *v. (1)* join, connect
Jungtinės Amerikos Valstijos United States of America
Jungtinių Tautų Organizacija United Nations
juodaodis, -ė *m. (1), f. (2)* black person
juodas, -a *adj. (1)* black
juodligė *f. (2)* anthrax
juodoji rinka black market
juokas *m. (1)* laughter
juokauti *v. (1)* joke
juokingas, -a *adj. (1)* funny
juoktis *v. (1)* laugh
jūra *f. (2)* sea
jūreivis, -ė *m. (1), f. (2)* sailor
juriskonsultas, -ė *m. (1), f. (2)* jurisconsult, legal adviser
jūrligė *f. (2)* seasickness
jūs *pron. pl.* you
juvelyras, -ė *m. (1), f. (2)* jeweler
juvelyriniai dirbiniai *pl.* jewelry

K

kabelinis, -ė *adj. (3)* cable
kabina *f. (2)* booth
kabinėtis *v. (1)* harass
kad *conj.* that
kada *adv.* when
kadaise *adv.* once (upon a time)
kadangi *conj.* because of, as
kadras *m. (1)* (film) exposure
kai *conj.* when
kailiniai *m. pl. (1)* fur coat
kailinis, -ė *adj. (3)* fur
kailis *m. (1)* fur
kaimas *m. (1)* village
kaimietis, -ė *m. (1), f. (2)* villager
kaimynas, -ė *m. (1), f. (2)* neighbor
kaina *f. (2)* price
kainoraštis *m. (1)* price list
kaip *adv.* how
kairė *f. (2)* left side
kajutė *f. (2)* cabin (on a ship)
kakava *f. (2)* cocoa, hot chocolate
kaklaraištis *m. (1)* tie
kaklas *m. (1)* neck
kakta *f. (2)* forehead
kalafioras *m. (1)* cauliflower
kalakutas *m. (1)* turkey
kalakutiena *f. (2)* turkey (meat)
kalba *f. (2)* language
kalbėti *v. (1)* speak
kalbininkas, -ė *m. (1), f. (2)* linguist
kalbotyra *f. (2)* linguistics
kalcis *m. (1)* calcium
kalė *vulg. f. (2)* bitch
Kalėdos *f. pl. (2)* Christmas
kalėjimas *m. (1)* prison, jail
kalendorius *m. (4)* calendar
kalėti *v. (2)* be imprisoned
kalinys, -ė *m. (1), f. (2)* prisoner
kalkuliatorius *m. (4)* calculator
kalnas *m. (1)* mountain
kalnuotas, -a *adj. (1)* mountainous, hilly
kalorija *f. (2)* calorie
kaloringas, -a *adj. (1)* caloric, nutritious
kaltas, -a *adj. (1)* guilty
kaltė *f. (2)* fault, guilt
kaltinti *v. (1)* accuse
kalva *f. (2)* hill
kalvis *m. (1)* blacksmith
kambarinė *f. (2)* maid
kambarinis, -ė *adj. (3)* indoor
kambarys *m. (1)* room
kamera *f. (2)* cell, camera
kamienas *m. (1)* (tree) trunk, stem
kaminas *m. (1)* chimney
kampanija *f. (2)* campaign
kampas *m. (1)* corner
kampinis, -ė *adj. (3)* corner
kamščiatraukis *m. (1)* corkscrew
kamštis *m. (1)* cork
kamuolys *m. (1)* ball
kanadietis, -ė *m. (1), f. (2)* Canadian
kanadietiškas, -a *adj. (1)* Canadian
kanalas *m. (1)* canal, channel
kanarėlė *f. (2)* canary
kanceliarija *f. (2)* office; chancellery
kandidatas, -ė *m. (1), f. (2)* candidate
kandis *f. (3)* moth
kankinti *v. (1)* torture

kanklės *f. pl. (2)* Lithuanian psaltery
kankorėžis *m. (1)* pine cone
kantrybė *f. (2)* patience
kantrus, -i *adj. (2)* patient
kapai *m. pl. (1)* cemetery
kapinės *f. pl. (2)* cemetery
kapas *m. (1)* grave
kapitalas *fin. m. (1)* capital
kapitalinis, -ė *adj. (3)* capital
kapitalistas, -ė *m. (1), f. (2)* capitalist
kapitalistinis, -ė *adj. (3)* capitalist
kapitonas, -ė *m. (1), f. (2)* captain
karalystė *f. (2)* kingdom, realm
karalienė *f. (2)* queen
karališkas, -a *adj. (1)* royal
karalius *m. (4)* king
karas *m. (1)* war
kardas *m. (1)* sword
kardinolas *m. (1)* cardinal
kareivinės *f. pl. (2)* soldier barracks
kareivis *m. (1)* soldier
kariauti *v. (1)* fight, make war
karieta *f. (2)* carriage, coach
karinė tarnyba military service
karininkas, -ė *m. (1), f. (2)* military officer
karinis, -ė *adj. (3)* military
kariuomenė *f. (2)* army
karjera *f. (2)* career
karklas *m. (1)* willow
karnavalas *m. (1)* carnival
karoliai *m. pl. (1)* beads
karpa *f. (2)* wart
karpis *m. (1)* carp
karstas *m. (1)* coffin
karščiuoti *v. (1)* have a fever
karštas, -a *adj. (1)* hot
karštligė *f. (2)* fever
karta *f. (2)* generation
kartais *adv.* sometimes
kartas *m. (1)* time (e.g., *šį kartą*—this time)
kartus, -i *adj. (2)* bitter
kartoti *v. (1)* repeat
kartu *adv.* together, jointly
karuselė *f. (2)* merry-go-round
karvė *f. (2)* cow
karvelis *m. (1)* pigeon
karžygys, -ė *m. (1), f. (2)* military hero
kas *pron.* who, what
kasa *f. (2)* box office; cash register; braid; pigtail; pancreas
kasdien *adv.* daily
kasdieniškas, -a *adj. (1)* ordinary, commonplace
kasyti *v. (3)* scratch
kąsnis *m. (1)* bite, piece
kaštonas *m. (1)* chestnut
katalikas, -ė *m. (1), f. (2)* Catholic
katalikybė *f. (2)* Catholicism
katalikiškas, -a *adj. (1)* Catholic
katė *f. (2)* cat
katedra *f. (2)* cathedral; department (at university)
kategorija *f. (2)* category
ką tik *part.* just, now
katinas *m. (1)* cat
kaukė *f. (2)* mask
kaukolė *f. (2)* skull
kaulas *m. (1)* bone
kauliukas *m. (1)* pit (of a fruit)
kava *f. (2)* coffee
kavinė *f. (2)* café, coffee shop
kavinukas *m. (1)* coffee pot
kėdė *f. (2)* chair
kefyras *m. (1)* kefir
keikti *v. (1)* curse, scold
keistas, -a *adj. (1)* strange, odd
keisti *v. (1)* change
keitimas *m. (1)* exchange
keleivinis, -ė *adj. (3)* passenger
keleivis, -ė *m. (1), f. (2)* passenger
keletas *pron. m. sg.* several
keli, -ios *pron. m. pl.* several
kelias *m. (1)* road
keliauti *v. (1)* travel
kėlinys *m. (1)* half-time
kelionė *f. (2)* journey, trip
kelioninis, -ė *adj. (3)* travel
kelmas *m. (1)* stump
kelnaitės *f. pl. (2)* panties, underwear
kelnės *f. pl. (2)* trousers, pants
keltas *m. (1)* ferry
kempinė *f. (2)* sponge
kenkti *v. (1)* sabotage; be injurious
kentėti *v. (1)* suffer
kepalas *m. (1)* loaf
kepėjas, -a *m. (1), f. (2)* baker
kepenys *f. pl. (3)* liver
kepykla *f. (2)* bakery
kepsnys *m. (1)* steak, roast meat
kepurė *f. (2)* cap
keramika *f. (2)* ceramics
keršyti *v. (1)* revenge oneself

keturi, -ios *num.* four
ketvirtadienis *m. (1)* Thursday
kiaulė *f. (2)* pig
kiauliena *f. (2)* pork
kiaušidė *med. f. (2)* ovary
kiaušinėlis *med. m. (1)* egg
kiaušinienė *f. (2)* omelet
kiaušinis *m. (1)* egg
kibiras *m. (1)* bucket
kiek *adv.* how many, how much
kiekis *m. (1)* quantity
kiemas *m. (1)* yard
kieno *pron.* whose
kietas, -a *adj. (1)* hard
kilimas *m. (1)* carpet
kilmė *f. (2)* origin
kilmingas, -a *adj. (1)* noble, of high descent
kilnus, -i *adj. (2)* generous, noble
kilogramas *m. (1)* kilogram
kinas *m. (1)* cinema
kinas, -ė *m. (1), f. (2)* Chinese
kiniškas, -a *adj. (1)* Chinese
kinoteatras *m. (1)* movie theater
kioskas *m. (1)* kiosk, newsstand
kirmėlė *f. (2)* worm
kirpėjas, -a *m. (1), f. (2)* hairdresser, barber
kirpykla *f. (2)* hair salon, barber's shop
kirpimas *m. (1)* haircut
kirpti *v. (1)* cut (with scissors)
kirvis *m. (1)* ax
kisielius *m. (4)* jelly-like cranberry drink
kišenė *f. (2)* pocket
kišeninis, -ė *adj. (3)* pocket
kišenvagis, -ė *m. (1), f. (2)* pickpocket
kyšininkas, -ė *m. (1), f. (2)* bribe-taker
kyšis *m. (1)* bribe
kiškis *m. (1)* hare
kištukas *col. m. (1)* plug
kitaip *adv.* differently, otherwise
kitas, -a *pron. m.* other
kitatautis, -ė *m. (1), f. (2)* foreigner
kitoks, -ia *pron. m.* different
klaida *f. (2)* mistake, error
klaidžioti *v. (1)* roam, wander
klasė *f. (2)* classroom, class
klasikas, -ė *m. (1), f. (2)* classic
klasikinis, -ė *adj. (3)* classic(al)
klausa *f. (2)* hearing
klausimas *m. (1)* question
klausyti *v. (3)* listen
klausti *v. (1)* ask, inquire
klaviatūra *f. (2)* keyboard
klebonas *m. (1)* parish priest
klestėti *v. (2)* prosper
klevas *m. (1)* maple tree
klientas, -ė *m. (1), f. (2)* client
klientūra *f. (2)* clientele
klijai *m. pl. (1)* glue
klijuoti *v. (1)* glue
klimatas *m. (1)* climate
klysti *v. (1)* be wrong, make mistakes
klubas *m. (1)* club; hip
klumpė *f. (2)* wooden shoe
klusnus, -i *adj. (2)* obedient
kmynas *m. (1)* caraway, cumin
knarkti *v. (1)* snore
knyga *f. (2)* book
knygynas *m. (1)* bookstore
ko *adv.* why, what
kodėl *adv.* why
koja *f. (2)* foot, leg
kojinė *f. (2)* stocking
kokybė *f. (2)* quality
kokybiškas, -a *adj. (1)* of high quality
koks, -ia *pron. m.* what (kind)
kol *conj.* while, until
koldūnai *m. pl. (1)* dumplings
kolega *m./f. (2)* colleague
kolekcija *f. (2)* collection
kolekcionierius, -ė *m. (4), f. (2)* collector
kolekcionuoti *v. (1)* collect
kolektyvas *m. (1)* collective body, coworkers
kolona *f. (2)* column
kolonija *f. (2)* colony
kolonizacija *f. (2)* colonization
kolūkis *arch. m. (1)* kolkhoz, collective farm
komanda *f. (2)* team, command
komandiruotė *f. (2)* business trip
komedija *f. (2)* comedy
komentuoti *v. (1)* comment
komercija *f. (2)* commerce
komercinis, -ė *adj. (3)* commercial
komfortas *m. (1)* luxury
komfortabilus, -i *adj. (2)* luxurious
komisaras, -ė *m. (1), f. (2)* commissar

komisas *m. (1)* consignment store, commission
komisija *f. (2)* commission, committee
komiškas, -a *adj. (1)* comic
komitetas *m. (1)* committee
komoda *f. (2)* chest of drawers
kompanija *f. (2)* company
kompasas *m. (1)* compass
kompensacija *f. (2)* compensation
kompensuoti *v. (1)* compensate
kompiuteris *m. (1)* computer
komplektas *m. (1)* set
kompotas *m. (1)* a drink made of stewed fruit
kompozitorius, -ė *m. (4), f. (2)* composer
komunikacija *f. (2)* communication
koncentracija *f. (2)* concentration
koncertas *m. (1)* concert
koncertuoti *v. (1)* give concerts
konditerija *f. (2)* confectionery
konferencija *f. (2)* conference
konfiskuoti *v. (1)* confiscate
konfliktas *m. (1)* conflict
konjakas *m. (1)* cognac
konkretus, -i *adj. (2)* concrete, specific
konkurencija *f. (2)* competition
konkurentas, -ė *m. (1), f. (2)* competitor
konkuruoti *v. (1)* compete
konservai *m. pl. (1)* canned food
konservatyvus, -i *adj. (2)* conservative
konservatorius, -ė *polit. m. (4), f. (2)* conservative
konspektuoti *v. (1)* take notes
konsulatas *m. (1)* consulate
konsultacija *f. (2)* consultation
konsultantas, -ė *m. (1), f. (2)* consultant, adviser
konsultuoti *v. (1)* advise
konsultuotis *v. (1)* consult, get advice
kontaktas *m. (1)* contact
kontaktiniai lęšiai contact lenses
kontaktuoti *v. (1)* contact
kontekstas *m. (1)* context
kontora *f. (2)* office, bureau
kontrabanda *f. (2)* contraband, smuggling
kontrabandininkas, -ė *m. (1), f. (2)* smuggler
kontrastas *m. (1)* contrast
kontrolė *f. (2)* control
kontroliuoti *v. (1)* control
kooperacija *f. (2)* cooperation
kooperuotis *v. (1)* cooperate
koordinuoti *v. (1)* coordinate
kopėčios *f. pl. (2)* ladder
kopija *f. (2)* copy
kopijuoti *v. (1)* copy
koplyčia *f. (2)* chapel
kopūstas *m. (1)* cabbage
korėjietis, -ė *m. (1), f. (2)* Korean
korėjietiškas, -a *adj. (1)* Korean
korektiškas, -a *adj. (1)* proper
korektorius, -ė *m. (4), f. (2)* proofreader
korespondencija *f. (2)* correspondence, mail
korespondentas, -ė *m. (1), f. (2)* correspondent, reporter
koridorius *m. (4)* corridor, passage
korta *f. (2)* card (for playing)
kosėti *v. (2)* cough
kostiumas *m. (1)* suit, costume
košė *f. (2)* porridge
kotas *m. (1)* handle
kotletas *m. (1)* cutlet
kova *f. (2)* struggle, fight
kovas *m. (1)* March; rook
kovoti *v. (1)* fight
kraitis *m. (1)* dowry
kramtyti *v. (3)* chew
kramtomoji guma chewing gum
kranas *m. (1)* tap, faucet; crane
krantas *m. (1)* bank, seashore
krapai *m. pl. (1)* dill
kraštas *m. (1)* edge; land, country
kraštotyra *f. (2)* study of local culture
kraštovaizdis *m. (1)* landscape, scenery
krata *f. (2)* search
kratos orderis search warrant
kraujagyslė *f. (2)* blood vessel
kraujas *m. (4)* blood
kraujospūdis *m. (1)* blood pressure
kraujuotas, -a *adj. (1)* bloody, stained with blood
kraujuoti *v. (1)* bleed
kraustytis *v. (3)* move to a new residence
krauti *v. (1)* load
krautuvė *f. (2)* store, shop
kreditas *m. (1)* credit
kreditinė kortelė credit card

kreditorius, -ė *m. (4), f. (2)* creditor
kreida *f. (2)* chalk
kreipti (dėmesį) *v. (1)* pay (attention)
kreivas, -a *adj. (1)* crooked, wry
kremas *m. (1)* cream
krepšininkas, -ė *m. (1), f. (2)* basketball player
krepšinio kamuolys basketball (ball)
krepšinis *m. (1)* basketball (game)
krešulys *m. (1)* clot of blood
kriauklė *f. (2)* shell; sink
kriaušė *f. (2)* pear
krienai *m. pl. (1)* horseradish
krikščionybė *f. (2)* Christianity
krikščionis, -ė *m. (1), f. (2)* Christian
krikščioniškas, -a *adj. (1)* Christian
krikštaduktė *f. (2)* Goddaughter
krikštamotė *f. (2)* Godmother
krikštas *m. (1)* baptism
krikštasūnis *m. (1)* Godson
krikštatėvis *m. (1)* Godfather
krikštynos *f. pl. (2)* baptism party, christening party
kriminalinis, -ė *adj. (3)* criminal
kristalas *m. (1)* crystal
kristi *v. (1)* fall, drop
kritika *f. (2)* criticism
kritikas, -ė *m. (1), f. (2)* critic
kritinis, -ė *adj. (3)* critical
krituliai *m. pl. (1)* precipitation
krizė *f. (2)* crisis
kryžius *m. (4)* cross
kronika *f. (2)* chronicle
krosnis *f. (3)* stove (covered with tiles)
krūmas *m. (1)* bush
kruopos *f. pl. (2)* grain; barley soup
kruopštus, -i *adj. (2)* thorough, meticulous
kruša *f. (2)* hail
krūtinė *f. (2)* chest, breast
krūtis *f. (3)* breast
krūva *f. (2)* pile
kruvinas, -a *adj. (1)* bloody, stained with blood
kubas *m. (1)* cube
kūdikis *m. (1)* baby
kūdikystė *f. (2)* infancy
kuklus, -i *adj. (2)* modest
kukurūzai *m. pl. (1)* corn
kulinaras, -ė *m. (1), f. (2)* chef, cook
kulinarinis, -ė *adj. (3)* culinary
kulka *f. (2)* bullet
kulkosvaidis *m. (1)* machine-gun
kulnas *m. (1)* heel
kultas *m. (1)* cult
kultūra *f. (2)* culture
kumelė *f. (2)* mare
kumpis *m. (1)* ham
kumštis *m. (1)* fist
kūnas *m. (1)* body
kunigaikštienė *f. (2)* duchess
kunigaikštis *m. (1)* duke
kunigas *m. (1)* priest (Roman Catholic)
kuprinė *f. (2)* backpack
kur *adv.* where
kuras *m. (1)* fuel
kurčias, -ia *adj. (1)* deaf
kūrėjas, -a *m. (1), f. (2)* creator, founder
kūrenti *v. (1)* heat
kūryba *f. (2)* creation, works
kūrybingas, -a *adj. (1)* creative
kuris, -i *pron. m.* which one
kurortas *m. (1)* health resort
kurti *v. (1)* create, found
kvadratas *m. (1)* square
kvailas, -a *adj. (1)* foolish, stupid
kvaišalai *m. pl. (1)* narcotics, drugs; alcoholic beverages
kvalifikacija *f. (2)* qualification
kvapas *m. (1)* smell, odor
kvepalai *m. pl. (1)* perfume
kvepėti *v. (1)* smell
kviesti *v. (1)* invite
kvitas *m. (1)* receipt
kvosti *v. (1)* question, interrogate
kvota *f. (2)* investigation, interrogation; *econ.* quota

L

laba diena! good afternoon!
labai *adv.* very
labanakt(is)! good night!
labas! hello!
labdara *f. (2)* charity
laboratorija *f. (2)* laboratory
lagaminas *m. (1)* suitcase
laida *f. (2)* issue
laidas *m. (1)* wire
laidoti *v. (1)* bury
laidotuvės *f. pl. (2)* funeral
laikas *m. (1)* time

laikinas, -a *adj. (1)* temporary
laikyti *v. (3)* keep; hold
laikotarpis *m. (1)* period, age
laikraštis *m. (1)* newspaper
laikrodis *m. (1)* watch; clock
laiku *adv.* in time, on time
laimė *f. (2)* happiness
laimėjimas *m. (1)* achievement; gain, prize
laimėti *v. (2)* win
laimingas, -a *adj. (1)* happy
laiminti *v. (1)* bless
laiptai *m. pl. (1)* stairs
laistyti *v. (3)* water (plants)
laisvalaikis *m. (1)* leisure
laisvas, -a *adj. (1)* free, liberated
laisvė *f. (2)* freedom
laiškanešys, -ė *m. (1), f. (2)* letter-carrier
laiškas *m. (1)* letter
laivas *m. (1)* ship
laivynas *m. (1)* fleet
lakas *m. (1)* varnish; hairspray; polish
lakūnas *m. (1)* pilot
langas *m. (1)* window
lankymas *m. (1)* visitation
lankyti *v. (3)* visit
lapas *m. (1)* leaf; sheet
lapė *f. (2)* fox
lapkritis *m. (1)* November
lašas *m. (1)* drop
lašėti *v. (1)* drip, drop
lašiniai *m. pl. (1)* bacon
lašiša *f. (2)* salmon
latvis, -ė *m. (1), f. (2)* Latvian
latviškas, -a *adj. (1)* Latvian
laukas *m. (1)* field
lauke *adv.* out(side)
laukiamasis *m. (1)* waiting room
laukinis, -ė *adj. (3), m. (1), f. (2)* wild, savage
laukti *v. (1)* wait
lauktuvės *f. pl. (2)* presents (from a trip)
laužas *m. (1)* bonfire
laužyti *v. (3)* break
lavonas *m. (1)* corpse
lazda *f. (2)* stick, cane
lažybos *f. pl. (2)* bet
lažintis *v. (1)* bet
ledai *m. pl. (1)* ice cream
ledas *m. (1)* ice
ledynas *m. (1)* glacier
legalizuoti *v. (1)* legalize
legalus, -i *adj. (2)* legal
legenda *f. (2)* legend
legendinis, -ė *adj. (3)* legendary
leidykla *f. (2)* publishing house
leidimas *m. (1)* edition; permission
leidinys *m. (1)* publication
leisti *v. (1)* allow, permit
leitenantas, -ė *m. (1), f. (2)* lieutenant
leksika *f. (2)* vocabulary
lektorius, -ė *m. (4), f. (2)* lecturer, reader
lėktuvas *m. (1)* plane
lėlė *f. (2)* doll
lempa *f. (2)* lamp
lengvas, -a *adj. (1)* light; easy
lenkas, -ė *m. (1), f. (2)* Pole
lenkiškas, -a *adj. (1)* Polish
lenktynės *f. pl. (2)* race
lenktis *v. (1)* bend (down), bow (down)
lenta *f. (2)* board
lepinti *v. (1)* spoil (a person)
lėšos *f. pl. (2)* means (monetary)
lėtas, -a *adj. (1)* slow
liaudis *f. (3)* people
liauka *f. (2)* gland
liautis *v. (1)* stop, cease
liberalas, -ė *polit. m. (1), f. (2)* liberal
lydeka *f. (2)* pike
lyderis, -ė *m. (1), f. (2)* leader
lydėti *v. (2)* accompany
liekana *f. (2)* remainder; remnant
lieknas, -a *adj. (1)* slender
liemenė *f. (2)* vest
liemuo *m. (5)* waist; trunk
liepa *f. (2)* lime (tree), linden (tree); July
liepsna *f. (2)* flame
liepti *v. (1)* order, tell
liesas, -a *adj. (1)* lean, thin
liesti *v. (1)* touch
lietingas, -a *adj. (1)* rainy
lietpaltis *m. (1)* raincoat
lietus *m. (4)* rain
lietuvaitė *f. (2)* Lithuanian girl
lietuvybė *f. (2)* Lithuanianism
lietuvis, -ė *m. (1), f. (2)* Lithuanian
lietuviškas, -a *adj. (1)* Lithuanian
liežuvauti *v. (1)* gossip
liežuvis *m. (1)* tongue
liftas *m. (1)* elevator

liftininkas, -ė *m. (1), f. (2)* elevator operator
lig(i) *adv.* until
lyg *part.* like, as
liga *f. (2)* illness
lygiai *adv.* equally, evenly
lygybė *f. (2)* equality
lyginti *v. (1)* compare; smooth; iron
lygintuvas *m. (1)* iron (for ironing)
lygis *m. (1)* level
ligoninė *f. (2)* hospital
ligonis, -ė *m. (1), f. (2)* patient
ligotas, -a *adj. (1)* ailing, unhealthy
lyguma *f. (2)* plain
lygus, -i *adj. (2)* flat; even; equal
likeris *m. (1)* liqueur
likimas *m. (1)* fate, destiny
likti *v. (1)* remain, stay
likutis *m. (1)* remainder, remnant
limitas *m. (1)* limit
limonadas *m. (1)* lemonade
lingvistas, -ė *m. (1), f. (2)* linguist
lingvistika *f. (2)* linguistics
linija *f. (2)* line
lininis, -ė *adj. (3)* linen
linkėjimai *m. pl. (1)* wishes, regards
linksmas, -a *adj. (1)* merry, joyful
linksminti *v. (1)* entertain, amuse
linksmintis *v. (1)* entertain oneself
lipti *v. (1)* climb
lyrika *f. (2)* lyric, poetry
lįsti *v. (1)* get (in/ into); bother
literatas, -ė *m. (1), f. (2)* writer, person of letters
lyti *v. (1)* rain
lytinis, -ė *adj. (3)* sexual
lytinis aktas (sexual) intercourse
lytinė liga sexual disease (STD)
lytis *f. (3)* sex; gender
litras *m. (1)* liter
lituanistas, -ė *m. (1), f. (2)* specialist in Lithuanian philology
lituanistika *f. (2)* Lithuanistics
liūdėti *v. (2)* sadness
liudijimas *m. (1)* certificate
liudininkas, -ė *m. (1), f. (2)* witness
liudyti *v. (1)* witness, testify
liūtas, -ė *m. (1), f. (2)* lion, -ess
liuteronas, -ė *m. (1), f. (2)* Lutheran
liuteroniškas, -a *adj. (1)* Lutheran
liūtis *f. (3)* heavy shower
lizdas *m. (1)* nest
lobis *m. (1)* treasure
logika *f. (2)* logic
logiškas, -a *adj. (1)* logic
lojalus, -i *adj. (2)* loyal
lokys *m. (1)* bear
lombardas *m. (1)* pawnshop
lopas *m. (1)* patch
(vaikų) lopšelis *m. (1)* nursery
lošėjas, -a *m. (1), f. (2)* player
lošti *v. (1)* play (cards)
loterija *f. (2)* lottery
loti *v. (1)* bark
lova *f. (2)* bed
lovatiesė *f. (2)* bedspread
lubos *f. pl. (2)* ceiling
lunatikas, -ė *m. (1), f. (2)* sleepwalker
luošas, -a *adj. (1)* cripple
lūpa *f. (2)* lip

M

mačas *m. (1)* match, contest
mada *f. (2)* fashion
madingas, -a *adj. (1)* fashionable
magistralė *f. (2)* highway
magistrantas, -ė *m. (1), f. (2)* graduate student (master's level)
magiškas, -a *adj. (1)* magic
magnetas *m. (1)* magnet
magnetofonas *m. (1)* tape-recorder, boombox
mainai *m. pl. (1)* exchange, barter
maistas *m. (1)* food
maistingas, -a *adj. (1)* nutritious
maišas *m. (1)* bag
maišyti *v. (3)* stir; impede
maištas *m. (1)* revolt, riot
maištauti *v. (1)* rebel
maištingas, -a *adj. (1)* rebellious
maištininkas, -ė *m. (1), f. (2)* rebel
maitinimas *m. (1)* feeding
maitinti *v. (1)* feed
majoras, -ė *mil. m. (1), f. (2)* major
makaronai *m. pl. (1)* noodles
malda *f. (2)* prayer
maldaknygė *f. (2)* prayer book
maldauti *v. (1)* beg
maldininkas, -ė *m. (1), f. (2)* pilgrim
malūnas *m. (1)* mill
mama *f. (2)* mother, Mom
mamytė *f. (2)* Mom
man *pron.* for me
mandagumas *m. (1)* politeness, courtesy
mandagus, -i *adj. (2)* polite, civil

mandarinas *m. (1)* tangerine, mandarin
manyti *v. (3)* think
mankšta *f. (2)* gymnastics, exercise
mano *pron.* my, mine
maras *m. (1)* plague
margarinas *m. (1)* margarine
margas, -a *adj. (1)* multicolored
marinuotas, -a *adj. (1)* pickled
marios *f. pl. (2)* lagoon
marlė *f. (2)* gauze
marmeladas *m. (1)* fruit jelly
marmuras *m. (1)* marble
marmurinis, -ė *adj. (3)* marble
marškiniai *m. pl. (1)* shirt, chemise
maršrutas *m. (1)* route, itinerary
marti *f. (2)* daughter-in-law
masažas *m. (1)* massage
masažistas, -ė *m. (1), f. (2)* masseur, -euse
masė *f. (2)* mass, weight
mastelis *m. (1)* scale
mąstymas *m. (1)* thinking
mąstyti *v. (3)* think, meditate, ponder
mašina *f. (2)* machine, car
mašinistas, -ė *m. (1), f. (2)* machinist
matematika *f. (2)* mathematics
materialinis, -ė *adj. (3)* material
materialistinis, -ė *adj. (3)* materialistic
matymas *m. (1)* vision, sight
matyti *v. (3)* see
matmenys *m. pl. (5)* measurement
matomas, -a *adj. (1)* visible
maudytis *v. (3)* bathe
maudymosi kostiumėlis swimming suit
mazgas *m. (1)* knot
mažas, -a *adj. (1)* little, small
mažakraujystė *med. f. (2)* anemia
mažametis, -ė *m. (1), f. (2)* juvenile
maždaug *adv.* approximately
mažėti *v. (1)* diminish, decrease
mažiausia *adv.* the least
mažylis, -ė *m. (1), f. (2)* baby
mažmeninis, -ė *adj. (3)* retail
mažuma *f. (2)* minority
mechanika *f. (2)* mechanics
mechanikas, -ė *m. (1), f. (2)* mechanic
mečetė *f. (2)* mosque
medalis *m. (1)* medal
medaus mėnuo honeymoon
medicina *f. (2)* medicine
mediena *f. (2)* timber
medikas, -ė *m. (1), f. (2)* physician; medical student
medinis, -ė *adj. (3)* wooden
medis *m. (1)* tree
medus *m. (4)* honey
medvilnė *f. (2)* cotton
medžiaga *f. (2)* material, fabric
medžioklė *f. (2)* hunt
medžioklinis, -ė *adj. (3)* hunting
medžiotojas, -a *m. (1), f. (2)* hunter
mėgdžioti *v. (1)* imitate
mėgėjiškas, -a *adj. (1)* amateur
mėginimas *m. (1)* attempt
mėginti *v. (1)* attempt
mėgti *v. (1)* like
megztinis *m. (1)* sweater
meilė *f. (2)* love
meilus, -i *adj. (2)* tender, affectionate, sweet
meilužis *m. (1)* lover
meilužė *f. (2)* mistress (lover)
melagingas, -a *adj. (1)* false, deceitful
melagis, -ė *m. (1), f. (2)* liar
melas *m. (1)* lie
mėlynakis, -ė *adj. (3)* blue-eyed
mėlynas, -a *adj. (1)* blue
mėlynė *f. (2)* bruise; blueberry
melstis *v. (1)* pray
meluoti *v. (1)* lie
menas *m. (1)* art
mėnesinis, -ė *adj. (3)* monthly
mėnesis *m. (1)* month
menininkas, -ė *m. (1), f. (2)* artist
meniškas, -a *adj. (1)* artistic
menkė *f. (2)* cod
menstruacijos *f. pl. (2)* menstruation
mėnulis *m. (1)* moon
mėnuo *m. (5)* month
mergaitė *f. (2)* girl (little)
mergina *f. (2)* girl (young); girlfriend
mes *pron.* we
mėsa *f. (2)* meat; flesh; pulp
mėsingas, -a *adj. (1)* meaty
mesti *v. (1)* throw
meška *f. (2)* bear
meškerė *f. (2)* fishing rod
meškerioti *v. (1)* fish
meškeriotojas, -a *m. (1), f. (2)* angler

mėšlas *m. (1)* dung, excrement
mėšlungis *m. (1)* cramp, convulsion
mėta *f. (2)* mint
metafora *f. (2)* metaphor
metai *m. pl. (1)* year
metalas *m. (1)* metal
metalinis, -ė *adj. (3)* metal
metas *m. (1)* time
metinės *f. pl. (2)* anniversary
mėtinis, -ė *adj. (3)* mint
metodas *m. (1)* method, way, mode
metras *m. (1)* meter
metraštis *m. (1)* chronicle
metro *m. (n.d.)* subway, the underground
midus *m. (4)* mead
miegas *m. (1)* sleep
miegmaišis *m. (1)* miegmaišis
miegoti *v. (1)* sleep
mieguistas, -a *adj. (1)* sleepy
mieguistumas *m. (1)* sleepiness, drowsiness
mielas, -a *adj. (1)* nice, sweet
mielės *f. pl. (2)* yeast
mielinis, -ė *adj. (3)* baked with yeast
miestas *m. (1)* town, city
miestelis *m. (1)* town (small)
miestietis, -ė *m. (1), f. (2)* city dweller
miežiai *m. pl. (1)* barley
migdolai *m. pl. (1)* almonds
migdolinis, -ė *adj. (3)* almond
mikrofonas *m. (1)* microphone
mikroskopas *m. (1)* microscope
mylėti *v. (2)* love
mylėtis *v. (2)* make love
mylia *f. (2)* mile
milijardas *m. (1)* billion
milijonas *m. (1)* million
milijonierius, -ė *m. (4), f. (2)* millionaire
mylimas, -a *adj. (1)* beloved, dear
mylimasis, -oji *adj. m.* sweetheart
milimetras *m. (1)* millimeter
miltai *m. pl. (1)* flour
milteliai *m. pl. (1)* powder
milžinas, -ė *m. (1), f. (2)* giant
milžiniškas, -a *adj. (1)* gigantic
mina *f. (2)* mine; (facial) expression
mineralas *m. (1)* mineral
mineralinis, -ė *adj. (3)* mineral
minia *f. (2)* crowd
ministerija *polit. f. (2)* ministry
ministras, -ė *polit. m. (1), f. (2)* minister
Ministras, -ė Pirmininkas, -ė *polit.* Prime Minister
minkštas, -a *adj. (1)* soft
mintis *f. (3)* thought
minusas *m. (1)* minus, drawback
minutė *f. (2)* minute
mirti *v. (1)* die
mirtinas, -a *adj. (1)* mortal (wound)
mirtis *f. (3)* death
misija *f. (2)* mission
misionierius, -ė *m. (4), f. (2)* missionary
mįslė *f. (2)* riddle
mįslingas, -a *adj. (1)* mysterious
mišios *f. pl. (2)* Mass (as in the liturgy of the Eucharist)
miškas *m. (1)* forest
miškingas, -a *adj. (1)* woody
miškininkystė *f. (2)* forestry
mišrainė *f. (2)* salad (usually potato)
mitas *m. (1)* myth
mitinis, -ė *adj. (3)* mythical
močiutė *f. (2)* granny
modelis *m. (1)* model, pattern, cut
modemas *m. (1)* modem
modernus, -i *adj. (2)* modern
modifikuoti *v. (1)* modify
mojuoti *v. (1)* wave
mokestis *m. (1)* tax, dues, fee
mokėti *v. (1)* pay; be able to (do something)
mokėtojas, -a *m. (1), f. (2)* payer
mokykla *f. (2)* school
mokymas *m. (1)* teaching
mokinys, -ė *m. (1), f. (2)* pupil, disciple, student (of school)
mokyti *v. (3)* teach
mokytis *v. (3)* learn
mokytojas, -a *m. (1), f. (2)* teacher
mokslas *m. (1)* science; education; learning
moksleivis, -ė *m. (1), f. (2)* pupil, student (of school)
mokslininkas, -ė *m. (1), f. (2)* scientist, scholar
mokslinis, -ė *adj. (3)* scientific, scholarly
molekulinis, -ė *adj. (3)* molecular
molis *m. (1)* clay
moliūgas *m. (1)* pumpkin
momentas *m. (1)* moment

monarchas, -ė *m. (1), f. (2)* monarch
monarchija *f. (2)* monarchy
moneta *f. (2)* coin
mongolas, -ė *m. (1), f. (2)* Mongolian
mongoliškas, -a *adj. (1)* Mongolian
monopolija *f. (2)* monopoly
moralė *f. (2)* morals
morka *f. (2)* carrot
mostas *m. (1)* gesture
moteris *f. (3)* woman
moteriškas, -a *adj. (1)* female, feminine
moteriškumas *m. (1)* femininity
motina *f. (2)* mother
motinystė *f. (2)* motherhood
motiniškas, -a *adj. (1)* motherly
motyvas *m. (1)* motive, cause
motociklas *m. (1)* motorcycle
motociklininkas, -ė *m. (1), f. (2)* motorcyclist
motoras *m. (1)* motor, engine
motorizuotas, -a *adj. (1)* motorized
motoroleris *m. (1)* scooter
mozaika *f. (2)* mosaic
mugė *f. (2)* fair
muilas *m. (1)* soap
muilinė *f. (2)* soap dish
muitas *m. (1)* duty (customs)
muitinė *f. (2)* customs
muitininkas, -ė *m. (1), f. (2)* customs officer
mūrinis, -ė *adj. (3)* brick, stone
murzinas, -a *adj. (1)* dirty
musė *f. (2)* fly
mūsų *pron.* our(s)
musulmonas, -ė *m. (1), f. (2)* Moslem
mušti *v. (1)* beat
muštynės *f. pl. (2)* (fist) fight
muštis *v. (1)* fight
muziejus *m. (4)* museum
muzika *f. (2)* music
muzikantas, -ė *m. (1), f. (2)* musician
muzikas, -ė *m. (1), f. (2)* musician

N

nacija *f. (2)* nation
nacionalinis, -ė *adj. (3)* national
nacionalistas, -ė *m. (1), f. (2)* nationalist
nacionalistinis, -ė *adj. (3)* nationalistic
nacionalizmas *m. (1)* nationalism
nacionalizuoti *v. (1)* nationalize
nacis, -ė *m. (1), f. (2)* nazi
nacistas, -ė *m. (1), f. (2)* nazi
nafta *f. (2)* oil
nagas *m. (1)* nail; claw
nagrinėti *v. (1)* analyze
naikinti *v. (1)* destroy, exterminate
naikintuvas *m. (1)* fighter jet
naivumas *m. (1)* naïveté
naivus, -i *adj. (2)* naïve
naktinis, -ė *adj. (3)* night
naktinis klubas night club
naktiniai marškiniai night gown
naktis *f. (3)* night
nakvynė *f. (2)* lodging for the night
nakvoti *v. (1)* spend the night
namai *m. pl. (1)* home, houses
namas *m. (1)* house
namie *adv.* at home
naminis, -ė *adj. (3)* domestic
namiškiai *m. pl. (1)* household
naras *m. (1)* diver
nardyti *v. (3)* dive
narys, -ė *m. (1), f. (2)* member
narkomanas, -ė *m. (1), f. (2)* drug addict
narkotikai *m. pl. (1)* drugs, narcotics
narkozė *med. f. (2)* anesthesia
narsus, -i *adj. (2)* courageous
naršyklė *f. (2)* web browser
narvas *m. (1)* cage
nasrai *m. pl. (1)* jaws
našlaitis, -ė *m. (1) f. (2)* orphan
našlys, -ė *m. (1) f. (2)* widower, widow
našumas *m. (1)* productivity
natiurmortas *m. (1)* still-life
natūra *f. (2)* nature
nauda *f. (2)* use, benefit
naudoti(s) *v. (1)* use
naujadaras *m. (1)* neologism
naujagimis, -ė *m. (1), f. (2)* newborn (child)
naujas, -a *adj. (1)* new
naujiena *f. (2)* news; novelty
naujovė *f. (2)* novelty
navigacija *f. (2)* navigation
ne *part.* no, not

nė *part.* no, not
neaiškus, -i *adj. (2)* vague, fishy
neapgalvotas, -a *adj. (1)* rash, hasty
neapykanta *f. (2)* hatred
neapsižiūrėti *v. (2)* overlook
neatidėliotinas, -a *adj. (1)* urgent
neatsargus, -i *adj. (2)* careless
nebe *part.* no more, no longer
nebent *part.* unless, except
nebylys, -ė *m. (1), f. (2)* mute person
nebūti *v. (1, irr.)* to not be
nedarbas *m. (1)* unemployment
nedaug *adv.* a little
nedegamas, -a *adj. (1)* fireproof
nedelsiant *adv.* immediately, without delay
nedoras, -a *adj. (1)* immoral; possessing evil intentions
nedrąsus, -i *adj. (2)* shy, bashful
negalima (it is) forbidden
negarbingas, -a *adj. (1)* infamous, unprincipled
negatyvas *m. (1)* negative
negilus, -i *adj. (2)* shallow; not deep
negirdėtas, -a *adj. (1)* unheard
negyvas, -a *adj. (1)* dead
negyvenamas, -a *adj. (1)* uninhibited
negu *part.* than
nei *part.* neither, than
neigiamai *adv.* negatively
neigti *v. (1)* deny
neįgyvendinamas, -a *adj. (1)* unrealizable
neilgai *adv.* not long
neįmanomas, -a *adj. (1)* impossible
neišauklėtas, -a *adj. (1)* ill-bread
neišgydomas, -a *adj. (1)* incurable
neištikimas, -a *adj. (1)* unfaithful
neišvengiamas, -a *adj. (1)* inevitable
nejaugi? *part.* really?
nekaip *adv.* poorly
nekaltas, -a *adj. (1)* innocent
nekenksmingas, -a *adj. (1)* harmless
nekęsti *v. (1)* hate
nė kiek not a bit
nekilnojamas turtas real estate
neklausyti *v. (3)* disobey
ne koks, -ia *adj. m.* not of the best quality
nelaimė *f. (2)* misfortune
nelaimingas, -a *adj. (1)* unhappy
nelauktas, -a *adj. (1)* unexpected
neleisti *v. (1)* forbid, not allow
neliečiamumas *m. (1)* immunity
nelygybė *f. (2)* inequality
nemalonė *f. (2)* disgrace
nemandagus, -i *adj. (2)* rude
nematytas, -a *adj. (1)* unseen
nemažas, -a *adj. (1)* not little
nemėgti *v. (1)* dislike
nemiga *f. (2)* insomnia
nemokamai *adv.* free of charge
nenuoširdus, -i *adj. (2)* insincere
nepageidaujamas, -a *adj. (1)* undesirable
nepagydomas, -a *adj. (1)* incurable
nepasisekti *v. (1)* fall through
nepasitikėti *v. (2)* distrust
nepataikyti *v. (3)* miss (the target)
nepatogus, -i *adj. (2)* uncomfortable; awkward
nepavojingas, -a *adj. (1)* safe, not dangerous
nepažįstamas, -a *adj. (1)* unknown, strange
neperšlampamas, -a *adj. (1)* waterproof
nepilnametis, -ė *m. (1)* minor, underage
nepriklausomas, -a *adj. (1)* independent
nepriklausomybė *f. (2)* independence
nėra *v.* there is/ are no
neramumai *m. pl. (1)* disturbance
nereikalingas, -a *adj. (1)* unnecessary
nerimas *m. (1)* anxiety
nėriniai *m. pl. (1)* lace
nervai *m. pl. (1)* nerves
nervingas, -a *adj. (1)* nervous
nes *conj.* because
nesąmonė *f. (2)* nonsense
nesąžiningas, -a *adj. (1)* dishonest
nesėkmė *f. (2)* failure
neseniai *adv.* recently
nesudėtingas, -a *adj. (1)* simple
nesuprantamas, -a *adj. (1)* incomprehensible
nesveikas, -a *adj. (1)* unhealthy
nėščia *adj. f. (1)* pregnant
nešiojamas kompiuteris laptop
nešti *v. (1)* carry

nėštumas *m. (1)* pregnancy
nešvarus, -i *adj. (2)* dirty
neteisybė *f. (2)* injustice
netekti *v. (1)* lose
netektis *f. (3)* loss
netyčia *adv.* unintentionally
netiesioginis, -ė *adj. (3)* indirect
netikėtas, -a *adj. (1)* unexpected
netikras, -a *adj. (1)* artificial, fake, uncertain
netinkamas, -a *adj. (1)* unfit, unsuitable
netoli *adv.* not far
neturtas *m. (1)* poverty
neturtingas, -a *adj. (1)* poor, not rich
neutralus, -i *adj. (2)* neutral
neužimtas, -a *adj. (1)* vacant, free
neužmirštamas, -a *adj. (1)* unforgettable
neva *part.* as if
nevalgomas, -a *adj. (1)* inedible
nevedęs *adj.* unmarried (man)
neviltis *f. (3)* despair
nežymus, -i *adj. (2)* insignificant
nežinomas, -a *adj. (1)* unknown
nežmoniškas, -a *adj. (1)* inhuman, brutal
niekada *adv.* never
niekaip *adv.* in no way
niekas *pron. m.* nothing, nobody
niekieno *pron. m.* nobody's
niekis *m. (1)* nothing, nevermind
niekur *adv.* nowhere
niežėti *v. (1)* itch
nykštys *m. (1)* thumb
nykti *v. (1)* disappear, become extinct
niūrus, -i *adj. (2)* gloomy
nokti *v. (1)* ripen
noras *m. (1)* wish, will
normalus, -i *adj. (2)* normal
nors *conj.* though
norvegas, -ė *m. (1), f. (2)* Norwegian
norvegiškas, -a *adj. (1)* Norwegian
nosinė *f. (2)* handkerchief
nosis *f. (3)* nose
notaras, -ė *m. (1), f. (2)* notary
nubausti *v. (1)* punish
nudegimas *m. (1)* burn, sunburn
nudegti *v. (1)* tan, get burned
nueiti *v. (1; irr.)* go away
nufotografuoti *v. (1)* photograph
nugalėti *v. (2)* overcome, defeat, win
nugalėtojas, -a *m. (1), f. (2)* conqueror, winner
nugara *f. (1)* back
nugarinė *f. (2)* sirloin, fillet
nulipti *v. (1)* come/ get down
nulis *m. (1)* zero
nuliūdęs, -usi *adj. m* sad
numeracija *f. (2)* numeration
numeris *m. (1)* number
numirėlis, -ė *m. (1), f. (2)* deceased
numirti *v. (1)* die
nuo *prep.* from
nuobodulys *m. (1)* boredom
nuobodus, -i *adj. (2)* boring
nuobodžiauti *v. (1)* be bored
nuodai *m. pl. (1)* poison
nuodėmė *f. (2)* sin
nuodingas, -a *adj. (1)* poisonous
nuodyti *v. (1)* poison
nuodugniai *adv.* thoroughly
nuodugnus, -i *adj. (2)* thorough
nuogas, -a *adj. (1)* naked
nuogybė *f. (2)* nudity
nuolaida *f. (2)* discount
nuolaidus, -i *adj. (2)* compliant; sloping
nuolat *adv.* constantly
nuoma *f. (2)* lease, rent
nuomininkas, -ė *m. (1), f. (2)* tenant
nuomonė *f. (2)* opinion
nuomoti *v. (1)* lease
nuomotis *v. (1)* rent
nuopelnas *m. (1)* merit
nuorašas *m. (1)* (longhand) copy
nuoroda *f. (2)* reference
nuorūka *f. (2)* cigarette-butt
nuosaikus, -i *adj. (2)* moderate
nuosavas, -a *adj. (1)* own
nuosavybė *f. (2)* property
nuoseklus, -i *adj. (2)* consistent
nuosprendis *m. (1)* (court) sentence
nuostaba *f. (2)* astonishment
nuostabus, -i *adj. (2)* wonderful
nuotaika *f. (2)* mood
nuotaka *f. (2)* bride
nuotykis *m. (1)* adventure
nuotolis *m. (1)* distance
nuotrauka *f. (2)* photograph
nuplėšti *v. (1)* tear off
nuplikti *v. (1)* grow bald
nuraminti *v. (1)* quiet, soothe

nurodymas *m. (1)* order; indication
nusibosti *v. (1)* bore, get sick of something
nusifotografuoti *v. (1)* get one's photograph taken
nusigerti *v. (1)* get drunk
nusiginklavimas *m. (1)* disarmament
nusiginkluoti *v. (1)* disarm
nusikalstamas, -a *adj. (1)* criminal
nusikalstamumas *m. (1)* criminality
nusikirpti *v. (1)* get one's hair cut
nusikratyti *v. (3)* get rid (of)
nusileisti *v. (1)* descend
nusilenkti *v. (1)* bow
nusilpti *v. (1)* weaken
nusiminti *v. (1)* despair
nusiraminti *v. (1)* calm
nusistatymas *m. (1)* attitude
nusisukti *v. (1)* turn away
nusivylimas *m. (1)* disappointment
nusivilti *v. (1)* be disappointed
nuskausminimas *m. (1)* anesthesia
nuskausminti *v. (1)* anesthetize
nuskęsti *v. (1)* drown
nuskriausti *v. (1)* hurt
nuskusti *v. (1)* shave off, peel
nuspręsti *v. (1)* decide
nustatytas, -a *adj. (1)* fixed, set
nustebimas *m. (1)* surprise
nustebinti *v. (1)* surprise
nušalti *v. (1)* catch cold
nušluostyti *v. (3)* wipe off
nušokti *v. (1)* jump off
nušveisti *v. (1)* polish
nutarimas *m. (1)* decision
nutarti *v. (1)* decide
nuteisti *v. (1)* sentence
nutraukti *v. (1)* break off, discontinue
nutrinti *v. (1)* erase, rub, sore
nuvesti *v. (1)* walk off, take away
nuvežti *v. (1)* drive/ take away
nuvilti *v. (1)* disappoint
nužudymas *m. (1)* murder
nužudyti *v. (3)* murder, assassinate

O

o *conj.* but, and, *inter.* oh
oazė *f. (2)* oasis
obelis *f. (3)* apple tree
objektas *m. (1)* object
objektyvus, -i *adj. (2)* objective
observatorija *f. (2)* observatory
obuolys *m. (1)* apple
oda *f. (2)* skin; leather
odinis, -ė *adj. (3)* leather
oficialus, -i *adj. (2)* official
oficiantas, -ė *m. (1), f. (2)* waiter
oho *inter.* ah!
oi *inter.* ouch!
okeanas *m. (1)* ocean
okulistas, -ė *med. m. (1), f. (2)* oculist
okupacija *f. (2)* occupation
okupacinis, -ė *adj. (3)* occupation
okupantas, -ė *m. (1), f. (2)* invader
okupuoti *v. (1)* occupy
ola *f. (2)* cave
olandas, -ė *m. (1), f. (2)* Dutch person
olandiškas, -a *adj. (1)* Dutch
olimpiada *f. (2)* Olympic games
olimpinis, -ė *adj. (3)* Olympic
omletas *m. (1)* omelette
opera *f. (2)* opera
operacija *f. (2)* operation; surgery
operacinė *f. (2)* operating room
operuoti *v. (1)* operate, perform a surgery
opijus *m. (4)* opium
opinija *f. (2)* public opinion
opiumas *m. (1)* opium
oponentas, -ė *m. (1), f. (2)* opponent, critic
opozicija *f. (2)* opposition
opozicinis, -ė *adj. (3)* opposition
optika *f. (2)* optics
optimistas, -ė *m. (1), f. (2)* optimist
optimistiškas, -a *adj. (1)* optimistic
oranžerija *f. (2)* greenhouse
oranžinis, -ė *adj. (3)* orange
oras *m. (1)* air weather
oratorius, -ė *m. (4), f. (2)* orator (public) speaker
orderis *m. (1)* warrant
organas *m. (1)* organ
organizacija *f. (2)* organization
organizatorius, -ė *m. (4), f. (2)* organizer
organizuoti *v. (1)* organize
orientacija *f. (2)* orientation
originalas *m. (1)* original
originalus, -i *adj. (2)* original
orkaitė *f. (2)* oven

orkestras *m. (1)* orchestra, band
oro linijos *f. pl. (2)* airline
oro uostas *m. (1)* airport
orumas *m. (1)* dignity
ovacijos *f. pl. (2)* ovation
ovalas *m. (1)* oval
ozonas *m. (1)* ozone
ožys *m. (1)* goat (male)
ožka *f. (2)* goat (female)

P

paaiškėti *v. (1)* turn out; clarify
paaiškinimas *m. (1)* explanation
paaiškinti *v. (1)* explain
paauglys, -ė *m. (1), f. (2)* teenager
paauglystė *f. (2)* adolescence
paauksuotas, -a *adj. (1)* gilded
paaukštinimas *m. (1)* promotion
pabaiga *f. (2)* end, conclusion
pabaigti *v. (1)* end
pabauda *f. (2)* fine, penalty
pabėgėlis, -ė *m. (1), f. (2)* fugitive, refugee
pabėgimas *m. (1)* escape
pabėgti *v. (1)* run away, escape
pablogėti *v. (1)* grow worse
pabrangti *v. (1)* rise in the price
pabrėžti *v. (1)* emphasize
pabučiuoti *v. (1)* kiss
pabusti *v. (1)* wake up
pabūti *v. (1)* stay for a while
pacientas, -ė *m. (1), f. (2)* patient
pačiūža *f. (2)* skate
padalijimas *m. (1)* division
padalyti *v. (1)* divide
padanga *f. (2)* tire
padangė *f. (2)* the skies
padarinys *m. (1)* consequence, result
padaryti *v. (3)* make
padaugėti *v. (1)* increase
padauginti *v. (1)* multiply
padavėjas, -a *m. (1), f. (2)* waiter
padažas *m. (1)* sauce, dressing, gravy
padegti *v. (1)* set on fire
padėjėjas, -a *m. (1), f. (2)* assistant
padėka *f. (2)* gratitude
padėklas *m. (1)* tray
padėkoti *v. (1)* thank
pademonstruoti *v. (1)* show, display
padėti *v. (1)* help; lay (down)
padėtis *f. (3)* position; location; condition
padidėjimas *m. (1)* increase
padidėti *v. (1)* increase
padirbtas, -a *adj. (1)* counterfeit
padirbti *v. (1)* counterfeit
padorus, -i *adj. (2)* decent
paduoti *v. (1)* give
padvėsti *v. (1)* die (about animals)
padvigubinti *v. (1)* double
paeiliui *adv.* in turn
pagadinti *v. (1)* spoil
pagal *prep.* according to
pagalba *f. (2)* assistance, help
pagaliau *adv.* finally
pagalvoti *v. (1)* think
pagaminti *v. (1)* manufacture, produce
pagarba *f. (2)* respect
pagarbus, -i *adj. (2)* respectful
pagauti *v. (1)* catch
pageidaujamas, -a *adj. (1)* desirable
pageidauti *v. (1)* wish
pageidavimas *m. (1)* wish
pagerbimas *m. (1)* celebration, homage, honor
pagerbti *v. (1)* honor
pagerėti *v. (1)* improve
pagerinti *v. (1)* improve
pagesti *v. (1)* become depraved, deteriorate
pagydyti *v. (3)* cure
pagydomas, -a *adj. (1)* curable
pagijimas *m. (1)* recovery
pagilinti *v. (1)* deepen
pagimdyti *v. (3)* give birth
pagyrimas *m. (1)* praise
pagirios *f. pl. (2)* hangover
pagirioti *v. (1)* have a hangover
pagirti *v. (1)* praise
pagyrūnas, -ė *m.(1), f. (2)* braggart
pagyti *v. (1)* recover
pagyvenęs, -usi *adj. m.* elderly
pagonybė *f. (2)* paganism
pagonis, -ė *m. (1), f. (2)* pagan
pagoniškas, -a *adj. (1)* pagan
pagrindas *m. (1)* foundation, base
pagrindinis, -ė *adj. (3)* fundamental
pagrįstas, -a *adj. (1)* well-grounded
pagrįsti *v. (1)* ground
pagrobėjas, -a *m. (1), f. (2)* kidnapper
pagrobti *v. (1)* seize, kidnap

pagunda *f. (2)* temptation
paguosti *v. (1)* comfort
pailgas, -a *adj. (1)* oblong
pailginti *v. (1)* make longer
pailsti *v. (1)* get tired
painus, -i *adj. (2)* complicated
pajamos *fin. f. pl. (2)* receipts, revenue
pajūris *m. (1)* seaside
pajusti *v. (1)* feel
pakaba *f. (2)* hanger
pakaitalas *m. (1)* substitute
pakartoti *v. (1)* repeat
pakeisti *v. (1)* change, substitute, replace
pakelė *f. (2)* roadside
pakenkti *v. (1)* harm
pakentėti *v. (1)* be patient
paketas *m. (1)* parcel, packet
pakilti *v. (1)* go up; climb; rise; advance
paklaida *mat. f. (2)* error
paklausa *f. (2)* demand
paklausti *v. (1)* ask
paklysti *v. (1)* lose one's way
paklodė *f. (2)* bed sheet
pakloti *v. (1)* make (the bed)
paklusnus, -i *adj. (2)* obedient
pakopa *f. (2)* step
pakrantė *f. (2)* (sea)coast
pakraštys *m. (1)* outskirts, rim
paktas *m. (1)* pact
pakulnė *f. (2)* heel
pakuoti *v. (1)* pack
pakviesti *v. (1)* invite
pakvietimas *m. (1)* invitation
pakvitavimas *m. (1)* receipt
pakvituoti *v. (1)* give a receipt
palaidas, -a *adj. (1)* loose
palaidinukė *f. (2)* blouse
palaikai *m. pl. (1)* remains
palaikyti *v. (3)* support, back up
palaiminimas *m. (1)* blessing
palaiminti *v. (1)* bless
palaipsniui *col. adv.* gradually
palangė *f. (2)* window-sill
palapinė *f. (2)* tent
palata *f. (2)* ward
palaukti *v. (1)* wait
paleisti *v. (1)* set free, release
palengva *adv.* little by little
paliaubos *f. pl. (2)* truce
palyda *f. (2)* escort
palydėti *v. (2)* escort, accompany
palydovas, -ė *m. (1), f. (2)* attendant, escort
paliesti *v. (1)* touch
palyginimas *m. (1)* comparison
palyginti *v. (1)* compare
palikimas *m. (1)* inheritance, heritage
palikti *v. (1)* leave
palikuonis, -ė *m. (1), f. (2)* descendant
palinkėti *v. (2)* wish
palmė *f. (2)* palm tree
paltas *m. (1)* coat
palūkanos *fin. f. pl. (2)* interest
pamaina *f. (2)* shift, change
pamaldos *f. pl. (2)* church service
pamatas *m. (1)* base, foundation (of a building)
pamažu *adv.* gradually
pamėgdžioti *v. (1)* imitate
pamėginti *v. (1)* try out, attempt
pamergė *f. (2)* bridesmaid
pamesti *v. (1)* lose; abandon
paminklas *m. (1)* monument
paminklinis, -ė *adj. (3)* memorial
pamiršti *v. (1)* forget
pamišėlis, -ė *m. (1), f. (2)* mad person
pamoka *f. (2)* lesson
pamokslas *m. (1)* sermon
pamotė *f. (2)* stepmother
panaikinti *v. (1)* abolish
panašumas *m. (1)* resemblance
panašus, -i *adj. (2)* alike
panaudoti *v. (1)* use
paneigimas *m. (1)* denial; negation
paneigti *v. (1)* deny; negate
panelė *f. (2)* young lady, miss
panika *f. (2)* panic
panorama *f. (2)* panorama
papartis *m. (1)* fern
papeikti *v. (1)* reprimand
paperkamas, -a *adj. (1)* bribable, corrupt
papietauti *v. (1)* have one's dinner
papildomas, -a *adj. (1)* additional
papirkti *v. (1)* bribe
papjauti *v. (1)* cut, butcher, kill
paplisti *v. (1)* spread
paplūdimys *m. (1)* beach
paprastas, -a *adj. (1)* ordinary, simple
paprašyti *v. (3)* ask
paprotys *m. (1)* custom
papūga *f. (2)* parrot

papulkininkis, -ė *m. (1), f. (2)* lieutenant-colonel
papuošalas *m. (1)* piece of jewelry
papuošti *v. (1)* decorate
papurtyti *v. (3)* shake
papusryčiauti *v. (1)* (have) breakfast
para *f. (2)* day (24 hours)
paradas *m. (1)* parade
paraidžiui *adv.* literally
paraiška *f. (2)* claim, application
paralelė *f. (2)* parallel
paralyžiuoti *v. (1)* paralyse
paralyžius *m. (4)* palsy, paralysis
parama *f. (2)* support
parapija *f. (2)* parish
parapijinis, -ė *adj. (3)* parish
parašas *m. (1)* signature
parašiutas *m. (1)* parachute
parašiutininkas, -ė *m. (1), f. (2)* parachuter
paraštė *f. (2)* margin
parausti *v. (1)* blush
parazitas, -ė *m. (1), f. (2)* parasite
pardavėjas, -a *m. (1), f. (2)* shop assistant, seller, vendor
pardavimas *m. (1)* selling, sale
parduoti *v. (1)* sell
parduotuvė *f. (2)* shop
pareiga *f. (2)* duty
pareigūnas, -ė *m. (1), f. (2)* officer
pareikalauti *v. (1)* demand
pareiškimas *m. (1)* application, declaration
pareiti *v. (1)* come back
paremti *v. (1)* support
parfumerija *f. (2)* perfumery
pargriūti *v. (1)* fall down
Paryžius *m. (4)* Paris
parkas *m. (1)* park
parlamentaras, -ė *m. (1), f. (2)* parliamentarian, member of parliament
parlamentas *m. (1)* parliament
parnešti *v. (1)* bring back
paroda *f. (2)* exhibition
parodija *f. (2)* parody
parodyti *v. (3)* show
partija *polit. f. (2)* party
partinis, -ė *polit. adj. (3)* party
partizanas, -ė *m. (1), f. (2)* partisan, guerrilla
partneris, -ė *m. (1), f. (2)* partner
paruošimas *m. (1)* preparation
paruošti *v. (1)* prepare
parvažiuoti *v. (1)* come (back)
pas *prep.* by, to, at
pasaga *f. (2)* horseshoe
pasak *prep.* according to
pasaka *f. (2)* fairy tale
pasakyti *v. (3)* say
pasakoti *v. (1)* narrate
pasala *f. (2)* ambush
pasaldinti *v. (1)* sweeten
pasamdyti *v. (3)* hire
pasąmonė *f. (2)* subconsciousness
pasąmoninis, -ė *adj. (3)* subconscious
pasas *m. (1)* passport
pasaugoti *v. (3)* look after
pasaulėžiūra *f. (2)* world outlook, worldview
pasaulinis, -ė *adj. (3)* world
pasekėjas, -a *m. (1), f. (2)* follower
pasenti *v. (1)* grow old
pasiekimas *m. (1)* achievement
pasiekti *v. (1)* reach
pasienietis, -ė *m. (1), f. (2)* border guard
pasienis *m. (1)* border, frontier
pasigailėjimas *m. (1)* mercy
pasigailėti *v. (2)* have pity
pasigerti *v. (1)* get drunk
pasiimti *v. (1)* take with oneself
pasikalbėti *v. (1)* have a talk
pasikeisti *v. (1)* change, exchange
pasilinksminimas *m. (1)* entertainment
pasimatymas *m. (1)* date (romantic)
pasinaudoti *v. (1)* take advantage
pasipriešinimas *m. (1)* resistance
pasipriešinti *v. (1)* resist
pasipuošti *v. (1)* dress up
pasirašyti *v. (3)* sign
pasirinkimas *m. (1)* choice
pasirodymas *m. (1)* appearance
pasirodyti *v. (3)* appear
pasiruošęs, -usi *adj.* ready
pasisekimas *m. (1)* success
pasisekti *v. (1)* turn out well, be a success
pasisiūlyti *v. (3)* volunteer
pasiskolinti *v. (1)* borrow
pasislėpti *v. (1)* hide (oneself)
pasistengti *v. (1)* do one's best
pasisveikinimas *m. (1)* greeting, saying "hello"
pasisveikinti *v. (1)* greet, say "hello"

pasisverti *v. (1)* weigh oneself
pasitaisyti *v. (3)* correct oneself; recover
pasitarimas *m. (1)* meeting, consultation, conference
pasiteirauti *v. (1)* ask, inquire
pasiteisinimas *m. (1)* excuse
pasitikėjimas *m. (1)* confidence
pasitikėti *v. (2)* rely; trust
pasitikti *v. (1)* meet
pasitraukti *v. (1)* step aside; retreat
pasiūla *f. (2)* supply
pasiūlymas *m. (1)* offer, proposal
pasiųsti *v. (1)* send
pasivaikščiojimas *m. (1)* stroll, walk
pasivaikščioti *v. (1)* take a walk
paskaita *f. (2)* lecture
paskaitininkas, -ė *m. (1), f. (2)* lecturer
paskambinti *v. (1)* call somebody on the phone
paskelbti *v. (1)* declare, announce
paskola *f. (2)* loan
paskubomis *adv.* in a hurry
paskui *adv.* afterwards
paskutinis, -ė *adj. (3)* last, latest; worst
paslapčia *adv.* secretly
paslaptingas, -a *adj. (1)* mysterious
paslaptis *f. (3)* mystery, secret
paslauga *f. (2)* service
paslėptas, -a *adj. (1)* hidden
paslysti *v. (1)* slip
pasmerkti *v. (1)* condemn
pasninkas *m. (1)* fast
pasninkauti *v. (1)* fast
paspringti *v. (1)* choke
pasta *f. (2)* paste
pastaba *f. (2)* remark
pastabus, -i *adj. (2)* observant
pastatas *m. (1)* building
pastatyti *v. (3)* build, erect; stage
pastebėti *v. (2)* notice
pastorius, -ė *m. (4), f. (2)* pastor
pastovus, -i *adj. (2)* constant
pastraipa *f. (2)* paragraph
pasukti *v. (1)* turn
pasveikinti *v. (1)* greet
pasveikti *v. (1)* recover
pašalpa *f. (2)* relief
paštas *m. (1)* mail; post office
pašto dėžutė mailbox
pašto ženklas post stamp
paštetas *m. (1)* pâté
paštininkas, -ė *m. (1), f. (2)* letter-carrier; mail(wo)man
pataisyti *v. (3)* repair, correct
patalynė *f. (2)* bedding
patarėjas, -a *m. (1), f. (2)* adviser
patarimas *m. (1)* advice
patarlė *f. (2)* proverb
patarti *v. (1)* advise; suggest
pateisinimas *m. (1)* justification
pateisinti *v. (1)* justify
patenkintas, -a *adj. (1)* content, satisfied
patentas *m. (1)* patent
patėvis *m. (1)* stepfather
pati *f. (2); pron. f.* wife; self
patiekalas *m. (1)* dish
patikimas, -a *adj. (1)* reliable
patiklus, -i *adj. (2)* credulous
patikrinimas *m. (1)* check-up, examination
patikrinti *v. (1)* check, examine
patikti *v. (1)* like
patylėti *v. (2)* be silent
patyręs, -usi *adj. m.* experienced
patirti *v. (1)* experience
patirtis *f. (3)* experience
patogus, -i *adj. (2)* convenient, comfortable
patranka *f. (2)* cannon
patrauklus, -i *adj. (2)* attractive
patriotas, -ė *m. (1), f. (2)* patriot
patriotinis, -ė *adj. (3)* patriotic
pats *pron. m.* self
patvarus, -i *adj. (2)* steady
patvinti *v. (1)* flood
patvirtinimas *m. (1)* confirmation
patvirtinti *v. (1)* confirm
paukštis *m. (1)* bird
pauzė *f. (2)* pause
pavadinimas *m. (1)* title, name
pavaduoti *v. (1)* act for somebody
pavaduotojas, -a *m. (1), f. (2)* assistant, vice- ; substitute (person)
pavaldus, -i *adj. (2)* subordinate
pavara *f. (2)* gear
pavardė *f. (2)* last name
pavargti *v. (1)* get tired
pavasaris *m. (1)* spring
paveikslas *m. (1)* picture
paveikti *v. (1)* influence
paveldėti *v. (2)* inherit
paveldimas, -a *adj. (1)* hereditary
pavėluoti *v. (1)* be late

pavidalas *m. (1)* form, shape
pavydas *m. (1)* jealousy, envy
pavydėti *v. (2)* be jealous, envy
pavydėtinas, -a *adj. (1)* enviable
pavyduliauti *v. (1)* be jealous, be envious
pavydus, -i *adj. (2)* jealous, envious
paviljonas *m. (1)* pavilion
paviršius *m. (4)* surface
pavyzdys *m. (1)* example
pavyzdžiui *adv.* for example, for instance
pavogti *v. (1)* steal
pavojingas, -a *adj. (1)* dangerous
pavojus *m. (4)* dangerous
pažadas *m. (1)* promise
pažadėti *v. (1)* promise
pažadinti *v. (1)* wake
pažanga *f. (2)* progress
pažangus, -i *adj. (2)* progressive
pažastis *f. (3)* armpit
pažeidimas *m. (1)* violation
pažeminimas *m. (1)* humiliation
pažeminti *v. (1)* lower, humiliate, demote
pažymėjimas *m. (1)* certificate
pažymys *m. (1)* grade, mark
pažinti *v. (2)* know, be acquainted
pažįstamas, -a *adj. (1), m. (1), f. (2)* familiar; acquaintance
pažiūra *f. (2)* attitude; outlook
pažodinis, -ė *adj. (3)* word for word, literal, verbatim
pečiai *m. pl. (1)* shoulders
pėda *f. (2)* foot
pedagogas, -ė *m. (1), f. (2)* pedagogue
pedikiūras *m. (1)* pedicure
pėdsakas *m. (1)* footprint
peilis *m. (1)* knife
peizažas *m. (1)* landscape
pelė *f. (2)* mouse
pelėda *f. (2)* owl
pelekas *m. (1)* fin
pelenai *m. pl. (1)* ashes
peleninė *f. (2)* ashtray
pelėsiai *m. pl. (1)* mold
pelkė *f. (2)* swamp
pelnas *m. (1)* profit, gain, return
pelningas, -a *adj. (1)* profitable
penalas *m. (1)* pencil-case
penicilinas *m. (1)* penicillin
penki, -ios *num.* five
penkiaaukštis *m. (1)* five-story building
penktadalis *m. (1)* one fifth
penktadienis *m. (1)* Friday
pensija *f. (2)* pension
pensininkas, -ė *m. (1), f. (2)* senior citizen, pensioner, retiree
per *prep.* through, across, because of
perbraukti *v. (1)* cross (through)
per daug too much, too many
perdavimas *m. (1)* transmission, transfer
perdėti *v. (1)* exaggerate
perduoti *v. (1)* pass/ give transmit
pereinamas, -a *adj. (1)* transitional
pereiti *v. (1)* get across, pass
perėja *f. (2)* crossing, pass
pergalė *f. (2)* victory
pergalingas, -a *adj. (1)* victorious
periodas *m. (1)* period
periodinis, -ė *adj. (3)* periodic(al)
periodiškas, -a *adj. (1)* periodic(al)
perkainojimas *m. (1)* revaluation, reappraisal
perkūnas *m. (1)* thunder
perlamutrinis, -ė *adj. (3)* mother-of-pearl
perlas *m. (1)* pearl
perlinis, -ė *adj. (3)* pearl
permaina *f. (2)* change
permainingas, -a *adj. (1)* changeable
permatomas, -a *adj. (1)* transparent
pernai *adv.* last year
pernakvoti *v. (1)* spend the night
pernykštis, -ė *adj. (3)* last year's
peroksidas *m. (1)* peroxide
perplaukti *v. (1)* swim across
perrengti *v. (1)* change somebody's clothes
persiauti *v. (1)* change one's shoes
persikas *m. (1)* peach
persikraustyti *v. (3)* move, change one's lodgings
persileidimas *med. m. (1)* miscarriage
persileisti *med. v. (1)* have a miscarriage
persirengti *v. (1)* change (one's clothes)
persistengti *v. (1)* overdo it
persišaldyti *v. (3)* catch cold
persiškas, -a *adj. (1)* Persian
persivalgyti *v. (3)* overeat
perskaityti *v. (3)* read

personalas *m. (1)* human resources, personnel
personalo skyrius human resources department
personažas *m. (1)* character, protagonist
perspėjimas *m. (1)* warning
perspektyva *f. (2)* perspective
perspėti *v. (1)* warn
peršlapti *v. (1)* get wet, get soaked
peršokti *v. (1)* jump over; skip over
peršviesti *v. (1)* X-ray
perteklius *m. (4)* surplus, abundance
pertrauka *f. (2)* break, intermission
pertvarkymas *m. (1)* reorganization
pertvarkyti *v. (3)* reform, reorganize
perukas *m. (1)* wig
perversmas *m. (1)* overturn
pervertinti *v. (1)* overestimate
peržiūra *f. (2)* review
pėsčias, -ia *adj. (1)* pedestrian
pesimistas, -ė *m. (1), f. (2)* pessimist
peteliškė *f. (2)* butterfly
peticija *f. (2)* petition
petražolė *f. (2)* parsley
pianinas *m. (1)* piano
pianistas, -ė *m. (1), f. (2)* pianist
piemuo, -enė *m. (5), f. (2)* shepherd
pienas *m. (1)* milk
pieniškas, -a *adj. (1)* milk, dairy
piešimas *m. (1)* drawing
piešti *v. (1)* draw, depict
pieštukas *m. (1)* pencil
pietauti *v. (1)* dine
pietietis, -ė *m. (1), f. (2)* southerner
pietinis, -ė *adj. (3)* southern
pietryčiai *m. pl. (1)* southeast
pietūs *m. pl. (4)* lunch; south
pietvakariai *m. pl. (1)* southwest
pieva *f. (2)* meadow
piginti *v. (1)* reduce the price
pigti *v. (1)* fall in price
pigus, -i *adj. (2)* cheap
piktas, -a *adj. (1)* angry
pykti *v. (1)* be angry
pyktis *m. (1)* anger
piktnaudžiauti *v. (1)* abuse, misuse
piktumas *m. (1)* malice
piktžolė *f. (2)* weed
pildyti *v. (3)* fill (a form)
pilietybė *f. (2)* citizenship
pilietinis, -ė *adj. (3)* civil
pilietis, -ė *m. (1), f. (2)* citizen
pilis *f. (3)* castle
piliulė *f. (2)* pill
pilkas, -a *adj. (1)* gray; dull
pilnas, -a *adj. (1)* full
pilotas, -ė *m. (1), f. (2)* pilot
pilti *v. (1)* pour
pilvas *m. (1)* stomach, belly
pincetas *m. (1)* tweezers
pingvinas *m. (1)* penguin
pinigai *m. pl. (1)* money
piniginė *f. (2)* wallet
piniginis, -ė *adj. (3)* monetary
pinti *v. (1)* weave; braid
pionierius, -ė *m. (4), f. (2)* pioneer
pipiras *m. (1)* pepper
pypkė *f. (2)* pipe
pyragaitis *m. (1)* pastry
pyragas *m. (1)* pie
pyragėlis *m. (1)* pastry
pirkėjas, -a *m. (1), f. (2)* buyer; customer
pirkinys *m. (1)* purchase
pirklys *m. (1)* merchant
pirkti *v. (1)* buy
pirmadienis *m. (1)* Monday
pirmagimis, -ė *m. (1), f. (2)* first-born
pirmarūšis, -ė *adj. (3)* of the best quality
pirmas, -a *num. (1)* first
pirmininkas, -ė *m. (1), f. (2)* chair (person)
pirmininkauti *v. (1)* preside (at a meeting)
pirmokas, -ė *m. (1), f. (2)* first grade student
piršlybos *f. pl. (2)* matchmaking
piršlys, -ė *m. (1), f. (2)* matchmaker
pirštas *m. (1)* finger
pirštinė *f. (2)* glove; mitten
pirštis *v. (1)* propose (in marriage)
pirtis *f. (3)* bathhouse
pistoletas *m. (1)* pistol
pižama *f. (2)* pajamas
pjaustyti *v. (3)* cut
pjesė *theat. f. (2)* play
pjūklas *m. (1)* saw
pjūvis *m. (1)* cut; section
plačiai *adv.* widely
plagijuoti *v. (1)* plagiarize
plakatas *m. (1)* poster
plaktukas *m. (1)* hammer

planas *m. (1)* plan
planeta *f. (2)* planet
planingas, -a *adj. (1)* systematic
plantacija *f. (2)* plantation
planuoti *v. (1)* plan
plaštaka *f. (2)* hand
plaštakė *f. (2)* butterfly
platforma *f. (2)* platform
platina *f. (2)* platinum
platus, -i *adj. (2)* wide
plaučiai *m. pl. (1)* lungs
plaučių uždegimas pneumonia
plaukai *m. pl. (1)* hair
plaukas *m. (1)* hair (one)
plaukikas, -ė *m. (1), f. (2)* swimmer
plaukti *v. (1)* swim
plaukuotas, -a *adj. (1)* hairy
plauti *v. (1)* rinse, wash
plentas *m. (1)* road, highway
plepėti *v. (1)* chatter
plėsti *v. (1)* expand
plėšikas, -ė *m. (1), f. (2)* robber
plėšimas *m. (1)* robbery
plėšrūnas, -ė *m. (1), f. (2)* predator
plėtoti *v. (1)* develop
pliažas *m. (1)* beach
plienas *m. (1)* steel
plieninis, -ė *adj. (3)* steel
plikas, -a *adj. (1)* bald; naked
plikė *f. (2)* bald patch/ head
plisti *v. (1)* spread
plyšys *m. (1)* crack
plyšti *v. (1)* tear
plyta *f. (2)* brick
plytinis, -ė *adj. (3)* brick
pliusas *m. (1)* plus, advantage
plojimas *m. (1)* applause
plokščias, -ia *adj. (1)* flat
plomba *f. (2)* seal, *med.* filling
plonas, -a *adj. (1)* thin, slender
plotas *m. (1)* area
plotis *m. (1)* width
plunksna *f. (2)* feather
plunksninė *f. (2)* pencil-case
pluta *f. (2)* crust
po *prep.* in, on, under
podukra *f. (2)* stepdaughter
poelgis *m. (1)* act, action
poema *f. (2)* poem
poetas, -ė *m. (1), f. (2)* poet
poetiškas, -a *adj. (1)* poetic
poezija *f. (2)* poetry
pogrindinis, -ė *adj. (3)* underground
pogrindis *m. (1)* underground
pogromas *m. (1)* pogrom, massacre
poilsiauti *v. (1)* rest (on vacation)
pokalbis *m. (1)* conversation
pokarinis, -ė *adj. (3)* post-war
pokeris *m. (1)* poker
pokštas *m. (1)* prank, joke
poleminis, -ė *adj. (3)* polemic, controversial
polemizuoti *v. (1)* argue
policija *f. (2)* police; police station
policininkas, -ė *m. (1), f. (2)* police officer
politika *f. (2)* politics
politikas, -ė *m. (1), f. (2)* politician
politiškas, -a *adj. (1)* political
politkalinys, -ė *m. (1), f. (2)* political prisoner
pomidoras *m. (1)* tomato
pomirtinis, -ė *adj. (3)* posthumous, after(life)
ponas *m. (1)* Mr., sir; master
ponia *f. (2)* Mrs., lady; mam
popierinis, -ė *adj. (3)* paper
popierius *m. (4)* paper
popietė *f. (2)* afternoon
popiežius *m. (4)* pope
populiarus, -i *adj. (2)* popular
pora *f. (2)* pair, couple
porcelianas *m. (1)* porcelain, china
porcelianinis, -ė *adj. (3)* porcelain
porcija *f. (2)* portion
poreikis *m. (1)* need, want
poryt *adv.* the day after tomorrow
pornografija *f. (2)* pornography
portfelis *m. (1)* briefcase
portjera *f. (2)* curtain
portretas *m. (1)* portrait
portugalas, -ė *m. (1), f. (2)* Portuguese
portugališkas, -a *adj. (1)* Portuguese
posakis *m. (1)* expression
posėdis *m. (1)* meeting
posmas *m. (1)* stanza, strophe
postas *m. (1)* post; position
posūkis *m. (1)* turn(ing)
posūnis *m. (1)* stepson
potencialus, -i *adj. (2)* potential
poteriai *m. pl. (1)* prayer
potraukis *m. (1)* inclination
potvynis *m. (1)* flood
povandeninis, -ė *adj. (3)* submarine
povas *m. (1)* peacock
poveikis *m. (1)* influence

poza *f. (2)* pose
pozicija *f. (2)* position
pozityvus, -i *adj. (2)* positive
pozuoti *v. (1)* pose
požeminis, -ė *adj. (3)* underground
požymis *m. (1)* indication, symptom, feature
požiūris *m. (1)* point of view; attitude
prabanga *f. (2)* luxury
prabangus, -i *adj. (2)* luxurious
pradedant beginning (with)
pradas *m. (1)* origin
pradėti *v. (1)* begin, start
pradinis, -ė *adj. (3)* initial, elementary
pradinė mokykla elementary school
pradurti *v. (1)* pierce
praeiti *v. (1; irr.)* pass; go by; be over
pragaras *m. (1)* hell
pragyvenimas *m. (1)* living
pragyventi *v. (1)* make a living
prajuokinti *v. (1)* make somebody laugh
prakaitas *m. (1)* sweat, perspiration
prakaituotas, -a *adj. (1)* sweaty
prakaituoti *v. (1)* perspire, sweat
prakeikimas *m. (1)* curse
praktiškas, -a *adj. (1)* practical
pralaimėjimas *m. (1)* loss
pralaimėti *v. (2)* lose
praleisti *v. (1)* let go past; omit, miss
pralošti *v. (1)* lose
pramiegoti *v. (1)* oversleep
praminti *v. (1)* name
pramoga *f. (2)* amusement; entertainment
pramonė *f. (2)* industry
pramoninis, -ė *adj. (3)* industrial
prancūzas, -ė *m. (1), f. (2)* French person
prancūziškas, -a *adj. (1)* French
pranešimas *m. (1)* lecture; report; notification; message
praraja *f. (2)* abyss
prarasti *v. (1)* lose
praryti *v. (1)* swallow
prasidėti *v. (1)* begin
prasimanymas *m. (1)* fiction; invention, fib
prasmė *f. (2)* sense
prasmingas, -a *adj. (1)* sensible
prastas, -a *adj. (1)* simple, plain
prašymas *m. (1)* request; application
prašyti *v. (3)* ask, invite
pratarmė *f. (2)* preface, foreword
pratimas *m. (1)* exercise
prausti *v. (1)* wash
praustis *v. (1)* wash oneself
pravardė *f. (2)* nickname
pravažiavimas *m. (1)* passage
pravažiuoti *v. (1)* pass by/ through, drive by/ through
prekė *f. (2)* goods, article, commodity
prekiauti *v. (1)* trade
prekyba *f. (2)* trade
prekybininkas, -ė *m. (1), f. (2)* (wholesale) dealer/ merchant; retailer
prekystalis *m. (1)* counter
premija *f. (2)* bonus, premium
premijuoti *v. (1)* give a bonus
premjera *f. (2)* premiere, opening night
premjeras, -ė *m. (1), f. (2)* prime minister
prenumerata *f. (2)* subscription
prenumeratorius, -ė *m. (4), f. (2)* subscriber
prenumeruoti *v. (1)* subscribe
prerija *f. (2)* prairie
presas *m. (1)* press
prestižas *m. (1)* prestige
pretendentas, -ė *m. (1)* claimant
pretenduoti *v. (1)* have a claim
pretenzija *f. (2)* claim; pretension
prezervatyvas *m. (1)* condom
prezidentas, -ė *m. (1), f. (2)* president
pribuvėja *f. (2)* midwife
pridėti *v. (1)* add
prie *prep.* at, by, to
priebalsė *f. (2)* consonant
priedanga *f. (2)* cover, shelter
priedas *m. (1)* addition; appendix
prieglauda *f. (2)* asylum
prieglobstis *m. (1)* shelter; refuge
prieiti *v. (1)* come up, approach
priėjimas *m. (1)* approach; access
priekaba *f. (2)* trailer
priekabiauti *v. (1)* harass
priekinis, -ė *adj. (3)* front
prielinksnis *m. (1)* preposition
priemiestinis, -ė *adj. (3)* suburban
priemiestis *m. (1)* suburb

priėmimas *m. (1)* reception
priemoka *f. (2)* additional payment
priemonė *f. (2)* means
prieplauka *f. (2)* dock
priepuolis *m. (1)* attack, fit
priesaga *f. (2)* suffix
priesaika *f. (2)* oath
prieskoniai *m. pl. (1)* spices
priestatas *m. (1)* extension; (building) annex
prieš *prep.* before, in front of, against
priešais *prep.* opposite, across the street
priešas, -ė *m. (1), f. (2)* enemy
priešingai *adv.* the other way (round), contrary
priešingas, -a *adj. (1)* opposite
priešininkas, -ė *m. (1), f. (2)* opponent
priešintis *v. (1)* oppose; resist
priešistorinis, -ė *adj. (3)* prehistoric
priešiškas, -a *adj. (1)* hostile
prieškarinis, -ė *adj. (3)* prewar
priešnuodis *m. (1)* antidote
prieštarauti *v. (1)* contradict
prietaisas *m. (1)* device; gear
prietema *f. (2)* dusk
prieveiksmis *m. (1)* adverb
priežiūra *f. (2)* supervision
priežodis *m. (1)* proverb
prigerti *v. (1)* drown
prigimtis *f. (3)* nature, character
priimamasis *m. (1)* waiting room
priimti *v. (1)* admit, accept, adopt
prijaukintas, -a *adj. (1)* tame, domestic
prijungti *v. (1)* attach; annex; connect
prijuostė *f. (2)* apron
prikalti *v. (1)* nail
priklausyti *v. (3)* belong
priklausomybė *f. (2)* dependence
primityvus, -i *adj. (2)* primitive
primokėti *v. (1)* pay in addition
princas *m. (1)* prince
princesė *f. (2)* princess
principas *m. (1)* principle
principingas, -a *adj. (1)* person of principle
prinokęs, -usi *adj.* ripe
prinokti *v. (1)* ripen
prioritetas *m. (1)* priority
pripažinimas *m. (1)* acknowledgment, recognition
priprasti *v. (1)* get accustomed
pripučiamas, -a *adj. (1)* inflatable
pripūsti *v. (1)* inflate
pririšti *v. (1)* tie, fasten
prisaikdinti *v. (1)* swear in
prisiliesti *v. (1)* touch
prisipažinimas *m. (1)* confession
prisipažinti *v. (1)* confess
prisistatyti *v. (3)* introduce oneself
pritapti *v. (1)* fit in
pritarimas *m. (1)* approval
pritarti *v. (1)* approve
pritūpti *v. (1)* squat
privalėti *v. (3)* must
privatus, -i *adj. (2)* private
priversti *v. (1)* force
privilegija *f. (2)* privilege
privilegijuotas, -a *adj. (1)* privileged
prizas *m. (1)* prize
prižadėti *v. (1)* promise
prižiūrėti *v. (2)* look after, supervise
prižiūrėtojas, -a *m. (1), f. (2)* supervisor
pro *prep.* through; by
proanūkis, -ė *m. (1), f. (2)* great-grandchild
problema *f. (2)* problem
problemiškas, -a *adj. (1)* problematic
procedūra *f. (2)* procedure
procentas *m. (1)* per cent
procesas *m. (1)* process
produktas *m. (1)* product
produktyvus, -i *adj. (2)* productive
profesija *f. (2)* profession
profesionalas, -ė *m. (1), f. (2)* professional
profesionalus, -i *adj. (2)* professional
profesorius, -ė *m. (4), f. (2)* professor
profilaktinis, -ė *adj. (3)* prophylactic
profilis *m. (1)* profile
proga *f. (2)* occasion
prognozė *f. (2)* forecast
programa *f. (2)* program
progresas *m. (1)* progress
progresuoti *v. (1)* progress
projektas *m. (1)* project

prokuratūra *f. (2)* prosecutor's office
prokuroras, -ė *m. (1), f. (2)* public prosecutor
proletaras, -ė *m. (1), f. (2)* proletarian
proletariškas, -a *adj. (1)* proletarian
propaganda *f. (2)* propaganda
proporcija *f. (2)* proportion, ratio
prorektorius, -ė *m. (4), f. (2)* vice chancellor
prosenelė *f. (2)* great-grandmother
prosenelis *m. (1)* great-grandfather
prospektas *m. (1)* avenue
prostitucija *f. (2)* prostitution
prostitutė *f. (2)* prostitute
protas *m. (1)* mind; intelligence
protekcija *f. (2)* protection
protestantas, -ė *m. (1), f. (2)* Protestant
protestas *m. (1)* protest
protestuoti *v. (1)* protest
protėvis *m. (1)* ancestor
protezas *m. (1)* prosthesis, dentures
protingas, -a *adj. (1)* clever
protinis, -ė *adj. (3)* mental; wisdom (tooth)
protokolas *m. (1)* protocol, minutes
provincialus, -i *adj. (2)* provincial
provincija *f. (2)* province
provokacija *f. (2)* provocation
provokuoti *v. (1)* provoke
prozininkas, -ė *m. (1), f. (2)* prose writer
prožektorius *m. (4)* searchlight
prūsas, -ė *m. (1), f. (2)* Prussian
psalmė *f. (2)* psalm
pseudonimas *m. (1)* pseudonym, pen-name
psichiatras, -ė *m. (1), f. (2)* psychiatrist
psichiatrija *med. f. (2)* psychiatry
psichinis, -ė *adj. (3)* mental, psychic
psichologas, -ė *m. (1), f. (2)* psychologist
psichologija *f. (2)* psychology
psichopatas, -ė *m. (1), f. (2)* psycho(path)
publika *f. (2)* public, audience
pudingas *m. (1)* pudding
pudra *f. (2)* powder (makeup/sugar)
pūga *f. (2)* snowstorm
puikus, -i *adj. (2)* splendid, wonderful
pūliai *m. pl. (1)* pus
pulkas *m. (1)* regiment; flock; crowd
pulsas *m. (1)* pulse
pulti *v. (1)* attack; rush (at), fall
pumpuras *m. (1)* bud
punktas *m. (1)* point; station; paragraph
punktyras *m. (1)* dotted line
punšas *m. (1)* punch
puodas *m. (1)* pot
puodelis *m. (1)* cup, mug
puodukas *m. (1)* cup, mug
puošnus, -i *adj. (2)* well-dressed
puošti *v. (1)* decorate
puota *f. (2)* feast, ball
puotauti *v. (1)* feast
pupa *f. (2)* bean
pupelė *f. (2)* kidney bean
purtyti *v. (3)* shake
purvas *m. (1)* dirt, filth
purvinas, -a *adj. (1)* dirty
purvinti *v. (1)* soil
pusantro *num.* one and a half
pusbrolis *m. (1)* cousin (male)
pusė *f. (2)* half, side
pusiasalis *m. (1)* peninsula
pusiaujas *m. (1)* equator
pusiaukelė *f. (2)* halfway
puskojinė *f. (2)* sock
puslapis *m. (1)* page
pūslė *f. (2)* blister, bladder
pusmetis *m. (1)* half year
pusnis *f. (3)* snow drift
pusnuogis, -ė *adj. (3)* half-naked
pusryčiai *m. pl. (1)* breakfast
pusryčiauti *v. (1)* (have) breakfast
pusseserė *f. (2)* cousin (female)
pūsti *v. (1)* blow
pusvalandis *m. (1)* half an hour
pušynas *m. (1)* pine forest
pušinis, -ė *adj. (3)* pine (wood)
pušis *f. (3)* pine (tree)
putpelė *f. (2)* quail

R

rabarbaras *m. (1)* rhubarb
rabinas *m. (1)* rabbi
racionalizacija *f. (2)* rationalization
racionalus, -i *adj. (2)* rational
radiatorius *m. (4)* radiator

radijas *m. (1)* radio
radikalas, -ė *polit. m. (1), f. (2)* radical
radikalus, -i *adj. (2)* radical
radinys *m. (1)* find
radioaktyvus, -i *adj. (2)* radioactive
rafinuotas, -a *adj. (1)* refined; fine
ragas *m. (1)* horn
ragauti *v. (1)* taste
ragelis *m. (1)* telephone receiver
raida *f. (2)* development
raidė *f. (2)* letter
raidynas *m. (1)* alphabet
raikyti *v. (3)* slice
rainelė *med. f. (2)* iris
raištis *m. (1)* band, bandage
raitas, -a *adj. (1)* on horseback
raitelis *m. (1)* rider
rajonas *m. (1)* district, region
raketa *f. (2)* rocket
raketė *f. (2)* racket
rakinti *v. (1)* lock
rakštis *f. (3)* splinter
raktas *m. (1)* key
ramentas *m. (1)* crutch
ramybė *f. (2)* peace
raminti *v. (1)* calm
ramstis *m. (1)* prop, support
ramus, -i *adj. (2)* calm
randas *m. (1)* scar
rangas *m. (1)* rank
rangovas, -ė *m. (1), f. (2)* contractor
ranka *f. (2)* hand; arm
rankena *f. (2)* handle
rankinis, -ė *adj. (3)* hand
rankogalis *m. (1)* cuff
rankovė *f. (2)* sleeve
rankraštis *m. (1)* manuscript
rankšluostis *m. (1)* towel
raportas *m. (1)* report
raportuoti *v. (1)* report
rasa *f. (2)* dew
rasinis, -ė *adj. (3)* racial
rąstas *m. (1)* log
rasti *v. (1)* find
rašalas *m. (1)* ink
rašyba *f. (2)* spelling
rašiklis *m. (1)* pen
rašymas *m. (1)* writing
rašinys *m. (1)* essay, composition
rašysena *f. (2)* handwriting
rašyti *v. (3)* write
rašytojas, -a *m. (1), f. (2)* writer
raštas *m. (1)* (hand)writing
raštelis *m. (1)* note
raštinė *f. (2)* office
raštingas, -a *adj. (1)* literate
raštingumas *m. (1)* literacy
ratas *m. (1)* wheel
rauda *f. (2)* lament
raudonas, -a *adj. (1)* red
raudonmedis *m. (1)* mahogany
raugėti *v. (1)* belch
raukšlė *f. (2)* wrinkle; crease
raukšlėtas, -a *adj. (1)* wrinkled
raumenys *m. pl. (5)* muscles
raupai *med. m. pl. (1)* smallpox
ravėti *v. (2)* weed
razina *f. (2)* raisin
rąžytis *v. (3)* stretch oneself
reabilitacija *f. (2)* rehabilitation
reabilituoti *v. (1)* rehabilitate
reaguoti *v. (1)* react, respond
reakcija *f. (2)* reaction
reaktyvinis lėktuvas jet plane
realybė *f. (2)* reality
realistas, -ė *m. (1), f. (2)* realist
realizuoti *v. (1)* realize, carry out
realus, -i *adj. (2)* real
recenzentas, -ė *m. (1), f. (2)* reviewer
recenzija *f. (2)* review
recenzuoti *v. (1)* review
receptas *m. (1)* recipe, prescription
redaguoti *v. (1)* edit
redaktorius, -ė *m. (4), f. (2)* editor
referatas *m. (1)* (term) paper
referendumas *m. (1)* referendum
refleksas *m. (1)* reflex
reforma *f. (2)* reform
reformacija *f. (2)* Reformation
reformuoti *v. (1)* reform
regėti *v. (2)* see
reginys *m. (1)* sight, spectacle
registracija *f. (2)* registration; check-in
registruoti *v. (1)* register
reguliarus, -i *adj. (2)* regular
reguliuoti *v. (1)* regulate
reikalas *m. (1)* affair, business matter
reikalauti *v. (1)* demand
reikalavimas *m. (1)* demand, request
reikalingas, -a *adj. (1)* necessary
reikėti *v. (1)* be necessary
reiklus, -i *adj. (2)* strict
reikmė *f. (2)* need
reikšmė *f. (2)* meaning, importance
reikšti *v. (1)* mean

reisas *m. (1)* run (bus/ train); trip
reiškinys *m. (1)* phenomenon
reklama *f. (2)* advertisement, advertising, commercial
reklamuoti *v. (1)* advertise
rekomendacija *f. (2)* recommendation
rekomenduoti *v. (1)* recommend
rekonstrukcija *f. (2)* reconstruction
rekordas *m. (1)* record
rekordininkas, -ė *m. (1), f. (2)* record-holder
rekordinis, -ė *adj. (3)* record
rėkti *v. (1)* cry, shout, scream
rektorius, -ė *m. (4), f. (2)* chancellor
religija *f. (2)* religion
religingas, -a *adj. (1)* religious (person)
religinis, -ė *adj. (3)* religious (book)
relikvija *f. (2)* relic
rėmai *m. pl. (1)* frame
rėmėjas, -a *m. (1), f. (2)* supporter, sponsor
remontas *m. (1)* repairs, maintenance
remontuoti *v. (1)* repair
remti *v. (1)* support
rėmuo *m. (5)* heartburn
Renesansas *m. (1)* Renaissance
rengėjas, -a *m. (1), f. (2)* organizer
rengti *v. (1)* prepare
rentgenas *m. (1)* X-ray
reorganizacija *f. (2)* reorganization
repatriantas, -ė *m. (1), f. (2)* repatriate
repeticija *f. (2)* rehearsal
repetuoti *v. (1)* rehearse
replės *f. pl. (2)* pliers, bender
reportažas *m. (1)* report(ing)
reporteris, -ė *m. (1), f. (2)* reporter
reprodukcija *f. (2)* reproduction
reputacija *f. (2)* reputation
respublika *f. (2)* republic
respublikonas, -ė *polit. m. (1), f. (2)* republican
restoranas *m. (1)* restaurant
resursai *m. pl. (1)* resources
retai *adv.* seldom, rarely
retas, -a *adj. (1)* rare; thin (cloth)
retkarčiais *adv.* now and then
retorika *f. (2)* rhetoric
retorinis, -ė *adj. (3)* rhetorical
revizorius, -ė *m. (4), f. (2)* inspector
revoliucija *f. (2)* revolution
revoliucinis, -ė *adj. (3)* revolutionary
revoliucionierius, -ė *m. (4), f. (2)* revolutionary
revolveris *m. (1)* revolver
rezervas *m. (1)* reserve(s)
rezervuaras *m. (1)* reservoir
rezervuotas, -a *adj. (1)* reserved (table)
rezervuoti *v. (1)* reserve
rezidencija *f. (2)* residence
reziumė *f. (2)* summary, resume
rezoliucija *f. (2)* resolution
rezultatas *m. (1)* result
režimas *m. (1)* regime
režisierius, -ė *m. (4), f. (2)* director, producer
riaušės *f. pl. (2)* disturbance(s)
riba *f. (2)* limit
ribotas, -a *adj. (1)* limited
ridikėlis *m. (1)* radish
riebalai *m. pl. (1)* fat, grease
riebaluotas, -a *adj. (1)* greasy
riebus, -i *adj. (2)* fat (food)
riekė *f. (2)* slice
riešas *m. (1)* wrist
riešutas *m. (1)* nut
riešutinis, -ė *adj. (3)* nut
ryklė *f. (2)* throat
ryklys *m. (1)* shark
riksmas *m. (1)* cry, scream
rimas *m. (1)* rhyme
rimbas *m. (1)* whip
rimtas, -a *adj. (1)* serious
rinka *f. (2)* market
rinkėjas, -a *m. (1), f. (2)* voter; collector
rinkinys *m. (1)* collection
rinkti *v. (1)* gather; collect; elect
rišykla *f. (2)* bookbinder's shop
ryškus, -i *adj. (2)* distinct; bright; vivid
rytas *m. (1)* morning
rytdiena *f. (2)* tomorrow
riteris *m. (1)* knight
ryti *v. (1)* swallow
rytietiškas, -a *adj. (1)* oriental
rytinis, -ė *adj. (3)* morning
ritmas *m. (1)* rhythm
ryt(oj) *adv.* tomorrow
rytojus *m. (4)* tomorrow
ritualas *m. (1)* ritual
rizika *f. (2)* risk
rizikingas, -a *adj. (1)* risky, hazardous

rizikuoti *v. (1)* risk
ryžiai *m. pl. (1)* rice
rytai *m. pl. (1)* east
rodyklė *f. (2)* arrow; index
rodiklis *m. (1)* indicator
rojus *m. (4)* paradise
romanas *m. (1)* novel; love affair
romantikas, -ė *m. (1), f. (2)* romantic
romantiškas, -a *adj. (1)* romantic
romas *m. (1)* rum
romėnas, -ė *m. (1), f. (2)* Roman
ropė *f. (2)* turnip
roplys *m. (1)* reptile
rozetė *f. (2)* outlet; *col.* socket
rozmarinas *m. (1)* rosemary
rožė *f. (2)* rose
rožinis, -ė *adj. (3)* pink
Rožinis *m. (1)* rosary
rūbai *m. pl. (1)* clothes
rubinas *m. (1)* ruby
rūbinė *f. (2)* coat check
rudas, -a *adj. (1)* brown
rudeninis, -ė *adj. (3)* autumn, fall
ruduo *m. (5)* autumn, fall
rugiagėlė *f. (2)* cornflower
rugiai *m. pl. (1)* rye
ruginis, -ė *adj. (3)* rye
rugpjūtis *m. (1)* August
rugsėjis *m. (1)* September
rūgštus, -i *adj. (2)* sour
rūkas *m. (1)* fog
rūkytas, -a *adj. (1)* smoked
rūkyti *v. (3)* smoke
ruletė *f. (2)* roulette
rūmai *m. pl. (1)* palace; mansion
rumunas, -ė *m. (1), f. (2)* Romanian
rumuniškas, -a *adj. (1)* Romanian
rungtynės *f. pl. (2)* contest; competition
rungtyniauti *v. (1)* compete
ruošti *v. (1)* prepare; make ready
ruoštis *v. (1)* get ready; keep house
rūpestingas, -a *adj. (1)* thoughtful
rūpestis *m. (1)* care; anxiety
rūpintis *v. (1)* look after
rupus, -i *adj. (2)* coarse
rupūžė *f. (2)* toad
rusas, -ė *m. (1), f. (2)* Russian
rūsys *m. (1)* cellar; basement
rusiškas, -a *adj. (1)* Russian
rūta *f. (2)* rue (Lithuanian national flower)
rutina *f. (2)* routine
rutulys *m. (1)* ball

S

sabotažas *m. (1)* sabotage
saga *f. (2)* button
saikingas, -a *adj. (1)* moderate
sąjūdis *m. (1)* movement
sąjunga *f. (2)* union, alliance
sąjungininkas, -ė *m. (1), f. (2)* ally
sakalas *m. (1)* falcon
sakyti *v. (3)* say
sakmė *f. (2)* legend
saksofonas *m. (1)* saxophone
sala *f. (2)* island
saldainis *m. (1)* sweet, candy
saldus, -i *adj. (2)* sweet
salė *f. (2)* hall
salieras *m. (1)* celery
sąlyga *f. (2)* condition
saliutas *m. (1)* salute
salonas *m. (1)* salon
salotos *f. pl. (2)* lettuce
samana *f. (2)* moss
samanotas, -a *adj. (1)* mossy
sąmata *fin. f. (2)* estimate
samdyti *v. (3)* hire
samdomas, -a *adj. (1)* hired
sąmojingas, -a *adj. (1)* witty
sąmokslas *m. (1)* conspiracy
sąnarys *m. (1)* joint
sanatorija *f. (2)* sanatorium
sandalas *m. (1)* sandal, sandalwood
sandara *f. (2)* structure
sandėlis *m. (1)* warehouse; storage room; pantry
sandėris *m. (1)* transaction
sanitaras, -ė *m. (1), f. (2)* nurse's aid
sankaba *f. (2)* clutch (of a car)
sankcija *f. (2)* sanction
sankryža *f. (2)* crossing
santarvė *f. (2)* accord, harmony
santaupos *f. pl. (2)* savings
santykiauti *v. (1)* correlate; have intercourse
santykiai *m. pl. (1)* relations
santrauka *f. (2)* summary
santuoka *f. (2)* marriage
santūrus, -i *adj. (2)* reserved
santvarka *f. (2)* system
sapnas *m. (1)* dream (in sleep)
sapnuoti *v. (1)* dream (in sleep)
sąrašas *m. (1)* list
sardinė *f. (2)* sardine
sargas, -ė *m. (1), f. (2)* guard
sarkastiškas, -a *adj. (1)* sarcastic

sąsiuvinis *m. (1)* notebook
sąskaita *f. (2)* bill
sąskrydis *m. (1)* meeting
satelitas *m. (1)* satellite
satelitinis, -ė *adj. (3)* satellite
satyra *f. (2)* satire
satyrinis, -ė *adj. (3)* satiric(al)
saugoti *v. (3)* keep guard; protect
saugus, -i *adj. (2)* safe
sauja *f. (2)* handful
saulė *f. (2)* sun
saulėgrąža *f. (2)* sunflower
saulėlydis *m. (1)* sunset
saulėtas, -a *adj. (1)* sunny
saulėtekis *m. (1)* sunrise
sausainis *m. (1)* biscuit, cracker
sausas, -a *adj. (1)* dry
sausis *m. (1)* January
sauskelnės *f. pl. (2)* diaper(s)
sausra *f. (2)* drought
savaime *adv.* by himself/ herself/ itself
savaip *adv.* in one's own way
savaitė *f. (2)* week
savaitgalis *m. (1)* weekend
savamokslis, -ė *m. (1), f. (2)* self-educated person
savanaudis, -ė *m. (1), f. (2)* selfish person
savanoris, -ė *m. (1), f. (2)* volunteer
savanoriškas, -a *adj. (1)* voluntary
savarankiškas, -a *adj. (1)* independent
sąvaržėlė *f. (2)* paper clip
savas, -a *adj. (1)* one's own
sąveika *f. (2)* interaction
savybė *f. (2)* peculiar quality
savigarba *f. (2)* self-respect
savikaina *f. (2)* cost; price
savikritika *f. (2)* self-criticism
savikritiškas, -a *adj. (1)* self-critical
savininkas, -ė *m. (1), f. (2)* owner
savivaldybė *f. (2)* local government
savižudybė *f. (2)* suicide
sąvoka *f. (2)* concept, notion
sąžinė *f. (2)* conscience
sąžiningas, -a *adj. (1)* honest
scena *theat. f. (2)* stage, scene
schema *f. (2)* scheme, diagram
sėdėti *v. (2)* sit
seifas *m. (1)* safe
Seimas *m. (1)* Lithuanian Parliament
sėkla *f. (2)* seed
seklys, -ė *m. (1), f. (2)* detective
sekmadieninis, -ė *adj. (3)* Sunday
sekmadienis *m. (1)* Sunday
sėkmė *f. (2)* success
sėkmingas, -a *adj. (1)* successful
sekretorius, -ė *m. (4), f. (2)* secretary
seksualinis, -ė *adj. (3)* sexual
seksualus, -i *adj. (2)* sexual
sekta *f. (2)* sect
sekti *v. (1)* follow; watch
sekundė *f. (2)* second
semestras *m. (1)* semester
seminaras *m. (1)* seminar
seminarija *f. (2)* seminary
seminaristas, -ė *m. (1), f. (2)* seminarian
senas, -a *adj. (1)* old
senatas *m. (1)* senate
senatorius, -ė *m. (4), f. (2)* senator
senatvė *f. (2)* old age
senelė *f. (2)* old woman; grandmother
senelis *m. (1)* old man; grandfather
seniena *f. (2)* antiquity
seniūnas, -ė *m. (1), f. (2)* village elder
senyvas, -a *adj. (1)* elderly
senoliai *m. pl. (1)* forefathers
senovė *f. (2)* olden times
senti *v. (1)* grow old
sentimentalus, -i *adj. (2)* sentimental
septyni, -ios *num.* seven
serbas, -ė *m. (1), f. (2)* Serb
serbentas *m. (1)* currant
serija *f. (2)* series
serijinis, -ė *adj. (3)* serial
servetėlė *f. (2)* napkin
seržantas, -ė *m. (1), f. (2)* sergeant
sesė *f. (2)* sister
sesija *f. (2)* session
sėslus, -i *adj. (2)* settled
sėsti *v. (1)* sit down
sesuo *f. (5)* sister
sezonas *m. (1)* season
sezoninis, -ė *adj. (3)* seasonal
sfera *f. (2)* sphere
siaubas *m. (1)* terror, horror
siaubingas, -a *adj. (1)* terrible, horrible
siauras, -a *adj. (1)* narrow
sidabras *m. (1)* silver
sidabrinis, -ė *adj. (3)* silver
siela *f. (2)* soul
siena *f. (2)* wall

sieninis, -ė *adj. (3)* wall
sietynas *m. (1)* chandelier
sifilis *med. m. (1)* syphilis
signalas *m. (1)* signal
signalizuoti *v. (1)* signal
sijonas *m. (1)* skirt
sykis *m. (1)* time
silkė *f. (2)* herring
silpnas, -a *adj. (1)* weak
silpnybė *f. (2)* weakness, weak point
simbolika *f. (2)* symbolics
simbolinis, -ė *adj. (3)* symbolic
simbolis *m. (1)* symbol
simfonija *f. (2)* symphony
simfoninis orkestras symphony orchestra
simpatiškas, -a *adj. (1)* likable, cute, pleasant
simptomas *m. (1)* symptom
sinagoga *f. (2)* synagogue
sinonimas *m. (1)* synonym
sirena *f. (2)* siren
sirgti *v. (1)* be ill
sirupas *m. (1)* syrup
sistema *f. (2)* system
situacija *f. (2)* situation
siūlas *m. (1)* thread
siūlė *f. (2)* seam; stitch
siūlyti *v. (3)* offer
siuntėjas, -a *m. (1), f. (2)* sender
siuntinys *m. (1)* parcel
siurblys *m. (1)* pump
siurprizas *m. (1)* surprise
siųsti *v. (1)* send
siūti *v. (1)* sew
siuvėjas, -a *m. (1), f. (2)* tailor; seamstress
siuvykla *f. (2)* tailor's shop
siuvinėtas, -a *adj. (1)* embroidered
siužetas *m. (1)* plot; subject
skaičiuoti *v. (1)* count
skaičius *m. (4)* number
skaidrė *f. (2)* slide
skaidrus, -i *adj. (2)* clear
skaitykla *f. (2)* reading room
skaitiklis *m. (1)* meter
skaitymas *m. (1)* reading
skaityti *v. (3)* read
skaitytojas, -a *m. (1), f. (2)* reader
skaitmeninis, -ė *adj. (3)* digital
skaitvardis *m. (1)* numeral
skalauti *v. (1)* rinse
skalbykla *f. (2)* laundromat
skalbimo mašina washing machine
skalbti *v. (1)* wash; do laundry
skalė *f. (2)* scale
skambutis *m. (1)* bell
skandalas *m. (1)* scandal
skandinavas, -ė *m. (1), f. (2)* Scandinavian
skandinaviškas, -a *adj. (1)* Scandinavian
skanus, -i *adj. (2)* delicious, tasty
skara *f. (2)* shawl
skardinė *f. (2)* can, tin
skaudėti *v. (1)* ache
skausmas *m. (1)* pain
skelbimas *m. (1)* ad; announcement
skeletas *m. (1)* skeleton
skeptikas, -ė *m. (1), f. (2)* skeptic
skerdykla *f. (2)* slaughterhouse
skersai *adv.* across
skersgatvis *m. (1)* by-street, lane
skersti *v. (1)* slaughter
skęsti *v. (1)* sink
skėtis *m. (1)* umbrella
skydas *m. (1)* shield
skiemuo *m. (5)* syllable
skiepas *m. (1)* vaccine
skiepyti *v. (1)* vaccinate
skiesti *v. (1)* dilute
skilandis *m. (1)* Lithuanian smoked sausage
skyryba *f. (2)* punctuation
skyrybos *f. pl. (2)* divorce
skyrius *m. (4)* department; chapter
skirstyti *v. (3)* distribute
skirti *v. (1)* separate; distinguish; allot; dedicate
skirtingas, -a *adj. (1)* different; diverse
skystas, -a *adj. (1)* liquid
skystis *m. (1)* fluid
sklerozė *med. f. (2)* sclerosis
skliausteliai *m. pl. (1)* parentheses
sklypas *m. (1)* lot, plot
skola *f. (2)* debt
skolingas, -a *adj. (1)* indebted
skolininkas, -ė *m. (1), f. (2)* debtor
skolinti *v. (1)* lend
skolintojas, -a *m. (1), f. (2)* lender
skoningas, -a *adj. (1)* tasteful
skonis *m. (1)* taste
skraidyti *v. (3)* fly
skrandis *m. (1)* stomach
skriausti *v. (1)* harm; hurt
skrybėlė *f. (2)* hat

skrydis *m. (1)* flight
skristi *v. (1)* fly
skrodimas *med. m. (1)* dissection; post-mortem examination
skruostas *m. (1)* cheek
skruzdė(lė) *f. (2)* ant
skubėti *v. (1)* hurry
skubus, -i *adj. (2)* urgent
skulptorius, -ė *m. (1), f. (2)* sculptor
skulptūra *f. (2)* sculpture
skundas *m. (1)* complaint
skurdas *m. (1)* poverty
skursti *v. (1)* be in need; be poor
skusti *v. (1)* shave; peel
skųsti *v. (1)* make a complaint
skustis *v. (1)* shave
skųstis *v. (1)* complain
skustuvas *m. (1)* razor
skutimosi kremas shaving cream
skvarbus, -i *adj. (2)* shrewd; piercing
skveras *m. (1)* square
slapčia *adv.* secretly
slaptas, -a *adj. (1)* secret
slaugas, -ė *m. (1), f. (2)* nurse; nurse's aid
slaugyti *v. (3)* nurse
slavas, -ė *m. (1), f. (2)* Slav
slaviškas, -a *adj. (1)* Slavic
slėnis *m. (1)* valley
slenkstis *m. (1)* threshold
slėpti *v. (1)* hide
slėptuvė *f. (2)* hiding place; shelter
slidės *f. pl. (2)* skis
slidinėjimas *m. (1)* skiing
slidinėti *v. (1)* ski
slidininkas, -ė *m. (1), f. (2)* skier
slidus, -i *adj. (2)* slippery
slysti *v. (1)* slide; slip
slyva *f. (2)* plum; plum tree
sloga *f. (2)* runny nose
slopinti *v. (1)* repress
sluoksnis *m. (1)* layer
smagiai *adv.* pleasantly
smakras *m. (1)* chin
smalsumas *m. (1)* curiosity
smalsus, -i *adj. (2)* curious
smaragdas *m. (1)* emerald
smarkus, -i *adj. (2)* strong; severe; heavy
smarvė *f. (2)* stink, bad odor
smaugti *v. (1)* strangle
smegenys *f. pl. (3)* brain
smeigtukas *m. (1)* pin
smėlėtas, -a *adj. (1)* sandy
smėlis *m. (1)* sand
smerkti *v. (1)* blame
smilkinys *m. (1)* temple (part of head)
smirdėti *v. (1)* stink
smokingas *m. (1)* tuxedo
smūgis *m. (1)* blow; stroke
smuikas *m. (1)* violin
smuikininkas, -ė *m. (1), f. (2)* violinist
smulkmena *f. (2)* detail
smulkus, -i *adj. (2)* small, petty, thin
smurtas *m. (1)* violence
snaigė *f. (2)* snowflake
snaiperis, -ė *m. (1), f. (2)* sniper
sniegas *m. (1)* snow
snigti *v. (1)* snow
snobas, -ė *m. (1), f. (2)* snob
socialdemokratas, -ė *polit. m. (1), f. (2)* Social Democrat
socialinis, -ė *adj. (3)* social
socialistas, -ė *m. (1), f. (2)* socialist
socializmas *m. (1)* socialism
sociologas, -ė *m. (1), f. (2)* sociologist
sociologija *f. (2)* sociology
sodas *m. (1)* garden
sodinti *v. (1)* plant
soja *f. (2)* soybean
solistas, -ė *m. (1), f. (2)* solist
sopranas *m. (1)* soprano
sostas *m. (1)* throne
sostinė *f. (2)* capital
sotus, -i *adj. (2)* full (after a meal); satiated
sovietinis *adj. (3)* Soviet
spalis *m. (1)* October
spalva *f. (2)* color
spalvingas, -a *adj. (1)* colorful
spalvotas, -a *adj. (1)* colored
spanguolė *f. (2)* cranberry
spanguolinis, -ė *adj. (3)* cranberry
sparnas *m. (1)* wing
spąstai *m. pl. (1)* trap
spauda *f. (2)* press
spausdinti *v. (1)* publish
spausdintuvas *m. (1)* printer
specialybė *f. (2)* specialty
specialistas, -ė *m. (1), f. (2)* specialist
specialus, -i *adj. (2)* special
speigas *m. (1)* hard frost
spektaklis *theat. m. (1)* play
spenelis *m. (1)* nipple

spėti *v. (1)* guess, suppose
spjaudyti *v. (3)* spit (often)
spjauti *v. (1)* spit
spyna *f. (2)* lock
spindėti *v. (2)* shine
spindulys *m. (1)* ray
spinta *f. (2)* cupboard; wardrobe
spiritas *m. (1)* alcohol
sportas *m. (1)* sport
sportininkas, -ė *m. (1), f. (2)* sports(wo)man
sportuoti *v. (1)* participate in sports
spręsti *v. (1)* decide; judge; discuss
sprogimas *m. (1)* explosion
sprogti *v. (1)* burst; explode
spuogas *m. (1)* pimple, zit
sraigė *f. (2)* snail
sritis *f. (3)* region; province; area (of inquiry)
sriuba *f. (2)* soup
srovė *f. (2)* current
stabdis *m. (1)* brake
stabdyti *v. (3)* stop
stabilus, -i *adj. (2)* stable
stabligė *med. f. (2)* tetanus
stačias, -ia *adj. (1)* upright, erect, standing
stačiatikis, -ė *m. (1), f. (2)* (Russian) Orthodox
stadionas *m. (1)* stadium
staiga *adv.* suddenly
staigmena *f. (2)* surprise
staigus, -i *adj. (2)* sudden
stalas *m. (1)* table
stalinis, -ė *adj. (3)* table
staltiesė *f. (2)* tablecloth
stambus, -i *adj. (2)* large, big
standartas *m. (1)* standard
standartinis, -ė *adj. (3)* standard
statyba *f. (2)* construction; building
statinė *f. (2)* barrel
statistika *f. (2)* statistics
statyti *v. (3)* build
statula *f. (2)* statue
statulėlė *f. (2)* statuette
status kampas right angle
statusas *m. (1)* status
statutas *m. (1)* statute
stebėti *v. (2)* observe
stebėtojas, -a *m. (1), f. (2)* observer
stebuklas *m. (1)* miracle
stebuklingas, -a *adj. (1)* miraculous, wonderful
steigėjas, -a *m. (1), f. (2)* founder
steigti *v. (1)* found; establish
stengtis *v. (1)* do one's best
sterilus, -i *adj. (2)* sterile
stiebas *m. (1)* stem; mast; stick
styga *f. (2)* string
styginis, -ė *adj. (3)* string
stiklas *m. (1)* glass
stiklinė *f. (2)* (drinking) glass
stiklinis, -ė *adj. (3)* glass
stilingas, -a *adj. (1)* stylish
stilistas, -ė *m. (1), f. (2)* stylist
stipendija *f. (2)* stipend; scholarship
stiprėti *v. (1)* become stronger
stiprumas *m. (1)* strength
stiprus, -i *adj. (2)* strong
stipti *v. (1)* die (about animals)
stogas *m. (1)* roof
stomatologas, -ė *m. (1), f. (2)* dentist
storas, -a *adj. (1)* thick; fat; deep (voice); heavy
stoti *v. (1)* stand; enter (the university)
stotis *f. (3)* station
stovėti *v. (2)* stand
stovykla *f. (2)* camp
straipsnis *m. (1)* article
strategija *f. (2)* strategy
strateginis, -ė *adj. (3)* strategic
strazdanotas, -a *adj. (1)* freckled
streikas *m. (1)* strike
strėlė *f. (2)* arrow
striukė *f. (2)* short coat
stuburas *m. (1)* vertebra; backbone
studentas, -ė *m. (1), f. (2)* student
studentiškas, -a *adj. (1)* student
studija *f. (2)* studio
studijos *f. pl. (2)* studies
studijuoti *v. (1)* study
stulpas *m. (1)* post; pole
su *prep.* with
suaugęs, -usi *adj.* grown-up, adult
subankrutuoti *v. (1)* become bankrupt
subjektas *m. (1)* subject
subrendęs, -usi *adj. m.* mature
subtilus, -i *adj. (2)* subtle
sudaryti *v. (3)* form; compose
sudaužyti *v. (3)* break
sudeginti *v. (1)* burn (down)
sudėti *v. (1)* put/ lay (together); add up
sudėtingas, -a *adj. (1)* complicated
sūdyti *v. (3)* salt
sudužti *v. (1)* break; crash
suėmimas *m. (1)* arrest

sugadinti *v. (1)* spoil
sugyvenamas, -a *adj. (1)* easy to live with
sugriauti *v. (1)* destroy
sugriūti *v. (1)* collapse
suimti *v. (1)* arrest
sukaktis *f. (3)* anniversary
sukapoti *v. (1)* chop
sukčiauti *v. (1)* cheat
sukilėlis, -ė *m. (1), f. (2)* rebel
sukilimas *m. (1)* rebellion
sukilti *v. (1)* rise in rebellion
suklaidinti *v. (1)* mislead
suklastoti *v. (1)* forge
suknelė *f. (2)* dress
suktas, -a *adj. (1)* sly
sūkurys *m. (1)* whirlpool; whirlwind
sula *f. (2)* sap (drink)
sulaužyti *v. (3)* break; infringe
sultingas, -a *adj. (1)* juicy
sultinys *m. (1)* broth
sultys *f. pl. (3)* juice
suma *f. (2)* sum; mass
sumaišyti *v. (3)* mix up
sumažėti *v. (1)* decrease
sumokėti *v. (1)* pay
sumuštinis *m. (1)* sandwich
sūnėnas *m. (1)* nephew
sunkus, -i *adj. (2)* heavy; difficult
sunkvežimis *m. (1)* truck
sūnus *m. (4)* son
suolas *m. (1)* bench
suomis, -ė *m. (1), f. (2)* Finn
suomiškas, -a *adj. (1)* Finnish
supakuoti *v. (1)* pack (up)
supelyti *v. (1)* grow moldy
supjaustyti *v. (3)* cut
suplyšti *v. (1)* tear
suprantamas, -a *adj. (1)* comprehensible; clear
suprasti *v. (1)* understand
suptis *v. (1)* swing; rock
sūpuoklės *f. pl. (2)* swing
surašymas *m. (1)* census
surašyti *v. (3)* make a list
sūris *m. (1)* cheese
sūrus, -i *adj. (2)* salty
susidraugauti *v. (2)* make friends
susidūrimas *m. (1)* collision
susidurti *v. (1)* collide; come across
susigiminiuoti *v. (1)* become related
susilpnėti *v. (1)* weaken
susirašinėti *v. (1)* correspond (through mail)
susirgti *v. (1)* fall ill
susirinkimas *m. (1)* meeting; gathering
susirinkti *v. (1)* gather
susisiekimas *m. (1)* communication; transportation
susišukuoti *v. (1)* comb one's hair
susitarimas *m. (1)* agreement
susituokti *v. (1)* marry
susivienyti *v. (1)* unite
susižadėti *v. (1)* become engaged
sustiprėti *v. (1)* strengthen; intensify
sušaudyti *v. (3)* shoot; execute
sušlapti *v. (1)* become wet
sutaisyti *v. (3)* repair
sutartis *f. (3)* agreement; contract
sutikimas *m. (1)* welcome; meeting; consent
sutikti *v. (1)* welcome; meet; agree
sutrukdyti *v. (3)* disturb
sutrumpinti *v. (1)* shorten
sutuoktinis, -ė *m. (1), f. (2)* spouse
sutuoktuvės *f. pl. (2)* wedding
sutvarkyti *v. (3)* arrange; put in order
sutvarstyti *v. (3)* bandage; dress
suvartojimas *m. (1)* consumption
suvartoti *v. (1)* consume
suvažiavimas *m. (1)* congress
suvenyras *m. (1)* souvenir
suvenyrinis, -ė *adj. (3)* souvenir
suverenitetas *m. (1)* sovereignty
suvienyti *v. (1)* unite
suvynioti *v. (1)* wrap up
sužadėtinis, -ė *m. (1), f. (2)* fiancé
sužadėtuvės *f. pl. (2)* engagement
sužavėti *v. (2)* charm
sužeisti *v. (1)* injure
sužinoti *v. (3)* find out
sužlugdyti *v. (3)* ruin
svaigalai *m. pl. (1)* alcoholic beverages
svainis *m. (1)* brother-in-law
svajonė *f. (2)* (day)dream
svajoti *v. (1)* (day)dream
svarba *f. (2)* importance
svarbus, -i *adj. (2)* important
svarstyklės *f. pl. (2)* scales
svečias *m. (1)* guest
svečiuotis *v. (1)* be a guest
sveikas, -a *adj. (1)* healthy
sveikata *f. (2)* health
sveikinimas *m. (1)* greeting
sveikinti *v. (1)* greet

sveikti *v. (1)* get better
svetainė *f. (2)* sitting room; salon; web page
svetimas, -a *adj. (1)* strange; belonging to someone else
svetimšalis, -ė *m. (1), f. (2)* foreigner; stranger
svetur *arch., adv.* abroad
sviestas *m. (1)* butter
sviestinis, -ė *adj. (3)* butter
svogūnas *m. (1)* onion
svogūninis, -ė *adj. (3)* onion
svoris *m. (1)* weight

Š

šachmatai *m. pl. (1)* chess
šachmatininkas, -ė *m. (1), f. (2)* chess player
šaka *f. (2)* branch
šaknis *f. (3)* root
šakutė *f. (2)* fork
šaldiklis *m. (1)* freezer
šaldytuvas *m. (1)* refrigerator
šalia *prep.* near by; close to
šaligatvis *m. (1)* sidewalk
šalikas *m. (1)* scarf
šalin *adv.* away; off
šalintis *v. (1)* avoid
šalis *f. (3)* side; land; country; part
šalmas *m. (1)* helmet
šaltas, -a *adj. (1)* cold
šaltiena *f. (2)* jellied meat
šaltinis *m. (1)* spring (water); source
šaltkalvis *m. (1)* locksmith
šamas *m. (1)* catfish
šampanas *m. (1)* champagne
šampūnas *m. (1)* shampoo
šansas *m. (1)* chance
šantažas *m. (1)* blackmail
šantažistas, -ė *m. (1), f. (2)* blackmailer
šantažuoti *v. (1)* blackmail
šarvai *m. pl. (1)* armor
šaudyti *v. (3)* shoot
šaudmenys *m. pl. (1)* ammunition
šauksmas *m. (1)* cry; call
šaukštas *m. (1)* spoon
šaukštelis *m. (1)* teaspoon
šaukti *v. (1)* cry
šaunus, -i *adj. (2)* awesome; great
še *part.* here (take it)
šefas, -ė *m. (1), f. (2)* boss
šeichas *m. (1)* sheik
šeima *f. (2)* family
šeimininkas *m. (1)* master; host; landlord
šeimininkė *f. (2)* hostess; landlady
šelpti *v. (1)* aid; support (financially)
(dantų) šepetėlis (tooth) brush
šepetys *m. (1)* brush
šerifas *m. (1)* sheriff
šerkšnas *m. (1)* frost (on trees/ windows)
šermenys *m. pl. (1)* funeral feast
šernas *m. (1)* wild boar
šerti *v. (1)* feed (animals)
šešėlis *m. (1)* shade; shadow
šeši, -ios *num.* six
šeštadienis *m. (1)* Saturday
šėtonas *m. (1)* Satan
šiaip *adv.* so; in general
šianakt *adv.* tonight
šiandien *adv.* today
šiapus *adv.* on this side
šiaudas *m. (1)* straw
šiaurė *f. (2)* north
šiaurinis, -ė *adj. (3)* northern
šiaurės rytai northeast
šiaurės vakarai northwest
šiek tiek a little; some
šiemet *adv.* this year
šienas *m. (1)* hay
šienauti *v. (1)* mow
šįkart *adv.* this time
šykštus, -i *adj. (2)* stingy; grudging
šildymas *m. (1)* heating
šilkas *m. (1)* silk
šilkinis, -ė *adj. (3)* silk
šiltas, -a *adj. (1)* warm
šiltnamis *m. (1)* greenhouse
šiluma *f. (2)* heat; warmth
šįmet *adv.* this year
šimtas *m. (1)* hundred
šimtmetis *m. (1)* century
šiokiadienis *m. (1)* weekday
šiokiadienis, -ė *adj. (3)* everyday
šypsena *f. (2)* smile
šypsotis *v. (3)* smile
širdingas, -a *adj. (1)* cordial
širdis *f. (3)* heart
šįryt *adv.* this morning
širma *f. (2)* screen
širšė *f. (2)* hornet
ši *pron. f.* this
šis *pron. m.* this
šiukšlės *f. pl. (2)* garbage

šiuolaikinis, -ė *adj. (3)* contemporary
šiurkštus, -i *adj. (2)* rough
škotas, -ė *m. (1), f. (2)* Scots(wo)man
škotiškas, -a *adj. (1)* Scottish
šlaitas *m. (1)* slope
šlamštas *m. (1)* trash
šlapias, -ia *adj. (1)* wet
šlapimas *m. (1)* urine
šlepetė *f. (2)* slipper
šliaužti *v. (1)* crawl
šlykštus, -i *adj. (2)* disgusting
šliurė *f. (2)* slipper
šlovė *f. (2)* glory
šluostytis *v. (3)* wipe oneself; dry oneself
šluota *f. (2)* broom
šmėkla *f. (2)* ghost; spirit
šneka *f. (2)* talk; chat
šnekėtis *v. (1)* talk
šnekus, -i *adj. (2)* talkative
šnervė *f. (2)* nostril
šnipas *m. (1)* spy; snout
šnipinėti *v. (1)* spy
šokas *m. (1)* shock
šokoladas *m. (1)* chocolate
šokoladinis, -ė *adj. (3)* chocolate
šokti *v. (1)* jump; dance
šonas *m. (1)* side
šonkaulis *m. (1)* rib
šparagai *m. pl. (1)* asparagus
špinatai *m. pl. (1)* spinach
štampas *m. (1)* stamp; cliché
šūkis *m. (1)* slogan
šukos *f. pl. (2)* comb
šukuotis *v. (1)* comb one's hair
šulinys *m. (1)* well
šuo *m. (5)* dog
šuoliais *adv.* at full gallop
šuolis *m. (1)* jump; leap
šūvis *m. (1)* shot
švara *f. (2)* cleanliness; neatness
švarkas *m. (1)* (suit) jacket
švarkelis *m. (1)* (woman's) (suit) jacket
švarus, -i *adj. (2)* clean; neat
švedas, -ė *m. (1), f. (2)* Swede
švediškas, -a *adj. (1)* Swedish
šveicaras, -ė *m. (1), f. (2)* Swiss
šveicariškas, -a *adj. (1)* Swiss
šveisti *v. (1)* scrub
švelnus, -i *adj. (2)* soft; tender
šventadienis *m. (1)* holiday
šventas, -a *adj. (1)* sacred; holy; saint; holiday
šventykla *f. (2)* sanctuary; temple
šventinis, -ė *adj. (3)* holiday; festive
šventvagystė *f. (2)* sacrilege; blasphemy
švęsti *v. (1)* celebrate
šviesa *f. (2)* light
šviesiaplaukis, -ė *adj. (3)* blonde
šviesoforas *m. (1)* traffic/ street lights
šviesus, -i *adj. (2)* light; bright
šviestuvas *m. (1)* chandelier; ceiling fixture
šviežias, -ia *adj. (1)* fresh
švilpti *v. (1)* whistle
švinas *m. (1)* lead
švininis, -ė *adj. (3)* lead
švisti *v. (1)* dawn
švyturys *m. (1)* beacon; lighthouse

T

tabakas *m. (1)* tobacco
tabletė *f. (2)* tablet; pill
taburetė *f. (2)* stool
tačiau *conj.* however; nevertheless
tad *conj.* so; therefore
tada *adv.* then
tai *pron.* that
taigi *conj.* thus
taika *f. (2)* peace
taikyti *v. (3)* aim
taiklus, -i *adj. (2)* accurate; well-aimed
taikomasis, -oji *adj.* applied
taikus, -i *adj. (2)* peaceful
taip *part.* yes; so; this way
taisyklė *f. (2)* rule
taisyklingas, -a *adj. (1)* regular; correct
taisyti *v. (3)* repair
taksofonas *m. (1)* pay phone
takas *m. (1)* path
taksi taxi
taktas *m. (1)* tact
taktiškas, -a *adj. (1)* tactful
talentas *m. (1)* talent
talentingas, -a *adj. (1)* talented; gifted
talka *f. (2)* (collective) assistance
talpa *f. (2)* capacity
talpus, -i *adj. (2)* capacious

tamsa *f. (2)* darkness
tamsiaplaukis, -ė *m. (1), f. (2); adj. (3)* dark-haired
tamsus, -i *adj. (2)* dark
tankas *m. (1)* tank
tankus, -i *adj. (2)* dense, thick
tapatybė *f. (2)* identity
tapyba *f. (2)* painting
tapyti *v. (3)* paint
tapytojas, -a *m. (1), f. (2)* painter (artist)
tapti *v. (1)* become
tarakonas *m. (1)* cockroach
tardyti *v. (3)* hold an inquest
tardytojas, -a *m. (1), f. (2)* investigator
taryba *f. (2)* council
tarybinis, -ė *adj. (3)* Soviet
tarimas *m. (1)* pronunciation
tarmė *f. (2)* dialect
tarnas, -aitė *m. (1), f. (2)* servant
tarnauti *v. (1)* serve
tarnautojas, -a *m. (1), f. (2)* employee
tarnyba *f. (2)* service job
tarnybinis, -ė *adj. (3)* official; work; office
tarp *prep.* between; among
tarpas *m. (1)* interval; space
tarpininkauti *v. (1)* mediate
tarpinis, -ė *adj. (3)* intermediate
tarpmiestinis, -ė *adj. (3)* intercity
tarptautinis, -ė *adj. (3)* international
tarsi *part.* as if; as though; like
tartis *f. (3)* pronunciation
ta *pron. f.* this; that
tas *pron. m.* this; that
taškas *m. (1)* point; period; spot; dot
taukai *m. pl. (1)* fat
taukuotas, -a *adj. (1)* greasy
taupyti *v. (3)* save
taurė *f. (2)* goblet; glass
taurelė *f. (2)* shot glass
tauta *f. (2)* nation
tautybė *f. (2)* nationality
tautietis, -ė *m. (1), f. (2)* compatriot
tautiškas, -a *adj. (1)* national
tautosaka *f. (2)* folklore
tavo *pron.* your(s)
teatras *m. (1)* theater
technika *f. (2)* technique; machinery
techninis, -ė *adj. (3)* technical; mechanical
technologija *f. (2)* technology
teigiamas, -a *adj. (1)* positive; affirmative
teiginys *m. (1)* thesis; proposition
teirautis *v. (1)* ask about; inquire
teisė *f. (2)* right; law
teisybė *f. (2)* truth
teisingas, -a *adj. (1)* just
teisingumas *m. (1)* justice; fairness
teisininkas, -ė *m. (1), f. (2)* lawyer
teisinti *v. (1)* justify
teisintis *v. (1)* justify oneself
teismas *m. (1)* court
teisti *v. (1)* convict
teisus, -i *adj. (2)* right
tekėti *v. (1)* flow; marry (for female)
tėkmė *f. (2)* flow
tekstas *m. (1)* text
tekstilė *f. (2)* textile
telefonas *m. (1)* telephone
telegrafas *m. (1)* telegraph
telegrama *f. (2)* telegram
televizija *f. (2)* television
televizorius *m. (4)* TV set
tema *f. (2)* subject; composition; school essay
tempas *m. (1)* rate; pace
temperatūra *f. (2)* temperature; fever
ten(ai) *adv.* there
tenisas *m. (1)* tennis
tenisininkas, -ė *m. (1), f. (2)* tennis player
tenkinti *v. (1)* satisfy
tenoras *m. (1)* tenor
teorija *f. (2)* theory
teorinis, -ė *adj. (3)* theoretic(al)
teoriškai *adv.* theoretically
tepalas *m. (1)* ointment; lubricant
(batų) tepalas shoe polish
teptukas *m. (1)* (painter's) brush
teritorija *f. (2)* territory
teritorinis, -ė *adj. (3)* territorial
terminas *m. (1)* date; term
terminologija *f. (2)* terminology
terminuotas, -a *adj. (1)* at a fixed date
termometras *m. (1)* thermometer
testamentas *m. (1)* (last) will
tęsti *v. (1)* continue
tešla *f. (2)* dough
teta *f. (2)* aunt
tėtė *m. (2)* dad

tėtis *m. (1)* dad
tėvai *m. pl. (1)* parents
tėvas *m. (1)* father
tėvynė *f. (2)* native land
tezė *f. (2)* thesis
tyčia *adv.* purposely; deliberately; for fun
tiek *adv.* so much, so many
tiekėjas, -a *m. (1), f. (2)* supplier; caterer
ties *prep.* over; by
tiesa *f. (2)* truth
tiesioginis, -ė *adj. (3)* direct
teisus, -i *adj. (2)* straight
tigras, -ė *m. (1), f. (2)* tiger
tik *part.* only; merely; just
tikėjimas *m. (1)* faith; belief
tikėti *v. (2)* believe
tikėtis *v. (2)* hope; expect
tikimybė *f. (2)* probability
tikintis, -i *adj. m.* religious; believing
tikintis, -i *m. (1), f. (2)* believer
tikras, -a *adj. (1)* real; true
tikrovė *f. (2)* reality
tikslas *m. (1)* aim; goal
tiktai *adv.* only; merely; just
tyla *f. (2)* silence
tylėti *v. (2)* be silent
tiltas *m. (1)* bridge
tylus, -i *adj. (2)* quiet
tymai *med. m. (1)* measles
tinginys, -ė *m. (1), f. (2)* lazy person
tingus, -i *adj. (2)* lazy
tinkamas, -a *adj. (1)* suitable
tinkas *m. (1)* plaster
tinklainė *med. f. (2)* retina
tinklas *m. (1)* net; network; web
tinklininkas, -ė *m. (1), f. (2)* volleyball player
tinklinis *m. (1)* volleyball
tinti *v. (1)* swell
tipas *m. (1)* type, character
tipiškas, -a *adj. (1)* typical
tiražas *m. (1)* circulation; number of prited copies in edition
tyrėjas, -a *adj. (1)* researcher; explorer
tyrimas *m. (1)* research; investigation; analysis; test
tyrinėti *v. (1)* research; explore
tirti *v. (1)* research; investigate
tirpalas *m. (1)* solution
tirpti *v. (1)* dissolve; melt
tirštas, -a *adj. (1)* thick
tirti *v. (1)* investigate; research
tįsti *v. (1)* stretch
titulas *m. (1)* title
tobulas, -a *adj. (1)* perfect
tobulybė *f. (2)* perfection
todėl *adv.* therefore; that's why
tokia *pron. f.* such
toks *pron. m.*such
tol until
toleruoti *v. (1)* tolerate
tolesnis, -ė *adj. (3)* farther; further
toliaregis, -ė *m. (1), f. (2)* farsighted
toli *adv.* far
tolimas, -a *adj. (1)* far; distant; remote
tomas *m. (1)* volume (of a book)
tona *f. (2)* ton
tonas *m. (1)* tone
tortas *m. (1)* cake
tostas *m. (1)* toast
totorius, -ė *m. (4), f. (2)* Tartar
totoriškas, -a *adj. (1)* Tartar
tradicija *f. (2)* tradition
tradicinis, -ė *adj. (3)* traditional
tragedija *f. (2)* tragedy
tragiškas, -a *adj. (1)* tragic
traktorininkas, -ė *m. (1), f. (2)* tractor driver
traktorius *m. (4)* tractor
tramdyti *v. (3)* tame
tramvajus *m. (4)* tram(way), streetcar
transliacija *f. (2)* broadcast
trapus, -i *adj. (2)* fragile; easy to fall apart
trąša *f. (2)* fertilizer
traukinys *m. (1)* train
trečdalis *m. (1)* one-third
trečiadienis *m. (1)* Wednesday
tremti *v. (1)* exile, deport
tremtinys, -ė *m. (1), f. (2)* deportee
treneris, -ė *m. (1), f. (2)* coach
trešnė *f. (2)* (sweet) cherry; cherry-tree
tręšti *v. (1)* fertilize
tribūna *f. (2)* tribune; platform; stand
tribunolas *m. (1)* tribunal
trikampis *m. (1)* triangle
trikampis, -ė *adj. (3)* triangular
trikojis *m. (1)* tripod
trimitas *m. (1)* trumpet
trynys *m. (1)* (egg) yolk
trinti *v. (1)* rub; grate
trintukas *m. (1)* eraser

trys *num.* three
triukšmas *m. (1)* noise
triukšmauti *v. (1)* make noise
triukšmingas, -a *adj. (1)* noisy
triušiena *f. (2)* rabbit (meat)
triušis *m. (1)* rabbit
troba *f. (2)* peasant house
trobelė *f. (2)* cabin; hut; shack
trofėjus *m. (4)* trophy
troleibusas *m. (1)* trolley(bus)
troškulys *m. (1)* thirst
trukdyti *v. (3)* disturb
trūkis *med. m. (1)* hernia
trūkti *v. (1)* lack; break
trumparegis, -ė *m. (1), f. (2)* nearsighted
trumparegystė *med. f. (2)* myopia; nearsightedness
trumpas, -a *adj. (1)* short
trupė *f. (2)* troupe; company (of actors)
trupėti *v. (1)* crumble
trupinys *m. (1)* crumb
truputis *m. (1)* a little, some
tu *pron.* you
tualetas *m. (1)* restroom, toilet
tualetinis popierius toilet paper
tuberkuliozė *med. f. (2)* tuberculosis
tūkstantis *m. (1)* thousand
tūkstantmetis *m. (1)* millennium
tulpė *f. (2)* tulip
tundra *f. (2)* tundra
tunelis *m. (1)* tunnel
tuoj(au) *adv.* immediately
tuoktis *v. (1)* marry somebody
tuomet *adv.* then
tupėti *v. (2)* squat; perch
turbūt *part.* probably
turbina *f. (2)* turbine
turėklai *m. pl. (1)* rail(ing)
turėti *v. (2)* have
turgus *m. (4)* market; bazaar
tūris *m. (1)* volume; capacity
turistas, -ė *m. (1), f. (2)* tourist
turistinis, -ė *adj. (3)* tourist
turizmas *m. (1)* tourism
turkas, -ė *m. (1), f. (2)* Turk
turkiškas, -a *adj. (1)* Turkish
turnyras *m. (1)* tournament
turtas *m. (1)* wealth; property; belongings
turtingas, -a *adj. (1)* rich
turtuolis, -ė *m. (1), f. (2)* rich person
tušas *m. (1)* mascara; ink; toner
tuščias, -ia *adj. (1)* empty
tuzinas *m. (1)* dozen
tvardytis *v. (3)* control oneself
tvarka *f. (2)* order
tvarkaraštis *m. (1)* schedule
tvarkingas, -a *adj. (1)* neat; tidy
tvarkyti *v. (3)* manage; be in charge; put in order; clean
tvarstis *m. (1)* bandage
tvartas *m. (1)* barn; cattle-shed; stable; pigsty
tvenkinys *m. (1)* pond
tvirtas, -a *adj. (1)* strong
tvirtinti *v. (1)* maintain; claim; approve
tvirtovė *f. (2)* fortress
tvora *f. (2)* fence

U, Ū, Ų

ugdyti *v. (3)* develop; train
ūgis *m. (1)* height (of person)
ugniagesys *m. (1)* fireman
ugnis *f. (3)* fire
ūkininkas, -ė *m. (1), f. (2)* farmer
ūkininkauti *v. (1)* manage a farm
ūkis *m. (1)* farm
ukrainietis, -ė *m. (1), f. (2)* Ukrainian
ukrainietiškas, -a *adj. (1)* Ukrainian
ūmus, -i *adj. (2)* quick-tempered
ungurys *m. (1)* eel
uniforma *f. (2)* uniform
uniforminis, -ė *adj. (3)* uniform
universalus, -i *adj. (2)* universal
universitetas *m. (1)* university
uodas *m. (1)* mosquito
uodega *f. (2)* tail
uoga *f. (2)* berry
uogauti *v. (1)* pick berries
uogienė *f. (2)* confiture; jam
uola *f. (2)* rock; cliff
uolėtas, -a *adj. (1)* rocky
uosis *m. (1)* ash-tree
uoslė *f. (2)* smell; flair
uostamiestis *m. (1)* seaport
uostas *m. (1)* port; harbor
uostyti *v. (3)* smell
uošvė *f. (2)* mother-in-law
uošvis *m. (1)* father-in-law
upė *f. (2)* river
upėtakis *m. (1)* trout

uraganas *m. (1)* hurricane; tornado
urgzti *v. (1)* growl; snarl
urna *f. (2)* urn
urvas *m. (1)* cave
urvinis, -ė *adj. (3)* cave
ūsai *m. pl. (1)* mustache
utėlė *f. (2)* louse
už *prep.* behind; beyond; for; than
užantspauduoti *v. (1)* seal
užaugti *v. (1)* grow up
uždanga *f. (2)* (theater) curtain
uždaryti *v. (3)* close; shut
uždarytas, -a *adj. (1)* closed
uždavinys *m. (1)* task; goal; exercise
uždegimas *med. m. (1)* inflammation
uždegti (šviesą) *v. (1)* switch on (the light)
uždėti *v. (1)* put on/ over; lay on/ over
uždirbti *v. (1)* earn
uždrausti *v. (1)* forbid; ban; prohibit
užeiga *f. (2)* inn
Užgavėnės *f. pl. (2)* Mardi Gras; Shrovetide
užgesinti *v. (1)* put out; switch off (the light)
užhipnotizuoti *v. (1)* hypnotize
užimtas, -a *adj. (1)* occupied
užimti *v. (1)* occupy
užjausti *v. (1)* symphatize with
užjūris *m. (1)* overseas
užkandinė *f. (2)* snack bar
užkandis *m. (1)* hors d'oeuvres; snack
užkąsti *v. (1)* have a snack
užkloti *v. (1)* cover
užkrečiamas, -a *adj. (1)* contagious; transmissible
užkrėsti *v. (1)* infect
užmiestis *m. (1)* outskirts of town; suburbs
užmiršti *v. (1)* forget
užmokestis *m. (1)* pay; wages
užmokėti *v. (1)* pay
užmušti *v. (1)* kill
užpakalis *m. (1)* behind; butt
užpernai *adv.* the year before last
užplombuoti *v. (1)* seal fill (a tooth)
užporyt *adv.* in three days
užpulti *v. (1)* attack; assault
užpūsti *v. (1)* blow out
užrakinti *v. (1)* lock
užrakintas, -a *adj. (1)* locked
užrašai *m. pl. (1)* notes; memoirs
užrašų knygelė pocket book
užsakymas *m. (1)* order
užsakyti *v. (3)* order
užsienietis, -ė *m. (1), f. (2)* foreigner
užsienietiškas, -a *adj. (1)* foreign
užsienis *m. (1)* abroad
užsikrėsti *v. (1)* get infected
užsimerkti *v. (1)* close one's eyes
užsirašyti *v. (3)* write down
užsispyręs, -usi *adj. m.* stubborn
užteršti *v. (1)* soil; litter
užtvanka *f. (2)* dam
užuojauta *f. (2)* sympathy; condolences; obituary
užuolaida *f. (2)* curtain; blind
užuomina *f. (2)* hint
užuovėja *f. (2)* place sheltered from the wind
užvalkalas *m. (1)* pillowcase

V

va *part.* there; here (when pointing)
vabalas *m. (1)* beetle; bug
vabzdys *m. (1)* insect
vadas, -ė *m. (1), f. (2)* commander; chief; leader
vadyba *f. (2)* management (field of)
vadybininkas, -ė *m. (1), f. (2)* manager
vadinti *v. (1)* call, name
vadovas, -ė *m. (1)* manager; leader; reference book
vadovauti *v. (1)* manage; lead
vadovėlis *m. (1)* textbook
vadovybė *f. (2)* management; administration
vagis *m. (3)* thief
vagystė *f. (2)* theft
vagonas *m. (1)* (train)car
vaidyba *f. (2)* acting
vaidila *m. (2)* pagan priest
vaidilutė *f. (2)* pagan priestess
vaidinimas *m. (1)* play; performance
vaidmuo *m. (5)* role; part
vaiduoklis *m. (1)* ghost; spirit
vaikaitis, -ė *m. (1), f. (2)* grandchild
vaikas *m. (1)* child

vaikinas *m. (1)* guy; boyfriend
vaikiškas, -a *adj. (1)* childish; children's
vaikystė *f. (2)* childhood
vaikščioti *v. (1)* walk
vainikas *m. (1)* wreath
vairas *m. (1)* (steering) wheel
vairuoti *v. (1)* drive; steer
vairuotojas, -a *m. (1), f. (2)* driver
vairuotojo pažymėjimas driver's license
vaisingas, -a *adj. (1)* fertile; productive
vaisingumas *m. (1)* fertility
vaisius *m. (1)* fruit
vaismedis *m. (1)* fruit-tree
vaistas *m. (1)* remedy; drug
vaistažolė *f. (2)* (medicinal) herb
vaistinė *f. (2)* pharmacy; drugstore
vaisvandeniai *m. pl. (1)* fruit drinks; fruit soda/ pop
vaisinis, -ė *adj. (3)* fruit
vaišės *f. pl. (2)* reception; refreshments
vaišingas, -a *adj. (1)* hospitable
vaišingumas *m. (1)* hospitality
vaišinti *v. (1)* treat; offer food and drink
vaivorykštė *f. (2)* rainbow
vaizdas *m. (1)* view
vaizdingas, -a *adj. (1)* picturesque
vaizduotė *f. (2)* imagination
vaizduoti *v. (1)* depict; picture
vajus *m. (4)* campaign
vakar *adv.* yesterday
vakaras *m. (1)* evening
vakarėlis *m. (1)* party
vakarienė *f. (2)* dinner (supper)
vakarietiškas, -a *adj. (1)* Western
vakarykštis, -ė *adj. (3)* yesterday's
vakarinis, -ė *adj. (3)* evening; west
valanda *f. (2)* hour, o'clock
valda *f. (2)* (territorial) possession
valdyba *f. (2)* board (of directors); administration
valdininkas, -ė *m. (1), f. (2)* official
valdytojas, -a *m. (1), f. (2)* manager
valdovas, -ė *m. (1), f. (2)* ruler
valdžia *f. (2)* state/ local power/ authority
valgiaraštis *m. (1)* menu
valgykla *f. (2)* cafeteria; eatery; canteen
valgis *m. (1)* food; dish
valgyti *v. (3)* eat
valgomas, -a *adj. (1)* edible
valgomasis *m. (1)* dining room
valia *f. (2)* will
valykla *f. (2)* cleaner's
valio! *inter.* hooray!
valyti *v. (3)* clean
valytojas, -a *m. (1), f. (2)* cleaning person
valiuta *f. (2)* currency
valsas *m. (1)* waltz
valsčius *m. (4)* (small rural) district
valstybė *f. (2)* state
valstybinis, -ė *adj. (3)* state
valstietis, -ė *m. (1), f. (2)* peasant
valstija *f. (2)* state (of the U.S.A.)
valtis *f. (3)* boat
vampyras *m. (1)* vampire
vamzdis *m. (1)* pipe
vanagas *m. (1)* hawk
vandenynas *m. (1)* ocean
vanduo *m. (5)* water
vapsva *f. (2)* wasp
vardadienis *m. (1)* nameday
vardas *m. (1)* name
vargingas, -a *adj. (1)* poor
vargonai *m. pl. (1)* organ
vargšas, -ė *m. (1), f. (2)* poor; poor thing
vargti *v. (1)* live in poverty; take trouble
varguomenė *f. (2)* the poor
variklis *m. (1)* motor; engine
varinis, -ė *adj. (3)* copper
varis *m. (1)* copper
varlė *f. (2)* frog
varlytė *f. (2)* bow tie
varna *f. (2)* crow
varnas *m. (1)* raven
varpa *f. (2)* ear (of a rye); penis
varpas *m. (1)* bell
varpinė *f. (2)* bell tower
varškė *f. (2)* farmer's cheese; cottage cheese
vartai *m. pl. (1)* gate
vartininkas, -ė *m. (1), f. (2)* gatekeeper
vartojimas *m. (1)* use; consumption
vartoti *v. (1)* use
vartotojas, -a *m. (1), f. (2)* consumer; user
varveklis *m. (1)* icicle
varvėti *v. (1)* drip
varžybos *f. pl. (2)* contest
varžovas, -ė *m. (1), f. (2)* rival
vasara *f. (2)* summer

vasarinis, -ė *adj. (3)* summer
vasaris *m. (1)* February
vaškas *m. (1)* wax
vaškinis, -ė *adj. (3)* wax
vata *f. (2)* cotton (ball(s))
vaza *f. (2)* vase
vazelinas *m. (1)* vaseline
vazonas *m. (1)* flower pot
važiuoti *v. (1)* go; drive
vedėjas, -a *m. (1), f. (2)* head; manager
vedęs *adj.* married
vedybos *f. pl. (2)* marriage
vegetaras, -ė *m. (1), f. (2)* vegetarian
vegetarinis, -ė *adj. (3)* vegetarian
veidas *m. (1)* face
veidmainis, -ė *m. (1), f. (2)* hypocrite
veidrodis *m. (1)* mirror
veikti *v. (1)* act; do
veislė *f. (2)* breed
veja *f. (2)* lawn
vėjaraupiai *med. m. pl. (1)* chicken pox
vėjas *m. (1)* wind
vekselis *m. (1)* promissory note
vėl *adv.* again
vėlai *adv.* late
vėliava *f. (2)* flag
Velykos *f. pl. (2)* Easter
velionis, -ė *m. (1), f. (2)* deceased
velnias *m. (1)* devil
veltui *adv.* for free; in vain
vėluoti *v. (1)* be late
vemti *v. (1)* vomit; throw up
vengti *v. (1)* avoid
vengras, -ė *m. (1), f. (2)* Hungarian
vengriškas, -a *adj. (1)* Hungarian
vėpla *m./f. (2)* gawk; gaper
vergas, -ė *m. (1), f. (2)* slave
vergija *f. (2)* slavery
vėrinys *m. (1)* necklace
verkti *v. (1)* cry, weep
verslas *m. (1)* business
verslininkas, -ė *m. (1), f. (2)* entrepreneur; business(wo)man
versti *v. (1)* force
vertė *f. (2)* value
vertėjas, -a *m. (1), f. (2)* translator; interpreter
vertybiniai popieriai *fin.* securities
vertikalus, -i *adj. (2)* vertical
vertimas *m. (1)* translation
vertinti *v. (1)* appraise; appreciate
vesti *v. (1)* marry; lead
vestuvės *f. pl. (2)* wedding
vėsus, -i *adj. (2)* chilly
veterinaras, -ė *m. (1), f. (2)* veterinarian
vėtra *f. (2)* storm, tempest
vežimas *m. (1)* cart
vėžys *m. (1)* cancer; crayfish
vežti *v. (1)* carry
videokasetė *f. (2)* videocassette
videomagnetofonas *m. (1)* VCR
vidinis, -ė *adj. (3)* internal
Viduramžiai *m. pl. (1)* Middle Ages
vidurdienis *m. (1)* noon
viduriai *m. pl. (1)* intestines
vidurinis, -ė *adj. (3)* middle
vidurys *m. (1)* middle
viduriavimas *m. (1)* diarrhea
viduriuoti *v. (1)* have diarrhea
vidurkis *m. (1)* average
vidus *m. (4)* interior; inside
viela *f. (2)* wire
vienas, -a *num. (1)* one; a; *adj. (1)* alone
vienatvė *f. (2)* solitude; loneliness
vienbalsiai *adv.* unanimously
viengungis, -ė *m. (1), f. (2)* single person; bachelor(ette)
vienybė *f. (2)* unity
vienintelis, -ė *adj. (3)* sole; only
vienišas, -a *adj. (1)* lonely; single
vienodas, -a *adj. (1)* the same
vienturtis, -ė *m. (1), f. (2)* the only child
vienuolė *f. (2)* nun
vienuolynas *m. (1)* monastery; convent
vienuolis *m. (1)* monk
viešas, -a *adj. (1)* public
viešbutis *m. (1)* hotel
Viešpats *m. (1)* Lord; ruler
vieta *f. (2)* place; seat; space; post/job
vietinis, -ė *adj. (3)* local
vykdyti *v. (3)* carry out; execute
vikšras *m. (1)* caterpillar
vykti *v. (1)* go; happen; occur
vila *f. (2)* villa
vilkas, -ė *m. (1), f. (2)* wolf
vilkti *v. (1)* drag
vilna *f. (2)* wool
vilnonis, -ė *adj. (3)* wool(en)
viltis *f. (3); v. (1)* hope

vynas *m. (1)* wine
vinis *f. (3)* nail
vynuogė *f. (2)* grape
vynuogynas *m. (1)* vineyard
violetinis, -ė *adj. (3)* violet; purple
violončelė *f. (2)* cello
violončelistas, -ė *m. (1), f. (2)* cellist
vyras *m. (1)* man; male; husband
virdulys *m. (1)* tea kettle
virėjas, -a *m. (1), f. (2)* cook
vyriausias, -ia *adj. (1)* head; senior
vyriausybė *f. (2)* government
vyriškas, -a *adj. (1)* masculine
virš *prep.* over; above
viršininkas, -ė *m. (1), f. (2)* boss
virškinti *v. (1)* digest
viršūnė *f. (2)* top; summit
viršus *m. (4)* top; upper part
viršvalandžiai *m. pl. (1)* overtime
virti *v. (1)* boil; cook
virtuvė *f. (2)* kitchen
virvė *f. (2)* rope
visada *adv.* always
visagalis, -ė *adj. (3)* almighty
visai *adv.* quite; entirely
visaip *adv.* in every possible way
visas, -a *adj. (1)* all; whole; entire
visata *f. (2)* universe
visgi *part.* however; still; nevertheless
visiškai *adv.* quite; entirely
viskas *m. (1)* everything; all
vyskupas *m. (1)* bishop
vyskupija *f. (2)* bishopric
visraktis *m. (1)* master key
vystyti *v. (3)* develop; change (the baby)
visuomenė *f. (2)* society
visuomet *adv.* always
visuotinis, -ė *adj. (3)* universal
visur *adv.* everywhere
viščiukas *m. (1)* chicken; chick
vyšnia *f. (2)* cherry; cherry-tree
višta *f. (2)* hen
vištiena *f. (2)* poultry; chicken (meat)
vitaminas *m. (1)* vitamin
vytis *m. (1)* knight (Lithuanian State emblem)
vitrina *f. (2)* window (of a shop)
viza *f. (2)* visa
vyzdys *m. (1)* pupil (of the eye)
vizitas *m. (1)* visit
vogti *v. (1)* steal
vokalinis, -ė *adj. (3)* vocal
vokas *m. (1)* envelope
vokietis, -ė *m. (1), f. (2)* German
vokiškas, -a *adj. (1)* German
vonia *f. (2)* bathroom; bathtub
voras *m. (1)* spider
voratinklis *m. (1)* web
vos *part.* hardly; almost
votis *f. (3)* abscess
voverė *f. (2)* squirrel
vualis *m. (1)* veil
vulgarus, -i *adj. (2)* vulgar

Z

zomšinis, -ė *adj. (3)* suede
zona *f. (2)* zone
zoologijos sodas zoo
zuikis *m. (1)* hare; rabbit

Ž

žadėti *v. (1)* promise
žadinti *v. (1)* wake
žadintuvas *m. (1)* alarm clock
žagsėti *v. (2)* hiccup; hiccough
žaibas *m. (1)* lightning
žaibiškas, -a *adj. (1)* quick (as lightning)
žaidėjas, -a *m. (1), f. (2)* player
žaidimas *m. (1)* game
žaislas *m. (1)* toy
žaizda *f. (2)* wound
žala *f. (2)* harm
žalias, -ia *adj. (1)* green
žaliava *f. (2)* raw material
žalingas, -a *adj. (1)* harmful
žaloti *v. (1)* damage; injure
žaltys *m. (1)* grass snake
žalumynai *m. pl. (1)* greens
žalvarinis, -ė *adj. (3)* brass
žandikaulis *m. (1)* jaw
žarna *f. (2)* intestine
žąsiena *f. (2)* goose (meat)
žąsis *f. (3)* goose
žemaitis, -ė *m. (1), f. (2)* inhabitant of Žemaitija (lowlander)
žemas, -a *adj. (1)* low; short; mean
žemdirbys, -ė *m. (1), f. (2)* farmer
žemdirbystė *f. (2)* agriculture
žemė *f. (2)* earth; land; soil

žemėlapis *m. (1)* map
žemės drebėjimas earthquake
žemyn *adv.* down(wards)
žemynas *m. (1)* continent
žeminti *v. (1)* humiliate
žemuma *f. (2)* lowland
žengti *v. (1)* step
ženklas *m. (1)* sign; signal
žentas *m. (1)* son-in-law
žibalas *m. (1)* kerosene
žibintas *m. (1)* lantern
žibuoklė *f. (2)* violet
žiburys *m. (1)* (small) light
žydas, -ė *m. (1), f. (2)* Jew
židinys *m. (1)* fireplace
žydiškas, -a *adj. (1)* Jewish
žydras, -a *adj. (1)* sky blue; *col.* homosexual
žiebtuvėlis *m. (1)* lighter
žiedas *m. (1)* ring
žiema *f. (2)* winter
žieminis, -ė *adj. (3)* winter
žievė *f. (2)* bark
žilas, -a *adj. (1)* gray(haired)
žymė *f. (2)* mark; sign
žingsnis *m. (1)* step; pace
žinia *f. (2)* message
žinios *f. pl. (2)* news
žiniasklaida *f. (2)* media
žinoma *adv.* certainly; of course
žinoti *v. (3)* know; be aware of
žinovas, -ė *m. (1), f. (2)* expert
žiogas *m. (1)* grasshopper
žiogelis *m. (1)* safety pin
žioplys, -ė *m. (1), f. (2)* fool
žiovauti *v. (1)* yawn
žirgas *m. (1)* horse
žirklės *f. pl. (2)* scissors
žirnis *m. (1)* pea
žiūrėti *v. (2)* look
žiurkė *f. (2)* rat
žiūronas *m. (1)* binocular
žiūrovas, -ė *m. (1), f. (2)* spectator; member of the audience
žlugti *v. (1)* fall (through/ down)
žmogus *m. (4)* human being; person
žmona *f. (2)* wife
žmonės *m. pl. (2)* people
žmoniškas, -a *adj. (1)* humane
žnybti *v. (1)* pinch
žodynas *m. (1)* dictionary; vocabulary
žodis *m. (1)* word
žolė *f. (2)* grass
žudikas, -ė *m. (1), f. (2)* killer
žudynės *f. pl. (2)* slaughter
žurnalas *m. (1)* magazine, journal
žurnalistas, -ė *m. (1), f. (2)* journalist
žūti *v. (1)* die; get killed
žuvėdra *f. (2)* seagull
žuvis *f. (3)* fish
žvaigždė *f. (2)* star
žvaigždėtas, -a *adj. (1)* starry
žvairas, -a *adj. (1)* cross-eyed
žvakė *f. (2)* candle
žvalgas, -ė *m. (1), f. (2)* spy; scout
žvalgybininkas, -ė *m. (1), f. (2)* secret agent
žvalus, -i *adj. (2)* cheerful
žvejys, -ė *m. (1), f. (2)* fisher(wo)man
žvilgsnis *m. (1)* glance, stare
žvyras *m. (1)* gravel
žvirblis *m. (1)* sparrow

ENGLISH-LITHUANIAN DICTIONARY

A

a vienas, -a
able (to be) *v. (2)* galėti
abortion *m. (1)* abortas
about *prep.* apie
above *adv.* aukštai, aukščiau; *prep.* virš
abroad *m. (1)* užsienis; *adv.* svetur
abuse *v. (1)* piktnaudžiauti
academy *f. (2)* akademija
accelerator *m. (4)* akseleratorius
accept *v. (1)* priimti
access *m. (1)* priėjimas
accident *f. (2)* avarija
accidentally *adv.* atsitiktinai
accompany *v. (2)* (pa)lydėti
accommodation *f. (2)* apsistojimo vieta
according to *prep.* pagal, pasak
account *f. (2)* ataskaita
accountant *m. (1), f. (2)* buhalteris, -ė
accounting *f. (2)* buhalterija
accurate *adj. (2)* taiklus, -i
accuse *v. (1)* kaltinti
ache *v. (1)* mausti, skaudėti
achievement *m. (1)* laimėjimas, pasiekimas
acknowledge *v. (1)* pripažinti
acknowledgment *m. (1)* pripažinimas
acquaintance *adj. (1)* pažįstamas, -a
across *adv.* skersai; *prep.* per
act *m. (1)* poelgis; *v. (1)* veikti
acting *f. (2)* vaidyba
action *m. (1)* poelgis
active *adj. (2)* aktyvus, -i; judrus, -i
actor *m. (4), f. (2)* aktorius, -ė
ad *m. (1)* skelbimas
adapter *techn. m. (1)* adapteris
add *v. (1)* pridėti
add up *v. (1)* sudėti
addition *m. (1)* priedas
additional *adj. (1)* papildomas, -a
address *m. (1)* adresas
addressee *m. (1), f. (2)* adresatas, -ė
adjective *m. (1)* būdvardis
administration *f. (2)* administracija, vadyba, vadovybė
admire *v. (2)* pasigėrėti
admit *v. (1)* priimti; tarti
adolescence *f. (2)* paauglystė
adopt *v. (1)* priimti
adopt (a boy) *v. (1)* įsūnyti; **~ a girl** *v. (1)* įdukrinti
adopted daughter *f. (2)* įdukra; **~ son** *m. (1)* įsūnis
adult *adj.* suaugęs, -usi
advance *v. (1)* pakilti
advance payment *m. (1)* avansas
advantage *m. (1)* pliusas
Advent *m. (1)* Adventas
adventure *f. (2)* avantiūra
adventurer *m. (1), f. (2)* avantiūristas, -ė
adverb *m. (1)* prieveiksmis
advertise *v. (1)* reklamuoti
advertisement *f. (2)* reklama
advertising *f. (2)* reklama
advice *m. (1)* patarimas
advise *v. (1)* konsultuoti, patarti
adviser *m. (1), f. (2)* patarėjas, -a
affair *m. (1)* reikalas
affectionate *adj. (2)* meilus, -i
after *prep.* po
afternoon *f. (2)* popietė
afterwards *adv.* paskui
again *adv.* vėl
against *prep.* prieš
age *m. (1)* laikotarpis, *(4)* amžius
agency *f. (2)* agentūra
agent *m. (1), f. (2)* agentas, -ė
agree *v. (1)* sutikti
agreement *m. (1)* susitarimas; *f. (3)* sutartis (contract)
agriculture *f. (2)* žemdirbystė
ah *inter.* oho
aid *v. (1)* šelpti
AIDS AIDS
ailing *adj. (1)* ligotas, -a
aim *m. (1)* tikslas; *v. (3)* taikyti
air *m. (1)* oras
airline *f. pl. (2)* oro linijos

airplane *m. (1)* lėktuvas
airport *m. (1)* oro uostas
alarm *m. (1)* aliarmas
alarm clock *m. (1)* žadintuvas
album *m. (1)* albumas
alcohol *m. (1)* alkoholis
alcoholic *m. (1), f. (2)* alkoholikas, -ė
alcoholic beverages *m. pl. (1)* svaigalai
alike *adj. (2)* panašus, -i
alive *adj. (1)* gyvas, -a
all *adj. (1)* visas, -a; *pron.* viskas
allergic *adj. (1)* alergiškas, -a
allergy *f. (2)* alergija
alliance *f. (2)* sąjunga
allot *v. (1)* skirti
allow *v. (1)* leisti
ally *m. (1), f. (2)* sąjungininkas, -ė
almighty *adj. (3)* visagalis, -ė
almond *adj. (3)* migdolinis, -ė
almonds *m. pl. (1)* migdolai
almost *part.* beveik, kone
aloe *m. (4)* alijošius
alone *adj. (1)* vienas, -a
alphabet *m. (1)* alfabetas, raidynas
already *adv.* jau
also *conj.* irgi
altar *m. (4)* altorius
aluminum *m. (1)* aliuminis
always *adv.* visada, visuomet
amateur *m. (1), f. (2)* mėgėjas, -a; *adj. (1)* mėgėjiškas, -a
ambassador *m. (4), f. (2)* ambasadorius, -ė
amber *m. (1)* gintaras; *adj. (3)* gintarinis, -ė
ambulance *f. (1)* greitoji pagalba
ambush *f. (2)* pasala
American *m. (1), f. (2)* amerikietis, -ė; *adj. (1)* amerikietiškas, -a
ammunition *m. pl. (1)* šaudmenys
among *prep.* tarp
amulet *m. (1)* amuletas
amuse *v. (1)* linksminti
amusement *f. (2)* pramoga
analysis *f. (2)* analizė; *m. (1)* tyrimas
analyst *m. (1), f. (2)* analitikas, -ė
analyze *v. (1)* nagrinėti
anarchy *f. (2)* anarchija
ancestor *m. (1)* protėvis
anchor *m. (1)* inkaras
and *conj.* bei; ir; o
anecdote *m. (1)* anekdotas
anemia *med. f. (2)* mažakraujystė
anesthesia *med. f. (2)* narkozė; *m. (1)* nuskausminimas
anesthetize *v. (1)* nuskausminti
angel *m. (1)* angelas
anger *m. (1)* pyktis
angler *m. (1), f. (2)* meškeriotojas, -a
angry *adj. (1)* piktas, -a; **to be ~** *v. (1)* pykti
animal *m. (1)* gyvulys
annex *m. (1)* priestatas; *v. (1)* prijungti
annexation *f. (2)* aneksija
anniversary *m. (1)* jubiliejus; *f. pl. (2)* metinės; *f. (3)* sukaktis
announce *v. (1)* paskelbti
announcement *m. (1)* skelbimas
annoy *v. (1)* erzinti
annul *v. (1)* anuliuoti
answer *v. (1)* atsiliepti; *v. (3)* atsakyti
ant *f. (2)* skruzdė(lė)
anthem *m. (1)* himnas
anthrax *f. (2)* juodligė
antibiotic *m. (1)* antibiotikas
antidote *m. (1)* priešnuodis
antiquity *f. (2)* seniena
anxiety *m. (1)* nerimas, rūpestis
anxious *adj. (2)* neramus, -i
apologize *v. (3)* atsiprašyti
apology *m. (1)* atsiprašymas
appeal *v. (1)* apeliuoti
appear *v. (3)* pasirodyti
appearance *m. (1)* pasirodymas (on stage); *f. (2)* išorė (look)
appendix *m. (1)* priedas
appetite *m. (1)* apetitas
applause *m. pl. (1)* aplodismentai; *m. (1)* plojimas
apple *m. (1)* obuolys
apple tree *f. (3)* obelis
application *m. (1)* pareiškimas, prašymas
applied *adj.* taikomasis, -oji
appointment *m. (1)* pasimatymas
appraise *v. (1)* vertinti
appreciate *v. (1)* vertinti
apprentice *m. (1)* pameistrys
approach *m. (1)* priėjimas; *v. (1)* prieiti
approval *m. (1)* pritarimas
approve *v. (1)* pritarti; tvirtinti
approximately *adv.* apytikriai, maždaug
apricot *m. (1)* abrikosas
April *m. (1)* balandis
apron *f. (2)* prijuostė

aquarium *m. (1)* akvariumas
arch *f. (2)* arka
archeologist *m. (1), f. (2)* archeologas, -ė
archeology *f. (2)* archeologija
architect *m. (1), f. (2)* architektas, -ė
architecture *f. (2)* architektūra
archive *m. (1)* archyvas
area *m. (1)* plotas
arena *f. (2)* arena
argue *v. (1)* ginčytis, polemizuoti
argument *m. (1)* argumentas; ginčas
aristocrat *m. (1), f. (2)* aristokratas, -ė
arm *f. (2)* ranka
armed *adj. (1)* ginkluotas, -a
armor *m. pl. (1)* šarvai
armpit *f. (3)* pažastis
army *f. (2)* armija, kariuomenė
aroma *m. (1)* aromatas
around *prep.* aplink
arrange *v. (3)* sutvarkyti
arrest *m. (1)* areštas, suėmimas; *v. (1)* areštuoti, suimti
arrival *m. (1)* atvykimas, atėjimas
arrive *v. (1)* atvykti
arrogance *f. (2)* arogancija; *m. (1)* išdidumas
arrogant *adj. (2)* išdidus, -i
arrow *f. (2)* rodyklė; strėlė
art *f. (2)* dailė; *m. (1)* menas
arteriosclerosis *med. f. (2)* arteriosklerozė
artery *f. (2)* arterija
article *m. (1)* straipsnis; gaminys
artificial *adj. (1)* netikras, -a
artist *m. (1), f. (2)* menininkas, -ė; dailininkas, -ė
artistic *adj. (1)* meniškas, -a
artist's studio *f. (2)* ateljė
as *conj.* kadangi; *part.* lyg; ~ **if** neva, tarsi; ~ **far** ~ *prep.* iki
ashes *m. pl. (1)* pelenai
ashtray *f. (2)* peleninė
ash tree *m. (1)* uosis
ask *v. (1)* (pa)klausti; *v. (3)* (pa)prašyti
ask about *v. (1)* teirautis
asparagus *m. pl. (1)* šparagai
aspirin *m. (1)* aspirinas
assailant *m. (1), f. (2)* užpuolikas, -ė
assassinate *v. (3)* nužudyti
assault *v. (1)* užpulti
assembly *f. (2)* asamblėja
assert *v. (1)* teigti
assistance *f. (2)* pagalba
assistant *m. (1), f. (2)* padėjėjas, -a, pavaduotojas, -a
associate *v. (1)* bendrauti
association *f. (2)* asociacija
assumption *f. (2)* prielaida
asthma *med. f. (2)* astma
astonishment *f. (2)* nuostaba
astronomer *m. (1), f. (2)* astronomas, -ė
astronomy *f. (2)* astronomija
asylum *f. (2)* prieglauda
at *prep.* prie, pas; ~ **all costs** *part.* žūtbūt; ~ **least** bent; ~ **home** *adv.* namie
atheism *m. (1)* ateizmas
atheist *m. (1), f. (2)* ateistas, -ė
athlete *m. (1), f. (2)* atletas, -ė
athletic *adj. (1)* atletiškas, -a
atmosphere *f. (2)* atmosfera
atom *m. (1)* atomas
atomic *adj. (3)* atominis, -ė
attach *v. (1)* prijungti
attack *m. (1)* priepuolis; *v. (1)* atakuoti, (už)pulti
attempt *m. (1)* bandymas, mėginimas; *v. (1)* (pa)mėginti; *v. (3)* bandyti
attendant *m. (1), f. (2)* palydovas, -ė
attention *m. (1)* dėmesys
attitude *m. (1)* nusistatymas; *f. (2)* pažiūra
attorney *m. (1), f. (2)* advokatas, -ė
attract *v. (1)* vilioti, traukti
attraction *f. (2)* trauka
attractive *adj. (2)* patrauklus, -i
audience *f. (2)* publika; audiencija
auditorium *f. (2)* auditorija
August *m. (1)* rugpjūtis
aunt *f. (2)* teta; *f. (2)* dėdienė (uncle's wife)
Australian *m. (1), f. (2)* australas, -ė; *adj. (1)* australiškas, -a
Austrian *m. (1), f. (2)* austras, -ė; *adj. (1)* austriškas, -a
author *m. (4), f. (2)* autorius, -ė
authority *m. (1)* autoritetas
autobiography *f. (2)* autobiografija
automobile *m. (1)* automobilis
autonomy *f. (2)* autonomija
autopsy *med. m. (1)* skrodimas
autumn *m. (5)* ruduo; *adj. (3)* rudeninis, -ė

avant-garde *m. (1)* avangardas
avenue *f. (2)* alėja; *m. (1)* prospektas
average *m. (1)* vidurkis
aviation *f. (2)* aviacija
avoid *v. (1)* šalintis, vengti
award *m. (1)* apdovanojimas
away *adv.* šalin
awesome *adj. (2)* šaunus, -i
awkward *adj. (2)* nepatogus, -i
ax *m. (1)* kirvis

B

baby *m. (1)* kūdikis
back *f. (1)* nugara; *adj. (3)* užpakalinis, -ė; *adv.* atgal
back up *v. (3)* palaikyti
backpack *f. (2)* kuprinė
backwards *adv.* atgal
bacon *m. pl. (1)* lašiniai
bacterium *f. (2)* bakterija
bad *adj. (1)* blogas, -a
badly *adv.* blogai
bag *m. (1)* maišas
baggage *m. (1)* bagažas; **~ claim** bagažo atsiėmimas
bait *m. (1)* jaukas
bake *v. (1)* iškepti
baker *m. (1), f. (2)* kepėjas, -a
bakery *f. (2)* kepykla
balance *f. (2)* pusiausvyra
balcony *m. (1)* balkonas
bald *adj. (1)* plikas, -a
ball *m. (1)* kamuolys; rutulys
ball (banquet) *f. (2)* puota; *col. m. (4)* balius
ballet *m. (1)* baletas
balloon *m. (1)* balionas
banana *m. (1)* bananas
band *m. (1)* raištis; orkestras
bandage *m. (1)* tvarstis, raištis; *v. (3)* sutvarstyti
bandit *m. (1), f. (2)* banditas, -ė
bank *fin. m. (1)* bankas; krantas (of a river)
banker *m. (1), f. (2)* bankininkas, -ė
banknote *m. (1)* banknotas
bankrupt (to become) *v. (1)* (su)bankrutuoti
bankruptcy *m. (1)* bankrotas
baptism *m. (1)* krikštas; **~ party** *f. pl. (2)* krikštynos
bar *m. (1)* baras
barber *m. (1), f. (2)* kirpėjas, -a
barber's shop *f. (2)* kirpykla
barefoot *adj. (1)* basas, -a
bargain *v. (1)* derėtis
bark *f. (2)* žievė; *v. (1)* loti
barley *m. pl. (1)* miežiai
barley soup *f. pl. (2)* kruopos
barn *m. (1)* tvartas
baroque *m. (1)* barokas
barrel *f. (2)* statinė
barricade *f. (2)* barikada
barrier *m. (1)* barjeras
barter *m. pl. (1)* mainai
base *f. (2)* bazė (military; commercial); *m. (1)* pagrindas; pamatas (of a building)
basketball *m. (1)* krepšinis; **~ player** *m. (1), f. (2)* krepšininkas, -ė
bathe *v. (3)* maudytis
bathhouse *f. (3)* pirtis
bathroom *m. (1)* tualetas
bathtub *f. (2)* vonia
battery *f. (2)* baterija
bazaar *m. (4)* turgus
be *v. (1, irr.)* būti
beach *m. (1)* paplūdimys, pliažas
beads *m. pl. (1)* karoliai
bean *f. (2)* pupa
bear *m. (1)* lokys; *f. (2)* meška; *v. (1)* pakęsti
beard *f. (2)* barzda
beat *v. (1)* mušti
beautiful *adj. (2)* gražus, -i
beautiful girl/ woman *f. (2)* gražuolė
beaver *m. (1)* bebras
because *conj.* nes; *adv.* todėl
because of *conj.* dėl, kadangi; *prep.* per
become *v. (1)* tapti
bed *f. (2)* lova
bedbug *f. (2)* blakė
bedding *f. (2)* patalynė
bedsheet *f. (2)* paklodė
bedspread *f. (2)* lovatiesė
bee *f. (2)* bitė
beef *f. (2)* jautiena
beefsteak *m. (1)* bifšteksas
beehive *m. (1)* avilys
beekeeper *m. (1), f. (2)* bitininkas, -ė
beer *m. (4)* alus
beet(root) *m. (1)* burokas
beetle *m. (1)* vabalas
before *prep.* prieš

beg *v. (1)* maldauti
beggar *m./f. (2)* elgeta
begin *v. (1)* pra(si)dėti
behavior *m. (1)* elgesys
behind *m. (1)* užpakalis; *prep.* už
belch *v. (1)* (atsi)raugėti
Belgian *m. (1), f. (2)* belgas, -ė; *adj. (1)* belgiškas, -a
belief *m. (1)* tikėjimas
believe *v. (2)* tikėti
bell *m. (1)* skambutis; varpas
bell tower *f. (2)* varpinė
belly *m. (1)* pilvas
belongings *m. (1)* turtas
beloved *adj. (1)* mylimas, -a
belt *m. (1)* diržas
bench *m. (1)* suolas
bend *v. (1)* lenkti; linkti; **~ down** *v. (1)* lenktis
benefit *f. (2)* nauda
berry *f. (2)* uoga
beside *adv.* greta
bet *f. pl. (2)* lažybos; *v. (1)* lažintis
betray *v. (1)* išduoti
better (to get) *v. (1)* sveikti
between *prep.* tarp
beyond *prep.* už
Bible *f. (2)* Biblija
bicycle *m. (1)* dviratis
big *adj. (3)* didelis, -ė; *adj. (2)* stambus, -i
bile *f. (3)* tulžis
bill *f. (2)* sąskaita
billion *m. (1)* milijardas
binocular *m. (1)* žiūronas
biographer *m. (1), f. (2)* biografas, -ė
biography *f. (2)* biografija
biologist *m. (1), f. (2)* biologas, -ė
biology *f. (2)* biologija
birch *m. (1)* beržas
bird *m. (1)* paukštis
birth *m. (1)* gimimas
birthday gimimo diena
birthday person *m. (1), f. (2)* jubiliatas, -ė
biscuit *m. (1)* sausainis
bishop *m. (1)* vyskupas
bitch **vlg.** *f. (2)* kalė
bite *m. (1)* kąsnis; *v. (1)* įkąsti
bitter *adj. (2)* kartus, -i
black *adj. (1)* juodas, -a
black person *m. (1), f. (2)* juodaodis, -ė
blackmail *m. (1)* šantažas; *v. (1)* šantažuoti
blackmailer *m. (1), f. (2)* šantažistas, -ė
black market juodoji rinka
blacksmith *m. (1)* kalvis
bladder *f. (2)* pūslė
blame *v. (1)* smerkti
blanket *f. (2)* antklodė
bleed *v. (1)* kraujuoti
bless *v. (1)* (pa)laiminti
blessing *m. (1)* palaiminimas
blind *f. (2)* užuolaida; *adj. (1)* aklas, -a
blink *v. (2)* mirksėti
blister *f. (2)* pūslė
block *m. (1)* blokas
blockade *f. (2)* blokada
blonde *m. (1), f. (2)* blondinas, -ė; *adj. (3)* šviesiaplaukis, -ė
blood *m. (4)* kraujas; **~ pressure** *m. (1)* kraujospūdis
blood test *m. (1)* (kraujo) tyrimas
blood vessel *f. (2)* kraujagyslė
bloody *adj. (1)* kraujuotas, -a, kruvinas, -a
blouse *f. (2)* palaidinukė
blow *m. (1)* smūgis; *v. (1)* pūsti; **~ out** *v. (1)* užpūsti
blue *adj. (1)* mėlynas, -a
blueberry *f. (2)* mėlynė
blue-eyed *adj. (3)* mėlynakis, -ė
blush *v. (1)* parausti
board *f. (2)* lenta; **~ of directors** *f. (2)* valdyba
boarding school *m. (1)* internatas
boat *f. (3)* valtis
body *m. (1)* kūnas; kolektyvas
boil *v. (1)* virti
boletus (a kind of mushroom) *m. (1)* baravykas
bomb *f. (2)* bomba
bond *fin. f. (2)* obligacija
bone *m. (1)* kaulas
bonfire *m. (1)* laužas
bonus *f. (2)* premija
book *f. (2)* knyga
bookbinder's shop *f. (2)* rišykla
bookkeeping *f. (2)* buhalterija
bookstore *m. (1)* knygynas
boombox *m. (1)* magnetofonas
booth *f. (2)* kabina
border *m. (1)* pasienis
border guard *m. (1), f. (2)* pasienietis, -ė

bored (to be) *v. (1)* nuobodžiauti
boredom *m. (1)* nuobodulys
boring *adj. (2)* nuobodus, -i
borrow *v. (1)* pasiskolinti
borsch (soup) *m. pl. (1)* barščiai
boss *m. (1), f. (2)* viršininkas, -ė; *col.* šefas, -ė, bosas, -ė
both *pron. f.* abi; *m.* abu
bother *v. (2)* įkyrėti; *(1)* lįsti
bottle *m. (1)* butelis
bottle-opener *m. (1)* atidarytuvas
bottom *m. (1)* dugnas
boulevard *m. (1)* bulvaras
bow *v. (1)* (nusi)lenkti;
~ **down** *v. (1)* lenktis
bow tie *f. (2)* varlytė
box *f. (2)* dėžė; **small** ~ dėžutė
box office *f. (2)* kasa
boxer *m. (1), f. (2)* boksininkas, -ė
boxing *m. (1)* boksas
boy *m. (1)* berniukas
boyfriend *m. (1)* vaikinas
braid *f. (2)* kasa; *v. (1)* pinti
brain *f. pl. (3)* smegenys
brake *m. (1)* stabdys
branch *m. (1)* filialas (of a company)
brass *adj. (3)* žalvarinis, -ė
brave *adj. (2)* drąsus, -i
bread *f. (2)* duona;
~ **store** *f. (2)* duoninė
break *f. (2)* pertrauka; *v. (3)* (su)daužyti, (su)laužyti; sudužti
breakfast *m. pl. (1)* pusryčiai
break in *v. (1)* įsilaužti;
~ **up** *v. (1)* išsiskirti
breast *f. (3)* krūtis; *f. (2)* krūtinė
breed *f. (2)* veislė
brewer *m. (1), f. (2)* aludaris, -ė
bribable *adj. (1)* paperkamas, -a
bribe *v. (1)* papirkti; *m. (1)* kyšis
bribe-taker *m. (1), f. (2)* kyšininkas, -ė
brick *f. (2)* plyta; *adj. (3)* mūrinis, -ė, plytinis, -ė
bride *f. (2)* nuotaka, jaunamartė
bridegroom *m. (1)* jaunikis
bridesmaid *f. (2)* pamergė
bridge *m. (1)* tiltas
briefcase *m. (1)* portfelis
bright *adj. (2)* ryškus, -i, šviesus, -i, skaistus, -i
brilliant *adj. (2)* genealus, -i
bring *v. (1)* atnešti;
~ **up** *v. (1)* auginti, išauklėti
British *m. (1), f. (2)* britas, -ė
broadcast *f. (2)* transliacija
bronchitis *med. m. (1)* bronchitas
broom *f. (2)* šluota
broth *m. (1)* sultinys
brother *m. (1)* brolis
brother-in-law *m. (1)* svainis
brown *adj. (1)* rudas, -a
bruise *f. (2)* mėlynė
brunette *m. (1), f. (2)* brunetas, -ė
brush *m. (1)* šepetys
bucket *m. (1)* kibiras
Buddhism *m. (1)* budizmas
Buddhist *m. (1), f. (2)* budistas, -ė
budget *m. (1)* biudžetas
buffet *m. (1)* bufetas
build *v. (3)* statyti
building *m. (1)* pastatas; *v. (3)* pastatyti
Bulgarian *m. (1), f. (2)* bulgaras, -ė; *adj. (1)* bulgariškas, -a
bull *m. (1)* jautis; *m. (4)* bulius
bullet *f. (2)* kulka
bulletin *m. (1)* biuletenis
bum *f. (2)* valkata
bunker *m. (1)* bunkeris
bureau *m. (1)* biuras; *f. (2)* kontora
bureaucrat *m. (1), f. (2)* biurokratas, -ė
burglar *m. (1), f. (2)* įsilaužėlis, -ė
burglary *m. (1)* apiplėšimas
burgundy (color) *adj./f. (n.d.) col.* bordo
burn *m. (1)* nudegimas; *v. (1)* degti
bury *v. (1)* laidoti
bus *m. (1)* autobusas
bus station (depot) autobusų stotis
bus stop autobuso stotelė
bush *m. (1)* krūmas
business *m. (1)* verslas, *col.* biznis; reikalas
business person *m. (1), f. (2)* verslininkas, -ė, *col. m. (4), f. (2)* biznierius, -ė
business trip *f. (2)* komandiruotė
business-like *adj. (1)* dalykiškas, -a
but *conj.* bet; o
butcher *v. (1)* papjauti
butt *m. (1)* užpakalis
butter *m. (1)* sviestas; *adj. (3)* sviestinis, -ė
butterfly *m. (1)* drugelis
button *f. (2)* saga
buy *v. (1)* pirkti
buyer *m. (1), f. (2)* pirkėjas, -a
by *prep.* pas; prie; šalia; ties; pro

by the way *part.* beje
by-street *m. (1)* skersgatvis

C

cabbage *m. (1)* kopūstas
cabin *f. (2)* trobelė; *f. (2)* kajutė (on a ship)
cable *adj. (3)* kabelinis, -ė
café *f. (2)* kavinė
cafeteria *f. (2)* valgykla
cage *m. (1)* narvas
cake *m. (1)* tortas
calcium *m. (1)* kalcis
calculator *m. (4)* kalkuliatorius
calendar *m. (4)* kalendorius
calf (of the leg) *f. (2)* blauzda
call *m. (1)* šaukimas, šauksmas; *v. (1)* vadinti; (pa)skambinti
caller *m. (1), f. (2)* interesantas, -ė
calm *v. (1)* (nusi)raminti; *adj. (2)* ramus, -i
calorie *f. (2)* kalorija
camera *f. (2)* kamera
camp *f. (2)* stovykla
campsite *f. (2)* poilsiavietė
campaign *f. (2)* kampanija; *m. (4)* vajus
can *f. (2)* skardinė
Canadian *m. (1), f. (2)* kanadietis, -ė; *adj. (1)* kanadietiškas, -a
canal *m. (1)* kanalas
canary *f. (2)* kanarėlė
cancel *v. (1)* atšaukti
cancer *m. (1)* vėžys
candidate *m. (1), f. (2)* kandidatas, -ė
candle *f. (2)* žvakė
candy *m. (1)* saldainis
cane *f. (2)* lazda
canned food *m. pl. (1)* konservai
cannon *f. (2)* patranka
canoe *f. (2)* baidarė
cap *f. (2)* kepurė
capacity *f. (2)* talpa
capital *fin. m. (1)* kapitalas; *f. (2)* sostinė; *adj. (3)* kapitalinis, -ė
capitalist *m. (1), f. (2)* kapitalistas, -ė; *adj. (3)* kapitalistinis, -ė
captain *m. (1), f. (2)* kapitonas, -ė
car *f. (2)* mašina; *m. (1)* automobilis
caraway *m. (1)* kmynas
carbohydrates *m. pl. (1)* angliavandeniai
card (for playing) *f. (2)* korta
cardinal *m. (1)* kardinolas
care *m. (1)* rūpestis
career *f. (2)* karjera
carefully *adv.* atsargiai
careless *adj. (2)* neatsargus, -i
caress *v. (1)* glamonėti, pamyluoti
carnival *m. (1)* karnavalas
carp *m. (1)* karpis
carpet *m. (1)* kilimas
carriage *f. (2)* karieta
carrot *f. (2)* morka
carry *v. (1)* nešti, vežti; ~ **out** *v. (1)* atlikti; *v. (3)* (į)vykdyti, realizuoti
cart *m. (1)* vežimas
case *m. (1)* atvejis; *f. (2)* byla
cash register *f. (2)* kasa
cast *med. m. (1)* gipsas
castle *f. (3)* pilis
cat *f. (2)* katė; *m. (1)* katinas
catch *v. (3)* gaudyti (to try); *(1)* pagauti; ~ **cold** *v. (3)* persišaldyti
category *f. (2)* kategorija
caterer *m. (1), f. (2)* tiekėjas, -a
caterpillar *m. (1)* vikšras
catfish *m. (1)* šamas
cathedral *f. (2)* katedra
Catholic *m. (1), f. (2)* katalikas, -ė; *adj. (1)* katalikiškas, -a
Catholicism *f. (2)* katalikybė
cauliflower *m. (1)* kalafioras
cause *m. (1)* motyvas
caution *m. (1)* atsargumas
cave *f. (2)* ola; *m. (1)* urvas; *adj. (3)* urvinis, -ė
caviar *m. pl. (1)* ikrai
CD kompaktinis diskas
CD player kompaktinių diskų grotuvas
cease *v. (1)* liautis
ceiling *f. pl. (2)* lubos; ~ **fixture** *m. (1)* šviestuvas
celebrate *v. (1)* švęsti
celebration *m. (1)* pagerbimas
celery *m. (1)* salieras
cell *f. (2)* celė, kamera
cellar *m. (1)* rūsys
cellist *m. (1), f. (2)* violončelistas, -ė
cello *f. (2)* violončelė
cement *m. (1)* cementas
cemetery *m. pl. (1)* kapai; *f. pl. (2)* kapinės
censorship *f. (2)* cenzūra
census *m. (1)* surašymas
cent *m. (1)* centas
center *m. (1)* centras

centimeter *m. (1)* centimetras
central *adj. (3)* centrinis, -ė
centralization *f. (2)* centralizacija
century *m. (4)* amžius;
m. (1) šimtmetis
ceramics *f. (2)* keramika
ceremony *f. (2)* ceremonija
certainly *adv.* būtinai, žinoma
certificate *m. (1)* liudijimas, pažymėjimas
chain *f. (2)* grandinė;
f. (2) grandinėlė (jewelry)
chair *f. (2)* kėdė
chair(person) *m. (1), f. (2)* pirmininkas, -ė
chalk *f. (2)* kreida
challenge *m. (1)* iššūkis
champagne *m. (1)* šampanas
champion *m. (1), f. (2)* čempionas, -ė
chance *m. (1)* šansas; atsitiktinumas
chancellor *m. (4), f. (2)* rektorius, -ė
chandelier *m. (1)* sietynas, šviestuvas
change *f. (2)* grąža; *f. (2)* pamaina; permaina; *v. (1)* (pa(si))keisti
change (one's clothes) *v. (1)* persirengti
change (the baby) *v. (3)* vystyti
change (one's shoes) *v. (1)* persiauti
change (somebody's clothes) *v. (1)* perrengti
channel *m. (1)* kanalas
chaos *m. (1)* chaosas
chapel *f. (2)* koplyčia
character *m. (1)* personažas; tipas;
f. (3) prigimtis
characteristic *f. (2)* ypatybė
charge *m. (1)* kaltinimas
charity *f. (2)* labdara, išmalda
charm *v. (2)* sužavėti
charms *m. pl. (1)* kerai
chat *f. (2)* šneka
cheap *adj. (2)* pigus, -i
cheat *v. (1)* sukčiauti
check *m. (1)* čekis; *v. (1)* patikrinti
check-in *f. (2)* registracija
checkmate *m. (1)* matas
check-up *m. (1)* (pa)tikrinimas
cheek *m. (1)* skruostas
cheerful *adj. (2)* žvalus, -i
cheese *m. (1)* sūris
chef *m. (1), f. (2)* kulinaras, -ė
chemistry *f. (2)* chemija
cherry *f. (2)* vyšnia;
~ **tree** *f. (2)* vyšnia
chess *m. pl. (1)* šachmatai;
~ **player** *m. (1), f. (2)* šachmatininkas, -ė
chest *f. (2)* krūtinė; *f. (2)* skrynia (box)
chest of drawers *f. (2)* komoda
chestnut *m. (1)* kaštonas
chew *v. (3)* kramtyti
chewing gum kramtomoji guma
chick *m. (1)* viščiukas
chicken *m. (1)* viščiukas;
f. (2) vištiena (meat)
chicken pox *med. m. pl. (1)* vėjaraupiai
chief *m. (1), f. (2)* vadas, -ė
child *m. (1)* vaikas
childbirth *m. (1)* gimdymas
childhood *f. (2)* vaikystė
childish *adj. (1)* vaikiškas, -a
childless *m. (1), f. (2);*
adj. (3) bevaikis, -ė
chilly *adj. (2)* vėsus, -i
chin *m. (1)* smakras
china *m. (1)* indas; porcelianas
Chinese *m. (1), f. (2)* kinas, -ė;
adj. (1) kiniškas, -a
chocolate *m. (1)* šokoladas;
adj. (3) šokoladinis, -ė
choice *m. (1)* pasirinkimas
choir *m. (1)* choras
choke *v. (1)* paspringti; dusti
chop *v. (1)* (su)kapoti
choreography *f. (2)* choreografija
chorus *m. (1)* choras
Christian *m. (1), f. (2)* krikščionis, -ė;
adj. (1) krikščioniškas, -a
Christianity *f. (2)* krikščionybė
Christmas *f. pl. (2)* Kalėdos
chronicle *f. (2)* kronika;
m. (1) metraštis
chronology *f. (2)* chronologija
church *f. (2)* bažnyčia; *f. (2)* cerkvė (Russian Orthodox)
church festival *m. pl. (1)* atlaidai
church service *f. pl. (2)* pamaldos
cigar *m. (1)* cigaras
cigarette *f. (2)* cigaretė;
~ **butt** *f. (2)* nuorūka
cinema *m. (1)* kinas
circle *m. (1)* apskritimas, būrelis
circulation *f. (2)* cirkuliacija;
m. (1) tiražas

circumstance *f. (2)* aplinkybė
circus *m. (1)* cirkas
citation *f. (2)* citata
cite *v. (1)* cituoti
citizen *m. (1), f. (2)* pilietis, -ė
citizenship *f. (2)* pilietybė
city *m. (1)* miestas; ~ **dweller** *m. (1), f. (2)* miestietis, -ė
civilization *f. (2)* civilizacija
civilized *adj. (1)* civilizuotas, -a
claim *f. (2)* paraiška; pretenzija
claimant *m. (1), f. (2)* pretendentas, -ė
clarify *v. (1)* paaiškėti
class *f. (2)* klasė
classic *m. (1), f. (2)* klasikas, -ė
classic(al) *adj. (3)* klasikinis, -ė
classroom *f. (2)* klasė
clause *m. (1)* teiginys
clay *m. (1)* molis
clean *v. (3)* (iš)valyti; tvarkyti; *adj. (2)* švarus, -i
cleaner's *f. (2)* valykla
cleaning person *m. (1), f. (2)* valytojas, -a
cleanliness *f. (2)* švara
clear *adj. (2)* aiškus, -i; skaidrus, -i; *adj. (1)* suprantamas, -a; giedras, -a, tyras, -a, grynas, -a
clever *adj. (1)* protingas, -a; *adj. (2)* apsukrus, -i, gudrus, -i
client *m. (1), f. (2)* klientas, -ė
cliff *f. (2)* uola
climate *m. (1)* klimatas
climb *v. (1)* lipti, kopti
clock *m. (1)* laikrodis
close *adj. (1)* artimas, -a; *v. (3)* uždaryti; *adv.* arti
close one's eyes *v. (1)* užsimerkti
closed *adj. (1)* uždarytas, -a
clot of blood *m. (1)* krešulys
cloth *m. (1)* audeklas, audinys; *f. (2)* drobė
clothes *m. pl. (1)* rūbai
clothing *f. (2)* apranga
cloud *m. (3)* debesis
clove *m. pl. (1)* gvazdikėliai
club *m. (1)* klubas, būrelis
clutch (of a car) *f. (2)* sankaba
coach *m. (1), f. (2)* treneris, -ė; *f. (2)* karieta
coal *f. (3)* anglis
coarse *adj. (2)* rupus, -i (miltai)
coat *m. (1)* paltas; ~ **check** *f. (2)* rūbinė
coat of arms *m. (1)* herbas
co-author *m. (4), f. (2)* bendraautoris, -ė
cocoa *f. (2)* kakava
cod *f. (2)* menkė
code *m. (1)* kodas; kodeksas
coffee *f. (2)* kava; ~ **pot** *m. (1)* kavinukas; ~ **shop** *f. (2)* kavinė
coffin *m. (1)* karstas
cognac *m. (1)* konjakas
coin *f. (2)* moneta
cold *adj. (1)* šaltas, -a
collapse *v. (1)* sugriūti
collar *f. (2)* apykaklė
colleague *m./f. (2)* kolega
collect *v. (1)* kolekcionuoti, rinkti
collection *f. (2)* kolekcija; *m. (1)* rinkinys
collective farm *m. (1)* kolūkis
collector *m. (4), f. (2)* kolekcionierius, -ė
collide *v. (1)* susidurti
collision *m. (1)* susidūrimas
colonization *f. (2)* kolonizacija
colony *f. (2)* kolonija
color *f. (2)* spalva
colored *adj. (1)* spalvotas, -a
colorful *adj. (1)* spalvingas, -a
colorless *adj. (3)* bespalvis, -ė
column *f. (2)* kolona
comb *f. pl. (2)* šukos
comb one's hair *v. (1)* susišukuoti
combination *m. (1)* derinys
come *v. (1; irr.)* ateiti; atvykti; ~ **back** *v. (1)* pareiti; ~ **down** *v. (1)* nulipti; ~ **up** *v. (1)* prieiti
comedian *m. (1)* komediantas, -ė
comedy *f. (2)* komedija
comfort *f. (2)* paguoda; *v. (1)* (pa)guosti
comfortable *adj. (2)* patogus, -i
comic *adj. (1)* komiškas, -a; *adj. (3)* humoristinis, -ė
coming *m. (1)* atėjimas
command *m. (1)* įsakymas; *f. (2)* komanda
commander *m. (1), f. (2)* vadas, -ė
comment *v. (1)* komentuoti
commerce *f. (2)* komercija
commercial *adj. (3)* komercinis, -ė
commissar *m. (1), f. (2)* komisaras, -ė
commission *f. (2)* komisija
commit an offense *v. (1)* nusižengti
committee *m. (1)* komitetas

common *adj. (1)* bendras, -a
commonplace *adj. (1)* kasdieniškas, -a
communication *f. (2)* komunikacija; *m. (1)* susisiekimas
community *f. (2)* bendrija
company *f. (2)* bendrovė, kompanija
compare *v. (1)* (pa)lyginti
comparison *m. (1)* palyginimas
compass *m. (1)* kompasas
compatriot *m. (1), f. (2)* tautietis, -ė
compensate *v. (1)* kompensuoti
compensation *f. (2)* kompensacija
compete *v. (1)* konkuruoti; rungtyniauti
competition *f. (2)* konkurencija; *f. pl. (2)* rungtynės
competitor *m. (1), f. (2)* konkurentas, -ė
complain *v. (1)* skųstis
complaint *m. (1)* skundas
completely *adv.* ištisai
compliant *adj. (2)* nuolaidus, -i
complicated *adj. (1)* sudėtingas, -a
compose *v. (3)* sudaryti
composer *m. (4), f. (2)* kompozitorius, -ė
composition *m. (1)* rašinys
computer *m. (1)* kompiuteris
concentration *f. (2)* koncentracija
concept *f. (2)* sąvoka
concert *m. (1)* koncertas
conclusion *f. (2)* išvada; pabaiga
concrete *m. (1)* betonas; *adj. (2)* konkretus, -i
condemn *v. (1)* pasmerkti
condition *f. (2)* sąlyga; būsena; būklė; *f. (3)* padėtis
condom *m. (1)* prezervatyvas
conduct *m. (1)* elgesys
conductor *m. (1), f. (2)* dirigentas, -ė
confectionery *f. (2)* cukrainė, konditerija
conference *f. (2)* konferencija
confess *v. (1)* prisipažinti
confession *f. (2)* išpažintis; *m. (1)* prisipažinimas
confidence *m. (1)* pasitikėjimas
confirm *v. (1)* patvirtinti
confirmation *m. (1)* patvirtinimas
confiscate *v. (1)* konfiskuoti
conflict *m. (1)* konfliktas
congress *m. (1)* suvažiavimas
conjugation *m. (1)* asmenavimas
connect *v. (1)* (pri)jungti; rišti
conscience *f. (2)* sąžinė
consent *m. (1)* sutikimas
consequence *m. (1)* padarinys
conservative *polit. m. (4), f. (2)* konservatorius, -ė; *adj. (2)* konservatyvus, -i
conserve *v. (1)* išsaugoti
consignment store *m. (1)* komisas
consistent *adj. (2)* nuoseklus, -i
consonant *f. (2)* priebalsė
conspiracy *m. (1)* sąmokslas
constant *adj. (2)* pastovus, -i
constantly *adv.* nuolat
construction *f. (2)* statyba
consulate *m. (1)* konsulatas
consult *v. (1)* konsultuotis
consultant *m. (1), f. (2)* konsultantas, -ė
consultation *f. (2)* konsultacija; *m. (1)* pasitarimas
consume *v. (1)* suvartoti
consumer *m. (1), f. (2)* vartotojas, -a
consumption *med. f. (2)* džiova; *m. (1)* (su)vartojimas (of products)
contact *m. (1)* kontaktas; *v. (1)* kontaktuoti
contact lenses kontaktiniai lęšiai
contagious *adj. (1)* užkrečiamas, -a
contemporary *adj. (3)* šiuolaikinis, -ė
content *adj. (1)* patenkintas, -a
contest *f. pl. (2)* rungtynės, varžybos; *m. (1)* mačas
context *m. (1)* kontekstas
continent *m. (1)* žemynas
continue *v. (1)* tęsti
contraband *f. (2)* kontrabanda
contract *f. (3)* sutartis
contractor *m. (1), f. (2)* rangovas, -ė
contradict *v. (1)* prieštarauti
contrary *adv.* priešingai
contrast *m. (1)* kontrastas
contribution *m. (1)* įnašas
control *f. (2)* kontrolė; *v. (1)* kontroliuoti
controversial *adj. (3)* poleminis, -ė
convenient *adj. (2)* patogus, -i
convent *m. (1)* vienuolynas
conversation *m. (1)* pokalbis, pašnekesys
convict *v. (1)* teisti
convince *v. (1)* įtikinti
convincing *adj. (1)* įtikinamas, -a

convulsion *m. (1)* mėšlungis
cook *m. (1), f. (2)* virėjas, -a, kulinaras, -ė; *v. (1)* virti
cool off *v. (1)* atvėsti
cooperate *v. (1)* kooperuotis, bendradarbiauti
coordinate *v. (1)* (su)derinti, koordinuoti
copper *m. (1)* varies; *adj. (3)* varinis, -ė
copy *f. (2)* kopija; *v. (1)* kopijuoti
cordial *adj. (1)* širdingas, -a
cork *m. (1)* kamštis
corkscrew *m. (1)* kamščiatraukis
corn *m. pl. (1)* kukurūzai; *m. (1)* grūdas
corner *m. (1)* kampas; *adj. (3)* kampinis, -ė
cornflower *f. (2)* rugiagėlė
corpse *m. (1)* lavonas
correct *v. (3)* ištaisyti, pataisyti; *adj. (1)* taisyklingas, -a
correspond *v. (1)* susirašinėti
correspondence *f. (2)* korespondencija
correspondent *m. (1), f. (2)* korespondentas, -ė
corrupt *adj. (1)* paperkamas, -a
cost *f. (2)* kaina
cost price *f. (2)* savikaina
costume *m. (1)* kostiumas
cottage cheese *f. (2)* varškė
cotton *f. (2)* medvilnė
cotton (ball(s)) *f. (2)* vata, vatelė
cough *v. (2)* kosėti
count *m. (1)* grafas; *v. (1)* skaičiuoti
counter *m. (1)* prekystalis
counterfeit *adj. (1)* padirbtas, -a; *v. (1)* padirbti
countess *f. (2)* grafienė
country *f. (3)* šalis
country code (for telephone) šalies kodas
countryside *m. (1)* kaimas
couple *f. (2)* pora
courage *f. (2)* drąsa
courageous *adj. (2)* drąsus, -i, narsus, -i
court *m. (1)* teismas; **~ sentence** *m. (1)* nuosprendis
courtesy *m. (1)* mandagumas
cousin *m. (1)* pusbrolis; *f. (2)* pusseserė
cover *f. (2)* (prie)danga; *v. (1)* užkloti; uždengti; *m. (1)* dangtis (lid)
cow *f. (2)* karvė
coward *m. (1), f. (2)* bailys, -ė
coworker *m. (1), f. (2)* bendradarbis, -ė
cozy *adj. (2)* jaukus, -i
crack *m. (1)* plyšys
cramp *m. (1)* mėšlungis
cranberry *f. (2)* spanguolė; *adj. (3)* spanguolinis, -ė
crane *m. (1)* kranas
crash *v. (1)* sudužti
crawl *v. (1)* šliaužti
crazy person *m. (1), f. (2)* beprotis, -ė
crease *f. (2)* raukšlė
create *v. (1)* kurti
creation *f. (2)* kūryba; *m. (1)* kūrimas
creative *adj. (1)* kūrybingas, -a
creator *m. (1), f. (2)* kūrėjas, -a
credit *m. (1)* kreditas
credit card kreditinė kortelė
creditor *m. (4), f. (2)* kreditorius, -ė
crew *m. (1)* ekipažas
criminal *adj. (3)* kriminalinis, -ė; *adj. (1)* nusikalstamas, -a
criminality *m. (1)* nusikalstamumas
cripple *adj. (1)* luošas, -a; *v. (1)* suluošinti
crisis *f. (2)* krizė
critic *m. (1), f. (2)* oponentas, -ė, kritikas, -ė
critical *adj. (3)* kritinis, -ė
criticism *f. (2)* kritika
crooked *adj. (1)* kreivas, -a
cross *m. (4)* kryžius
cross-eyed *adj. (1)* žvairas, -a
crossing *f. (2)* perėja; sankryža
crow *f. (2)* varna
crowd *f. (2)* minia
crumb *m. (1)* trupinys
crumble *v. (1)* trupėti; trupinti
crush *v. (3)* daužyti
crust *f. (2)* pluta
crutch *m. (1)* ramentas
cry *m. (1)* riksmas, šauksmas; *v. (1)* rėkti, šaukti; verkti
crystal *m. (1)* kristalas; krištolas; *adj. (3)* krištolinis, -ė
cube *m. (1)* kubas
cucumber *m. (1)* agurkas
cuff *m. (1)* rankogalis
culinary *adj. (3)* kulinarinis, -ė
cult *m. (1)* kultas

culture *f. (2)* kultūra
cultured/ educated person *m. (1), f. (2)* inteligentas, -ė
cup *m. (1)* puodelis, puodukas
curable *adj. (1)* pagydomas, -a
cure *v. (3)* pagydyti
curiosity *m. (1)* smalsumas
curious *adj. (2)* smalsus, -i
curly *adj. (1)* garbanotas, -a
currant *m. (1)* serbentas
currency *f. (2)* valiuta
current *f. (2)* srovė
curse *m. (1)* prakeikimas; *v. (1)* keikti
curtain *f. (2)* portjera, užuolaida
custom *m. (1)* paprotys
customer *m. (1), f. (2)* pirkėjas, -a
customs *f. (2)* muitinė
customs officer *m. (1), f. (2)* muitininkas, -ė
cut *m. (1)* pjūvis; *m. (1)* fasonas, modelis; *v. (3)* (su)pjaustyti; *v. (1)* kirpti (with scissors)
cute *adj. (1)* simpatiškas, -a
cutlet *m. (!)* kotletas
cycle *m. (1)* ciklas
cyclist *m. (1), f. (2)* dviratininkas, -ė
cynical *adj. (1)* ciniškas, -a
cyst *med. f. (2)* cista
czar *m. (1)* caras

D

dad *m. (2)* tėtė; *m. (1)* tėtis
daily *adv.* kasdien
dam *f. (2)* užtvanka
damp *adj. (1)* drėgnas, -a
dance *v. (1)* šokti
Dane *m. (1), f. (2)* danas, -ė
danger *m. (4)* pavojus
dangerous *adj. (1)* pavojingas, -a
dark *adj. (2)* tamsus, -i
darkness *f. (2)* tamsa
data *m. pl. (4)* duomenys
date *m. (1)* pasimatymas (romantic); terminas (due date); *f. (2)* data (day)
date (chronologically) *v. (1)* datuoti
daughter *f. (2)* dukra, duktė
daughter-in-law *f. (2)* marti
day *f. (2)* diena; para
daydream *v. (1)* svajoti
dead *adj. (1)* negyvas, -a
deaf *adj. (1)* kurčias, -ia
dear *adj. (1)* mylimas, -a; *adj. (2)* brangus, -i
dearly *adv.* brangiai
death *f. (3)* mirtis
debate *f. (2)* diskusija
debt *f. (2)* skola
debtor *m. (1), f. (2)* skolininkas, -ė
decade (ten years) *m. (1)* dešimtmetis
decay *v. (1)* irti
deceased *m. (1), f. (2)* numirėlis, -ė
deceitful *adj. (1)* melagingas, -a
deceive *v. (1)* apgauti
December *m. (1)* gruodis
decent *adj. (2)* padorus, -i
deception *f. (2)* apgaulė
decide *v. (1)* (nu)spręsti, nutarti
decision *m. (1)* nutarimas, sprendimas
deck (on a ship) *m. (1)* denis
declaration *f. (2)* deklaracija; *m. (1)* pareiškimas
declare *v. (1)* pareikšti; paskelbti
decorate *v. (1)* (pa)puošti
decrease *v. (1)* (su)mažėti
dedicate *v. (1)* dedikuoti; (pa)skirti
deer *m. (1), f. (2)* elnias, -ė
defeat *v. (2)* nugalėti
defect *m. (1)* defektas; *f. (2)* yda
defective *adj. (1)* ydingas, -a
defend *v. (1)* ginti
defendant *m. (1), f. (2)* atsakovas, -ė
defender *m. (1), f. (2)* gynėjas, -a
defense *f. (2)* gynyba
deficit *m. (1)* deficitas
delay *v. (1)* vilkinti
delegation *f. (2)* delegacija
delicious *adj. (2)* gardus, -i, skanus, -i
deliver *v. (1)* įteikti
demand *f. (2)* paklausa; *m. (1)* reikalavimas; *v. (1)* (pa)reikalauti
democracy *f. (2)* demokratija
democrat *polit. m. (1), f. (2)* demokratas, -ė
demolish *v. (1)* griauti
demote *v. (1)* pažeminti
demotion *m. (1)* pažeminimas
dense *adj. (2)* tankus, -i
density *m. (1)* tankumas
dentist *m. (1), f. (2)* dantistas, -ė, stomatologas, -ė
denture *m. (1)* protezas
deny *v. (1)* (pa)neigti
deodorant *m. (1)* dezodorantas

department *m. (4)* skyrius
department *m. (1)* fakultetas (at university); *m. (4)* skyrius (in a firm)
dependence *f. (2)* priklausomybė
dependent *m. (1), f. (2)* išlaikytinis, -ė
depict *v. (1)* vaizduoti; piešti
deport *v. (1)* tremti
deportation *m. (1)* ištrėmimas
deportee *m. (1), f. (2)* tremtinys, -ė
deposit *f. pl. (2)* nuosėdos; *fin. m. (1)* indėlis
depressed *adj. (1)* prislėgtas, -a
depth *m. (1)* gylis
descend *v. (1)* nusileisti
descendant *m. (1), f. (2)* palikuonis, -ė
description *m. (1)* aprašymas
desert *f. (2)* dykuma
design *m. (1)* dizainas
designer *m. (1), f. (2)* dizaineris, -ė
desirable *adj. (1)* pageidaujamas, -a
desire *m. (1)* geismas, troškimas; *v. (1)* geisti, trokšti
despair *f. (3)* neviltis; *v. (1)* nusiminti
dessert *m. (1)* desertas
destiny *m. (1)* likimas
destroy *v. (1)* (iš)naikinti; (su)griauti; *v. (3)* ardyti
detail *f. (2)* detalė, smulkmena
detective *m. (1), f. (2)* detektyvas, -ė; seklys, -ė
detergent skalbimo priemonė
deteriorate *v. (1)* (pa)gesti
detour *f. (2)* apylanka
devastate *v. (1)* niokoti
develop *v. (1)* plėtoti; *(3)* ugdyti, vystyti
development *f. (2)* raida; *m. (1)* pakilimas
device *m. (1)* prietaisas
devil *m. (1)* velnias
dew *f. (2)* rasa
diabetes *med. f. (2)* cukraligė; *m. (1)* diabetas
diabetic *m. (1), f. (2)* diabetikas, -ė
diagnosis *f. (2)* diagnozė
diagram *f. (2)* diagrama; schema
dial *v. (1)* rinkti
dialect *m. (1)* dialektas; *f. (2)* tarmė
dialing code *m. (1)* kodas
dialog *m. (1)* dialogas
diamond *m. (1)* deimantas, briliantas
diaper(s) *f. pl. (2)* sauskelnės
diarrhea *m. (1)* viduriavimas
diary *m. (1)* dienoraštis
dictionary *m. (1)* žodynas
die *v. (1)* (nu)mirti, žūti
different *adj. (1)* skirtingas, -a; *pron. m.* kitoks, *f.* kitokia
differently *adv.* kitaip
difficult *adj. (2)* sunkus, -i
digest *v. (1)* virškinti
digital *adj. (3)* skaitmeninis, -ė
dignity *m. (1)* orumas
dill *m. pl. (1)* krapai
dine *v. (1)* pietauti
dining room *m. (1)* valgomasis
dinner *m. pl. (4)* pietūs (lunch); *f. (2)* vakarienė (supper)
diphthong *m. (1)* dvibalsis
diploma *m. (1)* diplomas
diplomacy *f. (2)* diplomatija
diplomat *m. (1), f. (2)* diplomatas, -ė
diplomatic *adj. (1)* diplomatiškas, -a
direct *adj. (3)* tiesioginis, -ė
directions *f. (2)* instrukcija
director *m. (4), f. (2)* direktorius, -ė; režisierius, -ė (theater)
dirt *m. (1)* purvas
dirty *adj. (1)* purvinas, -a, murzinas, -a; *(2)* nešvarus, -i
disabled *adj. (1)* nedarbingas, -a; *(2)* neįgalus, -i
disagreement *m. (1)* nesutarimas
disappear *v. (1)* dingti, nykti
disappointed (to be) *v. (1)* nusivilti
disappointment *m. (1)* nusivylimas
disarm *v. (1)* nusiginkluoti
disarmament *m. (1)* nusiginklavimas
discipline *f. (2)* drausmė
disciplined *adj. (1)* drausmingas, -a
discontinue *v. (1)* nutraukti
discount *f. (2)* nuolaida
discovery *m. (1)* atradimas
discretion *f. (2)* nuožiūra
discriminate *v. (1)* diskriminuoti
discrimination *f. (2)* diskriminacija
discussion *f. (2)* diskusija
disgrace *f. (2)* negarbė; nemalonė
disgusting *adj. (2)* šlykštus, -i
dish *m. (1)* valgis, patiekalas; indas
dishonest *adj. (1)* nesąžiningas, -a
disinfect *v. (1)* dezinfekuoti
disk *m. (1)* diskas

dislike *v. (1)* nemėgti
disobedient *adj. (2)* neklusnus, -i
disobey *v. (3)* neklausyti
display *f. (2)* ekspozicija;
v.(1) pademonstruoti
disposition *m. (1)* charakteris, būdas
dissolve *v. (1)* tirpti
distance *m. (1)* atstumas, nuotolis;
f. (2) distancija
distant *adj. (1)* tolimas, -a
distinct *adj. (2)* ryškus, -i
distinguish *v. (1)* skirti
distort *v. (3)* iškraipyti
distribute *v. (3)* skirstyti
district *m. (1)* rajonas
distrust *v. (2)* nepasitikėti
disturb *v. (3)* (su)trukdyti
disturbance *m. pl. (1)* neramumai
dive *v. (3)* nardyti
diver *m. (1)* naras
diverse *adj. (1)* skirtingas, -a;
(2) įvairus, -i
divide *mat. v. (1)* (pa)dalyti
dividend *m. (1)* dividendas
division *mat. f. (2)* dalyba;
m. (1) padalijimas
divorce *f. (2)* ištuoka;
f. pl. (2) skyrybos;
v. (1) išsituokti, išsiskirti
divorced *adj.* išsiskyręs, -usi
do *v. (1)* veikti; *(3)* daryti
dock *f. (2)* prieplauka
doctor *m. (1), f. (2)* daktaras, -ė,
gydytojas, -a
document *m. (1)* dokumentas
dog *m. (5)* šuo
doll *f. (2)* lėlė
dollar *m. (1)* doleris
dolphin *m. (1)* delfinas
domestic *adj. (3)* naminis, -ė
donkey *m. (1)* asilas
door *f. pl. (3)* durys;
~ lock *f. (2)* spyna
doorman *m. (1), f. (2)* durininkas, -ė
dormitory *m. (1)* bendrabutis
dose *f. (2)* dozė
dot *m. (1)* taškas
double *v. (1)* padvigubinti
dough *f. (2)* tešla
down *m. (1)* pūkas
down(wards) *adv.* žemyn
dowry *m. (1)* kraitis
dozen *m. (1)* tuzinas
drag *v. (1)* vilkti, tempti
dragonfly *m. (1)* laumžirgis
drain *v. (1)* nusausinti
draw *v. (1)* piešti
drawback *m. (1)* minusas
drawing *m. (1)* piešimas
dread *v. (3)* bijoti
dream (in sleep) *m. (1)* sapnas;
v. (1) sapnuoti
dress *f. (2)* suknelė
dress up *v. (1)* pasipuošti
dressing *m. (1)* padažas
dressing gown *m. (1)* chalatas
dried toast *m. (1)* džiuvėsis
drill *m. (1)* grąžtas; muštras;
v. (1) gręžti
drink *v. (1)* gerti
drinking glass *f. (2)* stiklinė
drip *v. (1)* lašėti, varvėti
drive *v. (1)* vairuoti, važiuoti
driver *m. (1), f. (2)* vairuotojas, -a
driver's license vairuotojo
pažymėjimas
drop *m. (1)* lašas; *v. (1)* kristi; lašėti
drought *f. (2)* sausra
drown *v. (1)* prigerti, nuskęsti
drowsiness *m. (1)* mieguistumas
drug *m. (1)* vaistas
drug addict *m. (1), f. (2)*
narkomanas, -ė
drugs *m. pl. (1)* narkotikai
drugstore *f. (2)* vaistinė
drum *m. (1)* būgnas
drunk *adj. (1)* girtas, -a;
to get ~ *v. (1)* pasigerti
dry *v. (1)* džiūti; *adj. (1)* sausas, -a
duchess *f. (2)* hercogienė;
kunigaikštienė
due to *conj.* dėl
dues *m. (1)* mokestis
duke *m. (1)* hercogas; kunigaikštis
dumplings *m. pl. (1)* koldūnai
dung *m. (1)* mėšlas
during *prep.* per
dusk *f. (2)* prieblanda, prietema
Dutch *adj. (1)* olandiškas, -a;
~ person *m. (1), f. (2)* olandas, -ė
duty *f. (2)* pareiga; *m. (1)* muitas
(customs)
duty free *adj. (3)* bemuitis, -ė

E

eagle *m. (1)* erelis
ear *f. (3)* ausis

earl *m. (1)* grafas
early *adv.* anksti
earn *v. (1)* uždirbti
earring *m. (1)* auskaras
earth *f. (2)* žemė
earthquake žemės drebėjimas
east *m. pl. (1)* rytai
Easter *f. pl. (2)* Velykos
eastern *adj. (3)* rytietiškas, -a
easy *adj. (1)* lengvas, -a
eat *v. (3)* valgyti; *v. (1)* ėsti (speaking of animals)
ecology *f. (2)* ekologija
economical *adj. (2)* taupus, -i
economics *f. (2)* ekonomika
economist *m. (1), f. (2)* ekonomistas, -ė
economy *f. (2)* ekonomija
edge *m. (1)* kraštas
edible *adj. (1)* valgomas, -a
edit *v. (1)* redaguoti
edition *m. (1)* leidimas
editor *m. (4), f. (2)* redaktorius, -ė
educate *v. (1)* (iš)auklėti
education *m. (1)* išsilavinimas; mokslas
eel *m. (1)* ungurys
effect *m. (1)* efektas
effective *adj. (1)* efektingas, -a
effort *f. (2)* pastanga
egg *m. (1)* kiaušinis; **~ white** *m. (1)* (kiaušinio) baltymas; **~ yolk** *m. (1)* (kiaušinio) trynys
eggplant *m. (1)* baklažanas
eight *num.* aštuoni, -ios
elderly *adj. (1)* senyvas, -a
elect *v. (1)* rinkti
electrician *m. (1), f. (2)* elektrikas, -ė
electricity *f. (2)* elektra
elegance *f. (2)* elegancija
elegant *adj. (1)* elegantiškas, -a
elementary *adj. (3)* pradinis, -ė; **~ school** pradinė mokykla
elevator *m. (1)* liftas
elite *m. (1)* elitas; *adj. (3)* elitinis, -ė
elk *m. (1), f. (2)* briedis, -ė
eloquence *f. (2)* iškalba
eloquent *adj. (2)* iškalbus, -i
email elektroninis paštas; **~ address** elektroninio pašto adresas
embark *v. (1)* įlipti
embassy *f. (2)* ambasada, atstovybė
emblem *f. (2)* emblema
embrace *m. (1)* glėbys; *v. (1)* apkabinti
embroidered *adj. (1)* siuvinėtas, -a
emerald *m. (1)* smaragdas
emergency kritiška padėtis
emigrant *m. (1), f. (2)* emigrantas, -ė
emigration *f. (2)* emigracija
emission *f. (2)* emisija; *m. (1)* išleidimas
emotion *f. (2)* emocija
emotional *adj. (1)* emocingas, -a
emperor *m. (4), f. (2)* imperatorius, -ė
emphasize *v. (1)* pabrėžti
employee *m. (1), f. (2)* tarnautojas, -a
empty *adj. (1)* tuščias, -ia
encourage *v. (1)* padrąsinti, paskatinti, raginti
end *m. (1)* galas; *f. (2)* pabaiga; *v. (1)* pabaigti
ending *f. (2)* galūnė
endurance *f. (2)* ištvermė
endure *v. (1)* pakęsti
enemy *m. (1), f. (2)* priešas, -ė
energetic *adj. (1)* energingas, -a
energy *f. (2)* energija
engaged (to become) *v. (1)* susižadėti
engagement *f. pl. (2)* sužadėtuvės; *m. (1)* įsipareigojimas
engine *m. (1)* motoras, variklis
engineer *m. (4), f. (2)* inžinierius, -ė
English(wo)man *m. (1), f. (2)* anglas, -ė
English (language) anglų kalba
enough *adv.* gana
enter *v. (1, irr.)* įeiti
enterprise *f. (2)* įmonė
entertain *v. (1)* linksminti
entertainment *f. (2)* pramoga
enthusiasm *m. (1)* entuziazmas, pakilimas
enthusiast *m. (1), f. (2)* entuziastas, -ė
entire *adj. (1)* visas, -a
entirely *adv.* ištisai, visai, visiškai
entrance *m. (1)* įėjimas
entrepreneur *m. (1), f. (2)* verslininkas, -ė
envelope *m. (1)* vokas
envious *adj. (2)* pavydus, -i; **(to be)** *v. (1)* pavyduliauti

envy *m. (1)* pavydas; *v. (2)* pavydėti
epidemic *f. (2)* epidemija
epilepsy *med. f. (2)* epilepsija
episode *m. (1)* epizodas
equal *adj. (2)* lygus, -i
equality *f. (2)* lygybė
equally *adv.* lygiai
equator *m. (1)* pusiaujas
equipment *m. pl. (1)* įrengimai
era *f. (2)* era, epocha
erase *v. (1)* ištrinti, nutrinti
eraser *m. (1)* trintukas
erotic *adj. (1)* erotiškas, -a
error *mat. f. (2)* paklaida; *f. (2)* klaida
escape *m. (1)* pabėgimas
escort *m. (1), f. (2)* palydovas, -ė; *v. (2)* palydėti
especially *adv.* ypač
essay *f. (2)* apybraiža; *m. (1)* rašinys
essence *f. (2)* esmė
establish *v. (1)* steigti
estimate *f. (2)* sąmata; *v. (1)* įkainoti
Estonian *m. (1), f. (2)* estas, -ė; *adj. (1)* estiškas, -a
ethical *adj. (1)* etiškas, -a
ethics *f. (2)* etika
ethnographer *m. (1), f. (2)* etnografas, -ė
ethnography *f. (2)* etnografija
eulogy *f. (2)* panegirika
euro *m. (1)* euras
European *m. (1), f. (2)* europietis, -ė; *adj. (1)* europietiškas, -a
European Union Europos Sąjunga
evacuate *v. (1)* evakuoti(s)
evacuation *f. (2)* evakuacija
evaluate *v. (1)* įkainoti
evaporate *v. (1)* išgaruoti
even *adj. (2)* (to)lygus, -i
evening *m. (1)* vakaras; *adj. (3)* vakarinis, -ė
evenly *adv.* lygiai
event *m. (1)* atsitikimas, įvykis
everyday *adj. (3)* šiokiadienis, -ė
everything *m. (1)* viskas
everywhere *adv.* visur
evidence *m. (1)* įrodymas
evolution *f. (2)* evoliucija
exact *adj. (2)* tikslus, -i
exaggerate *v. (1)* perdėti
examination *m. (1)* egzaminas; patikrinimas
examine *v. (1)* patikrinti
example *m. (1)* pavyzdys; **(for)** *adv.* pavyzdžiui
except *part.* nebent
exceptional *adj. (1)* nepaprastas, -a
exchange *f. (2)* birža (stock); *m. pl. (1)* mainai; *v. (1)* iškeisti, pasikeisti
excise tax *m. (1)* akcizas
excite *v. (1)* sujaudinti
exclusive *adj. (3)* monopolinis, -ė
excrement *f. pl. (2)* išmatos
excursion *f. (2)* ekskursija
excuse *m. (1)* pasiteisinimas
execute *v. (3)* vykdyti; sušaudyti
execution *f. (2)* egzekucija
executioner *m. (1), f. (2)* budelis, -ė
exercise *m. (1)* pratimas, uždavinys; *f. (2)* mankšta
exhaust *v. (1)* nualinti
exhibition *f. (2)* paroda
exile *m. (1)* ištrėmimas; *v. (1)* tremti
exit *m. (1)* išėjimas
expand *v. (1)* (iš)plėsti
expansion *m. (1)* plėtimas
expel *v. (3)* išvaryti
expenditure *f. pl. (2)* išlaidos
expenses *f. pl. (2)* išlaidos
expensive *adj. (2)* brangus, -i
experience *f. (3)* patirtis; *v. (1)* patirti
experienced *adj.* patyręs, -usi
experiment *m. (1)* eksperimentas
expert *m. (1), f. (2)* ekspertas, -ė, žinovas, -ė, meistras, -ė
explain *v. (1)* išaiškinti, paaiškinti
explanation *m. (1)* paaiškinimas
explode *v. (1)* sprogti
exploit *v. (1)* išnaudoti
exploitation *m. (1)* išnaudojimas
explore *v. (1)* tyrinėti
explorer *adj. (1)* tyrinėtojas, -a
explosion *m. (1)* sprogimas
exposition *f. (2)* ekspozicija
expression *m. (1)* posakis
extend *v. (1)* pratęsti; išplėsti
exterior *f. (2)* išorė
exterminate *v. (1)* naikinti
extravagant *adj. (1)* ekstravagantiškas, -a
extreme *m. (1)* kraštutinumas
eye *f. (3)* akis
eyeglasses *m. pl. (1)* akiniai
eyelash *f. (2)* blakstiena
eyesight *m. (1)* regėjimas

F

fabric *f. (2)* medžiaga
face *m. (1)* veidas
fact *m. (1)* faktas
factory *m. (1)* fabrikas; *f. (2)* gamykla
facts *m. pl. (4)* duomenys
fade *v. (1)* blukti
failure *f. (2)* nesėkmė
faint *v. (1)* alpti
fair *f. (2)* mugė
fairness *m. (1)* teisingumas
fairy *f. (2)* fėja; ~ **tale** *f. (2)* pasaka
faith *m. (1)* tikėjimas
falcon *m. (1), f. (2)* sakalas
fall *m. (5)* ruduo; *v. (1)* kristi, pulti; *adj. (3)* rudeninis, -ė
fall in love *v. (2)* įsimylėti
false *adj. (1)* melagingas, -a
familiar *adj. (1)* pažįstamas, -a
family *f. (2)* šeima
fan *m. (1), f. (2)* mėgėjas, -a, gerbėjas, -a
fanatic *m. (1), f. (2)* fanatikas, -ė
fantastic *adj. (1)* pasakiškas, -a
fantasy *f. (2)* fantazija
far *adv.* toil; *adj. (1)* tolimas, -a
farm *f. (2)* ferma; *m. (1)* ūkis
farmer *m. (1), f. (2)* ūkininkas, -ė, fermeris, -ė, žemdirbys, -ė
farsighted *m. (1), f. (2)* toliaregis, -ė
farther *adj. (3)* tolesnis, -ė
fascism *m. (1)* fašizmas
fascist *m. (1), f. (2)* fašistas, -ė
fashion *f. (2)* mada
fashionable *adj. (1)* madingas, -a
fast *m. (1)* pasninkas; *v. (1)* pasninkauti; *adj. (1)* greitas, -a
fasten *v. (1)* pririšti, pritvirtinti
fat *m. pl. (1)* riebalai, taukai; *adj. (2)* riebus, -i (food); *adj. (1)* storas, -a (person)
fate *f. (2)* dalia; *m. (1)* likimas
father *m. (1)* tėvas
father-in-law *m. (1)* uošvis
faucet *m. (1)* čiaupas, kranas
fault *f. (2)* kaltė
favor *f. (2)* paslauga
favorable *adj. (2)* palankus, -i
favorite *adj. (1)* mėgstamas, -a
fax *m. (1)* faksas; ~ **machine** *m. (1)* faksas
fear *f. (2)* baimė; *v. (3)* bijoti
fearless *adj. (3)* bebaimis, -ė
feast *f. (2)* puota; *v. (1)* puotauti
feature *m. (1)* bruožas
February *m. (1)* vasaris
fee *m. (1)* mokestis
feed *v. (1)* maitinti
feel *v. (1)* pajusti, jausti; čiupinėti
feeling *m. (1)* jausmas
female *f. (3)* moteris (human); *f.* (2) patelė (animal)
feminine *adj. (1)* moteriškas, -a
femininity *m. (1)* moteriškumas
feminist *f. (2)* feministė, -as
fence *f. (2)* tvora
fern *m. (1)* papartis
ferocious *adj. (2)* nuožmus, -i
ferry *m. (1)* keltas
fertile *adj. (1)* vaisingas, -a; derlingas, -a
fertility *m. (1)* vaisingumas
fertilize *v. (1)* tręšti
fertilizer *f. (2)* trąša
festival *m. (1)* festivalis
festive *adj. (3)* šventinis, -ė
festivities *f. pl. (2)* iškilmės
fetch *v. (1)* atnešti
fever *f. (2)* karštligė; temperatūra
fiancé *m. (1), f. (2)* sužadėtinis, -ė
fiction *f. (2)* beletristika
fictitious *adj. (2)* fiktyvus, -i
field *m. (1)* laukas
fight *f. pl. (2)* muštynės; *v. (1)* muštis; kariauti, kovoti
fighter jet *m. (1)* naikintuvas
figure *f. (2)* figūra
file *f. (2)* byla
fill *v. (3)* pildyti (~ out a form); *v. (1)* prileisti
fillet *f. (2)* nugarinė
film *m. (1)* filmas
fin *m. (1)* pelekas
finally *adv.* pagaliau
finance(s) *m. pl. (1)* finansai
financial *adj. (3)* finansinis, -ė
financier *m. (1), f. (2)* finansininkas, -ė
find *v. (1)* rasti; ~ **out** *v. (3)* sužinoti
fine *f. (2)* (pa)bauda
fine arts *f. (2)* dailė
finger *m. (1)* pirštas
finish *v. (1)* baigti
Finn *m. (1), f. (2)* suomis, -ė
Finnish *adj. (1)* suomiškas, -a
fire *m. (1)* gaisras; *f. (3)* ugnis; *v. (1)* atleisti (from work)

fireman *m. (1)* gaisrininkas, ugniagesys
fireplace *m. (1)* židinys
fireproof *adj. (1)* nedegamas, -a
first *num.* pirmas, -a
first-born *m. (1), f. (2)* pirmagimis, -ė
fir tree *f. (2)* eglė
fish *f. (3)* žuvis; *v. (1)* meškerioti
fisher(wo)man *m. (1), f. (2)* žvejys, -ė
fishing rod *f. (2)* meškerė
fishy *adj. (2)* neaiškus, -i
fist *m. (1)* kumštis
fit *m. (1)* priepuolis; ~ **in** *v. (1)* pritapti
five *num.* penki, -ios
fix *v. (1)* fiksuoti
fixed *adj. (1)* nustatytas, -a
flag *f. (2)* vėliava
flame *f. (2)* liepsna
flash *m. (1)* blicas (photo camera)
flat *adj. (2)* lygus, -i
flea *f. (2)* blusa
fleet *m. (1)* laivynas
flesh *f. (2)* mėsa
flight *m. (1)* skrydis
flirt *m. (1)* flirtas; *v. (1)* flirtuoti
flood *m. (1)* potvynis; *v. (1)* apsemti; patvinti
floor *f. pl. (3)* grindys
flour *m. pl. (1)* miltai
flow *f. (2)* tėkmė; *v. (1)* tekėti
flower *f. (2)* gėlė; ~ **pot** *m. (1)* vazonas
flu *med. m. (1)* gripas
fluid *m. (1)* skystis
fly *f. (2)* musė; *v. (3)* skraidyti; *v. (1)* skristi
fog *m. (1)* rūkas; *f. (2)* migla
folklore *m. (1)* folkloras; *f. (2)* tautosaka
follow *v. (1)* sekti
follower *m. (1), f. (2)* pasekėjas, -a
food *m. (1)* maistas, valgis
fool *m./f. (2)* vėpla; *m. (1), f. (2)* žioplys, -ė
foolish *adj. (1)* kvailas, -a
foot *f. (2)* koja; pėda
football/ soccer *m. (1)* futbolas
footbridge *m. (1)* lieptas
footnote *f. (2)* išnaša
footprint *m. (1)* pėdsakas
footwear *f. (2)* avalynė
for *prep.* Už; *adv.* todėl; ~ **me** *pron.* man
forbid *v. (1)* (už)drausti, neleisti
force *v. (1)* (pri)versti
forecast *f. (2)* prognozė
forefathers *m. pl. (1)* senoliai
forehead *f. (2)* kakta
foreign *adj. (1)* užsienietiškas, -a
foreigner *m. (1), f. (2)* užsienietis, -ė
forest *f. (2)* giria; *m. (1)* miškas
forestry *f. (2)* miškininkystė
forever *adv.* amžinai
foreword *f. (2)* pratarmė
forge *v. (1)* suklastoti
forget *v. (1)* pamiršti, užmiršti
forgive *v. (1)* atleisti
forgiveness *m. (1)* atleidimas
fork *f. (2)* šakutė
form *f. (2)* forma (document); *m. (1)* pavidalas; *v. (1)* formuoti; *v. (3)* sudaryti
formal *adj. (2)* formalus, -i
fortress *f. (2)* tvirtovė
foster-daughter *f. (2)* įdukra; podukra
foster-son *m. (1)* įsūnis; posūnis
found *v. (1)* (į)kurti, steigti
foundation *m. (1)* pagrindas, pamatas
founder *m. (1), f. (2)* steigėjas, -a, kūrėjas, -a
four *num.* keturi, -ios
fox *f. (2)* lapė
fragile *adj. (2)* trapus, -i
frame *m. pl. (1)* rėmai; *v. (1)* įrėminti
fraud *f. (2)* apgaulė, afera
freckled *adj. (1)* strazdanotas, -a
free *adj. (1)* laisvas, -a, neužimtas, -a; ~ **of charge** *adv.* nemokamai, veltui
freedom *f. (2)* laisvė
freeze *v. (1)* užšalti
freezer *m. (1)* šaldiklis
French *adj. (1)* prancūziškas, -a; ~ **person** *m. (1), f. (2)* prancūzas, -ė
frequency *m. (1)* tankumas; dažnis (radio)
frequent *adj. (1)* dažnas, -a; *adj. (2)* tankus, -i
frequently *adv.* dažnai
fresh *adj. (1)* šviežias, -ia
Friday *m. (1)* penktadienis
friend *m. (1), f. (2)* draugas, -ė
frog *f. (2)* varlė

from *prep.* iš, nuo
front *m. (1)* frontas; priešaky; *adj. (3)* priekinis, -ė, priešakinis, -ė
frontier *m. (1)* pasienis
frost *m. (1)* šerkšnas
frown *v. (3)* raukytis
fruit *m. (1)* vaisius; *adj. (3)* vaisinis, -ė; ~ **tree** *m. (1)* vaismedis
fruit soda/ pop *m. pl. (1)* vaisvandeniai
fuel *m. pl. (1)* degalai; *m. (1)* kuras
fugitive *m. (1), f. (2)* bėglys, -ė, pabėgėlis, -ė
fulfill *v. (3)* įvykdyti; *v. (1)* atlikti
full *adj. (1)* pilnas, -a; *adj. (2)* sotus, -i (after a meal)
function *f. (2)* funkcija
fundamental *adj. (3)* pagrindinis, -ė
funeral *f. pl. (2)* laidotuvės; ~ **feast** *m. pl. (1)* šermenys
fungus *med. m. (1)* grybelis
funny *adj. (1)* juokingas, -a
fur *m. (1)* kailis; *adj. (3)* kailinis, -ė; ~ **coat** *m. pl. (1)* kailiniai
furniture *m. pl. (1)* baldai
further *adj. (3)* tolesnis, -ė
future *f. (3)* ateitis; *adj. (1)* būsimas, -a

G

gain *m. (1)* laimėjimas; *v. (1)* išlošti
game *m. (1)* žaidimas
gang *f. (2)* gauja
garage *m. (1)* garažas
garbage *f. pl. (2)* šiukšlės
garden *m. (1)* sodas
garlic *m. (1)* česnakas
garnish *m. (1)* garnyras
gas *f. pl. (2)* dujos; ~ **station** *f. (2)* degalinė
gasoline *m. (1)* benzinas
gatekeeper *m. (1), f. (2)* vartininkas, -ė
gates *m. pl. (1)* vartai
gather *v. (1)* (susi)rinkti
gathering *m. (1)* susirinkimas
gauze *f. (2)* marlė
gear *f. (2)* pavara
gem *m. (1)* brangakmenis
gender *f. (3)* lytis
gene *m. (1)* genas
genealogy *f. (2)* genealogija
general *adj. (1)* bendras, -a
generally *adv.* apskritai
generation *f. (2)* karta, generacija
generosity *m. (1)* dosnumas
generous *adj. (2)* dosnus, -i; kilnus, -i
genius *m. (4)* genijus
geography *f. (2)* geografija
German *m. (1), f. (2)* vokietis, -ė; *adj. (1)* vokiškas, -a
gesture *m. (1)* mostas
get *v. (1)* gauti; ~ **into** *v. (1)* įlipti
ghetto *m. (1)* getas
ghost *m. (1)* vaiduoklis
giant *m. (1), f. (2)* milžinas, -ė
gift *f. (2)* dovana
gifted *adj. (2)* gabus, -i; *adj. (1)* talentingas, -a
gigantic *adj. (1)* milžiniškas, -a
giggle *v. (1)* kikenti
gilded *adj. (1)* paauksuotas, -a
girl *f. (2)* mergaitė (little); *f. (2)* mergina (young woman)
girlfriend *f. (2)* mergina
give *v. (1)* (pa)duoti; teikti; ~ **back** *v. (1)* atiduoti; ~ **birth** *v. (3)* (pa)gimdyti
glacier *m. (1)* ledynas
glance *m. (1)* žvilgsnis
gland *f. (2)* liauka
glass *m. (1)* stiklas; *f. (2)* taurė; *adj. (3)* stiklinis, -ė
glasses *m. pl. (1)* akiniai
globe *m. (1)* gaublys
gloomy *adj. (2)* niūrus, -i
glorious *adj. (1)* šlovingas, -a
glory *f. (2)* šlovė
glove *f. (2)* pirštinė
glue *m. pl. (1)* klijai; *v. (1)* klijuoti
go *v. (1, irr.)* eiti; važiuoti; vykti; ~ **away** *v. (1; irr.)* nueiti
go crazy/ mad *v. (1)* išprotėti
goal *m. (1)* tikslas
goat *m. (1)* ožys; *f. (2)* ožka (she)
God *m. (1)* Dievas
god(dess) *m. (1), f. (2)* dievaitis, -ė
goddaughter *f. (2)* krikštaduktė
goddess *f. (2)* deivė
godfather *m. (1)* krikštatėvis
godmother *f. (2)* krikštamotė
godson *m. (1)* krikštasūnis
gold *m. (1)* auksas
golden *adj. (3)* auksinis, -ė
goldsmith *m. (1)* auksakalys
good *adj. (1)* geras, -a

good afternoon! laba diena!
goodbye! sudie! viso gero!
good night! labanakt(is)!
goods *f. (2)* prekė
goose *f. (3)* žąsis; **~ meat** *f. (2)* žąsiena
gossip *v. (1)* liežuvauti
gourmand *m. (1), f. (2)* gurmanas, -ė
govern *v. (3)* valdyti
government *f. (2)* vyriausybė
governor *m. (1), f. (2)* gubernatorius, -ė
grab *v. (1)* griebti
graceful *adj. (2)* grakštus, -i
grade *m. (1)* pažymys
gradually *adv.* palaipsniui
graduate student *m. (1), f. (2) col.* aspirantas, -ė
graduation *m. (1)* baigimas
grain *m. (1)* grūdas; *f. pl. (2)* kruopos
grammar *f. (2)* gramatika
grandchild *m. (1), f. (2)* vaikaitis, -ė
grandfather *m. (1)* senelis
grandmother *f. (2)* senelė
granite *m. (1)* granitas
granny *f. (2)* močiutė
grant *v. (1)* paskirti
grape *f. (2)* vynuog
grass *f. (2)* žolė
grass snake *m. (1)* žaltys
grasshopper *m. (1)* žiogas
grate *v. (1)* (su)tarkuoti
grateful *adj. (1)* dėkingas, -a
gratitude *f. (2)* padėka
gratuity *m. pl. (1)* arbatpinigiai
grave *m. (1)* kapas
gravel *m. (1)* žvyras
gravy *m. (1)* padažas
gray *adj. (1)* pilkas, -a; **~ haired** *adj. (1)* žilas, -a
grease *m. pl. (1)* riebalai
greasy *adj. (1)* riebaluotas, -a, taukuotas, -a
great *adj. (2)* šaunus, -i
great-grandchild *m. (1), f. (2)* proanūkis, -ė
great-grandfather *m. (1)* prosenelis
great-grandmother *f. (2)* prosenelė
greedy *adj. (2)* godus, -i
Greek *m. (1), f. (2)* graikas, -ė; *adj. (1)* graikiškas, -a
green *adj. (1)* žalias, -ia
greenhouse *m. (1)* šiltnamis
greens *m. pl. (1)* žalumynai
greet *v. (1)* (pa(si))sveikinti
greeting *m. (1)* sveikinimas
grief *m. (1)* sielvartas
ground *f. (2)* dirva; *v. (1)* pagrįsti
ground meat *m. (1)* faršas
grow old *v. (1)* senti; **~ up** *v. (1)* užaugti
growl *v. (1)* urgzti
grown-up *adj.* suaugęs, -usi
guarantee *f. (2)* garantija
guard *m. (1), f. (2)* sargas, -ė
guess *v. (1)* (at)spėti
guest *m. (1)* svečias
guide *m. (1), f. (2)* gidas, -ė
guilt *f. (2)* kaltė
guilty *adj. (1)* kaltas, -a
guitar *f. (2)* gitara
gums *med. f. pl. (2)* dantenos
gymnastics *f. (2)* mankšta
gypsy *m. (1), f. (2)* čigonas, -ė

H

habit *m. (1)* įprotis
hail *f. (2)* kruša
hair *m. pl. (1)* plaukai
haircut *m. (1)* kirpimas
hairdresser *m. (1), f. (2)* kirpėjas, -a
hairsalon *f. (2)* kirpykla
hairspray *m. (1)* lakas
hairy *adj. (1)* plaukuotas, -a
half *f. (2)* pusė
half an hour *m. (1)* pusvalandis
half year *m. (1)* pusmetis
half-time *m. (1)* kėlinys
halfway *f. (2)* pusiaukelė
hall *f. (2)* salė; halė
halva(h) *f. (2)* chalva
ham *m. (1)* kumpis
hammer *m. (1)* plaktukas
hand *f. (2)* plaštaka; ranka; *v. (1)* įteikti; *adj. (3)* rankinis, -ė
handful *f. (2)* sauja
handkerchief *f. (2)* nosinė
handle *m. (1)* kotas; *f. (2)* rankena
handsome *adj. (2)* gražus, -i
handwriting *m. (1)* braižas, raštas; *f. (2)* rašysena
handy *adj. (2)* parankus, -i
hang *v. (1)* (pa)kabinti; (pa)karti; *v. (3)* kaboti
hanger *f. (2)* pakaba

hangover *f. pl. (2)* pagirios
happen *v. (1)* vykti
happiness *f. (2)* laimė
happy *adj. (1)* laimingas, -a
harass *v. (1)* kabinėtis
harbor *m. (1)* uostas
hard *adj. (1)* kietas, -a
harden *v. (1)* sukietėti
hardly *adv.* kažin; *part.* vos
hare *m. (1)* kiškis, zuikis
harem *m. (1)* haremas
harm *f. (2)* žala, *v. (1)* pakenkti; skriausti
harmful *adj. (1)* žalingas, -a
harmless *adj. (1)* nekenksmingas, -a
harmony *f. (2)* harmonija; santarvė
harp *f. (2)* arfa
harvest *m. (4)* derlius
hasten *v. (1)* pagreitinti, paraginti; paskubėti
hasty *adj. (1)* skubotas, -a, neapgalvotas, -a
hat *f. (2)* skrybėlė
hate *v. (1)* nekęsti
hatred *f. (2)* neapykanta
have *v. (2)* turėti
hawk *m. (1)* vanagas
hay *m. (1)* šienas
hazardous *adj. (1)* rizikingas, -a
he *pron. m.* jis
head *f. (2)* galva; *m. (1), f. (2)* vedėjas, -a
headphones *f. pl. (2)* ausinės
health *f. (2)* sveikata
health resort *m. (1)* kurortas
healthy *adj. (1)* sveikas, -a
hear *v. (2)* girdėti
hearing *f. (2)* klausa
heart *f. (3)* širdis
heartbreak *f. (2)* širdgėla
heartburn *m. (5)* rėmuo
heat *f. (2)* šiluma; *v. (1)* kūrenti
heating *m. (1)* šildymas
heaven *m. (4)* dangus
heavenly *adj. (1)* dangiškas, -a
heavy *adj. (2)* sunkus, -i; smarkus, -i; *adj. (1)* storas, -a
hedgehog *m. (1)* ežys
heel *m. (1)* kulnas
height *m. (1)* aukštis, ūgis
heir *m. (1), f. (2)* įpėdinis, -ė
hell *m. (1)* pragaras
hello! labas! alio!
helmet *m. (1)* šalmas
help *v. (1)* padėti
helpless *adj. (3)* bejėgis, -ė
hemorrhoids *med. m. (4)* hemarojus
hen *f. (2)* višta
her(s) jos
herb (medicinal) *f. (2)* vaistažolė
herd *f. (2)* banda
here *adv.* čia
hereditary *adj. (1)* paveldimas, -a
heredity *m. (1)* paveldimumas
heritage *m. (1)* palikimas
hermit *m. (1), f. (2)* atsiskyrėlis, -ė
hernia *med. f. (2)* išvarža; *med. m. (1)* trūkis
hero *m. (1), f. (2)* didvyris, -ė
herring *f. (2)* silkė
hesitate *v. (1)* svyruoti
hiccup *v. (2)* žagsėti
hidden *adj. (1)* paslėptas, -a
hide *v. (1)* slėpti
high *adv.* aukštai
higher *adv.* aukščiau
highlander (inhabitant of Aukštaitija) *m. (1), f. (2)* aukštaitis, -ė
highway *f. (2)* magistralė; *m. (1)* plentas
hike *m. (1)* turistinis žygis (long)
hill *f. (2)* kalva
hilly *adj. (1)* kalnuotas, -a
him jį
hint *f. (2)* užuomina
hip *m. (1)* klubas
hire *v. (3)* (pa)samdyti
his jo
history *f. (2)* istorija
hockey *m. (1)* (ledo) ritulys; **~ player** *m. (1), f. (2)* (ledo) ritulininkas, -ė
hold *v. (3)* laikyti
hole *f. (2)* duobė
holiday *m. (1)* šventadienis; *adj. (3)* šventinis, -ė; *adj. (1)* šventas, -a
holy *adj. (1)* šventas, -a
home *m. pl. (1)* namai
homeless person *m. (1), f. (2)* benamis, -ė
homeopathy *f. (2)* homeopatija
homosexual *m. (1)* homoseksualas; *adj. (1) col.* žydras, -a
honest *adj. (1)* doras, -a; sąžiningas, -a
honey *m. (4)* medus
honeymoon medaus mėnuo
honor *f. (2)* garbė; *v. (1)* pagerbti

honorable *adj. (1)* garbingas, -a
hooligan *m. (1), f. (2)* chuliganas, -ė
hooray! valio!
hope *f. (3); v. (1)* viltis; *v. (2)* tikėtis
hopeless *adj. (1)* beviltiškas, -a
horn *m. (1)* ragas
hornet *f. (2)* širšė
horrible *adj. (2)* kraupus, -i, baisus, -i
horror *m. (1)* siaubas
hors d'oeuvres *m. (1)* užkandis
horse *m. (1)* arklys, žirgas
horse rider *m. (1), f. (2)* jojikas, -ė
horseradish *m. pl. (1)* krienai
horseshoe *f. (2)* pasaga
hospitable *adj. (1)* vaišingas, -a
hospital *f. (2)* ligoninė
hospitality *m. (1)* vaišingumas
host *m. (1)* šeimininkas
hostage *m. (1), f. (2)* įkaitas, -ė
hostel *m. (1)* hostelis
hostess *f. (2)* šeimininkė
hostile *adj. (1)* priešiškas, -a
hot *adj. (1)* karštas, -a
hot chocolate *f. (2)* kakava
hotel *m. (1)* viešbutis
hour *f. (2)* valanda
house *m. (1)* namas
household *m. pl. (1)* namiškiai
how *adv.* kaip
how many/ much *adv.* kiek
however *conj.* tačiau; *part.* visgi
hug *v. (1)* apkabinti
human being *m. (4)* žmogus
human resources *m. pl. (1)* kadrai; **~ department** kadrų skyrius
humane *adj. (1)* humaniškas, -a, žmoniškas, -a
humanitarian *m. (1), f. (2)* humanitaras, -ė
humid *adj. (1)* drėgnas, -a
humidity *f. (2)* drėgmė
humiliate *v. (1)* (pa)žeminti
humiliation *m. (1)* pažeminimas
humor *m. (1)* humoras
humorist *m. (1), f. (2)* humoristas, -ė
humorous *adj. (3)* humoristinis, -ė
hundred *m. (1)* šimtas
Hungarian *m. (1), f. (2)* vengras, -ė; *adj. (1)* vengriškas, -a
hunger *m. (1)* alkis, badas
hungry *adj. (1)* alkanas, -a
hunt *f. (2)* medžioklė
hunter *m. (1), f. (2)* medžiotojas, -a
hurricane *m. (1)* uraganas
hurry *v. (1)* skubėti
hurt *v. (1)* (nu)skriausti
husband *m. (1)* vyras
hut *f. (2)* lūšna, trobelė
hygiene *f. (2)* higiena
hygienic *adj. (1)* higieniškas, -a
hymn *m. (1)* himnas
hypnotize *v. (1)* užhipnotizuoti
hypocrite *m. (1), f. (2)* veidmainis, -ė
hysteria *med. f. (2)* isterija
hysterical *adj. (1)* isteriškas, -a

I

I *pron.* aš
ice *m. (1)* ledas; **~ cream** *m. pl. (1)* ledai
icicle *m. (1)* varveklis
icy *adj. (3)* ledinis, -ė
idea *m. (1)* sumanymas
identical *adj. (2)* tolygus, -i
identification *f. (2)* identifikacija
identify *v. (1)* atpažinti, identifikuoti
identity *f. (2)* tapatybė
idiot *m. (1), f. (2)* idiotas, -ė
idol *m. (1), f. (2)* stabas, dievaitis, -ė
if *conj.* jei, jeigu
ignore *v. (1)* ignoruoti
ill (to be) *v. (1)* sirgti
illegal *adj. (1)* neteisėtas, -a
illness *f. (2)* liga
illustrated *adj. (1)* iliustruotas, -a
illustration *f. (2)* iliustracija
image *m. (1)* atvaizdas
imaginary *adj. (1)* nebūtas, -a
imagination *f. (2)* vaizduotė, fantazija
imagine *v. (1)* įsivaizduoti
imitate *v. (1)* (pa)mėgdžioti
imitation *f. (2)* imitacija
immediately *adv.* nedelsiant, tuoj(au)
immigrant *m. (1), f. (2)* imigrantas, -ė
immigrate *v. (1)* imigruoti
immigration *f. (2)* imigracija
immunity *m. (1)* neliečiamumas
import *m. (1)* importas; *v. (1)* importuoti
importance *f. (2)* svarba, reikšmė
important *adj. (2)* svarbus, -i
imported *adj. (3)* importinis, -ė

impossible *adj. (1)* neįmanomas, -a
impressive *adj. (1)* įspūdingas, -a
imprison *v. (1)* įkalinti
imprisonment *f. (2)* nelaisvė
improve *v. (1)* pagerėti; pagerinti
improvement *m. (1)* pagerėjimas; pagerinimas
in *prep.* po; ~ **front of** *prep.* prieš; ~ **general** *adv.* apskritai; ~ **time** *adv.* laiku; ilgainiui
into *prep.* į
incident *m. (1)* atsitikimas
income *f. pl. (2)* įplaukos
incorporate *v. (1)* inkorporuoti
increase *m. (1)* padidėjimas; *v. (1)* (pa)daugėti, padidėti; padidinti
incurable *adj. (1)* neišgydomas, -a, nepagydomas, -a
independence *f. (2)* nepriklausomybė
independent *adj. (1)* nepriklausomas, -a; savarankiškas, -a
index *f. (2)* rodyklė
Indian *m. (1), f. (2)* indas, -ė; *adj. (1)* indiškas, -ė
indication *m. (1)* požymis; nurodymas
indicator *m. (1)* rodiklis
indirect *adj. (3)* netiesioginis, -ė
individual *m. (1)* individas; *adj. (2)* individualus, -i
indoor *adj. (3)* kambarinis, -ė
industrial *adj. (3)* pramoninis, -ė
industrious *adj. (2)* darbštus, -i
industry *f. (2)* pramonė
inedible *adj. (1)* nevalgomas, -a
inequality *f. (2)* nelygybė
inevitable *adj. (1)* neišvengiamas, -a
infamous *adj. (1)* negarbingas, -a
infancy *f. (2)* kūdikystė
infect *v. (1)* užkrėsti
infection *f. (2)* infekcija
infectious *adj. (3)* infekcinis, -ė
inflammation *med. m. (1)* uždegimas
inflatable *adj. (1)* pripučiamas, -a
inflate *v. (1)* pripūsti
inflation *f. (2)* infliacija
influence *f. (2)* įtaka; *m. (1)* poveikis; *v. (1)* paveikti
influential *adj. (1)* įtakingas, -a
information *f. (2)* informacija
informative *adj. (3)* informacinis, -ė
inhabitant *m. (1), f. (2)* gyventojas, -a
inherit *v. (2)* paveldėti
inheritance *m. (1)* palikimas
inhuman *adj. (1)* nežmoniškas, -a
initial *adj. (3)* pradinis, -ė
initiative *f. (2)* iniciatyva; *adj. (2)* iniciatyvus, -i
injection *med. f. (2)* injekcija
injure *v. (1)* sužeisti, žaloti
injury *f. (2)* skriauda
injustice *f. (2)* neteisybė
ink *m. (1)* rašalas
inn *f. (2)* užeiga
innocent *adj. (1)* nekaltas, -a
inquire *v. (1)* pasiteirauti, klausti
inquiry *m. (1)* tardymas
insanity *f. (2)* beprotystė
insect *m. (1)* vabzdys
insert *v. (1)* įterpti
insignificant *adj. (2)* nežymus, -i
insincere *adj. (2)* nenuoširdus, -i
insomnia *f. (2)* nemiga
inspection *f. (2)* inspekcija; revizija
inspector *m. (4), f. (2)* revizorius, -ė; kontrolierius, -ė
installment *f. (2)* įmoka
institute *m. (1)* institutas
instructions *f. (2)* instrukcija
instructor (in college) *m. (1), f. (2)* dėstytojas, -a
instrument *m. (1)* instrumentas, įrankis
insult *m. (1)* įžeidimas
insurance *m. (1)* draudimas
insure *v. (1)* apdrausti
integration *f. (2)* integracija
intellect *m. (1)* intelektas
intellectual *m. (1), f. (2)* intelektualas, -ė; *adj. (2)* intelektualus, -i
intelligence *m. (1)* išsilavinimas; protas
intend *v. (1)* ketinti
intensify *v. (1)* sustiprėti
interaction *f. (2)* sąveika
intercity *adj. (3)* tarpmiestinis, -ė
interest *fin. f. pl. (2)* palūkanos; *v. (1)* dominti
interested (to be) *v. (2)* domėtis
interesting *adj. (2)* įdomus, -i
interior *m. (4)* vidus
intermediary *m. (1), f. (2)* tarpininkas, -ė

intermediate *adj. (3)* tarpinis, -ė
intermission *f. (2)* pertrauka
internal *adj. (3)* vidinis, -ė
international *adj. (3)* tarptautinis, -ė
internet *m. (1)* internetas
interpreter *m. (1), f. (2)* vertėjas, -a
interrogate *v. (1)* kvosti
interrogation *f. (2)* kvota
interval *m. (1)* tarpas
interview *m. (n. d.)* interviu
intestine *f. (2)* žarna
intestines *m. pl. (1)* viduriai
intimate *adj. (2)* intymus, -i;
adj. (1) artimas, -a
introduction *m. (1)* įvadas;
f. (2) įžanga
invader *m. (1), f. (2)* okupantas, -ė
invasion *f. (2)* invazija
invent *v. (3)* prasimanyti;
v. (1) išrasti
invention *m. (1)* prasimanymas
inventor *m. (1), f. (2)* išradėjas, -a
inventory *m. (4)* inventorius
invest *v. (1)* investuoti
investigate *v. (1)* (iš)tirti
investigation *f. (2)* kvota;
m. (1) tyrimas; tardymas
investigator *m. (1), f. (2)*
tardytojas, -a
investment *f. (2)* investicija;
m. (1) indėlis
investor *m. (1), f. (2)* indėlininkas, -ė
invitation *m. (1)* pakvietimas
invite *v. (1)* (pa)kviesti
involuntary *adj. (1)* nevalingas, -a
iodine *m. (1)* jodas
iris *med. f. (2)* rainelė (of the eye)
Irish *m. (1), f. (2)* airis, -ė
iron *f. (3)* geležis; *v. (1)* lyginti;
m. (1) lygintuvas (for ironing)
ironic *adj. (1)* ironiškas, -a
irony *f. (2)* ironija
irregular *adj. (1)* netaisyklingas, -a
irresponsible *adj. (1)*
neatsakingas, -a
Islam *m. (1)* islamas
island *f. (2)* sala
isolate *v. (1)* izoliuoti
isolation *f. (2)* izoliacija
issue *m. (1)* išleidimas; *f. (2)* laida
Italian *m. (1), f. (2)* italas, -ė;
adj. (1) itališkas, -a
itch *v. (1)* niežėti
itinerary *m. (1)* maršrutas

J

jacket *m. (1)* švarkas
jaguar *m. (1)* jaguaras
jail *m. (1)* kalėjimas
January *m. (1)* sausis
Japanese *m. (1), f. (2)* japonas, -ė;
adj. (1) japoniškas, -a
jaw *m. (1)* žandikaulis
jaws *m. pl. (1)* nasrai
jazz *m. (1)* džiazas
jealous *adj. (2)* pavydus, -i;
(to be) *v. (2)* pavydėti
jealousy *m. (1)* pavydas
jeans *m. pl. (1)* džinsai;
adj. (3) džinsinis, -ė
jerk *m./f. (2)* akiplėša
jet plane reaktyvinis lėktuvas
Jew *m. (1), f. (2)* žydas, -ė
jewel *m. (1)* brangakmenis;
f. (2) brangenybė
jeweler *m. (1), f. (2)* juvelyras, -ė
jewelry *pl.* juvelyriniai dirbiniai
Jewish *adj. (1)* žydiškas, -a
job *f. (2)* tarnyba; *m. (1)* darbas
jog *v. (1)* bėgioti
joint *m. (1)* sąnarys; *v. (1)* jungti;
įstoti
joke *m. (1)* anekdotas; pokštas;
v. (1) juokauti
journal *m. (1)* žurnalas
journalist *m. (1), f. (2)* žurnalistas, -ė
journey *f. (2)* kelionė
joy *m. (1)* džiaugsmas
joyful *adj. (1)* linksmas, -a
judge *v. (1)* spręsti
juice *f. pl. (3)* sultys
juicy *adj. (1)* sultingas, -a
July *f. (2)* liepa
jump *m. (1)* šuolis; *v. (1)* šokti
June *m. (1)* birželis
jungle *f. pl. (2)* džiunglės
just *adj. (1)* teisingas, -a;
~ now *part.* ką tik
justice *m. (1)* teisingumas
justification *m. (1)* pateisinimas
justify *v. (1)* (pa)teisinti
juvenile *m. (1), f. (2)* mažametis, -ė

K

kayak *f. (2)* baidarė
keep *v. (3)* saugoti
kefir *m. (1)* kefyras

kerosene *m. (1)* žibalas
key *m. (1)* raktas
keyboard *f. (2)* klaviatūra
kidnapper *m. (1), f. (2)* pagrobėjas, -a
kidney *m. (1)* inkstas; **~ bean** *f. (2)* pupelė
kill *v. (1)* užmušti
killer *m. (1), f. (2)* žudikas, -ė
kilogram *m. (1)* kilogramas
kindness *m. (1)* gėris
king *m. (4)* karalius
kingdom *f. (2)* karalystė
kiosk *m. (1)* kioskas
kiss *m. (1)* bučinys, *col.* bučkis; *v. (1)* bučiuotis, pabučiuoti
kitchen *f. (2)* virtuvė
knife *m. (1)* peilis
knight *m. (1)* riteris
knight (Lithuanian State symbol) *m. (1)* vytis
knit *v. (1)* megzti
knot *m. (1)* mazgas
know *v. (2)* pažinti; *v. (3)* žinoti
kolkhoz *arch. m. (1)* kolūkis
Korean *m. (1), f. (2)* korėjietis, -ė; *adj. (1)* korėjietiškas, -a

L

label *f. (2)* etiketė
laboratory *f. (2)* laboratorija
lace *m. pl. (1)* nėriniai
lack *v. (1)* trūkti
ladder *f. pl. (2)* kopėčios
lady *f. (2)* ponia, dama
ladybug *f. (2)* boružė
lagoon *f. pl. (2)* marios
lake *m. (1)* ežeras
lakeside *f. (2)* paežerė
lamb *f. (2)* aviena
lamp *f. (2)* lempa
land *f. (2)* žemė; *m. (1)* kraštas; *f. (3)* šalis
landscape *m. (1)* kraštovaizdis, peizažas
lane *m. (1)* skersgatvis
language *f. (2)* kalba
lantern *m. (1)* žibintas
laptop (computer) nešiojamas kompiuteris
large *adj. (2)* stambus, -i
last *adj. (3)* paskutinis, -ė; **~ name** *f. (2)* pavardė; **~ year** *adv.* pernai
late *adv.* vėlai; **to be ~** *v. (1)* (pa)vėluoti
latest *adj. (3)* paskutinis, -ė
Latvian *m. (1), f. (2)* latvis, -ė; *adj. (1)* latviškas, -a
laugh *v. (1)* juoktis
laughter *m. (1)* juokas
laundromat *f. (2)* skalbykla
laundry (to do) *v. (1)* skalbti
law *m. (1)* įstatymas; *f. (2)* teisė
lawn *f. (2)* veja
lawyer *m. (1), f. (2)* teisininkas, -ė
lay (down) *v. (1)* (pa)dėti
layer *m. (1)* sluoksnis
layout *m. (1)* išdėstymas
lazy *adj. (2)* tingus, -i
lead *m. (1)* švinas; *v. (1)* vesti, vadovauti; *adj. (3)* švininis, -ė
leader *m. (1), f. (2)* lyderis, -ė; vadovas, -ė; vadas, -ė
leaf *m. (1)* lapas
lean *adj. (1)* liesas, -a
learn *v. (1)* išmokti; *v. (3)* mokytis
learning *m. (1)* mokslas
lease *f. (2)* nuoma; *v. (1)* (iš)nuomoti
leather *f. (2)* oda; *adj. (3)* odinis, -ė
leave *v. (1, irr.)* išeiti, palikti
lecture *f. (2)* paskaita; *m. (1)* pranešimas; **~ hall** *f. (2)* auditorija
lecturer *m. (1), f. (2)* dėstytojas, -a, paskaitininkas, -ė; *m. (4), f. (2)* lektorius, -ė
left side *f. (2)* kairė
leg *f. (2)* koja
legal *adj. (3)* įstatyminis, -ė, juridinis, -ė; *adj. (1)* teisėtas, -a; *adj. (2)* legalus, -i
legal adviser *m. (1), f. (2)* juriskonsultas, -ė
legalize *v. (1)* įteisinti, legalizuoti
legend *f. (2)* legenda, sakmė
legendary *adj. (3)* legendinis, -ė
legitimize *v. (1)* įteisinti
leisure *m. (1)* laisvalaikis
lemon *f. (2)* citrina
lemonade *m. (1)* limonadas
lend *v. (1)* skolinti
lender *m. (1), f. (2)* skolintojas, -a
lent *f. (2)* gavėnia
less mažiau
lesson *f. (2)* pamoka
letter *m. (1)* laiškas; *f. (2)* raidė

letter-carrier *m. (1), f. (2)* laiškanešys, -ė, paštininkas, -ė
lettuce *f. pl. (2)* salotos
level *m. (1)* lygis
liar *m. (1), f. (2)* melagis, -ė
liberal *polit. m. (1), f. (2)* liberalas, -ė
liberate *v. (1)* išlaisvinti, išvaduoti
librarian *m. (1), f. (2)* bibliotekininkas, -ė
library *f. (2)* biblioteka
lid *m. (1)* dangtis; viršelis
lie *m. (1)* melas; *v. (1)* meluoti; *v. (2)* gulėti; ~ **down** *v. (1)* (atsi)gulti
life *m. (1)* gyvenimas; *f. (2)* gyvybė
lift *v. (1)* pakelti
light *f. (2)* šviesa; *adj. (1)* lengvas, -a; *adj. (2)* šviesus, -i; ~ **the light** *v. (1)* uždegti (šviesą)
lighter *m. (1)* žiebtuvėlis
lighthouse *m. (1)* švyturys
lightning *m. (1)* žaibas
like *v. (1)* mėgti, patikti; *part.* lyg, tarsi
limb *f. (2)* galūnė
lime tree *f. (2)* liepa
limit *m. (1)* limitas; *f. (2)* riba
limitation *m. (1)* apribojimas
limited *adj. (1)* ribotas, -a
line *f. (2)* linija
linen *f. (2)* drobė; *m. pl. (1)* baltiniai; *adj. (3)* lininis, -ė
linguist *m. (1), f. (2)* kalbininkas, -ė, lingvistas, -ė
linguistics *f. (2)* kalbotyra, lingvistika
lion *m. (1)* liūtas
lioness *f. (2)* liūtė
lip *f. (2)* lūpa
liqueur *m. (1)* likeris
liquid *adj. (1)* skystas, -a
list *m. (1)* sąrašas
listen *v. (3)* klausyti
liter *m. (1)* litras
literacy *m. (1)* raštingumas
literate *adj. (1)* raštingas, -a
Lithuanian *m. (1), f. (2)* lietuvis, -ė; *adj. (1)* lietuviškas, -a
Lithuanian girl *f. (2)* lietuvaitė
Lithuanianism *f. (2)* lietuvybė
litter *v. (1)* užteršti
little *adj. (1)* mažas, -a; **a** ~ *m. (1)* truputis; *adv.* nedaug, šiek tiek
live *v. (1)* gyventi
lively *adj. (2)* judrus, -i
liver *f. pl. (3)* kepenys
load *v. (1)* (pri)krauti
loaf *m. (1)* kepalas
loan *f. (2)* paskola
local *adj. (3)* vietinis, -ė
location *f. (3)* padėtis
lock *f. (2)* spyna; *v. (1)* (už)rakinti
locked *adj. (1)* užrakintas, -a
locksmith *m. (1)* šaltkalvis
locomotive *m. (1)* garvežys
log *m. (1)* rąstas
logic *f. (2)* logika; *adj. (1)* logiškas, -a
loneliness *f. (2)* vienatvė
lonely *adj. (1)* vienišas, -a
long *adj. (1)* ilgas, -a
look *v. (2)* žiūrėti; ~ **after** *v. (1)* rūpintis; ~ **for** *v. (3)* ieškoti
loose *adj. (1)* palaidas, -a
Lord *m. (1)* Viešpats
lose *v. (1)* netekti, prarasti; pralošti; *v. (2)* pralaimėti
loss *f. (3)* netektis; *m. (1)* nuostolis; pralaimėjimas
lot *m. (1)* sklypas; *f. (2)* dalia
lottery *f. (2)* loterija
loud *adj. (2)* garsus, -i
love *f. (2)* meilė; *v. (2)* mylėti; ~ **affair** *m. (1)* romanas
lover *m. (1), f. (2)* meilužis, -ė
low *adj. (1)* žemas, -a
lowland *f. (2)* žemuma
loyal *adj. (2)* lojalus, -i
luck *f. (2)* palaima
luggage *m. (1)* bagažas
lunch *m. pl.* (4) pietūs
lungs *m. pl. (1)* plaučiai
Lutheran *m. (1), f. (2)* liuteronas, -ė; *adj. (1)* liuteroniškas, -a
luxurious *adj. (2)* komfortabilus, -i, prabangus, -i
luxury *m. (1)* komfortas; *f. (2)* prabanga

M

machine *f. (2)* mašina; ~ **gun** *m. (1)* kulkosvaidis
machinery *f. (2)* technika
machinist *m. (1), f. (2)* mašinistas, -ė
madness *m. (1)* pamišimas
magazine *m. (1)* žurnalas
magic *adj. (1)* magiškas, -a
magnet *m. (1)* magnetas

mahogany *m. (1)* raudonmedis
maid *f. (2)* kambarinė
mail *m. (1)* paštas; *f. (2)* korespondencija
mailbox pašto dėžutė
maintenance *m. (1)* išlaikymas
major *m. (1), f. (2)* majoras, -ė
majority *f. (2)* dauguma
make *v. (3)* (pa)daryti
make love *v. (2)* mylėtis
make-up *theat. m. (1)* grimas
male *m. (1)* vyras (human); patinas (animal)
man *m. (1)* vyras
manage *v. (3)* tvarkyti; *v. (1)* vadovauti
management *f. (2)* vadyba; vadovybė
manager *m. (1), f. (2)* vadybininkas, -ė, vadovas, -ė, valdytojas, -a, vedėjas, -a
maneuver *m. (1)* manevras
mansion *m. pl. (1)* rūmai
manufacture *v. (1)* pagaminti
manuscript *m. (1)* rankraštis
many *num.* daug
map *m. (1)* žemėlapis
maple tree *m. (1)* klevas
marble *m. (1)* marmuras
March *m. (1)* kovas
Mardi Gras *f. pl. (2)* Užgavėnės
mare *f. (2)* kumelė
margarine *m. (1)* margarinas
margin *f. (2)* paraštė
mark *f. (2)* žymė; *m. (1)* pažymys; *v. (1)* paženklinti
market *f. (2)* rinka; *m. (4)* turgus
marriage *f. (2)* santuoka; *f. pl. (2)* vedybos
married *adj.m.* vedęs (man); *adj. f.* ištekėjusi (woman)
marry *v. (1)* susituokti; vesti; (iš)tekėti
marsh *f. (2)* pelkė
mascara *m. (1)* tušas
masculine *adj. (1)* vyriškas, -a
mask *f. (2)* kaukė; masė
mass *f. pl. (2)* mišios
massacre *m. (1)* pogromas
massage *m. (1)* masažas
masseur, -euse *m. (1), f. (2)* masažistas, -ė
master *m. (1), f. (2)* meistras, -ė, šeimininkas, -ė, *m. (1)* ponas
master key *m. (1)* visraktis
match *m. (1)* degtukas; mačas
material *f. (2)* medžiaga; *adj. (3)* materialinis, -ė
materialistic *adj. (3)* materialistinis, -ė
mathematics *f. (2)* matematika
matter *m. (1)* reikalas; turinys
mattress *m. (1)* čiužinys
mature *v. (1)* bręsti; *adj.* subrendęs, -usi; *adj. (2)* brandus, -i
maybe *part.* gal
mead *m. (4)* midus
meadow *f. (2)* pieva
mean *v. (1)* reikšti
meaning *f. (2)* reikšmė
means *f. (2)* priemonė
measles *med. m. (1)* tymai
measure *m. (1)* matas; *v. (1)* išmatuoti
measurements *m. pl. (5)* matmenys
meat *f. (2)* mėsa
meaty *adj. (1)* mėsingas, -a
mechanic *m. (1), f. (2)* mechanikas, -ė
mechanical *adj. (3)* techninis, -ė
mechanics *f. (2)* mechanika
medal *m. (1)* medalis
media *f. (2)* žiniasklaida
mediate *v. (1)* tarpininkauti
medical student *m. (1), f. (2)* medikas, -ė
medicine *f. (2)* medicina
mediocre *adj. (1)* pusėtinas, -a
meditate *v. (3)* mąstyti
meet *v. (1)* pasitikti, sutikti
meeting *m. (1)* pasitarimas, posėdis, susirinkimas; sutikimas
melt *v. (1)* tirpti
member *m. (1), f. (2)* narys, -ė
memoirs *m. pl. (1)* atsiminimai, užrašai
memorial *adj. (3)* paminklinis, -ė
memory *f. (3)* atmintis
menstruation *f. pl. (2)* menstruacijos
mental *adj. (3)* protinis, -ė; psichinis, -ė
menu *m. (1)* valgiaraštis
merchant *m. (1)* pirklys
mercy *m. (1)* pasigailėjimas
merely *adv.* tiktai; *part.* tik
merit *m. (1)* nuopelnas
merry *adj. (1)* linksmas, -a
merry-go-round *f. (2)* karuselė
message *m. (1)* pranešimas; *f. (2)* žinia

messenger *m. (1), f. (2)* pasiuntinys, -ė; ryšininkas, -ė
metal *m. (1)* metalas; *adj. (3)* metalinis, -ė
metaphòr *f. (2)* metafora
meter *m. (1)* metras; skaitiklis
method *m. (1)* metodas
microphone *m. (1)* mikrofonas
microscope *m. (1)* mikroskopas
middle *m. (1)* vidurys; *adj. (3)* vidurinis, -ė
middleman *m. (1), f. (2)* tarpininkas, -ė
midwife *f. (2)* pribuvėja
mile *f. (2)* mylia
military *adj. (3)* karinis, -ė; ~ **duty** karinė prievolė; ~ **officer** *m. (1), f. (2)* karininkas, -ė
military service karinė tarnyba
milk *m. (1)* pienas; *adj. (1)* pieniškas, -a
mill *m. (1)* malūnas
millennium *m. (1)* tūkstantmetis
miller *m. (1), f. (2)* malūnininkas, -ė
millimeter *m. (1)* milimetras
million *m. (1)* milijonas
millionaire *m. (4), f. (2)* milijonierius, -ė
mind *m. (1)* protas
mine *f. (2)* mina; šachta; *pron.* mano
mineral *m. (1)* mineralas; *adj. (3)* mineralinis, -ė
minister *polit. m. (1), f. (2)* ministras, -ė
ministry *polit. f. (2)* ministerija
minor *m. (1), f. (2)* nepilnametis, -ė
minority *f. (2)* mažuma
mint *f. (2)* mėta; *adj. (3)* mėtinis, -ė
minus *m. (1)* minusas
minute *f. (2)* minutė; *adj. (2)* smulkus, -i
minutes *m. (1)* protokolas
miracle *m. (1)* stebuklas
miraculous *adj. (1)* stebuklingas, -a
mirror *m. (1)* veidrodis
miscarriage *med. m. (1)* persileidimas
misfortune *f. (2)* bėda, nelaimė
mislead *v. (1)* suklaidinti
miss *f. (2)* panelė; *v. (1)* praleisti
mission *f. (2)* misija
missionary *m. (4), f. (2)* misionierius, -ė
mistake *f. (2)* klaida
mistress *f. (2)* meilužė
mistrust *m. (1)* nepasitikėjimas
misuse *v. (1)* piktnaudžiauti
mitten *f. (2)* pirštinė
mix up *v. (3)* sumaišyti
mode *m. (1)* metodas
model *m. (1)* modelis
modem *m. (1)* modemas
moderate *adj. (2)* nuosaikus, -i; *adj. (1)* saikingas, -a
modern *adj. (2)* modernus, -i
modest *adj. (2)* kuklus, -i
modify *v. (1)* modifikuoti
mold *m. pl. (1)* pelėsiai
mole *m. (1)* apgamas
molecule *f. (2)* molekulė
mom *f. (2)* mama, mamytė
moment *m. (1)* momentas
monarch *m. (1), f. (2)* monarchas, -ė
monarchy *f. (2)* monarchija
monastery *m. (1)* vienuolynas
Monday *m. (1)* pirmadienis
monetary *adj. (3)* piniginis, -ė
money *m. pl. (1)* pinigai
Mongolian *m. (1), f. (2)* mongolas, -ė; *adj. (1)* mongoliškas, -a
monk *m. (1)* vienuolis
monkey *f. (2)* beždžionė
monopoly *f. (2)* monopolija
month *m. (5)* mėnuo; *m. (1)* mėnesis
monthly *adj. (3)* mėnesinis, -ė
monument *m. (1)* paminklas
mood *f. (2)* nuotaika
moon *m. (1)* mėnulis
morals *f. (2)* moralė, dorovė
more *part.* dar
morning *m. (1)* rytas; *adj. (3)* rytinis, -ė
mosaic *f. (2)* mozaika
Moslem *m. (1), f. (2)* musulmonas, -ė
mosque *f. (2)* mečetė
mosquito *m. (1)* uodas
moss *f. (2)* samana
mossy *adj. (1)* samanotas, -a
most daugiausia
moth *f. (3)* kandis
mother *f. (2)* mama, motina
motherhood *f. (2)* motinystė
mother-in-law *f. (2)* uošvė
motherly *adj. (1)* motiniškas, -a

mother-of-pearl *adj. (3)* perlamutrinis, -ė
motion *m. (1)* judesys
motivated *adj. (1)* motyvuotas, -a
motive *m. (1)* motyvas
motor *m. (1)* motoras, variklis
motorcycle *m. (1)* motociklas
motorcyclist *m. (1), f. (2)* motociklininkas, -ė
motorized *adj. (1)* motorizuotas, -a
mountain *m. (1)* kalnas; ~ **climber** *m. (1), f. (2)* alpinistas, -ė
mountainous *adj. (1)* kalnuotas, -a
mourn *v. (2)* gedėti
mourning *m. (1)* gedulas
mouse *f. (2)* pelė
move *v. (1)* pajudinti; sujaudinti; judėti; *v. (3)* persikraustyti; ~ **out** *v. (3)* išsikraustyti
movement *m. (1)* sąjūdis; judesys
movie *m. (1)* filmas
movie theater *m. (1)* kinoteatras
mow *v. (1)* šienauti
Mr. *m. (1)* ponas
Mrs. *f. (2)* ponia
Ms. *f. (2)* ponia
mud *m. (1)* dumblas
mug *m. (1)* bokalas; puodelis, puodukas
multicolored *adj.(1)* margas, -a
multiplication *mat. f. (2)* daugyba
multiply *v. (1)* (pa)dauginti
murder *m. (1)* nužudymas; *v. (3)* nužudyti
muscles *m. pl. (5)* raumenys
museum *m. (4)* muziejus
mushroom *m. (1)* grybas
music *f. (2)* muzika
musical *adj. (2)* muzikalus, -i
musician *m. (1), f. (2)* muzikantas, -ė, muzikas, -ė
must *v. (3)* privalėti
mustache *m. pl. (1)* ūsai
mustard *f. pl. (2)* garstyčios
mute person *m. (1), f. (2)* nebylys, -ė
my *pron.* mano
myopia *med. f. (2)* trumparegystė
mysterious *adj. (1)* mįslingas, -a, paslaptingas, -a
mystery *f. (3)* paslaptis
myth *m. (1)* mitas
mythical *adj. (3)* mitinis, -ė

N

nail *m. (1)* nagas; *f. (3)* vinis; *v. (1)* prikalti
naïve *adj. (2)* naivus, -i
naïveté *m. (1)* naivumas
naked *adj. (1)* nuogas, -a
name *m. (1)* pavadinimas; vardas; *v. (1)* praminti
nanny *f. (2)* auklė
napkin *f. (2)* servetėlė
narcotics *m. pl. (1)* narkotikai
narrow *adj. (1)* siauras, -a
nation *f. (2)* tauta, nacija
national *adj. (3)* nacionalinis, -ė; *adj. (1)* tautiškas, -a
nationalism *m. (1)* nacionalizmas
nationalist *m. (1), f. (2)* nacionalistas, -ė
nationalistic *adj. (3)* nacionalistinis, -ė
nationality *f. (2)* tautybė
nationalize *v. (1)* nacionalizuoti
native *adj.* gimtasis, -oji
Native American *m. (1), f. (2)* indėnas, -ė; *adj. (1)* indėniškas, -a
native land *f. (2)* tėvynė
natural *adj. (2)* natūralus, -i
nature *f. (2)* gamta; natūra; *m. (1)* pobūdis
nausea *m. (1)* šleikštulys
navel *f. (2)* bamba
navigation *f. (2)* navigacija
Nazi *m. (1)* nacis; *m. (1), f. (2)* nacistas, -ė
near *adv.* arti; *prep.* šalia
nearsighted *m. (1), f. (2)* trumparegis, -ė
nearsightedness *med. f. (2)* trumparegystė
neat *adj. (1)* tvarkingas, -a; *adj. (2)* švarus, -i
necessary *adj. (1)* reikalingas, -a; **(to be)** *v. (1)* reikėti
neck *m. (1)* kaklas
necklace *m. (1)* vėrinys
need *m. (1)* poreikis
needle *f. (2)* adata
needlework *m. (1)* rankdarbis
negative *m. (1)* negatyvas
negatively *adv.* neigiamai
negotiate *v. (1)* derėtis
negotiation *f. pl. (2)* derybos
negotiator *m. (1), f. (2)* derybininkas, -ė

neighbor *m. (1), f. (2)* kaimynas, -ė
neither *part.* nei
neologism *m. (1)* naujadaras
nephew *m. (1)* sūnėnas
nerves *m. pl. (1)* nervai
nervous *adj. (1)* nervingas, -a
nest *m. (1)* lizdas
net *m. (1)* tinklas
network *m. (1)* tinklas
neutral *adj. (2)* neutralus, -i
never *adv.* niekada
nevermind *m. (1)* niekis
nevertheless *conj.* tačiau; *part.* visgi
new *adj. (1)* naujas, -a
newborn *m. (1), f. (2)* naujagimis, -ė
newcomer *m. (1), f. (2)* ateivis, -ė
news *f. (2)* naujiena; *f. pl. (2)* žinios
newspaper *m. (1)* laikraštis
newsstand *m. (1)* kioskas
next *adj. (1)* sekantis, kitas
nice *adj. (1)* mielas, -a
nickname *f. (2)* pravardė
niece *f. (2)* dukterėčia
night *f. (3)* naktis; *adj. (3)* naktinis, -ė; ~ **club** naktinis klubas; ~ **gown** naktiniai marškiniai
nine *num.* devyni, -ios
nipple *m. (1)* spenelis
no *part.* nė, ne
no (. . . whatever) *pron. f.* jokia, *m.* joks
nobility *f. (2)* bajorija
noble *adj. (1)* kilmingas, -a; *adj. (2)* kilnus, -i
nobody *pron. m.* niekas
nobody's *pron. m.* niekieno
noise *m. (1)* triukšmas
noisy *adj. (1)* triukšmingas, -a
none *pron. f.* jokia, *m.* joks
nonsense *f. (2)* nesąmonė
noodles *m. pl. (1)* makaronai
noon *m. (1)* vidurdienis
normal *adj. (2)* normalus, -i
north *f. (2)* šiaurė
northeast šiaurės rytai
northern *adj. (3)* šiaurinis, -ė
northwest šiaurės vakarai
Norwegian *m. (1), f. (2)* norvegas, -ė; *adj. (1)* norvegiškas, -a
nose *f. (3)* nosis
nostril *f. (2)* šnervė
not *part.* nė, ne
not a bit nė kiek
notary *m. (1), f. (2)* notaras, -ė
note *m. (1)* raštelis
notebook *m. (1)* sąsiuvinis
notes *m. pl. (1)* užrašai
nothing *pron. m.* niekas
notice *v. (2)* pastebėti
notification *m. (1)* pranešimas
noun *m. (1)* daiktavardis
novel *m. (1)* romanas
novelty *f. (2)* naujovė, naujiena
November *m. (1)* lapkritis
now *adv.* dabar
nowhere *adv.* niekur
nuclear *adj. (3)* atominis, -ė
nudity *f. (2)* nuogybė
number *m. (1)* numeris; *m. (4)* skaičius
numeral *m. (1)* skaitvardis
nun *f. (2)* vienuolė
nurse *m. (1), f. (2)* slaugas, -ė; *v. (3)* slaugyti
nursery *m. (1)* (vaikų) lopšelis
nut *m. (1)* riešutas; *adj. (3)* riešutinis, -ė
nutrition *f. (2)* mityba
nutritious *adj. (1)* maistingas, -a, kaloringas, -a

O

oak *m. (1)* ąžuolas; *adj. (3)* ąžuolinis, -ė
oasis *f. (2)* oazė
oat *adj.* avižinis, -ė
oath *f. (2)* priesaika
obedient *adj. (2)* (pa)klusnus, -i
object *m. (1)* objektas; dalykas
objective *adj. (2)* objektyvus, -i
obligation *m. (1)* į(si)pareigojimas
observant *adj. (2)* pastabus, -i
observatory *f. (2)* observatorija
observe *v. (2)* stebėti
observer *m. (1), f. (2)* stebėtojas, -a
occasion *f. (2)* proga
occupation *f. (2)* okupacija; *adj. (3)* okupacinis, -ė
occupied *adj. (1)* užimtas, -a
occupy *v. (1)* okupuoti, užimti
ocean *m. (1)* vandenynas, okeanas
October *m. (1)* spalis
octopus *m. (1)* aštuonkojis
odor *m. (1)* kvapas
off *adv.* šalin

offense *f. (2)* skriauda
offer *m. (1)* pasiūlymas; *v. (3)* siūlyti
office *f. (2)* įstaiga, raštinė, kontora; kanceliarija; *m. (1)* biuras; *adj. (3)* tarnybinis, -ė
officer *m. (1), f. (2)* pareigūnas, -ė
official *m. (1), f. (2)* valdininkas, -ė; *adj. (2)* oficialus, -i
often *adv.* dažnai
oh *inter.* o
oil *f. (2)* nafta
ointment *m. (1)* tepalas
old *adj. (1)* senas, -a
Olympic *adj. (3)* olimpinis, -ė
Olympic games *f. (2)* olimpiada
omelet *f. (2)* kiaušinienė; *m. (1)* omletas
omit *v. (1)* praleisti
on *prep.* po; ~ **time** *adv.* laiku
one *num.* vienas, -a
onion *m. (1)* svogūnas
only *adj. (3)* vienintelis, -ė; *part.* tik; *adv.* tiktai
onto ant
open *adj. (1)* atdaras, -a; atviras, -a
opera *f. (2)* opera
operate *v. (1)* operuoti
operating room *f. (2)* operacinė
operation *f. (2)* operacija
opinion *f. (2)* nuomonė
opium *m. (4)* opijus
opponent *m. (1), f. (2)* oponentas, -ė, priešininkas, -ė
oppose *v. (1)* priešintis
opposite *adj. (1)* priešingas, -a; *prep.* prieš(ais)
opposition *f. (2)* opozicija; *adj. (3)* opozicinis, -ė
oppress *v. (1)* engti
optimist *m. (1), f. (2)* optimistas, -ė
option *fin. m. (1)* pasirinkimas
or *prep.* arba
orange *adj. (3)* oranžinis, -ė
orator *m. (4), f. (2)* oratorius, -ė
orchestra *m. (1)* orkestras
order *m. (1)* įsakymas, nurodymas, potvarkis; užsakymas; ordinas; *v. (1)* liepti; *v. (3)* užsakyti
ordinary *adj. (1)* kasdieniškas, -a, paprastas, -a
organ *m. (1)* organas; *m. pl. (1)* vargonai (musical instrument)
organization *f. (2)* organizacija
organize *v. (1)* organizuoti
organizer *m. (4), f. (2)* organizatorius, -ė
oriental *adj. (1)* rytietiškas, -a
orientation *f. (2)* orientacija
origin *f. (2)* kilmė
original *m. (1)* originalas; *adj. (2)* originalus, -i
orphan *m. (1) , f. (2)* našlaitis, -ė
other *pron. m.* kitas, -a
otherwise *adv.* kitaip
ouch *inter.* oi
our(s) *pron.* mūsų
out(side) adv. lauke
outlet *f. (2)* rozetė (electrical)
outlook *f. (2)* pažiūra
outskirts *m. (1)* pakraštys
ovary *med. f. (2)* kiaušidė
ovation *f. pl. (2)* ovacijos
oven *f. (2)* orkaitė
over *prep.* ties, virš
overestimate *v. (1)* pervertinti
overseas *m. (1)* užjūris
oversleep *v. (1)* pramiegoti
overtime *m. pl. (1)* viršvalandžiai
owl *f. (2)* pelėda
own *adj. (1)* nuosavas, -a
owner *m. (1), f. (2)* savininkas, -ė
oyster *f. (2)* austrė
ozone *m. (1)* ozonas

P

pace *m. (1)* tempas
pack *v. (1)* (su)pakuoti
package *m. (1)* įpakavimas; paketas
packing *m. (1)* įpakavimas
pact *m. (1)* paktas
paddle *m. (1)* irklas
pagan *m. (1), f. (2)* pagonis, -ė; *adj. (1)* pagoniškas, -a
paganism *f. (2)* pagonybė
page *m. (1)* puslapis
pain *m. (1)* skausmas
painkiller nuskausminamieji (vaistai)
paint *m. pl. (1)* dažai; *v. (3)* dažyti; tapyti
painter *m. (1), f. (2)* dailininkas, -ė, tapytojas, -a; dažytojas, -a
painting *m. (1)* paveikslas
pair *f. (2)* pora
pajamas *f. (2)* pižama
palace *m. pl. (1)* rūmai

palm (of a hand) *m. (1)* delnas
palm tree *f. (2)* palmė
palsy *m. (4)* paralyžius
pancake *m. (1)* blynas
pancreas *f. (2)* kasa
panic *f. (2)* panika
panorama *f. (2)* panorama
panties *f. pl. (2)* kelnaitės
pantry *m. (1)* sandėliukas
pants *f. pl. (2)* kelnės
paper *m. (4)* popierius; *adj. (3)* popierinis, -ė
paperclip *f. (2)* sąvaržėlė
parachute *m. (1)* parašiutas
parade *m. (1)* paradas
paradise *m. (4)* rojus
paragraph *f. (2)* pastraipa; *m. (1)* paragrafas; punktas
paralyze *v. (1)* paralyžiuoti
parasite *m. (1), f. (2)* parazitas, -ė
parcel *m. (1)* paketas, siuntinys
parentheses *m. pl. (1)* skliausteliai
parents *m. pl. (1)* tėvai
Paris *m. (4)* Paryžius
parish *f. (2)* parapija; *adj. (3)* parapijinis, -ė
Parisian *m. (1), f. (2)* paryžietis, -ė
park *m. (1)* parkas
parliament *m. (1)* parlamentas
parody *f. (2)* parodija; *v. (1)* parodijuoti
parrot *f. (2)* papūga
parsley *f. (2)* petražolė
part *f. (3)* dalis; *m. (5)* vaidmuo
participate *v. (1)* dalyvauti
partisan *m. (1), f. (2)* partizanas, -ė
partner *m. (1), f. (2)* partneris, -ė
party *polit. f. (2)* partija; *m. (1)* vakarėlis, pobūvis; *polit. adj. (3)* partinis, -ė
pass *v. (1; irr.)* praeiti
pass/ give *v. (1)* perduoti
passenger *m. (1), f. (2)* keleivis, -ė; *adj. (3)* keleivinis, -ė
passive *adj. (2)* neveiklus, -i, pasyvus, -i
passport *m. (1)* pasas
paste *f. (2)* pasta
pastor *m. (4)* pastorius, -ė
pastry *m. (1)* pyragaitis, pyragėlis
patch *m. (1)* lopas
pâté *m. (1)* paštetas
patent *m. (1)* patentas
path *m. (1)* takas
pathetic *adj. (1)* patetiškas, -a
patience *f. (2)* kantrybė
patient *m. (1), f. (2)* pacientas, -ė, ligonis, -ė; *adj. (2)* kantrus, -i
patriot *m. (1), f. (2)* patriotas, -ė
patriotic *adj. (3)* patriotinis, -ė
pattern *m. (1)* modelis
pause *f. (2)* pauzė
pavilion *m. (1)* paviljonas
pawnshop *m. (1)* lombardas
pay *m. (1)* užmokestis; *v. (1)* atsilyginti, (su)mokėti, užmokėti; ~ **phone** *m. (1)* taksofonas
payer *m. (1), f. (2)* mokėtojas, -a
payment *f. (2)* išmoka, įmoka
pea *m. (1)* žirnis
peace *f. (2)* taika; ramybė
peaceful *adj. (2)* taikus, -i
peach *m. (1)* persikas
pear *f. (2)* kriaušė
pearl *m. (1)* perlas; *adj. (3)* perlinis, -ė
peasant *m. (1), f. (2)* valstietis, -ė
pedestrian *adj. (1)* pėsčias, -ia
pedicure *m. (1)* pedikiūras
peel *v. (1)* (nu)skusti
peer (of the same age) *m. (1), f. (2)* bendraamžis, -ė
pen *f. (2)* plunksna; *m. (1)* rašiklis
penalty *f. (2)* (pa)bauda
pencil *m. (1)* pieštukas
penguin *m. (1)* pingvinas
penicillin *m. (1)* penicilinas
peninsula *m. (1)* pusiasalis
penis *f. (2)* varpa
pen-name *m. (1)* pseudonimas
pension *f. (2)* pensija
pensioner *m. (1), f. (2)* pensininkas, -ė
people *f. (3)* liaudis; *m. pl. (2)* žmonės
pepper *m. (1)* pipiras
per cent *m. (1)* procentas
perfect *adj. (1)* tobulas, -a
perfection *f. (2)* tobulybė
performance *m. (1)* vaidinimas
performer *m. (1), f. (2)* atlikėjas, -a
perfume *m. pl. (1)* kvepalai
period *m. (1)* laikotarpis, periodas; taškas; *f. (2)* fazė; *f. pl. (2)* menstruacijos
periodic(al) *adj. (3)* periodinis, -ė
permission *m. (1)* leidimas
peroxide *m. (1)* peroksidas
Persian *adj. (1)* persiškas, -a

persistent *adj. (2)* atkaklus, -i
person *m. (5)* asmuo; *m. (4)* žmogus
personnel *m. (1)* personalas
perspective *f. (2)* perspektyva
perspire *v. (1)* prakaituoti
persuade *v. (1)* įkalbėti, įtikinti
pervert *m. (1), f. (2)* iškrypėlis, -ė
pessimist *m. (1), f. (2)* pesimistas, -ė
petition *f. (2)* peticija
petrol *m. (1)* benzinas
pharmacist *m. (1), f. (2)* farmacininkas, -ė
pharmacy *f. (2)* vaistinė
phase *f. (2)* fazė
phenomenon *m. (1)* reiškinys
philosopher *m. (1), f. (2)* filosofas, -ė
photo camera *m. (1)* fotoaparatas
photograph *f. (2)* nuotrauka, fotografija; *v. (1)* nufotografuoti
phrase *f. (2)* frazė
physical *adj. (3)* fizinis, -ė
physician *m. (1), f. (2)* medikas, -ė
physicist *m. (1), f. (2)* fizikas, -ė
physics *f. (2)* fizika
pianist *m. (1), f. (2)* pianistas, -ė
piano *m. (1)* pianinas
pickled *adj. (1)* marinuotas, -a
pickpocket *m. (1), f. (2)* kišenvagis, -ė
picture *m. (1)* paveikslas; *v. (1)* vaizduoti
picturesque *adj. (1)* vaizdingas, -a
pie *m. (1)* pyragas
piece *m. (1)* gabalas; kąsnis
pierce *v. (1)* pradurti
piercing *adj. (2)* skvarbus, -i
pig *m. (1)* paršas; *f. (2)* kiaulė
pigeon *m. (1)* balandis, karvelis
pike *f. (2)* lydeka
pile *f. (2)* krūva
pilgrim *m. (1), f. (2)* maldininkas, -ė
pill *f. (2)* piliulė
pillowcase *m. (1)* užvalkalas
pilot *m. (1)* lakūnas, pilotas, -ė
pimple *m. (1)* spuogas
pin *m. (1)* smeigtukas
pine *f. (3)* pušis (tree); **~ cone** *m. (1)* kankorėžis; **~ wood** *adj. (3)* pušinis, -ė
pink *adj. (3)* rožinis, -ė
pioneer *m. (4), f. (2)* pionierius, -ė
pipe *f. (2)* pypkė; *m. (1)* vamzdis
pistol *m. (1)* pistoletas
pit *f. (2)* duobė; *m. (1)* kauliukas (of a fruit)
pitchfork *f. pl. (2)* šakės
pity *v. (2)* gailėtis
place *f. (2)* vieta
plague *m. (1)* maras
plain *f. (2)* lyguma; *m. (1)* planas, sumanymas; *v. (1)* planuoti
plane *m. (1)* lėktuvas
planet *f. (2)* planeta
plant *m. (1)* augalas; *f. (2)* gamykla; *v. (1)* (pa)sodinti
plaster *m. (1)* gipsas; tinkas
plastic *adj. (1)* plastiškas, -a
platform *f. (2)* platforma; tribūna
platinum *f. (2)* platina
play *theat. f. (2)* pjesė; *theat. m. (1)* spektaklis, vaidinimas; *v. (1)* lošti; *v. (1)* groti (music)
player *m. (1), f. (2)* žaidėjas, -a, lošėjas, -a
pleasantly *adv.* smagiai
please *v. (1)* įtikti
pliers *f. pl. (2)* replės
plot *m. (1)* siužetas; sklypas; *f. (2)* intriga
ploughman *m. (1)* artojas
plug *col. m. (1)* kištukas
plum/ plum tree *f. (2)* slyva
plural *f. (2)* daugiskaita
plus *m. (1)* pliusas
pneumonia *med.* plaučių uždegimas
pocket *f. (2)* kišenė; *adj. (3)* kišeninis, -ė
pocketbook užrašų knygelė
poem *m. (1)* eilėraštis; *f. (2)* poema
poet *m. (1), f. (2)* poetas, -ė
poetic *adj. (1)* poetiškas, -a
poetry *f. (2)* poezija
pogrom *m. (1)* pogromas
point *m. (1)* punktas, taškas; **~ of view** *m. (1)* požiūris
poison *m. pl. (1)* nuodai; *v. (1)* nuodyti
poisonous *adj. (1)* nuodingas, -a
poker *m. (1)* pokeris
pole *m. (1)* ašigalis; stulpas
Pole *m. (1), f. (2)* lenkas, -ė
police /police station *f. (2)* policija
police officer *m. (1), f. (2)* policininkas, -ė
Polish *adj. (1)* lenkiškas, -a
polish *m. (1)* lakas; *v. (1)* nušveisti
polite *adj. (2)* mandagus, -i

politeness *m. (1)* mandagumas
political *adj. (1)* politiškas, -a
political prisoner *m. (1), f. (2)* politkalinys, -ė
politician *m. (1), f. (2)* politikas, -ė
politics *f. (2)* politika
pond *m. (1)* tvenkinys
pool *m. (1)* biliardas
poor *m. (1), f. (2)* vargšas, -ė; *adj. (1)* neturtingas, -a, vargingas, -a
poorly *adv.* nekaip
pope *m. (4)* popiežius
popular *adj. (2)* populiarus, -i
porcelain *m. (1)* porcelianas; *adj. (3)* porcelianinis, -ė
pork *f. (2)* kiauliena
pornography *f. (2)* pornografija
porridge *f. (2)* košė
port *m. (1)* uostas
portion *f. (2)* porcija
portrait *m. (1)* portretas
Portuguese *m. (1), f. (2)* portugalas, -ė; *adj. (1)* portugališkas, -a
pose *f. (2)* poza; *v. (1)* pozuoti
position *f. (3)* padėtis; *f. (2)* pozicija; *m. (1)* postas
positive *adj. (2)* pozityvus, -i; *adj. (1)* teigiamas, -a
possibility *f. (2)* galimybė
post *m. (1)* postas; stulpas; **~ office** *m. (1)* paštas; **~ stamp** pašto ženklas; **~card** *m. (1)* atvirukas
poster *m. (1)* plakatas
posthumous *adj. (3)* pomirtinis, -ė
postpone *v. (1)* nukelti
post-war *adj. (3)* pokarinis, -ė
pot *m. (1)* puodas
potato *f. (2)* bulvė; *adj. (3)* bulvinis, -ė
potential *adj. (2)* potencialus, -i
poultry *f. (2)* vištiena
pour *v. (1)* pilti
poverty *m. (1)* skurdas, neturtas
powder *m. pl. (1)* milteliai; *f. (2)* pudra
power *f. (2)* galia; **~ plant** *f. (2)* jėgainė
powerful *adj. (1)* galingas, -a
practical *adj. (1)* praktiškas, -a
prairie *f. (2)* prerija
praise *m. (1)* pagyrimas; *v. (1)* pagirti
pray *v. (1)* melstis
prayer *f. (2)* malda
prayer book *f. (2)* maldaknygė
precipitation *m. pl. (1)* krituliai
predator *m. (1), f. (2)* plėšrūnas, -ė
predecessor *m. (1), f. (2)* pirmtakas, -ė
predict *v. (1)* išpranašauti
preface *f. (2)* pratarmė
pregnancy *m. (1)* nėštumas
pregnant *adj. f. (1)* nėščia
prehistoric *adj. (3)* priešistorinis, -ė
prep school *f. (2)* gimnazija
preparation *m. (1)* paruošimas
prepare *v. (1)* paruošti, rengti, ruošti
preposition *m. (1)* prielinksnis
prescription *m. (1)* receptas
present (gift) *f. (2)* dovana
presently *adv.* dabar
preserve *v. (1)* išsaugoti
preside (at a meeting) *v. (1)* pirmininkauti
president *m. (1), f. (2)* prezidentas, -ė
press *m. (1)* presas; *f. (2)* spauda (media)
prestige *m. (1)* prestižas
pretend *v. (1)* apsimesti
prewar *adj. (3)* prieškarinis, -ė
price *f. (2)* kaina; **~list** *m. (1)* kainoraštis
pride *m (1)* išdidumas
priest (Roman Catholic) *m. (1)* kunigas
primary *adj. (3)* pirminis, -ė
prime minister *m. (1), f. (2)* premjeras, -ė
primitive *adj. (2)* primityvus, -i
prince *m. (1)* princas, karalaitis
princess *f. (2)* princesė, karalaitė
principle *m. (1)* principas (moral); *m. (4), f. (2)* direktorius, -ė (head)
print *v. (1)* atspausdinti, išspausdinti
printer *m. (1)* spausdintuvas
priority *m. (1)* prioritetas
prism *f. (2)* prizmė
prison *m. (1)* kalėjimas
prisoner *m. (1)* kalinys, -ė
private *adj. (2)* privatus, -i
privilege *f. (2)* privilegija
privileged *adj. (1)* privilegijuotas, -a
prize *m. (1)* prizas, laimėjimas
probability *f. (2)* tikimybė

probably *part.* turbūt
problem *f. (2)* problema; *m. (1)* uždavinys
problematic *adj. (1)* problemiškas, -a
procedure *f. (2)* procedūra
process *m. (1)* procesas
producer *m. (4), f. (2)* režisierius, -ė
product *m. (1)* produktas, gaminys
production *f. (2)* gamyba
productive *adj. (2)* produktyvus, -i
productivity *m. (1)* našumas
profession *f. (2)* profesija
professional *m. (1), f. (2)* profesionalas, -ė; *adj. (2)* profesionalus, -i
professor *m. (4), f. (2)* profesorius, -ė
profile *m. (1)* profilis
profit *m. (1)* pelnas
profitable *adj. (1)* pelningas, -a
program *f. (2)* programa
progress *f. (2)* pažanga; *m. (1)* progresas; *v. (1)* progresuoti
progressive *adj. (2)* pažangus, -i
prohibition *m. (1)* draudimas
project *m. (1)* projektas
proletarian *m. (1), f. (2)* proletaras, -ė; *adj. (1)* proletariškas, -a
promise *m. (1)* pažadas; *v. (1)* (pa)žadėti, prižadėti
promissory note *m. (1)* vekselis
promote *v. (1)* pakelti
promotion *m. (1)* paaukštinimas
pronoun *m. (1)* įvardis
pronounce *v. (1)* (iš)tarti
pronunciation *m. (1)* tarimas
proof *m. (1)* įrodymas
proofreader *m. (4), f. (2)* korektorius, -ė
propaganda *f. (2)* propaganda
proper *adj. (1)* korektiškas, -a; doras, -a
property *f. (2)* nuosavybė; *m. (1)* turtas
prophylactic *adj. (3)* profilaktinis, -ė
proportion *f. (2)* proporcija
proposal *m. (1)* pasiūlymas
propose (in marriage) *v. (1)* pirštis
prosecutor's office *f. (2)* prokuratūra
prosper *v. (2)* (su)klestėti
prosthesis *m. (1)* protezas
prostitute *f. (2)* prostitutė
prostitution *f. (2)* prostitucija
protection *f. (2)* protekcija; apsauga
protein *m. pl. (1)* baltymai
protest *m. (1)* protestas; *v. (1)* protestuoti
Protestant *m. (1), f. (2)* protestantas, -ė
protocol *m. (1)* protokolas
proud *adj. (2)* išdidus, -i
proverb *f. (2)* patarlė
provide (for) *m. (1)* aprūpinti
Providence *m./f. (2)* Apvaizda
province *f. (2)* provincija; *f. (3)* sritis
provincial *m. (1), f. (2)* provincialas, -ė; *adj. (2)* provincialus, -i
provocation *f. (2)* provokacija
provoke *v. (1)* provokuoti
prudence *m. (1)* atsargumas
Prussian *m. (1), f. (2)* prūsas, -ė
psalm *f. (2)* psalmė
pseudonym *m. (1)* pseudonimas
psychiatrist *m. (1), f. (2)* psichiatras, -ė
psychiatry *med. f. (2)* psichiatrija
psychic *adj. (3)* psichinis, -ė
psycho(path) *m. (1), f. (2)* psichopatas, -ė
psychologist *m. (1), f. (2)* psichologas, -ė
psychology *f. (2)* psichologija
pub *f. (2)* aludė; *m. (1)* baras
public *f. (2)* publika; *adj. (1)* viešas, -a; **~ prosecutor** *m. (1), f. (2)* prokuroras, -ė
publication *m. (1)* leidinys
publish *v. (1)* spausdinti
publishing house *f. (2)* leidykla
pudding *m. (1)* pudingas
puddle *f. (2)* bala
pull *v. (1)* traukti
pulse *m. (1)* pulsas
pump *m. (1)* siurblys
pumpkin *m. (1)* moliūgas
punch *m. (1)* punšas
punctuation *f. (2)* skyryba
punish *v. (1)* (nu)bausti
punishment *f. (2)* bausmė
pupil *m. (1), f. (2)* mokinys, -ė, moksleivis, -ė; *m. (1)* vyzdys (of the eye)

purchase *m. (1)* pirkinys
pure *adj. (1)* grynas, -a, tyras, -a
purple *adj. (3)* violetinis, -ė
purposely *adv.* tyčia
pus *m. pl. (1)* pūliai

Q

quail *f. (2)* putpelė
qualification *f. (2)* kvalifikacija
quality *f. (2)* kokybė
quantity *m. (1)* kiekis
quarrel *m. (1)* barnis, kivirčas; *v. (1)* bartis, kivirčytis
queen *f. (2)* karalienė
question *m. (1)* klausimas; *v. (1)* kvosti
quick *adj. (1)* greitas, -a
quiet *adj. (2)* tylus, -i
quite *adv.* visai, visiškai
quote *v. (1)* cituoti

R

rabbi *m. (1)* rabinas
rabbit *m. (1)* triušis; ~ **meat** *f. (2)* triušiena
race *f. pl. (2)* lenktynės
racial *adj. (3)* rasinis, -ė
racket *f. (2)* raketė
radiator *m. (4)* radiatorius
radical *polit. m. (1), f. (2)* radikalas, -ė; *adj. (2)* radikalus, -i
radio *m. (1)* radijas
radioactive *adj. (2)* radioaktyvus, -i
radish *m. (1)* ridikėlis
rag *m. (1)* skuduras
rail(ing) *m. pl. (1)* turėklai
railway *m. (1)* geležinkelis; ~ **station** geležinkelio stotis
rain *m. (4)* lietus; *v. (1)* lyti
rainbow *f. (2)* vaivorykštė
raincoat *m. (1)* lietpaltis
rainy *adj. (1)* lietingas, -a
raise *v. (1)* auginti
raisin *f. (2)* razina
ram *m. (1)* avinas
rank *m. (1)* rangas
ransom *f. (2)* išpirka
rape *m. (1)* išprievartavimas; *v. (1)* išprievartauti
rare *adj. (1)* retas, -a
rash *adj. (1)* neapgalvotas, -a
raspberry *f. (2)* avietė
rat *f. (2)* žiurkė
rate *m. (1)* tempas
ratio *f. (2)* proporcija
rational *adj. (2)* racionalus, -i
rationalization *f. (2)* racionalizacija
rave *v. (2)* kliedėti
raven *m. (1)* varnas
raw material *f. (2)* žaliava
ray *m. (1)* spindulys
razor *m. (1)* skustuvas
reach *v. (1)* pasiekti
react *v. (1)* reaguoti
reaction *f. (2)* reakcija
read *v. (3)* (per)skaityti
reader *m. (1), f. (2)* skaitytojas, -a
reading *m. (1)* skaitymas
ready *adj.* pasiruošęs, -usi
real *adj. (2)* realus, -i; *adj. (1)* tikras, -a; ~ **estate** nekilnojamas turtas
realist *m. (1), f. (2)* realistas, -ė
reality *f. (2)* tikrovė, realybė
realize *v. (1)* įgyvendinti, realizuoti
really? *part.* nejaugi? tikrai?
reason *f. (3)* išmintis
rebel *m. (1), f. (2)* maištininkas, -ė, sukilėlis, -ė; *v. (1)* maištauti
rebellion *m. (1)* sukilimas
rebellious *adj. (1)* maištingas, -a
rebirth *m. (1)* atgimimas
rebuild *v. (3)* atstatyti
recall *v. (1)* atšaukti
receipt *m. (1)* kvitas, pakvitavimas
receipts *fin. f. pl. (2)* pajamos, įplaukos
receive *v. (1)* gauti
receiver *m. (1), f. (2)* gavėjas, -a
recently *adv.* neseniai
reception *m. (1)* priėmimas; *f. pl. (2)* vaišės
recipe *m. (1)* receptas
recognition *m. (1)* pripažinimas
recommend *v. (1)* rekomenduoti
recommendation *f. (2)* rekomendacija
reconstruction *f. (2)* rekonstrukcija
record *m. (1)* rekordas; *adj. (3)* rekordinis, -ė; ~ **holder** *m. (1), f. (2)* rekordininkas, -ė
recover *v. (1)* (pa)gyti, (pa)sveikti; atsigauti; *v. (3)* pasitaisyti

recovery *m. (1)* pagijimas
recruit *v. (1)* užverbuoti
red *adj. (1)* raudonas, -a
reference *f. (2)* nuoroda;
~ **book** *m. (1), f. (2)* vadovas, -ė
referendum *m. (1)* referendumas
refined *adj. (1)* rafinuotas, -a
reflect *v. (2)* atspindėti
reflection *m. (1)* atvaizdas
reflex *m. (1)* refleksas
reform *f. (2)* reforma;
v. (1) reformuoti; *v. (3)* pertvarkyti
Reformation *f. (2)* reformacija
refresh *v. (1)* gaivinti
refreshments *f. pl. (2)* vaišės
refrigerator *m. (1)* šaldytuvas
refuge *m. (1)* prieglobstis
refugee *m. (1), f. (2)* pabėgėlis, -ė
refuse *v. (3)* atsisakyti
regardless of napaisant
regards *m. pl. (1)* linkėjimai
regime *m. (1)* režimas
regiment *m. (1)* pulkas
region *f. (3)* sritis; *m. (1)* rajonas
register *v. (1)* (į)registruoti
registration *f. (2)* registracija
regular *adj. (2)* reguliarus, -i;
adj. (1) taisyklingas, -a
regulate *v. (1)* reguliuoti
rehabilitate *v. (1)* reabilituoti
rehabilitation *f. (2)* reabilitacija
rehearsal *f. (2)* repeticija
rehearse *v. (1)* repetuoti
relations *m. pl. (1)* santykiai
relative *m./f. (2)* giminė
relax *v. (1)* atsipalaiduoti
release *v. (1)* paleisti (a prisoner);
išleisti (a CD)
reliable *adj. (1)* patikimas, -a
relic *f. (2)* relikvija
relief *f. (2)* pašalpa
religion *f. (2)* religija
religious *adj.* tikintis, -i
reluctantly *adv.* nenoromis
rely *v. (2)* pasitikėti
remain *v. (1)* likti
remainder *f. (2)* liekana;
m. (1) likutis
remains *m. pl. (1)* palaikai
remark *f. (2)* pastaba
remedy *m. (1)* vaistas
remembrance *m. (1)*
prisiminimas; *m. (1)* likutis
remote *adj. (1)* tolimas, -a
renew *v. (1)* atnaujinti
rent *f. (2)* nuoma; *v. (1)* nuomoti(s)
reorganization *m. (1)* pertvarkymas;
f. (2) reorganizacija
reorganize *v. (3)* pertvarkyti
repair *v. (3)* (pa)taisyti, sutaisyti;
v. (1) remontuoti
repairs *m. (1)* remontas
repatriate *m. (1), f. (2)*
repatriantas, -ė
repeat *v. (1)* (pa)kartoti
replace *v. (1)* pakeisti
report *f. (2)* ataskaita;
m. (1) raportas; pranešimas;
v. (1) raportuoti
report(ing) *m. (1)* reportažas
reporter *m. (1), f. (2)* reporteris, -ė,
korespondentas, -ė
represent *v. (1)* atstovauti
representative *m. (1), f. (2)*
atstovas, -ė
repress *v. (1)* slopinti
reprimand *m. (1)* papeikimas;
v. (1) papeikti
reproduction *f. (2)* reprodukcija
reptile *m. (1)* roplys
republic *f. (2)* respublika
republican *polit. m. (1), f. (2)*
respublikonas, -ė
reputation *f. (2)* reputacija
request *m. (1)* prašymas,
reikalavimas
rescue *v. (1)* (iš)gelbėti
research *m. (1)* tyrimas;
v. (1) tyrinėti, tirti
researcher *adj. (1)* tyrėjas, -a
resemblance *m. (1)* panašumas
reservation *f. (2)* rezervacija
reserve *f. (2)* atsarga;
v. (1) rezervuoti
reserve(s) *m. (1)* rezervas
reserved *adj. (1)* rezervuotas, -a
(table); *adj. (2)* santūrus, -i
(person)
reservoir *m. (1)* rezervuaras
residence *f. (2)* rezidencija
resign *v. (1)* atsistatydinti
resist *m. (1), f. (2)* priešininkas, -ė;
v. (1) pasipriešinti
resistance *m. (1)* pasipriešinimas
resolution *f. (2)* rezoliucija;
m. (1) ryžtas
resources *m. pl. (1)* resursai
respect *f. (2)* pagarba
respectful *adj. (2)* pagarbus, -i
respond *v. (1)* reaguoti

responsibility *f. (2)* atsakomybė
responsible *adj. (1)* atsakingas, -a
rest *v. (2)* ilsėtis
restaurant *m. (1)* restoranas
restless *adj. (2)* neramus, -i
restriction *m. (1)* apribojimas
result *m. (1)* rezultatas
resume *f. (2)* reziumė
retail *adj. (3)* mažmeninis, -ė
retina *med. f. (2)* tinklainė
retreat *v. (1)* pasitraukti
retribution *m. (1)* atpildas
return *m. (1)* grįžimas; *fin.* pelnas; *v. (1)* grįžti; *v. (1)* atiduoti (~ something)
revaluation *m. (1)* perkainojimas
revenge oneself *v. (1)* keršyti
review *f. (2)* peržiūra; recenzija; *v. (1)* recenzuoti
reviewer *m. (1), f. (2)* recenzentas, -ė
revival *m. (1)* atgimimas
revolt *m. (1)* maištas; *v. (1)* papiktinti
revolution *f. (2)* revoliucija
revolutionary *m. (4), f. (2)* revoliucionierius, -ė; *adj. (3)* revoliucinis, -ė
revolver *m. (1)* revolveris
rhetoric *f. (2)* retorika
rhetorical *adj. (3)* retorinis, -ė
rhubarb *m. (1)* rabarbaras
rhyme *m. (1)* rimas
rhythm *m. (1)* ritmas
rib *m. (1)* šonkaulis
rice *m. pl. (1)* ryžiai
rich *adj. (1)* turtingas, -a
riddle *f. (2)* mįslė
ride on horseback *v. (1)* jodinėti
rider *m. (1)* raitelis
ridicule *v. (1)* išjuokti
rifle(wo)man)) *m. (1), f. (2)* šaulys, -ė
right *f. (2)* teisė; *adj. (2)* teisus, -i; **~ angle** status kampas; **~ side** *f. (2)* dešinė
ring *m. (1)* žiedas
rinse *v. (1)* skalauti; išplauti
riot *m. (1)* maištas
ripe *adj.* prinokęs, -usi
ripen *v. (1)* (pri)nokti
rise *m. (1)* pakilimas; *v. (1)* pakilti
risk *f. (2)* rizika; *v. (1)* rizikuoti
risky *adj. (1)* rizikingas, -a
ritual *m. (1)* ritualas
rival *m. (1), f. (2)* varžovas, -ė
river *f. (2)* upė
riverside *m. (1)* paupys
roach *m. (1)* tarakonas
road *m. (1)* kelias; plentas
roadside *f. (2)* pakelė
roam *v. (1)* klaidžioti
roast meat *m. (1)* kepsnys
rob *v. (1)* plėš(ikau)ti
robber *m. (1), f. (2)* plėšikas, -ė
robbery *m. (1)* (api)plėšimas
robe *m. (1)* chalatas
rock *f. (2)* uola; *v. (1)* suptis
rocket *f. (2)* raketa
rocky *adj. (1)* uolėtas, -a
rod *f. (2)* rykštė
role *theat. f. (2)* rolė; *m. (5)* vaidmuo
Roman *m. (1), f. (2)* romėnas, -ė
Romanian *m. (1), f. (2)* rumunas, -ė; *adj. (1)* rumuniškas, -a
romantic *m. (1), f. (2)* romantikas, -ė; *adj. (1)* romantiškas, -a
roof *m. (1)* stogas
room *m. (1)* kambarys; *f. (2)* patalpa
rooster *m. (1)* gaidys
root *f. (3)* šaknis
rope *f. (2)* virvė
rosary *m. (1)* Rožinis
rose *f. (2)* rožė
rosemary *m. (1)* rozmarinas
rot *v. (1)* pūti
rough *adj. (2)* šiurkštus, -i
roulette *f. (2)* ruletė
round *adj. (1)* apskritas, -a; *adj. (2)* apvalus, -i
route *m. (1)* maršrutas
routine *f. (2)* rutina
royal *adj. (1)* karališkas, -a
royalties *m. (1)* honoraras
rub *v. (1)* trinti
rubber *f. (2)* guma; *adj. (3)* guminis, -ė
ruby *m. (1)* rubinas
rude *adj. (2)* nemandagus, -i, įžūlus, -i
rue *f. (2)* rūta
ruin *v. (3)* sužlugdyti
rule *f. (2)* taisyklė
ruler *m. (1), f. (2)* valdovas, -ė; *m. (1)* Viešpats
rum *m. (1)* romas
rumor *m. (1)* gandas
run *m. (1)* reisas; *v. (1)* bėgti; **~ away** *v. (1)* pabėgti

runner *m. (1), f. (2)* bėgikas, -ė
runny nose *f. (2)* sloga
rural *adj. (1)* kaimiškas, -a
Russian *m. (1), f. (2)* rusas, -ė;
adj. (1) rusiškas, -a; ~ **Orthodox** *m. (1), f. (2)* stačiatikis, -ė
rye *m. pl. (1)* rugiai;
adj. (3) ruginis, -ė

S

sabotage *m. (1)* sabotažas
sacred *adj. (1)* šventas, -a
sacrifice *f. (2)* auka
sacrilege *f. (2)* šventvagystė
sad *adj. (2)* graudus, -i;
adj.(1) liūdnas, -a
saddle *m. (1)* balnas
safe *m. (1)* seifas;
adj. (1) nepavojingas, -a;
adj. (2) saugus, -i
safety pin *m. (1)* žiogelis
sail *f. (2)* burė
sailing *m. (1)* buriavimas
sailor *m. (1)* jūreivis
saint *adj. (1)* šventas, -a
salad (usually potato) *f. (2)* mišrainė
salary *f. (2)* alga; *m. (1)* atlyginimas
sale *m. (1)* pardavimas
salmon *f. (2)* lašiša
salon *m. (1)* salonas; *f. (2)* svetainė
salt *f. (2)* druska; *v. (3)* sūdyti
salty *adj. (2)* sūrus, -i
sanction *f. (2)* sankcija
sanctuary *f. (2)* šventykla
sand *m. (1)* smėlis
sandal *m. (1)* sandalas
sandals *f. pl. (2)* basutės
sandalwood *m. (1)* sandalas
sandwich *m. (1)* sumuštinis
sandy *adj. (1)* smėlėtas, -a
sap *f. (2)* sula
sarcastic *adj. (1)* sarkastiškas, -a
sardine *f. (2)* sardinė
satan *m. (1)* šėtonas
satanic *adj. (1)* šėtoniškas, -a
satellite *m. (1)* satelitas;
adj. (3) satelitinis, -ė
satin *m. (1)* satinas
satire *f. (2)* satyra
satiric(al) *adj. (3)* satyrinis, -ė
satisfy *v. (1)* tenkinti
Saturday *m. (1)* šeštadienis
sauce *m. (1)* padažas
sausage *f. (2)* dešra
save *v. (3)* taupyti; *v. (1)* išgelbėti
savings *f. pl. (2)* santaupos
saw *m. (1)* pjūklas
saxophone *m. (1)* saksofonas
say *v. (3)* (pa)sakyti
scab *m. (1)* šašas
scale *m. (1)* mastelis; *f. (2)* skalė
scales *f. pl. (2)* svarstyklės
scandal *m. (1)* skandalas
Scandinavian *m. (1), f. (2)* skandinavas, -ė;
adj. (1) skandinaviškas, -a
scar *m. (1)* randas
scarf *m. (1)* šalikas
scarlet fever *med. f. (2)* skarlatina
scene *theat. f. (2)* scena
scenery *m. (1)* kraštovaizdis;
theat. f. (2) dekoracija
schedule *m. (1)* tvarkaraštis
scheme *f. (2)* schema
scholar *m. (1), f. (2)* mokslininkas, -ė
scholarship *f. (2)* stipendija
school *f. (2)* mokykla
science *m. (1)* mokslas; ~ **fiction** *f. (2)* fantastika
scientific *adj. (3)* mokslinis, -ė
scientist *m. (1), f. (2)* mokslininkas, -ė
scissors *f. pl. (2)* žirklės
sclerosis *med. f. (2)* sklerozė
scold *v. (1)* barti, keikti
scooter *m. (1)* motoroleris
Scots(wo)man *m. (1), f. (2)* škotas, -ė
Scottish *adj. (1)* škotiškas, -a
scout *m. (1), f. (2)* žvalgas, -ė
scratch *v. (3)* kasyti
scream *m. (1)* riksmas; *v. (1)* rėkti
screen *m. (1)* ekranas; *f. (2)* širma
screwdriver *m. (1)* atsuktuvas
scrub *v. (1)* šveisti
sculptor *m. (1), f. (2)* skulptorius, -ė
sculpture *f. (2)* skulptūra
sea *f. (2)* jūra
seacoast *f. (2)* pakrantė
seagull *f. (2)* žuvėdra
seal *f. (2)* plomba; *v. (1)* užantspauduoti, užplombuoti
seam *f. (2)* siūlė
seamstress *m. (1), f. (2)* siuvėjas, -a
seaport *m. (1)* uostamiestis

search *f. (2)* krata; *v. (3)* ieškoti; ~ **warrant** kratos orderis
searchlight *m. (4)* prožektorius
seashore *m. (1)* krantas
seasickness *f. (2)* jūrligė
seaside *m. (1)* pajūris
season *m. (1)* sezonas
seasonal *adj. (3)* sezoninis, -ė
seat *f. (2)* vieta; *v. (1)* pasodinti
second *f. (2)* sekundė
secret *f. (3)* paslaptis; *adj. (1)* slaptas, -a; ~ **agent** *m. (1), f. (2)* žvalgybininkas, -ė
secretary *m. (4), f. (2)* sekretorius, -ė
secretly *adv.* (pa)slapčia
sect *f. (2)* sekta
section *m. (1)* pjūvis
secular *adj. (3)* pasaulietinis, -ė
securities *fin.* vertybiniai popieriai
security *f. (2)* apsauga
security alarm/ system *f. (2)* signalizacija
see *v. (3)* matyti; *v. (2)* regėti
seed *f. (2)* sėkla
seize *v. (1)* pagrobti
select *v. (1)* parinkti
self *f. (2); pron. f.* pati; *m.* pats; ~ **criticism** *f. (2)* savikritika; ~ **respect** *f. (2)* savigarba
selfish person *m. (1), f. (2)* savanaudis, -ė
sell *v. (1)* parduoti
seller *m. (1), f. (2)* pardavėjas, -a
semester *m. (1)* semestras
seminar *m. (1)* seminaras
seminary *f. (2)* seminarija
senate *m. (1)* senatas
senator *m. (4), f. (2)* senatorius, -ė
send *v. (1)* (at)siųsti, pasiųsti
sender *m. (1), f. (2)* siuntėjas, -a
senior *adj. (1)* vyriausias, -ia; ~ **citizen** *m. (1), f. (2)* pensininkas, -ė
sense *f. (2)* prasmė; *m. (1)* jausmas
sensible *adj. (1)* prasmingas, -a
sensitive *adj. (2)* jautrus, -i
sentence *v. (1)* nuteisti
sentimental *adj. (2)* sentimentalus, -i
separate *v. (1)* skirti; *adj. (1)* atskiras, -a
September *m. (1)* rugsėjis
sequel *m. (1)* tęsinys
Serb *m. (1), f. (2)* serbas, -ė
serene *adj. (1)* giedras, -a
serf *m. (1), f. (2)* baudžiauninkas, -ė
serfdom *f. (2)* baudžiava
sergeant *m. (1), f. (2)* seržantas, -ė
serial *adj. (3)* serijinis, -ė
series *f. (2)* serija
serious *adj. (1)* rimtas, -a
sermon *m. (1)* pamokslas
servant *m. (1), f. (2)* tarnas, -aitė
serve *v. (1)* tarnauti
service *m. (1)* aptarnavimas; *f. (2)* paslauga; tarnyba; ~ **staff** aptarnaujantis personalas
session *f. (2)* sesija
set *theat. f. (2)* dekoracija; *m. (1)* komplektas; *adj. (1)* nustatytas, -a
settle *v. (1)* įsikurti
seven *num.* septyni, -ios
several *pron. m. sg.* keletas; *pron. m. pl.* keli, -ios
severe *adj. (2)* smarkus, -i
sew *v. (1)* siūti
sex *f. (3)* lytis
sexual *adj. (3)* lytinis, -ė, seksualinis, -ė; *adj. (2)* seksualus, -i; ~ **disease (STD)** lytinė liga
sexual intercourse lytinis aktas
Seym (Lithuanian Parliament) *m. (1)* Seimas
shack *f. (2)* lūšna, trobelė
shade *m. (1)* šešėlis; atspalvis, niuansas
shadow *m. (1)* šešėlis
shake *v. (3)* (pa)purtyti
shallow *adj. (2)* negilus, -i
shame *f. (2)* gėda
shampoo *m. (1)* šampūnas
share *f. (3)* dalis
shark *m. (1)* ryklys
sharp *adj. (2)* aštrus, -i
sharpen *v. (1)* galąsti
shave *v. (1)* skusti
shaving cream skutimosi kremas
shawl *f. (2)* skara
she *pron. f.* ji
sheep *f. (3)* avis
sheik *m. (1)* šeichas
shell *f. (2)* kriauklė
shelter *m. (1)* prieglobstis; *f. (2)* priedanga, slėptuvė
shepherd *m. (5), f. (2)* piemuo, -enė
sheriff *m. (1)* šerifas
shield *m. (1)* skydas
shift *f. (2)* pamaina
shin *f. (2)* blauzda

shine *v. (1)* blizgėti; šviesti; *v. (2)* spindėti
ship *m. (1)* laivas
shirt *m. pl. (1)* marškiniai
shiver *m. (1)* drebulys, šiurpas
shock *m. (1)* šokas
shoe *m. (1)* batas; ~ **polish** (batų) tepalas
shoot *v. (3)* (su)šaudyti; *v. (1)* filmuoti
shop *f. (2)* parduotuvė; ~ **assistant/ keeper** *m. (1), f. (2)* pardavėjas, -a
shopping *m. (1)* apsipirkimas; *v. (1)* apsipirkti
short *adj. (1)* trumpas, -a; žemas, -a
shortage *m. (1)* trūkumas
shorten *v. (1)* sutrumpinti
shot *m. (1)* šūvis; ~ **glass** *f. (2)* taurelė
shoulders *m. pl. (1)* pečiai
shout *v. (1)* rėkti
show *v. (3)* parodyti
shower *m. (1)* dušas
shut *v. (3)* uždaryti
shy *adj. (2)* nedrąsus, -i
sick sergantis, -i
side *m. (1)* šonas; *f. (2)* pusė
sidewalk *m. (1)* šaligatvis
sigh *m. (1)* atodūsis
sight *m. (1)* reginys; matymas
sign *f. (2)* iškaba; žymė; *m. (1)* ženklas; *v. (3)* pasirašyti
signal *m. (1)* signalas; *m. (1)* ženklas; *v. (1)* signalizuoti
signature *m. (1)* parašas
silence *f. (2)* tyla
silk *m. (1)* šilkas; *adj. (3)* šilkinis, -ė
silver *m. (1)* sidabras; *adj. (3)* sidabrinis, -ė
simple *adj. (1)* (pa)prastas, -a, nesudėtingas, -a
simplicity *m. (1)* paprastumas
sin *f. (2)* nuodėmė
sing *v. (1)* giedoti
singer *m. (1), f. (2)* dainininkas, -ė
single *adj. (1)* vienišas, -a; ~ **person** *m. (1), f. (2)* viengungis, -ė
sink *f. (2)* kriauklė; *v. (1)* skęsti
sir *m. (1)* ponas
siren *f. (2)* sirena
sirloin *f. (2)* nugarinė
sister *f. (2)* sesė; *f. (5)* sesuo
sister-in-law (brother's wife) *f. (2)* brolienė
sit *v. (2)* sėdėti; ~ **down** *v. (1)* (atsi)sėsti
sitting room *f. (2)* svetainė
situation *f. (2)* situacija
six *num.* šeši, -ios
size *m. (1)* dydis
ski *v. (1)* slidinėti
skier *m. (1), f. (2)* slidininkas, -ė
skiing *m. (1)* slidinėjimas
skin *f. (2)* oda
skirt *m. (1)* sijonas
skis *f. pl. (2)* slidės
skull *f. (2)* kaukolė
sky *m. (4)* dangus
skyscraper *m. (1)* dangoraižis
slaughter *f. pl. (2)* žudynės; *v. (1)* skersti
slaughterhouse *f. (2)* skerdykla
Slav *m. (1), f. (2)* slavas, -ė
slave *m. (1), f. (2)* vergas, -ė
slavery *f. (2)* vergija
Slavic *adj. (1)* slaviškas, -a
sleep *m. (1)* miegas; *v. (1)* miegoti
sleeping bag *m. (1)* miegmaišis
sleeping car miegamasis vagonas (train)
sleepiness *m. (1)* mieguistumas
sleepless *adj. (3)* bemiegis, -ė
sleepwalker *m. (1), f. (2)* lunatikas, -ė
sleepy *adj. (1)* mieguistas, -a
sleeve *f. (2)* rankovė
sleeveless *adj. (3)* berankovis, -ė
slender *adj. (1)* lieknas, -a, plonas, -a
slice *f. (2)* riekė; *v. (3)* raikyti
slide *f. (2)* skaidrė; *v. (1)* slysti
slip *v. (1)* (pa)slysti
slipper *f. (2)* šlepetė, šliurė
slippery *adj. (2)* slidus, -i
slogan *m. (1)* šūkis
slope *m. (1)* šlaitas
sloping *adj. (2)* nuolaidus, -i
slow *adj. (1)* lėtas, -a
sly *adj. (1)* suktas, -a
small *adj. (2)* smulkus, -i; *adj. (1)* mažas, -a
smallpox *med. m. pl. (1)* raupai
smell *m. (1)* kvapas; *f. (2)* uoslė; *v. (1)* kvepėti; *v. (3)* uostyti
smile *f. (2)* šypsena; *v. (3)* šypsotis
smoke *m. pl. (1)* dūmai; *v. (3)* rūkyti

smoked *adj. (1)* rūkytas, -a
smuggler *m. (1), f. (2)* kontrabandininkas, -ė
smuggling *f. (2)* kontrabanda
snack *m. (1)* užkandis; *v. (1)* užkandžiauti; ~ **bar** *f. (2)* užkandinė
snail *f. (2)* sraigė
snake *f. (2)* gyvatė
sneeze *m. (1)* čiaudulys; *v. (2)* čiaudėti
sniper *m. (1), f. (2)* snaiperis, -ė
snob *m. (1), f. (2)* snobas, -ė
snore *v. (1)* knarkti
snout *m. (1)* snukis; šnipas
snow *m. (1)* sniegas; *v. (1)* snigti; **~drift** *f. (3)* pusnis; **~flake** *f. (2)* snaigė; **~storm** *f. (2)* pūga
so *adv.* šiaip; *conj.* tad; *part.* taip; ~ **many** *adv.* tiek; ~ **much** *adv.* tiek
soap *m. (1)* muilas; ~ **dish** *f. (2)* muilinė
sober *adj. (2)* blaivus, -i
soccer *m. (1)* futbolas; ~ **match** futbolo rungtynės
social *adj. (3)* socialinis, -ė
Social Democrat *polit. m. (1), f. (2)* socialdemokratas, -ė
socialism *m. (1)* socializmas
socialist *m. (1), f. (2)* socialistas, -ė
society *f. (2)* visuomenė
sociologist *m. (1), f. (2)* sociologas, -ė
sociology *f. (2)* sociologija
sock *f. (2)* puskojinė
sodium *m. (1)* natris
soft *adj. (1)* minkštas, -a; *adj. (2)* švelnus, -i
soften *v. (1)* minkštėti
softness *m. (1)* švelnumas
soil *f. (2)* žemė, dirva; *v. (1)* purvinti, užteršti
soldier *m. (1)* kareivis; ~ **barracks** *f. pl. (2)* kareivinės
sole *adj. (3)* vienintelis, -ė
solist *m. (1), f. (2)* solistas, -ė
solitude *f. (2)* vienatvė
solution *m. (1)* tirpalas
some *m. (1)* truputis; šiek tiek
sometimes *adv.* kartais
son *m. (4)* sūnus
song *f. (2)* daina
son-in-law *m. (1)* žentas
soothe *v. (1)* nuraminti
soprano *m. (1)* sopranas
sorry atsiprašau
soul *f. (2)* siela
sound *m. (1)* garsas
soundless *adj. (3)* begarsis, -ė
soup *f. (2)* sriuba
sour *adj. (2)* rūgštus, -i; ~ **cream** *f. (2)* grietinė
source *m. (1)* šaltinis
south *m. pl. (4)* pietūs; *adj. (3)* pietinis, -ė
southeast *m. pl. (1)* pietryčiai
southern *adj. (3)* pietinis, -ė
southerner *m. (1), f. (2)* pietietis, -ė
southwest *m. pl. (1)* pietvakariai
souvenir *m. (1)* suvenyras; *adj. (3)* suvenyrinis, -ė
sovereign *adj. (2)* suverenus, -i
sovereignty *m. (1)* suverenitetas
Soviet *f. (2)* taryba; *adj. (3)* tarybinis, -ė
soybean *f. (2)* soja
space *f. (2)* erdvė; vieta; *m. (1)* tarpas
Spaniard *m. (1), f. (2)* ispanas, -ė
Spanish *adj. (1)* ispaniškas, -a
sparrow *m. (1)* žvirblis
speak *v. (1)* kalbėti
special *adj. (2)* specialus, -i
specialist *m. (1), f. (2)* specialistas, -ė
specialty *f. (2)* specialybė
specific *adj. (1)* specifiškas, -a; *adj. (2)* konkretus, -i
spectacle *m. (1)* reginys
spectacles *m. pl. (1)* akiniai
spectator *m. (1), f. (2)* žiūrovas, -ė
spell *m. pl. (1)* kerai
spelling *f. (2)* rašyba
spend *v. (1)* praleisti
sphere *f. (2)* sfera
sphinx *m. (1)* sfinksas
spices *m. pl. (1)* prieskoniai
spicy *adj. (2)* aštrus, -i
spider *m. (1)* voras
spinach *m. pl. (1)* špinatai
spirit *f. (2)* dvasia
spirituality *m. (1)* dvasingumas
spit *v. (3)* spjaudyti
splash *v. (3)* taškyti
splendid *adj. (2)* puikus, -i, prašmatnus, -i
splendor *f. (2)* puikybė
splinter *f. (3)* rakštis

spoil *v. (1)* lepinti, pagadinti, sugadinti
sponge *f. (2)* kempinė
sponsor *m. (1), f. (2)* rėmėjas, -a
spoon *m. (1)* šaukštas
sport *m. (1)* sportas
sports(wo)man *m. (1), f. (2)* sportininkas, -ė
spot *f. (2)* dėmė; *m. (1)* taškas
spouse *m. (1), f. (2)* sutuoktinis, -ė
spread *v. (1)* (pa)plisti
spring *m. (1)* pavasaris; *m. (1)* šaltinis (water)
sprout *m. (1)* daigas
spy *m. (1), f. (2)* šnipas, -ė, žvalgas, -ė; *v. (1)* šnipinėti
square *f. (2)* aikštė; *m. (1)* skveras; kvadratas
squat *v. (1)* pritūpti; *v. (2)* tupėti
squirrel *f. (2)* voverė
stab *v. (1)* durti; papjauti
stabilize *v. (1)* stabilizuoti
stable *f. (2)* arklidė; *m. (1)* tvartas; *adj. (2)* stabilus, -i
stack *f. (3)* šūsnis
stadium *m. (1)* stadionas
stage *theat. f. (2)* scena; *v. (3)* pastatyti
stain *f. (2)* dėmė
stained *adj. (1)* dėmėtas, -a
stairs *m. pl. (1)* laiptai
stamp *m. (1)* štampas
stand *f. (2)* tribūna; *m. (1)* stendas; *v. (2)* stovėti; *v. (2)* stovėti; **~ up** *v. (1)* atsistoti
standard *f. (2)* norma; *m. (1)* standartas; *adj. (3)* standartinis, -ė
star *f. (2)* žvaigždė
stare *m. (1)* žvilgsnis
starry *adj. (1)* žvaigždėtas, -a
start *v. (1)* pradėti
starvation *m. (1)* badas
starve *v. (1)* badauti
state *f. (2)* būsena, būklė; valstybė; valstija; *adj. (3)* valstybinis, -ė; **~ emblem** *m. (1)* herbas
station *f. (3)* stotis
statistics *f. (2)* statistika; *adj. (3)* statistinis, -ė
statue *f. (2)* statula
statuette *f. (2)* statulėlė
status *m. (1)* statusas
statute *m. (1)* įstatymas
stay *v. (1)* likti
steady *adj. (2)* patvarus, -i
steak *m. (1)* kepsnys
steal *v. (1)* (pa)vogti
steam *m. (1)* garas
steel *m. (1)* plienas; *adj. (3)* plieninis, -ė
steer *v. (1)* vairuoti
steering wheel *m. (1)* vairas
stem *m. (1)* stiebas; kamienas
step *f. (2)* pakopa; *m. (1)* žingsnis; *v. (1)* žengti
stepdaughter *f. (2)* podukra
stepfather *m. (1)* patėvis
stepmother *f. (2)* pamotė
stepson *m. (1)* posūnis
sterile *adj. (2)* sterilus, -i
stick *f. (2)* lazda; *m. (1)* pagalys
still *part.* dar; visgi
still-life *m. (1)* natiurmortas
sting *v. (1)* įgelti; įkąsti
stingy *adj. (2)* šykštus, -i
stink *f. (2)* smarvė; *v. (1)* smirdėti, dvokti
stir *v. (3)* maišyti; *v. (1)* pajudinti
stocking *f. (2)* kojinė
stomach *m. (1)* pilvas; skrandis; **~ ache** pilvo/ skrandžio skausmas
stone *m. (5)* akmuo; *adj. (3)* mūrinis, -ė
stool *f. (2)* taburetė
stop *v. (1)* liautis (yourself); *v. (3)* stabdyti (somebody/ something else)
storage room *m. (1)* sandėlis
store *f. (2)* krautuvė, parduotuvė
storm *f. (2)* audra, vėtra
story *f. (2)* istorija
straight *adj. (2)* teisus, -i
strange *adj. (1)* keistas, -a (odd); svetimas, -a, nepažįstamas, -a (unknown)
strangle *v. (1)* (pa)smaugti
strategic *adj. (3)* strateginis, -ė
strategy *f. (2)* strategija
straw *m. (1)* šiaudas
strawberry *f. (2)* braškė
stream *m. (1)* srautas
street *f. (2)* gatvė; **~ smart** *adj. (2)* apsukrus, -i, gudrus, -i
streetcar *m. (4)* tramvajus
strength *f. (2)* jėga; *m. (1)* stiprumas
strengthen *v. (1)* sustiprėti
strenuous *adj. (1)* įtemptas, -a

stretch *v. (1)* tempti; tįsti;
 ~ **oneself** *v. (3)* rąžytis
strict *adj. (1)* griežtas, -a;
 adj. (2) reiklus, -i
strike *m. (1)* streikas; *v. (1)* suduoti
string *f. (2)* styga;
 adj. (3) styginis, -ė
striped *adj. (1)* dryžuotas, -a
stroke *m. (1)* smūgis;
 v. (3) paglostyti
stroll *m. (1)* pasivaikščiojimas
strong *adj. (2)* smarkus, -i, stiprus, -i;
 adj. (1) tvirtas, -a
structure *f. (2)* sandara
struggle *f. (2)* kova
stubborn *adj.* užsispyręs, -usi
student *m. (1), f. (2)* studentas, -ė;
 adj. (1) studentiškas, -a
studies *f. pl. (2)* studijos
studio *f. (2)* studija
study *v. (1)* studijuoti
stump *m. (1)* kelmas
stupid *adj. (1)* kvailas, -a
sturgeon *m. (1)* eršketas
style (of a dress) *m. (1)* fasonas
stylish *adj. (1)* stilingas, -a
stylist *m. (1), f. (2)* stilistas, -ė
subconscious *adj. (3)*
 pasąmoninis, -ė
subconsciousness *f. (2)* pasąmonė
subject *m. (1)* subjektas; siužetas;
 f. (2) tema
sublease *f. (2)* subnuoma
submarine *adj. (3)* povandeninis, -ė;
 ~ **ship** povandeninis laivas
subordinate *adj. (2)* pavaldus, -i
subscribe *v. (1)* prenumeruoti
subscriber *m. (4), f. (2)*
 prenumeratorius, -ė
subscription *f. (2)* prenumerata
subsidiary *m. (1)* filialas
subsidy *f. (2)* dotacija
substitute *m. (1)* pakaitalas,
 surogatas; *v. (1)* pakeisti
subtle *adj. (2)* subtilus, -i
suburb *m. (1)* priemiestis
suburban *adj. (3)* priemiestinis, -ė
subway *m. (n.d.)* metro
success *m. (1)* pasisekimas;
 f. (2) sėkmė
successful *adj. (1)* sėkmingas, -a
such *pron. f.* tokia, *pron. m.* toks
sudden *adj. (2)* staigus, -i
suddenly *adv.* staiga
suede *adj. (3)* zomšinis, -ė
suffer *v. (1)* (nu)kentėti, kęsti
suffix *f. (2)* priesaga
suffocate *v. (1)* dusti, trokšti
sugar *m. (4)* cukrus
suicide *f. (2)* savižudybė
suit *m. (1)* kostiumas
suitable *adj. (1)* tinkamas, -a
suitcase *m. (1)* lagaminas
sum *f. (2)* suma
summary *f. (2)* reziumė, santrauka
summer *f. (2)* vasara;
 adj. (3) vasarinis, -ė
summit *f. (2)* viršūnė
summons *m. (1)* šaukimas
sun *f. (2)* saulė
sunblock kremas nuo saulės
sunburn *m. (1)* nudegimas
Sunday *m. (1)* sekmadienis;
 adj. (3) sekmadieninis, -ė
sunflower *f. (2)* saulėgrąža
sunglasses akiniai nuo saulės
sunny *adj. (1)* saulėtas, -a
sunrise *m. (1)* saulėtekis
sunset *m. (1)* saulėlydis
supervise *v. (2)* prižiūrėti
supervision *f. (2)* priežiūra
supervisor *m. (1), f. (2)*
 prižiūrėtojas, -a
supplier *m. (1), f. (2)* tiekėjas, -a
supply *f. (2)* pasiūla; parama
support *m. (1)* ramstis; *v. (1)*
 (pa)remti, šelpti; *v. (3)* palaikyti
supporter *m. (1), f. (2)* rėmėjas, -a
suppose *v. (1)* tarti
surface *m. (4)* paviršius
surgeon *m. (1), f. (2)* chirurgas, -ė
surgery *med. f. (2)* operacija;
 chirurgija
surplus *m. (4)* perteklius
surprise *m. (1)* nustebimas;
 siurprizas; *f. (2)* staigmena;
 v. (1) nustebinti
suspect *m. (1), f. (2)* įtariamasis,
 -oji; *v. (1)* įtarti
suspicion *m. (1)* įtarimas
suspicious *adj. (1)* įtartinas, -a
swallow *v. (1)* (pra)ryti, nuryti
swamp *f. (2)* pelkė
swan *f. (2)* gulbė
swear in *v. (1)* prisaikdinti
sweat *m. (1)* prakaitas;
 v. (1) prakaituoti
sweater *m. (1)* megztinis
sweaty *adj. (1)* prakaituotas, -a
Swede *m. (1), f. (2)* švedas, -ė

Swedish *adj. (1)* švediškas, -a
sweet *m. (1)* saldainis;
adj. (2) saldus, -i; meilus, -i;
adj. (1) mielas, -a
sweeten *v. (1)* pasaldinti
sweetener *m. (1)* saldiklis
sweetheart *adj.* mylimasis, -oji
swell *v. (1)* (iš)tinti
swelling *m. (1)* ištinimas
swim *v. (1)* plaukti
swimmer *m. (1), f. (2)* plaukikas, -ė
swimming pool *m. (1)* baseinas
swimming suit maudymosi kostiumėlis
swing *f. pl. (2)* sūpuoklės;
v. (1) suptis
Swiss *m. (1), f. (2)* šveicaras, -ė;
adj. (1) šveicariškas, -a
switch *m. (1)* jungiklis;
~ **off** *v. (1)* išjungti; ~ **on the light** *v. (1)* uždegti šviesą
sword *m. (1)* kardas
syllable *m. (5)* skiemuo
symbol *m. (1)* simbolis
symbolic *adj. (3)* simbolinis, -ė
sympathy *f. (2)* užuojauta
symphony *f. (2)* simfonija;
~ **orchestra** simfoninis orkestras
symptom *m. (1)* simptomas, požymis
synagogue *f. (2)* sinagoga
synonym *m. (1)* sinonimas
syphilis *med. m. (1)* sifilis
syrup *m. (1)* sirupas
system *f. (2)* santvarka; sistema
systematic *adj. (1)* planingas, -a

T

table *m. (1)* stalas; *adj. (3)* stalinis, -ė; ~ **of contents** *m. (1)* turinys
tablecloth *f. (2)* staltiesė
tact *m. (1)* taktas
tactful *adj. (1)* taktiškas, -a
tail *f. (2)* uodega
tailor *m. (1), f. (2)* siuvėjas, -a
tailor's shop *f. (2)* siuvykla
take *v. (1)* imti;
~ **a walk** *v. (1)* pasivaikščioti;
~ **advantage** *v. (1)* pasinaudoti;
~ **away** *v. (1)* paimti, atimti;
~ **care (of)** *v. (1)* globoti;
~ **notes** *v. (1)* konspektuoti;
~ **off** *v. (3)* išvykti; pakilti (plane);
~ **part** *v. (1)* dalyvauti
talent *m. (1)* talentas
talented *adj. (1)* talentingas, -a
talk *f. (2)* šneka; *v. (1)* šnekėtis
talkative *adj. (2)* šnekus, -i
tall *adj. (1)* aukštas, -a
tame *v. (3)* tramdyti;
adj. (1) prijaukintas, -a
tan *v. (1)* nudegti
tangerine *m. (1)* mandarinas
tank *m. (1)* tankas; bakas
tap *m. (1)* čiaupas, kranas
tape-recorder *m. (1)* magnetofonas
tapestry *m. (1)* gobelenas
tar *f. (2)* smala
Tartar *m. (4), f. (2)* totorius, -ė;
adj. (1) totoriškas, -a
taste *m. (1)* skonis; *v. (1)* ragauti
tasteful *adj. (1)* skoningas, -a
tasteless *adj. (3)* beskonis, -ė
tax *m. (1)* mokestis; ~ **free** *adj. (1)* neapmokestinamas, -a
taxi taksi
tea *f. (2)* arbata; ~ **kettle** *m. (1)* virdulys
teach *v. (3)* dėstyti, mokyti
teacher *m. (1), f. (2)* mokytojas, -a
teaching *m. (1)* mokymas
team *f. (2)* komanda; brigada
teapot *m. (1)* arbatinukas
tear *f. (2)* ašara; *v. (1)* (su)plyšti
tease *v. (1)* erzinti
teaspoon *m. (1)* šaukštelis
technical *adj. (3)* techninis, -ė
technique *f. (2)* technika
technology *f. (2)* technologija
teeth *m. pl. (3)* dantys
teenager *m. (1), f. (2)* paauglys, -ė
telecommunications
telegram *f. (2)* telegrama
telegraph *m. (1)* telegrafas
telephone *m. (1)* telefonas;
~ **receiver** *m. (1)* ragelis
television *f. (2)* televizija
tell *v. (1)* liepti
temper *m. (1)* būdas, charakteris
temperature *f. (2)* temperatūra
tempest *f. (2)* vėtra
temple *m. (1)* smilkinys;
f. (2) šventykla
temporary *adj. (1)* laikinas, -a
tempt *v. (3)* gundyti
temptation *f. (2)* pagunda
ten *num.* dešimt
tenant *m. (1), f. (2)* nuomininkas, -ė
tender *adj. (2)* meilus, -i, švelnus, -i

tennis *m. (1)* tenisas; ~ **player** *m. (1), f. (2)* tenisininkas, -ė
tenor *m. (1)* tenoras
tense *adj. (1)* įtemptas, -a
tension *f. (2)* įtampa
tent *f. (2)* palapinė
term *m. (1)* terminas; ~ **paper** *m. (1)* referatas
terminology *f. (2)* terminologija
terrible *adj. (2)* baisus, -i; *adj. (1)* siaubingas, -a
territorial *adj. (3)* teritorinis, -ė
territory *f. (2)* teritorija
terror *m. (1)* siaubas
test *m. (1)* tyrimas
testify *v. (1)* (pa)liudyti
tetanus *med. f. (2)* stabligė
text *m. (1)* tekstas
textbook *m. (1)* vadovėlis
textile *f. (2)* tekstilė
than *part.* negu; *prep.* už
thank *v. (1)* (pa)dėkoti; ~ **you** *inter.* ačiū
thanks dėkui
that *pron. f.* ana, *m.* anas; *conj.* kad; *pron.* tai; *pron. f.* ta, *m.* tas; ~ **one** *pron. f.* ana, *m.* anas
theater *m. (1)* teatras
theft *f. (2)* vagystė
then *adv.* tada, tuomet
theoretic(al) *adj. (3)* teorinis, -ė
theoretically *adv.* teoriškai
theory *f. (2)* teorija
there *adv.* ten(ai)
therefore *conj.* tad
thermometer *m. (1)* termometras
these *m.* šie, *f.* šios
thesis *m. (1)* teiginys; *f. (2)* tezė
they *pron. m. pl.* jie; *pron. f. pl.* jos
thick *adj. (1)* storas, -a; tirštas, -a; *adj. (2)* tankus, -i
thief *m. (1), f. (2)* vagis, -ilė
thin *adj. (1)* plonas, -a, liesas, -a; retas, -a; *adj. (2)* smulkus, -i
thing *m. (1)* daiktas; dalykas
think *v. (3)* manyti, mąstyti; *v. (1)* pagalvoti
thinking *m. (1)* mąstymas
thirst *m. (1)* troškulys
thirsty ištroškęs, -usi
this *pron. f.* ši, *m.* šis;
thorough *adj. (2)* kruopštus, -i, nuodugnus, -i
thoroughly *adv.* nuodugniai
though *conj.* nors
thought *f. (3)* mintis
thoughtful *adj. (1)* rūpestingas, -a
thousand *num. m. (1)* tūkstantis
thread *m. (1)* siūlas
threat *m. (1)* grasinimas; *f. (2)* grėsmė
threaten *v. (1)* grasinti
three *num.* trys
threefold *adj. (1)* trigubas, -a
threshold *m. (1)* slenkstis
throat *f. (2)* gerklė, ryklė
throne *m. (1)* sostas
through *prep.* per, pro
throw *v. (1)* mesti; ~ **away** *v. (1)* išmesti
thumb *m. (1)* nykštys
thunder *m. (1)* griaustinis, perkūnas; *v. (1)* griaudėti, griausti
Thursday *m. (1)* ketvirtadienis
thus *conj.* taigi
tick *f. (2)* erkė
ticket *m. (1)* bilietas
tickle *v. (1)* kutenti
tidy *adj. (1)* tvarkingas, -a
tie *m. (1)* kaklaraištis; *v. (1)* (pri)rišti
tiger *m. (1), f. (2)* tigras, -ė
tile *f. (2)* čerpė
timber *f. (2)* mediena
time *m. (1)* laikas; metas; *m. (1)* sykis
tin box *f. (2)* skardinė
tiny *adj. (1)* mikroskopinis, -ė
tip *m. pl. (1)* arbatpinigiai
tire *f. (2)* padanga
tired (to get) *v. (1)* pavargti
title *m. (1)* pavadinimas; titulas
to *prep.* prie; pas
to (direction) *prep.* į
toad *f. (2)* rupūžė
toast *m. (1)* tostas
tobacco *m. (1)* tabakas
today *adv.* šiandien
together *adv.* kartu
toilet *m. (1)* tualetas; ~ **paper** tualetinis popierius
tolerable *adj. (1)* pakenčiamas, -a
tolerate *v. (1)* toleruoti
tomato *m. (1)* pomidoras
tomorrow *f. (2)* rytdiena; *m. (4)* rytojus; *adv.* ryt(oj)
ton *f. (2)* tona
tone *m. (1)* tonas
tongue *m. (1)* liežuvis
tonight *adv.* šianakt

tonsillitis *med. f. (2)* angina
too much per daug
tool *m. (1)* įrankis
tooth *m. (3)* dantis
toothbrush *m. (1)* (dantų) šepetėlis
toothpaste dantų pasta
top *f. (2)* viršūnė; *m. (4)* viršus
tornado *m. (1)* uraganas
torture *v. (1)* kankinti
touch *m. (1)* prisilietimas;
v. (1) čiupinėti, (pa)liesti, prisiliesti
tourism *m. (1)* turizmas
tourist *m. (1), f. (2)* turistas, -ė;
adj. (3) turistinis, -ė
tournament *m. (1)* turnyras
towel *m. (1)* rankšluostis
tower *m. (1)* bokštas
town *m. (1)* miestas
town (small) *m. (1)* miestelis
toy *m. (1)* žaislas
tractor *m. (4)* traktorius;
~ **driver** *m. (1), f. (2)* traktorininkas, -ė
trade *f. (2)* prekyba; *v. (1)* prekiauti
tradition *f. (2)* tradicija
traditional *adj. (3)* tradicinis, -ė
traffic *m. (1)* eismas**;**
~ **lights** *m. (1)* šviesoforas
tragedy *f. (2)* tragedija
tragic *adj. (1)* tragiškas, -a
trailer *f. (2)* priekaba
train *m. (1)* traukinys; *v. (3)* ugdyti;
v. (1) auklėti; ~ **car** *m. (1)* vagonas
train station traukinių/geležinkelio stotis
trait *m. (1)* bruožas
traitor *m. (1), f. (2)* išdavikas, -ė
tram(way) *m. (4)* tramvajus
tramp *f. (2)* valkata
transaction *m. (1)* sandėris
transfer *m. (1)* perdavimas
transitional *adj. (1)* pereinamas, -a
translation *m. (1)* vertimas
translator *m. (1), f. (2)* vertėjas, -a
transmission *m. (1)* perdavimas
transmit *v. (1)* perduoti
transparent *adj. (1)* permatomas, -a
transplant *med. v. (1)* persodinti
transport *m. (1)* transportas;
v. (1) pervežti
transportation *m. (1)* susisiekimas
trap *m. pl. (1)* spąstai
trash *m. (1)* šlamštas
travel *v. (1)* keliauti;
adj. (3) kelioninis, -ė
traveler *m. (1)* keliautojas, -a
traveler's check kelioninis čekis
tray *m. (1)* padėklas
treasure *f. (2)* brangenybė;
m. (1) lobis
treasurer *m. (1), f. (2)* iždininkas, -ė
treasury *m. (1)* iždas
treat *med. v. (3)* gydyti;
v. (1) vaišinti
tree *m. (1)* medis;
~ **trunk** *m. (1)* kamienas
trial *m. (1)* bandymas
triangle *m. (1)* trikampis
triangular *adj. (3)* trikampis, -ė
tribunal *m. (1)* tribunolas
tribune *f. (2)* tribūna
tribute *f. (2)* duoklė
trip *f. (2)* ekskursija, kelionė;
m. (1) reisas
tripod *m. (1)* trikojis
trolley(bus) *m. (1)* troleibusas
trophy *m. (4)* trofėjus;
adj. (3) trofėjinis, -ė
trouble *f. (2)* bėda
troupe *f. (2)* trupė
trousers *f. pl. (2)* kelnės
trout *m. (1)* upėtakis
truce *f. pl. (2)* paliaubos
truck *m. (1)* sunkvežimis
true *adj. (1)* tikras, -a
trumpet *m. (1)* trimitas
trunk *m. (5)* liemuo
trust *v. (2)* pasitikėti
truth *f. (2)* teisybė, tiesa
tuberculosis *med. f. (2)* tuberkuliozė
Tuesday *m. (1)* antradienis
tulip *f. (2)* tulpė
tumor *med. m. (1)* auglys
tundra *f. (2)* tundra
tunnel *m. (1)* tunelis
turbine *f. (2)* turbina
Turk *m. (1), f. (2)* turkas, -ė
turkey *m. (1)* kalakutas;
~ **meat** *f. (2)* kalakutiena
Turkish *adj. (1)* turkiškas, -a
turn *v. (1)* pasukti;
~ **around** *v. (1)* atsisukti;
~ **away** *v. (1)* nusisukti;
~ **into** *v. (1)* pavirsti;
~ **off** *v. (1)* išjungti;
~ **out** *v. (1)* paaiškėti

turn(ing) *m. (1)* posūkis
turnip *f. (2)* ropė
tuxedo *m. (1)* frakas, smokingas
TV set *m. (1)* televizorius
tweezers *m. (1)* pincetas
twin *m. (1), f. (2)* dvynys, -ė
two *num.* du, dvi
type *m. (1)* tipas
typical *adj. (1)* tipiškas, -a

U

ugly *adj. (2)* bjaurus, -i
Ukrainian *m. (1), f. (2)* ukrainietis; *adj. (1)* ukrainietiškas, -a
umbrella *m. (1)* skėtis
unacceptable *adj. (1)* nepriimtinas, -a
unanimously *adv.* vienbalsiai
unarmed *adj. (3)* beginklis, -ė
unbutton *v. (1)* atsegti
uncertain *adj. (1)* netikras, -a
uncle *m. (2)* dėdė
uncomfortable *adj. (2)* nepatogus, -i
uncover *v. (1)* atidengti
under *prep.* po
underage *m. (1), f. (2)* nepilnametis, -ė
underground *m. (1)* pogrindis; *adj. (3)* pogrindinis, -ė; požeminis, -ė
understand *v. (1)* suprasti
underwear *f. pl. (2)* kelnaitės
unemployed *m. (1), f. (2)* bedarbis, -ė
unemployment *m. (1)* nedarbas
unexpected *adj. (1)* netikėtas, -a, nelauktas, -a
unfaithful *adj. (1)* neištikimas, -a
unfit *adj. (1)* netinkamas, -a
unfortunately *inter.* deja
unhappy *adj. (1)* nelaimingas, -a
unhealthy *adj. (1)* nesveikas, -a, ligotas, -a
uniform *f. (2)* uniforma; *adj. (3)* uniforminis, -ė; *adj. (2)* tolygus, -i
uninhibited *adj. (1)* negyvenamas, -a
unintentionally *adv.* netyčia
union *f. (2)* sąjunga
unite *v. (1)* su(si)vienyti
United Nations Jungtinių Tautų Organizacija
United States of America (USA) Jungtinės Amerikos Valstijos (JAV)
unity *f. (2)* vienybė
universal *adj. (2)* universalus, -i; *adj. (3)* visuotinis, -ė
universe *f. (2)* visata
university *m. (1)* universitetas
unknown *adj. (1)* nepažįstamas, -a, nežinomas, -a
unleash *v. (1)* atrišti
unless *part.* nebent
unlike *adj. (2)* nepanašus, -i
unload *v. (1)* iškrauti
unmarried *adj.* nevedęs (man); *adj.* netekėjusi (woman)
unnecessary *adj. (1)* nereikalingas, -a
unpack *v. (1)* išpakuoti
unsuitable *adj. (1)* netinkamas, -a
untie *v. (1)* atrišti
until *adv.* lig(i) tol; *prep.* iki; *conj.* kol
unusual *adj. (1)* nepaprastas, -a
unveil *v. (1)* atidengti
unworthy *adj. (1)* nevertas, -a
upright *adj. (1)* stačias, -ia
upwards *adv.* aukštyn
urgent *adj. (1)* neatidėliotinas, -a; *adj. (2)* skubus, -i
urgently *adv.* primygtinai
urine *m. (1)* šlapimas
urn *f. (2)* urna
use *f. (2)* nauda; *m. (1)* vartojimas; *v. (1)* naudoti(s), panaudoti, vartoti
user *m. (1), f. (2)* vartotojas, -a
usual *adj. (1)* įprastas, -a

V

vacant *adj. (1)* neužimtas, -a
vacation *f. pl. (2)* atostogos
vaccinate *v. (1)* skiepyti
vaccine *m. (1)* skiepas
vague *adj. (2)* neaiškus, -i; *adj. (1)* neapibrėžtas, -a
valley *m. (1)* slėnis
valuable *adj. (1)* vertingas, -a
value *f. (2)* vertė

various *adj. (2)* įvairus, -i
vase *f. (2)* vaza
vaseline *m. (1)* vazelinas
VCR *m. (1)* videomagnetofonas
vegetable *f. (2)* daržovė
vegetarian *m. (1), f. (2)* vegetaras, -ė; *adj. (3)* vegetarinis, -ė
veil *m. (1)* šydas, vualis
vein *f. (2)* gysla
vendor *m. (1), f. (2)* pardavėjas, -a
vertebrae *m. (1)* stuburas
vertical *adj. (2)* vertikalus, -i
very *adv.* labai
vest *f. (2)* liemenė
vet(erinary) *m. (1), f. (2)* veterinaras, -ė
victim *f. (2)* auka
victorious *adj. (1)* pergalingas, -a
victory *f. (2)* pergalė
videocassette *f. (2)* videokasetė
view *m. (1)* vaizdas
villa *f. (2)* vila
village *m. (1)* kaimas
villager *m. (1), f. (2)* kaimietis, -ė
vineyard *m. (1)* vynuogynas
violation *m. (1)* pažeidimas
violence *m. (1)* smurtas
violet *f. (2)* žibuoklė; *adj. (3)* violetinis, -ė
violin *m. (1)* smuikas
violinist *m. (1), f. (2)* smuikininkas, -ė
virtue *f. (2)* dorybė
visa *f. (2)* viza
visible *adj. (1)* matomas, -a
vision *m. (1)* matymas
visit *m. (1)* vizitas; *v. (3)* lankyti
visitation *m. (1)* lankymas
visitor *m. (1), f. (2)* interesantas, -ė
vitamin *m. (1)* vitaminas
vocabulary *f. (2)* leksika
vocal *adj. (3)* vokalinis, -ė
vodka *f. (2)* degtinė
voice *m. (1)* balsas
volleyball *m. (1)* tinklinis; **~ player** *m. (1), f. (2)* tinklininkas, -ė
volume *m. (1)* tomas; tūris
voluntary *adj. (1)* savanoriškas, -a
volunteer *m. (1), f. (2)* savanoris, -ė; *v. (3)* pasisiūlyti
vomit *v. (1)* vemti
voter *m. (1), f. (2)* rinkėjas, -a
voting *m. (1)* balsavimas
vowel (letter) *f. (2)* balsė
vulgar *adj. (2)* vulgarus, -i

W

wade *v. (3)* braidyti
wages *m. (1)* užmokestis
waist *m. (5)* liemuo
wait *v. (1)* (pa)laukti
waiter *m. (1), f. (2)* padavėjas, -a, oficiantas, -ė
waiting room *m. (1)* laukiamasis, priimamasis
wake *v. (1)* (pa)žadinti; **~ up** *v. (1)* pabusti
walk *v. (1, irr.)* eiti; *v. (1)* vaikščioti;
wall *f. (2)* siena; *adj. (3)* sieninis, -ė
wallet *f. (2)* piniginė
waltz *m. (1)* valsas
wander *v. (1)* klaidžioti
want *f. (2)* reikmė; *v. (2)* norėti
war *m. (1)* karas
ward *f. (2)* palata
wardrobe *f. (2)* spinta
warehouse *m. (1)* sandėlis
warm *adj. (1)* šiltas, -a
warmth *f. (2)* šiluma
warn *v. (1)* įspėti, perspėti
warning *m. (1)* įspėjimas, perspėjimas
warrant *m. (1)* orderis
warranty *f. (2)* garantija
wart *f. (2)* karpa
wash *v. (1)* (iš)skalbti; prausti; (iš)plauti; **~ oneself** *v. (1)* praustis
washing machine skalbimo mašina
wasp *f. (2)* vapsva
waste *f. pl. (2)* atliekos
watch *m. (1)* laikrodis
water *m. (5)* vanduo; *v. (3)* laistyti (plants)
watercolor *f. (2)* akvarelė
waterproof *adj. (1)* neperšlampamas, -a
wave *f. (2)* banga; *v. (1)* mojuoti
wax *m. (1)* vaškas; *adj. (3)* vaškinis, -ė
way *m. (1)* metodas
we *pron.* mes
weak *adj. (1)* silpnas, -a

weaken *v. (1)* nusilpti, susilpnėti
weakness *f. (2)* silpnybė
wealth *m. (1)* turtas
weapon *m. (1)* ginklas
wear *v. (1)* nešioti (clothes); *v. (2)* avėti (shoes, boots)
weather *m. (1)* oras
wedding *f. pl. (2)* sutuoktuvės, vestuvės
Wednesday *m. (1)* trečiadienis
weed *f. (2)* piktžolė; *v. (2)* ravėti
week *f. (2)* savaitė
weekday *m. (1)* šiokiadienis
weekend *m. (1)* savaitgalis
weep *v. (1)* verkti
weight *m. (1)* svoris; *f. (2)* masė
welcome *m. (1)* sutikimas; *v. (1)* sutikti
well *m. (1)* šulinys; *adv.* gerai
west *adj. (3)* vakarinis, -ė
western *adj. (1)* vakarietiškas, -a
wet *adj. (1)* šlapias, -ia; **to become ~** *v. (1)* sušlapti
what *adv.* ko; *pron.* kas
what (kind) *pron. m.* koks, -ia
wheel *m. (1)* ratas
wheelchair *m. (1)* vežimėlis
when *adv.* kada; *conj.* kai
where *adv.* kur
which one *pron. m.* kuris, -i
while *conj.* kol
whip *m. (1)* bizūnas, botagas, rimbas
whirlpool *m. (1)* sūkurys
white *adj. (1)* baltas, -a; *m. (1), f. (2)* baltaodis, -ė (person)
who *pron.* kas
whole *adj. (1)* visas, -a
wholesale *adj. (3)* didmeninis, -ė; **~ dealer/ merchant** *m. (1), f. (2)* prekybininkas, -ė
whose *pron.* kieno
why *adv.* kodėl
wide *adj. (2)* platus, -i
widely *adv.* plačiai
widow *f. (2)* našlė
widower *m. (1)* našlys
width *m. (1)* plotis
wife *f. (2)* žmona
wig *m. (1)* perukas
wild *adj. (3)* laukinis, -ė; **~ boar** *m. (1)* šernas
will *f. (2)* valia; *m. (1)* noras
willow *m. (1)* gluosnis, karklas
win *v. (1)* išlošti; *v. (2)* laimėti, nugalėti
wind *m. (1)* vėjas
window *m. (1)* langas; *f. (2)* vitrina (of a shop)
windowsill *f. (2)* palangė
windy *adj. (1)* vėjuotas, -a
wine *m. (1)* vynas
wing *m. (1)* sparnas
winner *m. (1), f. (2)* nugalėtojas, -a
winter *f. (2)* žiema; *adj. (3)* žieminis, -ė
wire *m. (1)* laidas; *f. (2)* viela
wisdom *f. (3)* išmintis
wise *adj. (1)* išmintingas, -a
wish *m. (1)* noras, pageidavimas; *v. (1)* pageidauti; *v. (2)* palinkėti
wishes *m. pl. (1)* linkėjimai
with *prep.* su
without *prep.* be
witness *m. (1), f. (2)* liudininkas, -ė; *v. (1)* (pa)liudyti
witty *adj. (1)* sąmojingas, -a
wolf *m. (1), f. (2)* vilkas, -ė
woman *f. (3)* moteris
womb *f. (2)* gimda
wonderful *adj. (2)* nuostabus, -i, puikus, -i; *adj. (1)* stebuklingas, -a
wooden *adj. (3)* medinis, -ė
woodpecker *m. (1)* genys
woody *adj. (1)* miškingas, -a
wool *f. (2)* vilna
wool(en) *adj. (3)* vilnonis, -ė
word *m. (1)* žodis
work *m. (1)* darbas; *v. (1)* dirbti; *adj. (3)* darbinis, -ė, tarnybinis, -ė
worker *m. (1), f. (2)* darbininkas, -ė
works *f. (2)* kūryba
world *adj. (3)* pasaulinis, -ė
worm *f. (2)* kirmėlė; *m. (1)* kirminas
worthless *adj. (3)* bevertis, -ė
worthy *adj. (1)* vertas, -a
wound *f. (2)* žaizda
wrap up *v. (1)* suvynioti
wreath *m. (1)* vainikas
wreck *f. (2)* avarija
wrinkle *f. (2)* raukšlė
wrinkled *adj. (1)* raukšlėtas, -a
wrist *m. (1)* riešas
write *v. (3)* rašyti; **~ down** *v. (3)* už(si)rašyti
writer *m. (1), f. (2)* rašytojas, -a, literatas, -ė
writing *m. (1)* rašymas
wrong (to be) *v. (1)* klysti
wry *adj. (1)* kreivas, -a

X

X-ray *v. (1)* peršviesti; *m. (1)* rentgenas

Y

yacht *f. (2)* jachta
yard *m. (1)* kiemas
yawn *v. (1)* žiovauti
year *m. pl. (1)* metai
yeast *f. pl. (2)* mielės
yellow *adj. (1)* geltonas, -a
yes *part.* taip
yesterday *adv.* vakar
yesterday's *adj. (3)* vakarykštis, -ė
you *pron.* tu, *pl.* jūs
young *adj. (1)* jaunas, -a
your(s) *pron.* tavo
youth *f. (2)* jaunystė

Z

zero *num. m. (1)* nulis
zone *f. (2)* zona
zoo zoologijos sodas

PHRASEBOOK CONTENTS

Getting Started

Everyday words and phrases— Kasdieniai žodžiai ir frazės

Yes.	**Taip.**
No.	**Ne.**
Maybe.	**Gal/ Galbūt.**
Please.	**Prašau.**
Thank you.	**Ačiū.**
Thank you very much.	**Labai ačiū.**
Here you are.	**Prašau/Prašom.**
You are welcome.	**Nėra už ką.**
No problem.	**Jokių problemų.**
Great.	**Puiku.**
OK.	**Gerai.**
Excuse me.	**Atsiprašau/ Atleiskite.**
I am very sorry.	**Labai atsiprašau.**
Cheers!	**Į sveikatą!**
Bless you!	**Į sveikatą!**

Being understood—Kad jus suprastų

I (we) do not speak Lithuanian.
Nekalbu (nekalbame) lietuviškai.

Do you speak English?
Ar kalbate angliškai?

I (we) do not understand.
Nesuprantu (nesuprantame).

I (we) understand.
Suprantu (suprantame).

Can you understand me?
Ar galite mane suprasti?

Did I say [that] correctly?
Ar aš teisingai pasakiau?

Speak slower, please.
Prašau kalbėti lėčiau.

Repeat, please.
Prašau pakartoti.

Can you [do that] slower, please?
Gal galite lėčiau?

Can you write that down, please?
Gal galite užrašyti?

Can you help me, please?
Gal galite man padėti?

Does anyone speak English here?
Ar kas nors čia kalba angliškai?

Could you please translate that for me?
Gal galėtumėte man tai išversti?

Greetings and exchanges—Pasisveikinimas

Good morning.
Labas rytas.

Good afternoon.
Laba diena.

Good evening.
Labas vakaras.

Hi!
Labas!

Hello!
Sveikas! (sing. m.)/ **Sveika!** (sing. f.)/ **Sveiki!** (pl. m.)/ **Sveikos!** (pl. f.)

Welcome!
Sveiki atvykę!

How are you?
Kaip laikotės?/ Kaip sekasi?

Great.
Puikiai.

Fine, thanks.
Ačiū, gerai.

So so.
Šiaip sau.

And you?
O jums?

It's good to see you (again).
Malonu jus (vėl) matyti.

Same here.
Man taip pat.

How is your wife (husband) ?
Kaip (laikosi) jūsų žmona (vyras)?

What's new?
Kas naujo?

Good night.
Labanakt.

Good-bye.
Sudie/Viso gero.

See you (soon).
Iki (greito) pasimatymo.

Bye.
Iki.

Have a nice day!
Geros dienos!

Have a nice evening!
Gero vakaro!

Sweet dreams!
Saldžių sapnų!

Have a nice trip!
Laimingos kelionės!

Common questions—Klausimai

Who?	**Kas?**
What?	**Kas?**
Where?	**Kur?**
Where is/are. . .?	**Kur yra. . .?**
When?	**Kada?**
How?	**Kaip?**
How much/many?	**Kiek?**
Why?	**Kodėl?**
Which?	**Kuris?** (m.)/ **Kuri?** (f.)
What for?	**Už ką?**
To whom?	**Kam?**
With whom?	**Su kuo?**
Where from?	**Iš kur?**

Where is the bathroom?
Kur tualetas?

What happened?
Kas atsitiko?

Is anything wrong?
Ar kas nors negerai?

What (who) is this?
Kas tai?

Who's there?
Kas ten?

Who did this?
Kas tai padarė?

How much do I have to pay?
Kiek turiu mokėti?

How much does it cost?
Kiek tai kainuoja?

How long will it take?
Kiek tai užtruks?

What time do you close?
Kada baigiate darbą?

What does this mean?
Ką tai reiškia?

What does the word âraktasÂ mean?
Ką reiškia žodis âraktasÂ?

Do you mind if I smoke?
Ar jūs neprieštarausite, jei užsirūkysiu?

Where could I . . .
Kur galėčiau . . .

. . . make a call?
. . . paskambinti?

. . . buy a postcard?
. . . nusipirkti atviruką?

. . . buy some postage stamps?
. . . nusipirkti pašto ženklų?

Asking the time—Teiraujantis laiko

What time is it?
Kiek valandų?

I do not have a watch.
Neturiu laikrodžio.

watch/clock	**laikrodis**
hour	**valanda**
minute	**minutė**
second	**sekundė**

It is (now) . . .
(Dabar) . . .

. . . six (o'clock).
. . . šešios (valandos).

. . . six (o'clock) thirty (minutes).
. . . šešios (valandos) trisdešimt (minučių)/ pusė septynių.

. . . ten (minutes) after two.
. . . dešimt (minučių) po dviejų.

. . . ten (minutes) to two.
. . . be dešimt (minučių) dvi.

. . . nine sharp.
. . . lygiai devynios.

. . . noon.
. . . vidurdienis/ dvylika (valandų) (dienos).

. . . midnight.
. . . vidurnaktis/ dvylika (valandų) (nakties).

. . . almost four (o'clock).
. . . beveik keturios (valandos).

already	**jau**
immediately	**tuojau (pat)/ tučtuojau**
soon	**greitai**
in half an hour	**už pusvalandžio**
half an hour	**pusvalandis**
in an hour	**po valandos**
in two hours	**po dviejų valandų**
this morning	**šį rytą**
after lunch	**po pietų**
tonight	**šį vakarą**
in the evening	**vakare**
at night	**naktį**
today	**šiandien**
tomorrow	**rytoj**
yesterday	**vakar**
the day after tomorrow	**poryt**
the day before yesterday	**užvakar**
in two days	**po poros/ po dviejų dienų**
in a week	**po savaitės**
in a month	**po mėnesio**
in half a year	**po pusmečio**
in a year	**po metų**
a year ago	**prieš metus**

two months ago	**prieš pora/ prieš du mėnesius**
early	**anksti**
late	**vėlai**
just in time	**pačiu laiku**

Common Problems—Problemos

My wallet (purse) got stolen.
Pavogė mano piniginę (rankinuką).

I cannot find my passport.
Nerandu savo paso.

I (we) got into an accident.
Patekau (patekome) į avariją.

I (we) got lost.
Pasiklydau (pasiklydome).

I cannot remember my address.
Neprisimenu savo adreso.

I lost my credit cards.
Pamečiau savo kreditines korteles.

I need to contact American Express.
Turiu susisiekti su American Express.

I need a lawyer.
Man reikia advokato.

Small Talk

Introduction—Pažintis

(Very) nice to meet you.
(Labai) malonu (susipažinti).

The pleasure is mine.
Ir man malonu.

I've heard much about you.
Esu daug apie jus girdėjęs (m.)/ **girdėjusi** (f.).

Let me introduce you to . . .
Leiskite jums pristatyti . . .

. . . my wife.	**. . . mano žmoną.**
. . . my husband.	**. . . mano vyrą.**
. . . my friend Dalia.	**. . . mano draugę Dalią.**

This is my son (daughter).
Tai mano sūnus (dukra).

I'd like you to meet my sister.
Norėčiau supažindinti jus su savo seserimi.

My name is . . .
Mano vardas . . .

What is your name?
Koks jūsų vardas?

Here is my card.
Štai mano kortelė.

May I have your card, please?
Gal galėčiau gauti jūsų kortelę?

May I call you?
Ar galėčiau jums paskambinti?

I'd like to take you out to dinner (lunch).
Norėčiau pakviesti jus kartu pavakarieniauti (papietauti).

It was (very) nice (to meet you).
Buvo (labai) malonu (susipažinti).

Occupations—Profesijos

I am a teacher.
Aš mokytojas (m.)/ **mokytoja** (f.).

I am a student.
Aš studentas (m.)/ **studentė** (f.).

I am studying finance.
Studijuoju finansus.

What do you do for living?
Kokia jūsų profesija?

Where do you work?
Kur jūs dirbate?

I am unemployed.
Aš bedarbis (m.)/ **bedarbė** (f.).

I am a housewife.
Esu namų šeimininkė.

I work part-time.
Dirbu puse etato.

How long have you been working at this place?
Kiek laiko dirbate šioje vietoje?

Do you have a university degree?
Ar esate baigęs (m.)/ **baigusi** (f.) **universitetą?**

What was (is) your major?
Ką studijavote (studijuojate)?

What university did you go to?
Kuriame universitete studijavote?

accountant	**buhalteris** (m.)/ **buhalterė** (f.)
actor/ actress	**aktorius** (m.)/ **aktorė** (f.)
administrator	**administratorius** (m.)/ **administratorė** (f.)
architect	**architektas** (m.)/ **architektė** (f.)
army officer	**karininkas** (m.)/ **karininkė** (f.)
artist	**menininkas** (m.)/ **menininkė** (f.)
attorney	**advokatas, teisininkas** (m.)/ **advokatė, teisininkė** (f.)
banker	**bankininkas** (m.)/ **bankininkė** (f.)
bartender	**barmenas** (m.)/ **barmenė** (f.)
businessman	**verslininkas** (m.)
businesswoman	**verslininkė** (f.)
construction worker	**statybininkas** (m.)/ **statybininkė** (f.)
economist	**ekonomistas** (m.)/ **ekonomistė** (f.)
dancer	**šokėjas** (m.)/ **šokėja** (f.)
designer	**dizaineris** (m.)/ **dizainerė** (f.)
doctor	**gydytojas** (m.)/ **gydytoja** (f.)
driver	**vairuotojas** (m.)/ **vairuotoja** (f.)
engineer	**inžinierius** (m.)/ **inžinierė** (f.)
factory worker	**fabriko darbininkas** (m.)/ **darbininkė** (f.)
financier	**finansininkas** (m.)/ **finansininkė** (f.)
hairdresser	**kirpėjas** (m.)/ **kirpėja** (f.)
interpreter	**vertėjas** (m.)/ **vertėja** (f.)
journalist	**žurnalistas** (m.)/ **žurnalistė** (f.)
lawyer	**advokatas, teisininkas** (m.)/ **advokatė, teisininkė** (f.)
manager	**vadybininkas** (m.)/ **vadybininkė** (f.)
musician	**muzikantas** (m.)/ **muzikantė** (f.)

nanny	**auklė** (f.)
nurse	**medicinos sesuo** (f.)
painter	**dailininkas** (m.)/ **dailininkė** (f.)
poet	**poetas** (m.)/ **poetė** (f.)
police officer	**policininkas** (m.)/ **policininkė** (f.)
politician	**politikas** (m.)/ **politikė** (f.)
professor	**profesorius** (m.)/ **profesorė** (f.)
scholar	**mokslininkas** (m.)/ **mokslininkė** (f.)
scientist	**mokslininkas** (m.)/ **mokslininkė** (f.)
secretary	**sekretorius** (m.)/ **sekretorė** (f.)
shop assistant	**pardavėjas** (m.)/ **pardavėja** (f.)
surgeon	**chirurgas** (m.)/ **chirurgė** (f.)
student	**studentas** (m.)/ **studentė** (f.)
teacher	**mokytojas** (m.)/ **mokytoja** (f.)
translator	**vertėjas** (m.)/ **vertėja** (f.)
waiter, -ress	**padavėjas** (m.)/ **padavėja** (f.)
writer	**rašytojas** (m.)/ **rašytoja** (f.)

Countries and nationalities—Šalys ir tautybės

I am an American.
Aš amerikietis (m.)/ **amerikietė** (f.).

I am an American of a Lithuanian heritage.
Aš—lietuvių kilmės amerikietis (m.)/ **amerikietė** (f.).

Africa	**Afrika**
African	**afrikietis** (m.)/ **afrikietė** (f.)
Albania	**Albanija**
Albanian	**albanas** (m.)/ **albanė** (f.)
America	**Amerika**
American	**amerikietis** (m.)/ **amerikietė** (f.)
Armenia	**Armėnija**
Armenian	**armėnas** (m.)/ **armėnė** (f.)
Australia	**Australija**
Australian	**australas** (m.)/ **australė** (f.)
Austria	**Austrija**
Austrian	**austras** (m.)/ **austrė** (f.)

Belgium	**Belgija**
Belgian	**belgas** (m.)/ **belgė** (f.)
Bulgaria	**Bulgarija**
Bulgarian	**bulgaras** (m.)/ **bulgarė** (f.)
Byelorussia	**Baltarusija, Gudija**
Byelorussian	**baltarusis** (m.), **baltarusė** (f.), **gudas** (m.), **gudė** (f.)
Canada	**Kanada**
Canadian	**kanadietis** (m.)/ **kanadietė** (f.)
China	**Kinija**
Chinese	**Kinas** (m.)/ **Kinė** (f.)
Czech	**Čekija**
Czech	**čekas** (m.)/ **čekė** (f.)
Denmark	**Danija**
Danish	**danas** (m.)/ **danė** (f.)
England	**Anglija**
English	**anglas** (m.)/ **anglė** (f.)
Estonia	**Estija**
Estonian	**estas** (m.)/ **estė** (f.)
Europe	**Europa**
European	**europietis** (m.)/ **europietė** (f.)
Finland	**Suomija**
Finnish	**suomis** (m.)/ **suomė** (f.)
France	**Prancūzija**
French	**prancūzas** (m.)/ **prancūzė** (f.)
Georgia	**Gruzija**
Georgian	**gruzinas** (m.)/ **gruzinė** (f.)
Great Britain	**Didžioji Britanija**
British	**britas** (m.)/ **britė** (f.)
Greece	**Graikija**
Greek	**graikas** (m.)/ **graikė** (f.)
Holland	**Olandija**
Dutch	**olandas** (m.)/ **olandė** (f.)
Hungary	**Vengrija**
Hungarian	**vengras** (m.)/ **vengrė** (f.)
India	**Indija**
Indian	**indas** (m.)/ **indė** (f.)
Ireland	**Airija**
Irish	**airis** (m.)/ **airė** (f.)

Israel	**Izraelis**
Israeli, Jewish	**izraelitas, žydas** (m.)/ **izraelitė, žydė** (f.)
Italy	**Italija**
Italian	**italas** (m.)/ **italė** (f.)
Japan	**Japonija**
Japanese	**japonas** (m.)/ **japonė** (f.)
Latvia	**Latvija**
Latvian	**latvis** (m.)/ **latvė** (f.)
Lithuania	**Lietuva**
Lithuanian	**lietuvis** (m.)/ **lietuvė** (f.)
Mexico	**Meksika**
Mexican	**meksikietis** (m.)/ **meksikietė** (f.)
Norway	**Norvegija**
Norvegian	**norvegas** (m.)/ **norvegė** (f.)
Poland	**Lenkija**
Polish	**lenkas** (m.)/ **lenkė** (f.)
Prussia	**Prūsija**
Prussian	**prūsas** (m.)/ **prūsė** (f.)
Romania	**Rumunija**
Romanian	**rumunas** (m.)/ **rumunė** (f.)
Russia	**Rusija**
Russian	**rusas** (m.)/ **rusė** (f.)
Scotland	**Škotija**
Scottish	**škotas** (m.)/ **škotė** (f.)
Serbia	**Serbija**
Serbian	**serbas** (m.)/ **serbė** (f.)
Slovakia	**Slovakija**
Slovakian	**slovakas** (m.)/ **slovakė** (f.)
Spain	**Ispanija**
Spanish	**ispanas** (m.)/ **ispanė** (f.)
Sweden	**Švedija**
Swedish	**švedas** (m.)/ **švedė** (f.)
Switzerland	**Šveicarija**
Swiss	**šveicaras** (m.)/ **šveicarė** (f.)
Turkey	**Turkija**
Turkish	**turkas** (m.)/ **turkė** (f.)
Ukraine	**Ukraina**
Ukrainian	**ukrainietis** (m.)/ **ukrainietė** (f.)

United States of America (U.S.A) **Jungtinės Amerikos Valstijos (JAV)**
American **amerikietis** (m.)/ **amerikietė** (f.)

Age—Amžius

How old are you?
Kiek jums metų?

I am . . . **Man . . .**
. . . eighteen. **. . . aštuoniolika.**
. . . twenty-one. **. . . dvidešimt vieneri.**
. . . thirty. **. . . trisdešimt.**
. . . forty-five. **. . . keturiasdešimt penkeri.**

We are the same age.
Mes bendraamžiai.

I was born in 1970.
Aš gimiau 1970 (tūkstantis devyni šimtai septyniasdešimtaisiais) metais.

When is your birthday?
Kada jūsų gimtadienis?

My birthday is August 1st.
Mano gimtadienis rugpjūčio pirmą (dieną).

Family—Šeima

Are you married?
Ar jūs vedęs (m.)/ **ištekėjusi** (f.)**?**

No, I am not married/ No, I am single.
Ne, aš nevedęs (m.)/ **netekėjusi** (f.).

(I am not married, but) I have a girlfriend/ boyfriend.
(Aš nevedęs (m.)/ **netekėjusi** (f.), **bet) turiu merginą/ vaikiną.**

I am engaged.
Aš susižadėjęs (m.)/ **susižadėjusi** (f.).

I am a widower/ widow.
Aš našlys/ našlė.

I am divorced.
Aš išsiskyręs (m.)/ **išsiskyrusi** (f.)

I am separated from my wife/ husband.
Gyvenu atskirai nuo žmonos/ vyro.

I live with my girlfriend/ boyfriend.
Gyvenu su savo mergina/ vaikinu.

I am gay/ lesbian.
Aš gėjus/ lesbietė.

I have a partner.
Turiu partnerį (m.)/ **partnerę** (f.).

Do you have any children?
Ar turite vaikų?

Yes, they live separately.
Taip, jie gyvena atskirai.

Yes, I have two little children: a girl and a boy.
Taip, turiu du mažus vaikus: mergaitę ir berniuką.

Here are their photos.
Štai jų nuotraukos.

And here is my wife/ husband.
O štai mano žmona/ vyras.

Is your family large?
Ar jūsų šeima didelė?

We have three children.
Turime tris vaikus.

My wife is pregnant (again).
Mano žmona (vėl) laukiasi.

aunt	**teta**
boy	**berniukas**
boyfriend	**vaikinas, draugas**
brother	**brolis**
brother-in-law	**sesers vyras**
cousin	**pusbrolis** (m.)/ **pusseserė** (f.)
dad	**tėtis, tėtė, tėvelis**
daughter	**dukra, duktė**
daughter-in-law	**marti**
father	**tėvas**
father-in-law	**uošvis**
girl	**mergaitė**
girlfriend	**mergina, draugė, panelė**
granddaughter	**anūkė, vaikaitė**
grandfather	**senelis**
grandmother	**močiutė, senelė**
grandparents	**seneliai**
grandson	**anūkas, vaikaitis**
husband	**vyras**
mom	**mama, mamytė**
mother	**motina**
mother-in-law	**anyta (husband's mother), uošvė (wife's mother)**
nephew	**sūnėnas**
niece	**dukterėčia**
only child	**vienturtis** (m.)/ **vienturtė** (f.)
parents	**tėvai**
relative	**giminaitis** (m.)/ **giminaitė** (f.)
sister	**sesuo**
son	**sūnus**
son-in-law	**žentas**
spouse	**sutuoktinis** (m.)/ **sutuoktinė** (f.)
uncle	**dėdė**
wife	**žmona**

Weather—Oras

The best time to travel in Lithuania is summer, especially July as this is the warmest month of the year (avg. temperature +20.5 C). However, please bear in mind that summer nights usually are much cooler than are summer days. The coldest month of the year is February (avg. temperature –4.2 C).

What a beautiful day!
Kokia graži diena!

What is the weather like today?
Koks šiandien oras?

Is it going . . .	**Ar gali . . .**
. . . to rain?	**. . . lyti?**
. . . to snow?	**. . . snigti?**

Will it be much colder at night?
Ar naktį bus daug vėsiau?

It is . . . (today).	**(Šiandien) . . .**
. . . quite cool	**. . . gana vėsu.**
. . . very hot	**. . . labai karšta.**
. . . raining	**. . . lyja.**
. . . pouring	**. . . pliaupia lietus.**
. . . snowing	**. . . sninga.**
. . . gloomy	**. . . apsiniaukę.**
. . . cloudy	**. . . debesuota.**
. . . sunny	**. . . saulėta.**
. . . lightning	**. . . žaibuoja.**
. . . foggy	**. . . rūkas.**
. . . windy	**. . . vėjuota.**
. . . drizzling	**. . . dulksnoja.**
. . . thawing	**. . . atodrėkis.**
. . . freezing	**. . . šąla.**

It will get warmer (colder) later in the day.
Dieną atšils (atšals).

It's minus ten (degrees).
Minus dešimt (laipsnių).

It's ten degrees below zero.
Dešimt laipsnių šalčio.

It's plus twenty (degrees).
Plius dvidešimt (laipsnių).

It's twenty degrees above zero.
Dvidešimt laipsnių šilumos.

It's too hot (cold).
Per karšta (šalta).

What a pleasant breeze!
Koks malonus vėjelis!

cloud	**debesis**
damp	**drėgna**
degree	**laipsnis**
flood	**potvynis**
fog	**rūkas**
heat	**karštis**
ice	**ledas**
moon	**mėnulis**
moonlight	**mėnesiena**
sky	**dangus**
snow	**sniegas**
storm	**audra**
sun	**saulė**
temperature	**temperatūra**
thermometer	**termometras**
thunder	**griaustinis**
weather	**oras**
weather forecast	**orų prognozė**
wind	**vėjas**

The sky is . . .	**Dangus (yra) . . .**
. . . blue.	**. . . žydras.**
. . . clear.	**. . . giedras.**
. . . without a cloud.	**. . . be debesėlio.**
. . . gray.	**. . . pilkas.**
. . . cloudy.	**. . . apsiniaukęs.**

What is the water temperature (today)?
Kokia (šiandien) vandens temperatūra?

The wind is from . . .	**Vėjas iš . . .**
. . . the South.	**. . . pietų.**
. . . the North.	**. . . šiaurės.**
. . . the East.	**. . . rytų.**
. . . the West.	**. . . vakarų.**

The wind is (very) strong.
Vėjas (labai) stiprus.

Expressing one's first impressions about country and people— Pirmieji įspūdžiai apie šalį ir žmones

I like it here (very much).
Man čia (labai) patinka.

I do not like it here (very much).
Man čia (labai) nepatinka.

People are very kind.
Žmonės labai malonūs.

Life is (much) slower-paced here than in America.
Gyvenimo tempai čia (daug) lėtesni nei Amerikoje.

The girls are very beautiful.
Merginos labai gražios.

Many girls look like models.
Daug merginų atrodo lyg manekenės.

I'll tell my friends to come here.
Pakviesiu savo draugus čia apsilankyti.

I miss ice-cubes in my drinks.
Savo gėrimuose pasigendu ledo.

Lithuania is a (very) beautiful country.
Lietuva (labai) graži šalis.

I will definitely return.
Aš būtinai sugrįšiu.

It is a small country.
Tai maža šalis.

Lithuanian is a (very) difficult language.
Lietuvių kalba (labai) sunki.

I liked the sea very much.
Man labai patiko jūra.

The water was warm (cold).
Vanduo buvo šiltas (šaltas).

It surprised me that there are no mountains in Lithuania.
Mane nustebino, kad Lietuvoje nėra kalnų.

I liked (did not like) the food here.
Man čia patiko (nepatiko) maistas.

There are many good shops and boutiques (in large cities).
(Dideliuose miestuose) daug gerų parduotuvių.

At the Airport

At the moment, there are no direct flights from the United States to Lithuania. Therefore, you will need to fly through a major European hub such as Frankfurt, London, Amsterdam, or Copenhagen, etc. Most international flights arrive at the *Vilniaus oro uostas* (Vilnius Airport). Some go to Kaunas and Palanga.

Vilnius Airport is located within the city limits and can be reached by a city bus. However, taking a taxi will be much more convenient and not very expensive. Try to establish a fare before getting into a cab as some taxi drivers might attempt to rip off a foreigner. A ride to Old Town should cost you about 15 Litas.

If you are a citizen of the United States, you do not need a visa to enter Lithuania and travel within the country as a tourist. If you plan on working in the country for an extended period of time, you will need to secure a visa and a work permit.

While in Lithuania, expect to travel by car, bus, or train.

Arrival—Atvykimas

Hello.
Laba diena.

I am an American (Canadian, British, Australian).
Aš amerikietis (kanadietis, anglas, australas) (m.)/
amerikietė (kanadietė, anglė, australė) (f.).

Here is my passport.
Štai mano pasas.

I came on business.
Atvažiavau verslo reikalais.

I am a tourist.
Aš turistas (m.)/**turistė** (f.).

I am a student.
Aš studentas (m.)/**studentė** (f.).

I am on vacation.
Atostogauju.

We are on vacation.
Atostogaujame.

I (we) have relatives in Lithuania.
Lietuvoje turiu (turime) giminių.

I (we) have friends in Lithuania.
Lietuvoje turiu (turime) draugų.

Customs—Muitinė

I (we) have no goods to declare.
Deklaruojamų prekių neturiu (neturime).

Do I (we) have to declare this?
Ar turiu (turime) tai deklaruoti?

These are gifts.
Čia dovanos.

These are samples.
Tai pavyzdžiai.

These are my personal belongings.
Čia yra mano asmeniniai daiktai.

That is not my suitcase.
Šis lagaminas ne mano.

Problems—Problemos

I have lost my passport.
Pamečiau savo pasą.

I have lost my ticket.
Pamečiau bilietą.

Nobody was (t)here to pick me up.
Niekas manęs nepasitiko.

My suitcase got lost.
Mano lagaminas dingo.

Where is the currency exchange?
Kur valiutos keitykla?

I need to get to the American (Canadian, British, Australian) Embassy.
Turiu patekti į Amerikos (Kanados, Anglijos, Australijos) ambasadą.

I am (we are) late.
Vėluoju (vėluojame).

I am (we are) in a hurry.
Skubu (skubame).

Where is . . . ?	**Kur yra . . .?**
. . . a phone?	**. . . telefonas?**
. . . a restroom?	**. . . tualetas?**
. . . a bank?	**. . . bankas?**
. . . an information desk?	**. . . informacija?**
. . . a bar?	**. . . baras?**
. . . a restaurant?	**. . . restoranas?**
. . . the police?	**. . . policija?**
. . . a pharmacy?	**. . . vaistinė?**
. . . a (luggage) storage room?	**. . . saugojimo kamera?**

Where can I buy a phone card?
Kur galiu nusipirkti telefono kortelę?

I must exchange some money.
Man reikia išsikeisti pinigų.

I need an English translator.
Man reikia anglų kalbos vertėjo.

I need a doctor.
Man reikia gydytojo.

I (we) got robbed (i.e., some of my property got stolen).
Mane (mus) apvogė.

Is this a bus to the city?
Ar tai autobusas į miestą?

Luggage—Bagažas

I cannot find my suitcases.
Nerandu savo lagaminų.

Where is my luggage?
Kur mano bagažas?

One suitcase (bag) is missing.
Trūksta vieno lagamino (krepšio).

That is . . .
Tai . . .

. . . a large (black) suitcase.
. . . didelis (juodas) lagaminas.

. . . small (gray) suitcase.
. . . mažas (pilkas) lagaminas.

. . . brown (leather) backpack.
. . . ruda (odinė) kuprinė.

My suitcase is damaged.
Mano lagaminas apgadintas.

Could somebody?
Gal kas nors man galėtų padėti?

Could you help me, please?
Gal galėtumėte man padėti?

I need a porter.
Man reikia nešiko.

Thank you.
Ačiū./ Dėkoju.

Be careful with that.
Būkite atsargus (m.)/ **atsargi** (f.) **su tuo.**

Please, take this all to the cab.
Prašau viską nuneškite į taksi.

No, thank you.
Ne, ačiū.

That, I will carry myself.
Tą aš pats (m.)/**pati** (f.) **panešiu.**

How much do I owe you?
Kiek esu skolingas (m.)/ **skolinga** (f.)?

How much do I have to pay?
Kiek turiu mokėti?

Nothing.
Nieko.

Departure-Išvykimas

Vilnius airport is small; therefore, even for an international flight, you may arrive only an hour prior to the scheduled departure time.

For flights within Europe, you will be allowed up to 20 kg of luggage for Economy Class and up to 30 kg for Business Class. If you are flying directly to North America, you will be allowed more luggage. For exact specifications, please check with the airline you are flying.

Can I (we) check in my/our bags?
Ar galiu (galime) priduoti savo bagažą?

Could I (we) fly first class?
Ar galėčiau (galėtume) skristi pirma klase?

How much do I (we) have to pay for the upgrade?
Kiek turiu (turime) mokėti už klasės pakeitimą?

Could I get a . . . seat, please?
Gal gaučiau vietą. . .?

. . . window . . . **. . . prie lango.**
. . . an aisle . . . **. . . prie praėjimo.**

Is smoking allowed on the plane?
Ar lėktuve galima rūkyti?

Your luggage is too heavy.
Jūsų bagažas per sunkus.

There is a charge for additional weight.
Už papildomą svorį reikia primokėti.

How much do I (we) have to pay for the additional weight?
Kiek turiu (turime) primokėti už papildomą svorį?

Can I (we) change the departure . . .
Ar galiu (galime) pakeisti išvykimo . . .

. . . day?	**. . . dieną?**
. . . time?	**. . . laiką?**
. . . airlines?	**. . . aviakompaniją?**

What you may hear—Ką galite išgirsti

Attention! Attention!
Dėmesio! Dėmesio!

Ladies and gentlemen, . . .
Ponios ir ponai, . . .

. . . flight number . . . has arrived from Frankfurt.
. . . lėktuvas iš Frankfurto, reiso numeris . . . , nusileido.

. . . a flight number . . . is leaving for Frankfurt in 30 minutes.
. . . lėktuvas į Frankfurtą, reiso numeris . . . , išvyksta už trisdešimt minučių.

. . . passengers taking a flight #LK 741 to Helsinki are invited to check-in.
. . . keleivius, skrendančius į Helsinkį, reiso numeriu LK 741, kviečiame registruotis.

Attention! Attention! Mr. Jonas Kielaitis, who is traveling to Helsinki, your party is waiting for you at the information desk.
Dėmesio! Dėmesio! Ponas Jonas Kielaiti, keliaujantis į Helsinkį, jūsų laukia prie informacijos.

Living Arrangements

Hotel—Viešbutis

In Lithuania, taxes are already included in the price. Therefore, unless you order extra services, you will pay only the quoted price.

Are there any vacant rooms?
Ar yra laisvų kambarių?

There should be a room reserved on my name.
Man turėtų būti rezervuotas kambarys.

My name is . . .
Aš esu . . .

I (we) will be staying at the hotel for . . .
Viešbutyje gyvensiu (gyvensime) . . .

. . . just one day.	**. . . tik vieną dieną.**
. . . a couple of days.	**. . . pora dienų.**
. . . a week.	**. . . savaitę.**
. . . ten days.	**. . . dešimt dienų.**

There are four of us.
Mes keturiese.

Do you have any . . .
Ar turite . . .

. . . single rooms?
. . . vienviečių kambarių.

. . . double rooms with a bath?
. . . dviviečių kambarių su vonia?

. . . any rooms with two beds?
. . . kambarių su dviem lovom?

. . . any rooms with a double bed?
. . . kambarių su viena plačia lova?

May I (we) see the room?
Ar galėčiau (galėtume) apžiūrėti kambarį?

How much do you charge per room per night?
Kiek kainuoja kambarys parai?

Do I (we) pay now or at departure?
Ar mokėti turiu (turime) dabar, ar kai išsiregistruosiu (išsiregistruosime)?

I'll pay with a credit card.
Mokėsiu kredito kortele.

I need a bed for a child.
Man reikia lovos vaikui.

Does this room have a bath or a shower?
Ar šiame numeryje yra vonia ar dušas?

Does the price include breakfast?
Ar į kainą įeina pusryčiai?

Is there a charge for parking?
Ar reikia mokėti už mašinos stovėjimo vietą?

Is it OK to smoke in the room?
Ar kambaryje galima rūkyti?

What floor is my room on?
Kuriame aukšte mano kambarys?

Can I (we) order in-room breakfast?
Ar galiu (galime) užsisakyti pusryčius į kambarį?

Is there . . . in the hotel?	**Ar viešbutyje yra. . .?**
. . . currency exchange . . .	**. . . valiutos keitykla**
. . . a gym . . .	**. . . sporto salė**
. . . a swimming pool . . .	**. . . baseinas**
. . . a beauty salon . . .	**. . . grožio salonas**
. . . a hair salon . . .	**. . . kirpykla**

. . . a laundry service . . .	**. . . skalbykla**
. . . a playroom for children . . .	**. . . vaikų žaidimų kambarys**
. . . an internet café?	**. . . interneto kavinė?**

Is there anybody to supervise the children?
Ar vaikus kas nors prižiūri?

Is there . . . in the room?	**Ar kambaryje yra . . .?**
. . . air conditioning . . .	**. . . oro kondicionierius**
. . . a minibar . . .	**. . . mini baras**
. . . a refrigerator . . .	**. . . šaldytuvas**
. . . an iron . . .	**. . . lygintuvas**
. . . a hairdryer . . .	**. . . plaukų džiovintuvas**
. . . a TV set . . .	**. . . televizorius**
. . . cable TV . . .	**. . . kabelinė televizija**
. . . TV guide . . .	**. . . televizijos programa**
. . . a room service menu . . .	**. . . siūlomų paslaugų sąrašas**
. . . an internet connection . . .	**. . . internetinis ryšys**
. . . robes and slippers . . .	**. . . chalatai ir šlepetės**
. . . any tourist information . . .	**. . . turistinės informacijos**

We would like to have rooms on the same floor.
Norėtume kambarių tame pačiame aukšte.

Is there a phone in the room?
Ar kambaryje yra telefonas?

How do I place a local call?
Kaip rinkti vietinį numerį?

I need an area code for this city, please.
Prašyčiau šio miesto kodo.

I need to place an international call.
Turiu paskambinti į užsienį.

Where can I buy a phone card?
Kur galiu nusipirkti telefono kortelę?

I need . . .	**Man reikia . . .**
. . . a taxi.	**. . . taksi.**
. . . a fax machine.	**. . . fakso.**
. . . to find this person.	**. . . rasti šį žmogų.**

Do I have any messages?
Ar man palikta žinučių?

Where could I get a newspaper in English?
Kur galėčiau gauti laikraštį anglų kalba?

Where could I buy some flowers (wine)?
Kur galėčiau nusipirkti gėlių (vyno)?

When does the hotel close for the night?
Kada viešbutis uždaromas nakčiai?

We are open 24 hours a day.
Dirbame visą parą.

Do I leave my room key here?
Ar palikti kambario raktą čia?

No.	**Ne.**
Yes.	**Taip.**

Can I get an additional key?
Ar galiu gauti dar vieną raktą?

When does the restaurant (bar) close?
Kada uždaromas restoranas (baras)?

When is the . . .	**Kada . . .**
. . . breakfast?	**. . . pusryčiai?**
. . . lunch?	**. . . pietūs?**
. . . dinner?	**. . . vakarienė?**

Bed & Breakfast

Most Bed & Breakfast places in Lithuania are rooms in private apartments or houses. The prices usually range from $10 to $25 per person per night, depending on the city, the location within the city, and the condition of the apartment/house. Bed & Breakfast is a cheap alternative to a hotel and is a good way of learning more about native Lithuanians and their manner of living.

You can find B&Bs not only in Vilnius, Kaunas, or Klaipėda, but also in most other Lithuanian cities. Seaside resort B&Bs such as those Palanga and Neringa attract many native Lithuanians from all over the country. If you are on a budget, you may find a bed in a multiple occupancy room in Palanga for only $5 a night. However, you must keep in mind that the more expensive B&Bs are usually nicer. Also, please be prepared to face the fact that not all Bed & Breakfast owners speak fluent English.

If you are very concerned about your comfort, a hotel is your best bet. Like elsewhere in the world, the more luxurious the hotel, the more expensive it is.

Making Reservations—Rezervacijos

Hello!
Laba diena!

I am . . .
Aš esu . . .

Do you have any rooms available?
Ar turite laisvų kambarių?

I would like to reserve a room.
Norėčiau užsisakyti kambarį.

I was quoted a lower price over the phone.
Telefonu man buvo pasakyta žemesnė kaina.

Does your hotel have a web page?
Ar jūsų viešbutis turi interneto svetainę (interneto puslapį)?

Do you have any student discounts?
Ar studentams taikomos nuolaidos?

No.
Ne.

Yes, but only if you have an ISIC card.
Taip, bet tik su ISIC kortele.

Do you have an ISIC card?
Ar turite ISIC kortelę?

Yes, I do.
Taip, turiu.

Could somebody pick me (us) up in the airport?
Ar kas nors galėtų sutikti mane (mus) oro uoste?

It would be best for you to catch a taxi.
Jums būtų geriausia važiuoti taksi.

Service—Aptarnavimas

I need . . .	**Man reikia . . .**
. . . more towels.	**. . . daugiau rankšluosčių.**
. . . some toilet paper.	**. . . tualetinio popieriaus.**
. . . a toothbrush.	**. . . dantų šepetėlio.**
. . . one more blanket.	**. . . dar vienos antklodės.**
. . . one more pillow.	**. . . dar vienos pagalvės.**
. . . an ashtray.	**. . . peleninės.**
. . . some hangers for clothes.	**. . . pakabų drabužiams.**

. . . some note paper. **. . . popieriaus laiškams.**
. . . post stamps. **. . . pašto ženklų.**

Do you have any of today's newspapers in English?
Ar turite šios dienos laikraščių anglų kalba?

Please wake me up at 7 A.M.
Prašau mane pažadinti septintą valandą ryto.

Where could I send a fax?
Kur galėčiau išsiųsti faksą?

How much does it cost?
Kiek tai kainuoja?

Please send this fax for me.
Prašau išsiųskite šį faksą.

I am expecting a fax.
Laukiu fakso.

Can I pay with a credit card?
Ar galiu mokėti kredito kortele?

I need to have my suit pressed (dry cleaned).
Mano kostiumą reikia išlyginti (išvalyti).

Please charge this to my room.
Prašau įtraukite tai į mano kambario sąskaitą.

Can I use my personal computer here?
Ar galiu čia naudotis savo asmeniniu kompiuteriu?

Is there an internet connection in my room?
Ar mano kambaryje yra internetinis ryšys?

Can I call abroad from my room?
Ar galiu skambinti į užsienį iš savo kambario?

How do I use the phone?
Kaip naudotis telefonu?

May I get a phone book, please?
Gal galėčiau gauti telefonų knygą?

I need to charge these batteries.
Man reikia pakrauti šias baterijas.

Can you recommend a good Lithuanian restaurant?
Gal galite rekomenduoti gerą lietuvišką restoraną?

Can I leave this in the safe?
Ar galiu tai palikti seife?

I want to have my things back from the safe.
Noriu pasiimti savo daiktus iš seifo.

Problems—Problemos

I want to speak to your boss.
Noriu pasikalbėti su jūsų viršininku.

He (she) spoke rudely to me.
Jis (ji) šiurkščiai su manimi kalbėjo.

There are no towels in the bathroom.
Vonioje nėra rankšluosčių.

The bathroom is dirty.
Vonia nešvari.

The restroom (shower) is dirty.
Tualetas (dušas) nešvarus.

My room key doesn't work.
Mano kambario raktas nerakina.

My neighbors are making a lot of noise.
Mano kaimynai labai triukšmauja.

It's too cold (hot) in my room.
Mano kambaryje per šalta (karšta).

I cannot open the window.
Negaliu atidaryti lango.

The lamp is not working.
Lempa neveikia.

There is no hot (cold) water.
Nėra karšto (šalto) vandens.

The room has not been cleaned.
Kambarys nebuvo išvalytas.

Some of my things are missing.
Keletas mano daiktų dingo.

My daughter is sick.
Mano dukra serga.

I (we) need a doctor.
Man (mums) reikia gydytojo.

Checking Out—Išsiregistravimas

At what time do I (we) have to check out?
Kada reikia išsiregistruoti?

Can I leave my luggage with you until 6 P.M.?
Ar galiu palikti savo bagažą pas jus iki šeštos valandos vakaro?

Can you call me a taxi, please?
Gal galite iškviesti man taksi?

I (we) would like to stay an extra night.
Norėčiau (norėtume) pasilikti dar vienai parai.

Can I have the bill, please?
Prašau sąskaitą.

Thank you. We had a pleasant stay in your hotel.
Ačiū. Buvo malonu apsistoti jūsų viešbutyje.

Staying with friends—Gyvenant pas draugus

If you want to explore culture, staying with Lithuanian friends will give you a much more realistic picture of what Lithuania is all about than staying at a hotel. Please keep in mind, however, that not all Lithuanians speak English. Younger people are more likely to be fluent or semi-fluent in English than are their parents and grandparents.

When staying with a family, it is customary to bring a "thank you" gift. You are likely to hear "***Oi, nereikėjo***" (i.e., Oh, there was no need to), but the gift(s) will be gladly accepted. If you didn't bring anything from your home country, you can always go to a local grocery store and get some good ground coffee and a bottle of foreign alcohol (e.g., brandy). Most Lithuanians are real "coffee addicts" and will be happy with such "thank you" gifts. If your hosts are not rich, and you are staying for a few days and eating a lot of home-cooked meals, you may also offer to pay for the groceries used in preparation of these meals. Taking your friends out for a dinner in a restaurant may be a nice gesture on your part as well.

Lithuanians are known for their hospitality. Unless the hostess has lived in the United States for an extended period of time, she is likely to force food on you. Some people may also try to force alcohol on you. To "survive," you need to learn how to stay "***Ne, ačiū***" (i.e., No, thank you) and "***Ačiū, užteks***" (i.e., Thanks, that will be enough). On the other hand, it is considered rude of a guest to roam in the refrigerator looking for food, unless, of course, the hosts have specifically asked you to help yourself to whatever is in the refrigerator. If no such permission was granted and you are not alone in the house, it is best to ask for food and/or drink.

The most popular Lithuanian toasts are "***Į sveikatą!***" (To [your] health!) and "***Už jus!***" (To you!). People may offer you homemade cider or gira (i.e., a Lithuanian drink made from rye bread and honey). If you do not feel comfortable drinking these drinks, ask your hosts to get you some mineral water. Lithuanians usually do not put ice cubes into their drinks; so be prepared for this inconvenience.

If a national dish is offered, either wait for the native Lithuanians to start eating it, or ask for "directions." If you start first, you risk an embarrassment because you are likely to eat in a different way than the locals.

If your friends have an apartment in a Soviet-style high-rise, you are almost certain to find a bathroom consisting of two separate rooms. One is called "***vonia***" (i.e., bathroom) and includes a bathtub, a sink, and often a washing machine. The other, called "***tualetas***" (i.e., restroom), is very small and includes a toilet. Private homes usually have American-style bathrooms consisting of one larger room. It can be referred to either as "*vonia*" or as "*tualetas*." The most polite expression indicating that you want to use a restroom is "***Norėčiau nusiplauti rankas***" (i.e., I would like to wash my hands).

Phone calls are very expensive by Lithuanian standards. Therefore, your hosts will be happy if you avoid outgoing calls. To make everyone happy, you may either rent a mobile (cell) phone (with a mobile card (e.g., Extra)) or buy a phone card and use public payphones. Payphone cards come in different denominations and can be purchased at *Lietuvos spauda* kiosks or at post offices. In Lithuania, you will not have to pay for incoming calls; however, outgoing calls, especially those made to a mobile phone, will cost you a small fortune. If calling a mobile phone or a foreign number from a payphone, buy a high denomination calling card (e.g., 100 credits)—the credits will disappear very quickly.

This is your room.
Tai jūsų kambarys.

Can I leave my things here?
Ar galiu čia palikti savo daiktus?

I'd like to wash my hands.
Norėčiau nusiplauti rankas.

Where is the restroom?
Kur tualetas?

Here/ there
Čia/ ten.

These towels are for you.
Šie rankšluosčiai jums.

Here is your key.
Čia jūsų raktas.

We go to bed at 11 P.M.
Mes einame miegoti vienuoliktą.

This is a small gift for you.
Tai maža dovanėlė jums.

Thank you.
Ačiū.

Thank you very much.
Labai ačiū.

There was no need to.
Nereikėjo.

These are my family photos.
Tai mano šeimos nuotraukos.

Do you want anything to eat (drink)?
Ar norite valgyti (gerti)?

I am hungry.
Aš alkanas (m.)/**alkana** (f.)

I want something to eat (to drink).
Noriu valgyti (gerti).

Did anybody call me?
Ar man niekas neskambino?

What did they say?
Ką sakė?

I want to find this person.
Noriu surasti šį žmogų.

Could you help me call him (her)?
Gal galėtumėte man padėti jam (jai) paskambinti?

Could I use your phone, please?
Gal galėčiau pasinaudoti jūsų telefonu?

That is a local call.
Tai vietinis skambutis.

I will pay for my calls.
Aš apmokėsiu savo pokalbius.

Is there a payphone near by?
Ar netoliese yra taksofonas?

Where can I buy a phone card?
Kur galiu nusipirkti taksofono kortelę?

I want to wash some clothes.
Noriu išsiskalbti keletą drabužių

I need . . . — **Man reikia . . .**
. . . an iron. — **. . . lygintuvo.**
. . . a hairdryer. — **. . . plaukų džiovintuvo.**
. . . a nail polish remover. — **. . . nagų lako valiklio.**
. . . scissors. — **. . . žirklių.**
. . . shoe polish. — **. . . batų tepalo.**
. . . a needle and some thread. — **. . . adatos ir siūlo.**

I want to buy . . . — **Noriu nusipirkti . . .**
. . . some souvenirs. — **. . . suvenyrų.**
. . . some amber. — **. . . gintarų.**

Could you recommend any store?
Gal galėtumėte rekomenduoti kokią parduotuvę?

Do we have time?
Ar turime laiko?

How do I get to the (city) center from here?
Kaip patekti į (miesto) centrą iš čia?

Where can I buy bus (trolley) tickets?
Kur galiu nusipirkti autobuso (troleibuso) bilietų?

Could you call a taxi for me, please?
Gal galėtumėte man iškviesti taksi?

I am meeting a friend at seven o'clock.
Septintą valandą susitinku su draugu (m.)/ **drauge** (f.).

I need to go to the American (British, Canadian, Australian) Embassy.
Turiu nueiti į Amerikos (Anglijos, Kanados, Australijos) ambasadą.

I had a very nice stay with you.
Buvo labai malonu pas jus pasisvečiuoti.

Please visit me in my country.
Prašau mane aplankyti mano šalyje.

You may stay with me.
Galėsite apsistoti mano namuose.

Renting an apartment (house)— Nuomojant butą (namą)

When do I have to pay the rent?
Kada turiu mokėti nuomą?

Does the rent include utilities?
Ar į nuomą įeina komunaliniai patarnavimai?

Is the apartment (house) furnished?
Ar butas (namas) su baldais?

Is there . . .	**Ar yra . . .**
. . . a phone?	**. . . telefonas?**
. . . a TV set?	**. . . televizorius?**
. . . a cable TV?	**. . . kabelinė televizija?**
. . . internet connection?	**. . . interneto ryšys?**

Can I call you at this number?
Ar galiu jums skambinti šiuo numeriu?

Could you send a repairman, please?
Ar galėtumėte atsiųsti meistrą?

The toilet is clogged.
Tualetas užsikimšo.

There is a leak under the kitchen sink.
Po virtuvės kriaukle bėga vanduo.

The faucet leaks water.
Iš krano laša.

There is no hot (cold) water.
Nėra karšto (šalto) vandens.

There is no water.
Nėra vandens.

We need two sets of keys.
Mums reikia dviejų raktų.

Where is the key for this door?
Kur šių durų raktas?

What's this?
Kas čia?

Could you help me (us) find a cleaning lady, please?
Gal galėtumėte padėti man (mums) rasti ateinančią valytoją?

Around the House—Namuose

apartment	**butas**
room	**kambarys**
door	**durys**
ceiling	**lubos**
floor	**grindys**
wall	**siena**
window	**langas**
balcony	**balkonas**
bathroom	**vonia**
bath	**vonia**
detergent	**skalbimo priemonė**
faucet	**kranas**
mirror	**veidrodis**
rug	**kilimėlis**
shelf	**lentyna**
shower	**dušas**
shower curtain	**dušo užuolaida**

sink	**kriauklė**
soap	**muilas**
sponge	**kempinė**
toothbrush	**dantų šepetėlis**
toothpaste	**dantų pasta**
towel	**rankšluostis**
bathroom (toilet)	**tualetas**
toilet paper	**tualetinis popierius**
children's room	**vaikų kambarys**
kitchen	**virtuvė**
dessert spoon	**šaukštelis**
fork	**šakutė**
glass	**stiklinė**
knife	**peilis**
plate	**lėkštė**
pot	**puodas**
sauce/frying pan	**keptuvė**
shot glass	**taurelė**
(table) spoon	**šaukštas**
wine glass	**vyno taurė**
living room	**svetainė**
painting	**paveikslas**
storage room	**sandėliukas**
vacuum cleaner	**dulkių siurblys**
wallpaper	**tapetai**

Furniture—Baldai

armchair	**fotelis**
bed	**lova**
bedspread	**lovatiesė**
pillow	**pagalvė**
sheet	**paklodė**
blanket	**antklodė**
bookcase	**knygų spinta**
bookcase & dresser unit	**sekcija**
ceiling fixture	**šviestuvas**
chair	**kėdė**

closet	**spintelė**
coffee table	**staliukas (kavai)**
curtains	**užuolaidos**
dresser	**indauja**
flower plant	**gėlė**
ironing board	**lyginimo lenta**
lamp	**lempa**
mirror	**veidrodis**
painting	**paveikslas**
side table	**staliukas**
sofa	**sofa**
table	**stalas**
wallpaper	**tapetai**
wardrobe	**(rūbų) spinta**

Camping—Kempingas

Camping is not very popular in Lithuania. Some campgrounds are located around Vilnius, and some are near the Baltic Sea. Although they are not very well equipped, most have electricity and covered shower and toilet areas (sometimes inadequate for the number of campers). Better campgrounds have satellite TV, guarded parking, and sauna. In some campgrounds, you can rent water bikes, yachts and even go for a ride in a hot air balloon.

Off-ground camping is getting more and more difficult in Lithuania as most scenic land now is individually owned.

Where is the nearest campground?
Kur artimiausias kempingas?

Can we pitch our tent here?
Ar galime čia pasistatyti palapinę?

Can we park our camper here?
Ar galime čia pasistatyti namelį?

Can we light a fire?
Ar galime susikurti laužą?

How much will we have to pay per day (week)?
Kiek reikės mokėti už parą (savaitę)?

Is there electricity on the campground?
Ar kempinge yra elektros?

Where do I pay?
Kur turiu sumokėti?

When do I need to pay?
Kada turiu sumokėti?

Where can I buy some groceries?
Kur galiu nusipirkti maisto produktų?

Is there a restaurant near by?
Ar netoliese yra restoranas?

Is this the drinking water?
Ar tai geriamas vanduo?

Where is the shower?
Kur dušas?

Is there any hot water?
Ar yra karšto vandens?

Where are the bathrooms?
Kur tualetai?

Where can we wash our dishes, please?
Kur galėtume susiplauti indus?

Where are the garbage containers?
Kur šiukšlių konteineriai?

Is there . . . on the campground?
Ar kempinge yra . . .

. . . a swimming pool	**. . . baseinas?**
. . . television	**. . . televizija?**
. . . a swing set	**. . . sūpynės?**

air mattress	**pripučiamas čiužinys**
backpack	**kuprinė**
corkscrew	**kamščiatraukis**
camp-fire	**laužas**
candle	**žvakė**
bottle opener	**(butelių) atidarytuvas**
can opener	**(konservų) atidarytuvas**
fire	**ugnis**
garbage	**šiukšlės**
flashlight	**žibintuvėlis**
folding chair	**sudedama kėdė**
folding table	**sudedamas stalas**
frying pan	**keptuvė**
knife	**peilis**
lock	**spyna**
matches	**degtukai**
medications	**vaistai**
plate	**lėkštė**
pot	**puodas**
rope	**virvė**
sleeping bag	**miegmaišis**
sunblock lotion	**kremas nuo saulės**
tent	**palapinė**
thermos flask	**termosas**
water	**vanduo**

Childcare—Vaikų priežiūra

I am looking for a babysitter . . .
Ieškau auklės . . .

. . . for this evening.	**. . . šiam vakarui.**
. . . for three hours.	**. . . trims valandoms.**

My son (daughter) is 5 years old.
Mano sūnui (dukrai) penkeri.

My son (daughter) goes to bed at nine.
Mano sūnus (dukra) eina miegoti devintą.

Here is the food/toys.
Čia maistas/žaislai.

This milk needs to be warmed.
Šis pienas turi būti pašildytas.

Where could I . . .	**Kur galėčiau . . .**
. . . get some diapers?	**. . . gauti sauskelnių?**
. . . get some baby food?	**. . . gauti vaikų maistelio?**
. . . feed the baby?	**. . . pamaitinti kūdikį?**
. . . change the baby?	**. . . pervilkti/pervystyti kūdikį?**

My child is ill.
Mano vaikas serga.

We need a doctor.
Mums reikia gydytojo.

At a Bank—Banke

Changing money—Valiutos keitimas

The Lithuanian Litas has a fixed exchange rate with the Euro; therefore, if the US dollar is low compared to the Euro, your travel expenses in Lithuania will be higher than if the situation were reverse.

Where is the nearest currency exchange?
Kur artimiausia valiutos keitykla?

I'd like to change this amount for Litas.
Norėčiau išsikeisti šią sumą į litus.

I'd like to cash these traveler's checks.
Norėčiau išgryninti šiuos kelioninius čekius.

What's the exchange rate?
Koks keitimo kursas?

What bank has the best exchange rate?
Kuriame banke geriausias kursas?

Where is the nearest branch of this bank?
Kur artimiausias šio banko skyrius?

Please give me a hundred Litas in ten Litas bills.
Prašau man duoti šimtą litų dešimties litų banknotais.

Can you please break this hundred dollar bill into fifty dollars worth of Litas and fifty US dollars?
Prašau iškeisti šį šimto dolerių banknotą į litus taip, kad man dar liktų penkiasdešimt Amerikos dolerių.

Please give me half of this amount in Litas and half in Latvian Latas (Euros).
Prašau, duokite pusę šios sumos litais ir pusę Latvijos latais (eurais).

The exchange rate is not favorable today.
Keitimo kursas šiandien nepalankus.

Opening an account—Sąskaitos atidarymas

I'd like to open an account in . . .
Norėčiau atidaryti sąskaitą . . .

. . . Litas.	**. . . litais.**
. . . dollars.	**. . . doleriais.**
. . . Euros.	**. . . eurais.**

I want to deposit this amount.
Noriu padėti šią sumą.

I need a debit card.
Man reikia atsiskaitymo kortelės.

What's the yearly fee for the card?
Koks metinis mokestis už kortelę?

I'd like to get a credit card.
Norėčiau gauti kredito kortelę.

Do you have any information in English?
Ar turite informacijos anglų kalba?

What is the annual percentage rate for a CD?
Kokios metinės palūkanos už terminuotą indėlį?

It depends on the currency and the length of a CD.
Priklauso nuo valiutos ir indėlio laikymo trukmės.

Please sign here.
Prašau pasirašyti čia.

Please write down the bank code and other information necessary for money to be transferred to my account from abroad.
Prašau užrašyti banko kodą ir kitą informaciją, reikalingą pinigams pervesti į mano sąskaitą iš užsienio.

Getting Around

Public transportation in Lithuania—Viešasis transportas Lietuvoje

In Lithuania, public transportation is well-developed and not expensive. Please be advised that you will need different tickets for buses and trolleybuses.

Tickets can be purchased at any *Lietuvos spauda* kiosk usually for less than 1 Litas each. Tickets can also be obtained from bus drivers for the exact change. Once inside the bus or the trolley, do not forget to punch your ticket to validate it. If your ticket is not valid, you may get fined.

Monthly passes can also be purchased at *Lietuvos spauda* kiosks. They do not need to be punched.

Minibuses (*mikroautobusai*) are a faster yet more expensive means of transportation than are buses and trolleybuses. Here, you do not need a ticket, only 1–2 Litas in cash, depending on the city. Also, you must loudly inform the driver when you want to get off.

Commuting via inter-city trains and buses costs about the same. All train tickets must be purchased at the ticket office, and some bus tickets may be bought on the bus. Express buses tend to be slightly more expensive yet much more convenient as they do not stop at every little town on the way.

In bus stations, you may encounter private drivers who solicit passengers to travel with them for the price of a bus ticket. For safety reasons, it is best that you stick with the "official" transportation as some people may try to take advantage of foreigners.

Asking directions—Kur yra . . . ?

Excuse me, where is . . .	**Atsiprašau, kur yra . . .**
. . . the restroom?	**. . . tualetas?**
. . . the post office?	**. . . paštas?**
. . . the train station?	**. . . geležinkelio stotis?**
. . . the bus station?	**. . . autobusų stotis?**
. . . hotel “Artis”?	**. . . viešbutis “Artis”?**
. . . Pilies Street?	**. . . Pilies gatvė?**
. . . this street?	**. . . ši gatvė?**
. . . the police?	**. . . policija?**
. . . the nearest bank?	**. . . artimiausias bankas?**
. . . the center of the city?	**. . . miesto centras?**
. . . the Opera/ Ballet Theater?	**. . . Operos ir baleto teatras?**
. . . the monument to Frank Zappa?	**. . . paminklas Frankui Zapai?**

I am lost.
Aš pasiklydau.

Please show me this place on the map.
Prašau parodyti man šią vietą žemėlapyje.

Is this . . .	**Ar tai . . .**
. . . the Gate of Dawn?	**. . . Aušros Vartai?**
. . . the Cathedral?	**. . . Katedra?**
. . . St. Anne’s Church?	**. . . Šventos Onos bažnyčia?**

Will I get to the Vilnius University if I take this street?
Ar, eidamas (m.)/ **eidama** (f.) **šia gatve, pateksiu į Vilniaus universitetą?**

How do I get to . . .
Kaip nuvykti į . . .

. . . the nearest internet café?
. . . artimiausią interneto kavinę?

. . . the Old Town?
. . . senamiestį?

. . . the airport?
. . . į oro uostą?

Is it far?
Ar tai toli?

Can I walk, or is better to take a bus?
Ar galiu nueiti, ar geriau važiuoti autobusu?

What bus should I take?
Kuriuo autobusu važiuoti?

Where do I get off?
Kur man išlipti?

What is here to see?
Ką čia verta pamatyti?

I am looking for . . .	**Ieškau . . .**
. . . a good clothing store.	**. . . geros rūbų parduotuvės.**
. . . a good restaurant.	**. . . gero restorano.**
. . . a pharmacy.	**. . . vaistinės.**

What can you recommend?
Ką galite rekomenduoti?

avenue	**alėja**
block	**kvartalas**
boulevard	**bulvaras**
bridge	**tiltas**
building	**pastatas**
castle	**pilis**
cemetery	**kapinės**
church	**bažnyčia**
city hall	**rotušė**
corner	**kampas**
crossing	**perėja**

crossroad	**sankryža**
downtown	**miesto centras**
monument	**paminklas**
museum	**muziejus**
river	**upė**
square	**skveras, aikštė**
statue	**statula**
street	**gatvė**
theater	**teatras**
tower	**bokštas**
traffic lights	**šviesoforas**
straight ahead	**tiesiai**
to the left	**į kairę**
to the right	**į dešinę**
back	**atgal**
go	**eikite**
turn	**pasukite**
go back	**grįžkite atgal**

Ask the police officer.
Paklauskite policininko.

I'll show you the way.
Aš jus palydėsiu.

By taxi—Taksi

Cab ride fares vary depending on the city and the taxi company. Generally, it is much cheaper to call a taxi from a phone (a payphone will do the trick) than to pick one up at a taxi stand or to hail one on the street.

No tips are expected, but will be greatly appreciated. However, as a foreigner, you may be overcharged; thus try to negotiate the price before you get into the cab. In case of emergency (e.g., you miss the last bus/train to the city you are staying at), you can even take a cab home. It should not cost you more than traveling longer distances with a cab in New York City or Chicago. For example, a 55 km ride should not cost you more than 60 Litas (less than $20). Do not let the taxi driver know that you missed your last bus/train and try to negotiate as much as possible. Some cab companies give out discount cards each time you take a cab (e.g., you get one free ride for ten collected cards).

Could you call a taxi for me, please?
Gal galėtumėte man iškviesti taksi?

What taxi company would you recommend?
Kurią taksi firmą rekomenduotumėte?

What do you charge for one kilometer?
Kiek turiu mokėti už vieną kilometrą?

Where can I get a taxi?
Kur galiu rasti taksi?

I am in a (big) hurry.
Aš (labai) skubu.

I am late.
Vėluoju.

We are late.
Vėluojame.

Please hurry!
Prašau, paskubėkite!

Here is the address.
Štai adresas.

Please wait here.
Prašau čia palaukti.

What do I owe you?
Kiek aš jums skolingas (m.)/ **skolinga** (f.)?

What do I have to pay?
Kiek turiu mokėti?

Keep the change.
Grąžą pasilikite.

Please stop here.
Prašau sustoti čia.

Don't drive around!
Nevažinėkite aplink!

There must be a shorter way!
Turi būti trumpesnis kelias!

By bus/trolley—Autobusas/troleibusas

You can purchase bus and trolley tickets at any *Lietuvos spauda* kiosk. If you are willing to pay slightly more, you may purchase a ticket from the driver once on the bus/trolley.

City buses and trolleys tend to be crowded, so please watch your purses and wallets, especially when you are getting on/off the bus/trolley. It is usually young teenagers who will attempt (often successfully) to steal your money. If you can afford it, minibuses (*mikroautobusai*) and cabs present a much faster and safer option.

If traveling to another city, board a bus in the bus station. For some buses, you will need to buy tickets at the ticket office, for some from the driver on the bus. Express buses are usually better than regular ones as they do not stop in every little village on the way. Minibuses (*mikroautobusai*) are fast and convenient too. If you need to get off at some village, do not take an express bus. Furthermore, tell the driver your destination when you board the bus as he may not stop there otherwise.

Where is a bus stop?
Kur autobusų stotelė?

Does this bus go downtown?
Ar šis autobusas važiuoja į miesto centrą?

When is the next bus to Kaunas?
Kada kitas autobusas į Kauną?

I am going to this address.
Važiuoju šiuo adresu.

Please tell me where to get off.
Prašau pasakyti, kur man išlipti.

One bus/trolley ticket, please.
Prašau vieną autobuso/troleibuso bilietą.

How much is it?
Kiek kainuoja?

When is the last bus to Panevėžys?
Kada išvyksta paskutinis autobusas į Panevėžį?

By train—Traukinys

Some trains in Lithuania have no assigned seats and no classes. Therefore, the earlier you board these trains, the better seat you will get.

One ticket to Marijampolė, please.
Prašau vieną bilietą į Marijampolę.

When is the next train to Vilnius?
Kada išvyksta kitas traukinys į Vilnių?

When is the last train to Warsaw?
Kada išvyksta paskutinis traukinys į Varšuvą?

Is this a sleeper train?
Ar šiame traukinyje yra miegamieji vagonai?

How long will the trip last?
Kiek užtruks kelionė?

Where is the time-table?
Kur tvarkaraštis?

Do you have any discounts for students (children)?
Ar studentams (vaikams) taikote nuolaidas?

Where is the luggage storage?
Kur bagažo saugykla?

I want to leave this bag here.
Noriu čia palikti šį krepšį.

When does the train arrive?
Kada traukinys atvyksta?

Where do I need to go to board the train, please?
Kur man eiti, kad surasčiau traukinį?

Is this the train to Alytus?
Ar šis traukinys į Alytų?

Is this seat free?
Ar ši vieta laisva?

May I sit here?
Ar galiu čia atsisėsti?

Are we in Kaunas yet?
Ar mes jau Kaune?

What town is this?
Koks tai miestas?

I have lost my ticket.
Pamečiau bilietą.

Do you mind if I close (open) the window?
Ar neprieštarausite, jei uždarysiu (atidarysiu) langą?

Can you help me, please?
Gal galite man padėti?

carriage	**vagonas**
compartment	**kupė**
conductor	**palydovas** (m.)/ **palydovė** (f.)
passenger	**keleivis** (m.)/ **keleivė** (f.)
platform	**peronas, kelias**
railway	**geležinkelis**
station	**stotis**
ticket	**bilietas**
ticket office	**bilietų kasa**
ticket inspector	**kontrolierius** (m.)/ **kontrolierė** (f.)
train	**traukinys**

Driving

Renting a car—Mašinos nuoma

You can rent a car at Budget, Hertz, Avis, and a plethora of local companies, many of which offer free hotel/airport delivery, unlimited mileage, and optional chauffeur service. Inquire about possible tours of Vilnius and other cities. However, be prepared to empty your wallets as car rentals are quite expensive in Lithuania (i.e., on average, about $40/day).

I would like to rent a car.
Norėčiau išsinuomoti mašiną.

Do you have anything cheaper?
Ar turite ką nors pigiau?

I want . . .
Noriu . . .

. . . a luxury car.
. . . prabangios mašinos.

. . . a small (large) car.
. . . mažos (didelės) mašinos.

. . . a car with an automatic stick shift.
. . . mašinos su automatine pavarų dėže.

What are the color choices?
Koks spalvų pasirinkimas?

What insurance do you offer?
Kokį draudimą siūlote?

Do you have any discounts?
Ar siūlote nuolaidų?

Do you have unlimited mileage?
Ar kilometražas neribotas?

Do I have to pay in advance?
Ar reikia mokėti iš anksto?

I can pay with a credit card, can't I?
Galiu mokėti kredito kortele, ar ne?

Do I have to return the car here?
Ar mašiną čia turiu grąžinti?

Can I leave the car at the airport?
Ar galiu palikti mašiną oro uoste?

I would like to hire a chauffeur . . .
Norėčiau pasisamdyti vairuotoją . . .

. . . for two days. **. . . porai dienų.**
. . . for a week. **. . . savaitei.**

Please deliver the car to my hotel tomorrow at 8 A.M.
Prašau pristatyti mašiną man į viešbutį rytoj aštuntą ryto.

Asking for directions—Kur yra . . .?

Where is the nearest gas station?
Kur artimiausia degalinė?

Does this road go to Klaipėda?
Ar tai kelias į Klaipėdą?

Do I need to turn here?
Ar turiu čia pasukti?

Excuse me, where is downtown?
Atsiprašau, kur miesto centras?

How do I get onto the highway?
Kaip išvažiuoti į greitkelį?

How far is Telšiai?
Kiek kilometrų iki Telšių?

Go straight ahead.
Važiuokite tiesiai.

Turn left at the traffic lights.
Prie šviesoforo pasukite į kairę.

Traffic—Eismas

When is the rush hour?
Kada piko valandos?

Is this a one-way road?
Ar čia vienos krypties eismas?

What is the speed limit here?
Koks čia leistinas greitis?

Is the road wet?
Ar kelias šlapias?

Are the roads cleared?
Ar keliai nuvalyti?

Parking—Automobilių stovėjimo vieta

Where is the nearest (guarded) parking lot?
Kur artimiausia (saugoma) mašinų stovėjimo aikštelė?

Where can I park my car?
Kur galiu pasistatyti mašiną?

Can I park here?
Ar galiu čia pasistatyti mašiną?

How much does one hour (day) cost?
Kiek kainuoja viena valanda (para)?

Can I leave the car over-night?
Ar galiu palikti mašiną nakčiai?

Is it safe?
Ar tai saugu?

Weather conditions—Oro sąlygos

The roads are . . .	**Keliai . . .**
. . . wet.	**. . . šlapi.**
. . . slippery.	**. . . slidūs.**

Be careful!
Būkite atsargūs!

Drive carefully!
Važiuokite atsargiai!

Is it very slippery?
Ar labai slidu?

Is it very windy?
Ar labai vėjuota?

It is raining.
Lyja.

It is snowing.
Sninga.

At the gas station—Degalinėje

Can I pay with the credit card?
Ar galiu mokėti kredito kortele?

Fill the tank, please.
Prašau pripilti pilną baką benzino.

Could you clean the windshield, please?
Gal galėtumėte nuplauti priekinį stiklą?

Is there a car wash here?
Ar čia yra mašinų plovykla?

How much does it cost?
Kiek tai kainuoja?

Breakdowns and repairs—
Mašinos gedimai ir remontas

I have a flat tire.
Sprogo padanga.

Can you help me, please?
Gal galite man padėti?

Something happened to my car.
Kažkas atsitiko mano mašinai.

My car has broken down.
Mano mašina sugedo.

Something is wrong with the engine.
Kažkas atsitiko varikliui.

Where is the nearest garage?
Kur artimiausias autoservisas?

I have run out of gas.
Baigėsi benzinas.

Can I buy some gas from you?
Gal galėčiau iš jūsų nusipirkti truputį benzino?

Could you tow my car, please?
Gal galėtumėte patempti mano mašiną?

I need a phone.
Man reikia telefono.

How long will it take to repair my car?
Kiek laiko taisys mano mašiną?

I have no spare parts.
Neturiu atsarginių dalių.

I have locked myself out of the car.
Užsitrenkiau mašinos dureles.

I have left my keys inside.
Palikau raktus mašinoje.

Accidents and the police—
Nelaimingi atsitikimai ir policija

There is an accident.
Įvyko avarija.

Call . . .	**Iškvieskite . . .**
. . . the police!	**. . . policiją!**
. . . the ambulance!	**. . . greitąją pagalbą!**

Can you be my witness, please?
Ar sutinkate būti mano liudininku?

Who was driving?
Kas buvo už vairo?

Are you hurt?
Ar jūs sužeistas (m.)/ **sužeista** (f.)**?**

Is anybody hurt?
Ar yra sužeistų?

Can you speak?
Ar galite kalbėti?

Don't move.
Nejudėkite.

What is your name and address?
Koks jūsų vardas ir adresas?

I did not notice him (her).
Aš jo (jos) nepastebėjau.

You were speeding.
Jūs viršijote leistiną greitį.

May I see your driver's license, please?
Prašau parodyti savo vairuotojo pažymėjimą.

I am a foreigner.
Aš užsienietis (m.)/ **užsienietė** (f.)**.**

I didn't drink any alcoholic beverages.
Aš negėriau alkoholinių gėrimų.

I did not see the sign.
Nemačiau kelio ženklo.

It was too slippery.
Buvo per slidu.

I was driving only at 60 km/h.
Važiavau tik 60 km/h (šešiasdešimties kilometrų per valandą) greičiu.

My tire burst.
Sprogo padanga.

I lost control of my car.
Nesuvaldžiau mašinos.

That is a rental car.
Tai išnuomota mašina.

Car Parts

accelerator	**akseleratorius**
air filter	**oro filtras**
alarm (system)	**signalizacija**
antenna	**antena**
antifreeze	**aušinamasis skystis**
automatic	**automatinis** (m.)/ **automatinė** (f.)
axle	**ašis**
battery	**akumuliatorius**
brakes	**stabdžiai**
brights	**tolimos šviesos**
bulb	**lemputė**
car	**mašina**
carburetor	**karbiuratorius**
chassis	**važiuoklė**
cylinder	**cilindras**
door	**durelės**
engine	**variklis**
exhaust pype	**dujų išmetimo vamzdis**
gas	**benzinas**
gas tank	**benzino bakas**
gear	**pavara**
gear box	**pavarų dėžė**
gearshift	**pavarų perjungimo svirtis**
hand (emergency) brake	**rankinis stabdis**
hazard lights	**avarinės šviesos**
headlights	**priekiniai žibintai**
heating system	**šildymo sistema**

hood	**kapotas**
horn	**signalas**
to press the horn	**signalizuoti**
hose	**žarna**
ignition	**degimas**
ignition key	**užvedimo raktelis**
jack	**keltuvas/ domkratas** (col.)
lights	**šviesos**
mirror	**veidrodėlis**
oil	**alyva**
pedal	**pedalas**
pump	**siurblys/ pompa**
radiator	**radiatorius**
screwdriver	**atsuktuvas**
seat	**vieta**
seat belt	**(saugos) diržas**
spare parts	**atsarginės dalys**
spare tire	**atsarginė padanga**
spark plug	**žvakė**
speedometer	**spidometras**
starter	**starteris**
steering wheel	**vairas**
tire	**padanga**
tools	**įrankiai**
trunk	**bagažinė**
water	**vanduo**
wheel	**ratas**
windshield	**priekinis stiklas**
(windshield) wipers	**valytuvai**
wrench	**raktas**

Food and Drink

What and when Lithuanians eat— Ką ir kada valgo lietuviai

Lunch (*pietūs*) is the main meal of the day. It is eaten sometime between noon and 2 P.M. Traditionally, Lithuanians eat soup first. Herring, which may be served in a variety of ways, is a popular appetizer. If a meat dish is eaten afterwards, it is served with a vegetable salad or fresh cut vegetables and potatoes, rice, or noodles.

Lithuanians usually do not top every meal with pastries and cakes; however, most people will have a cup of coffee or hot tea after lunch. Fresh fruit is a "dessert" of choice for many. Nevertheless, richer desserts are gladly consumed at parties and on weekends.

Lithuanian breakfast (*pusryčiai*) is similar to American lunch. In cities, most people eat open sandwiches with cheese or smoked sausage (usually, not on the same sandwich) topped with a slice of tomato or fresh (or pickled) cucumber. Hardboiled or fried eggs and Lithuanian-style omelets are popular breakfast choices as well. In villages, people tend to eat richer breakfast than do people in towns. Younger people, especially in cities, often opt for an American-style light breakfast consisting of cereal and/or yogurt and/or fruits and a cup of coffee or tea.

Dinner (*vakarienė*) is eaten sometime between 6 P.M. and 8 P.M. and is usually lighter than lunch. Most Lithuanians stay away from rich foods at night. Sometimes a leftover soup from lunch makes a dinner.

Lithuanians consume a lot of potatoes, and most national dishes are made from potatoes. Also, Lithuanians eat plenty of rye or "black" bread (*juoda duona*).

FOOD AND DRINK

Lithuanians drink less water than do Americans. However, they eat plenty of soups. Many women watch their figures and prefer salads to meat. Nevertheless, there are not many vegetarians in Lithuania.

Generally, meals in Lithuanian restaurants are served in smaller portions than in American restaurants. Yet, unlike in the United States, in Lithuania people do not take leftovers home.

Tips are not expected. However, if you leave one, it will be greatly appreciated. A 10% tip will be perceived as a very generous one, especially if your bill is large. For tourists' convenience, most restaurants in large cities will have Lithuanian-English menus.

Some national dishes such as *cepelinai* (i.e., potato paste Zeppelins stuffed with meat) or *šaltibarščiai* (i.e., cold beet soup) may be a challenge to eat. To avoid embarrassment, ask the waiter or observe the locals eat the same dish.

Food—Maistas

almonds **migdolai**
appetizer **užkandis**
apple **obuolys**
apricot **abrikosas**
banana **bananas**
beans **pupelės**
beef **jautiena**
beets **burokėliai**
biscuit **sausainis**
blackcurrant **juodieji serbentai**
blueberries **mėlynės**
bread **duona**
broth **sultinys**
butter **sviestas**
cabbage **kopūstai**
cake **tortas**

calamari	**kalmarai**
candy	**saldainis**
carbohydrates	**angliavandeniai**
carp	**karpis**
carrots	**morkos**
cauliflower	**žiediniai kopūstai/ kalafiorai**
caviar (black/ red)	**ikrai (juodieji/ raudonieji)**
celery	**salierai**
cereal	**dribsniai, javainiai**
cheese	**sūris**
cheeseburger	**sūrainis/ mėsainis su sūriu**
cherries	**vyšnios**
chewing gum	**kramtomoji guma**
chicken	**vištiena**
chips	**traškučiai**
chocolate	**šokoladas**
cod	**menkė**
corn	**kukurūzai**
cornflakes	**kukurūzų lazdelės**
cottage cheese	**varškė**
crab	**krabas**
crackers	**krekeriai**
cream	**grietinėlė**
cucumber	**agurkas**
cutlet	**kotletas**
duck	**antis, antiena**
eel (smoked)	**ungurys (rūkytas)**
fat	**riebalai**
fish	**žuvis**
fish fingers	**žuvų piršteliai**
french fries	**bulvių lazdelės**
fruit	**vaisiai**
garlic	**česnakas**
goose	**žąsis, žąsiena**
grapefruit	**greipfrutas**
grapes	**vynuogės**
gravy	**padažas**
green peas	**žirneliai**

green/ red/ yellow pepper	**žaliasis/ raudonasis/ geltonasis pipiras**
greens	**žalumynai**
ham	**kumpis**
hamburger	**mėsainis**
hazelnuts	**lazdyno riešutai**
herring	**silkė**
horseradish	**krienai**
hot chocolate	**kakava**
hot dog	**dešrainis**
ice cream	**ledai**
jam	**džemas**
jelly	**želė**
kipper	**rūkyta silkė**
kiwi	**kivis**
lamb	**aviena**
leek	**poras**
lemon	**citrina**
lettuce	**salotos**
lobster	**vėžys**
mackarel	**skumbrė**
mashed potatoes	**bulvių košė**
margarine	**margarinas**
mayonnaise	**majonezas**
meat	**mėsa**
milk	**pienas**
mushrooms	**grybai**
mustard	**garstyčios**
noodles	**makaronai**
nuts	**riešutai**
oil	**aliejus**
olives	**alyvuogės**
omelet	**omletas**
onion	**svogūnas**
orange	**apelsinas**
oysters	**austrės**
pancakes	**blynai**
pasta	**makaronų mišrainė**
pâté	**paštetas**
peach	**persikas**

peanuts **žemės riešutai**
pear **kriaušė**
peas **žirneliai**
pepper **pipirai**
perch **ešerys**
pie **pyragas**
pike **lydeka**
pineapple **ananasas**
plaice **plekšnė**
plum **slyva**
pork **kiauliena**
porridge **košė**
potato **bulvė**
potato pancakes **bulviniai blynai**
poultry **paukštiena**
prawns **(didelės) krevetės**
preserves **uogienė**
protein **baltymai**
pudding **pudingas**
raisins **razinos**
raspberries **avietės**
rice **ryžiai**
rye bread **juoda duona**
roast meat **kepsnys**
salad **salotos**
salmon **lašiša**
salt **druska**
sandwich **sumuštinis**
sardine **sardinė**
sauce **padažas**
sauerkraut **rauginti kopūstai**
sausage **dešra, dešrelė**
scrambled eggs **plakta kiaušinienė**
seasoning **prieskoniai**
shrimps **krevetės**
smoked fish **rūkyta žuvis**
soup **sriuba**
sour cream **grietinė**
spices **prieskoniai**
spinach **špinatai**

steak	**steikas/ kepsnys**
stew	**troškinys**
strawberries	**braškės**
sturgeon	**eršketas**
sugar	**cukrus**
tangerine	**mandarinas**
tart	**pyragaitis**
toast	**skrebutis**
tomato	**pomidoras**
trout	**upėtakis**
tuna	**tunas**
turkey	**kalakutas, kalakutiena**
veal	**veršiena**
vegetables	**daržovės**
vinegar	**actas**
walnuts	**graikiniai riešutai**
watermelon	**arbūzas**
whipped cream	**plakta grietinėlė**
yogurt	**jogurtas**

Ordering food—Patiekalų užsakymas

One more menu, please.
Prašau dar vieną meniu.

Do you have a menu in English, please?
Gal turite meniu anglų kalba?

I am vegetarian.
Aš vegetaras (m.)/ **vegetarė** (f.).

What would you recommend?
Ką pasiūlytumėte?

I would like to try some national dishes.
Norėčiau paragauti nacionalinių patiekalų.

What soup is the best?
Kuri sriuba skaniausia?

I'd like to have some chicken dish.
Norėčiau vištienos patiekalo.

Is this fresh?
Ar tai šviežia?

Is it very spicy?
Ar tai labai aštru?

I'll try that.
Pabandysiu.

I am allergic to peanuts.
Aš alergiškas (m.)/ **alergiška** (f.) **žemės riešutams.**

We are ready to order.
Mes jau galime užsisakyti.

I did not order this.
Aš šito neužsisakiau.

The bill, please.
Prašau sąskaitą.

We are in a (big) hurry.
Mes (labai) skubame.

We would like to pay separately.
Mokėsime atskirai.

Drinks—Gėrimai

alcohol **alkoholis**
beer **alus**
Bloody Mary **Kruvinoji Merė**
brandy **brendis**
cacao **kakava**
champagne **šampanas**
cocktail **kokteilis**

coffee	**kava**
cognac	**konjakas**
coke	**kokakola**
gin	**džinas**
gin & tonic	**džinas su tonika**
ground coffee	**malta kava**
hot chocolate	**kakava**
instant coffee	**tirpioji kava**
juice	**sultys**
liquor	**likeris**
milk	**pienas**
mineral water	**mineralinis (vanduo)**
sparkling	**gazuotas**
spring	**šaltinio**
orange juice	**apelsinų sultys**
port	**portveinas**
red wine	**raudonasis vynas**
rum	**romas**
rum & coke	**romas su kokakola**
sangria	**sangrija**
soda	**limonadas**
sparkling wine	**putojantis vynas**
tea	**arbata**
with lemon	**su citrina**
with milk	**su pienu**
with honey	**su medum**
tonic	**tonikas**
vodka	**degtinė**
water	**vanduo**
white wine	**baltasis vynas**
wine	**vynas**
dessert	**desertinis**
dry	**sausas**
Muscat	**muskatinis**
sweet	**saldus**
table	**stalo**
whisky	**viskis**

Ordering drinks—Gėrimų užsakymas

What would you like to drink?
Ką gersite?

One beer, please.
Prašau vieną alaus.

One more.
Dar vieną.

The same please.
Prašau to paties.

What (dark/light) beer is the best in Lithuania?
Kuris (tamsusis/ šviesusis) alus geriausias Lietuvoje?

May we have the menu, please.
Prašau paduoti mums meniu (valgiaraštį).

Black coffee, please.
Prašau juodos kavos.

May I have some milk with my coffee?
Gal gaučiau pieno kavai?

Two cups of green tea, please.
Prašau du puodelius žaliosios arbatos.

A glass of cold mineral water.
Stiklinę šalto mineralinio.

A bottle of red (white) wine.
Butelį raudonojo (baltojo) vyno.

Three glasses of white wine.
Tris taures baltojo vyno.

A glass of orange juice and a glass of peach juice.
Stiklinę apelsinų sulčių ir stiklinę persikų sulčių.

A hundred grams of cherry liquor.
Šimtą gramų vyšnių likerio.

Coke with (without) ice.
Kokakolos su ledais (be ledų).

Paying the bill—Sąskaitos apmokėjimas

The bill, please.
Prašau sąskaitą.

I'll pay.
Aš mokėsiu.

That's my treat.
Aš vaišinu.

I'll pay for the drinks.
Aš sumokėsiu už gėrimus.

We'll pay separately.
Mokėsime atskirai.

Please bring separate bills.
Gal galite atnešti atskiras sąskaitas?

What do I have to pay?
Kiek turiu mokėti?

What do I owe you?
Kiek aš skolingas (m.)/ **skolinga** (f.)?

Twenty Litas and sixty cents.
Dvidešimt litų ir šešiasdešimt centų.

I'll pay with a card.
Mokėsiu kortele.

Complaints and compliments—
Skundai ir pagyrimai

Could you please hurry up? We have been waiting for a long time.
Gal galėtumėte paskubėti? Mes jau seniai laukiame.

It's very good.
Labai skanu.

Excellent!
Puiku!

So so.
Šiaip sau.

It's interesting.
Įdomu.

The soup is cold.
Sriuba atšalusi.

Please bring another setting.
Prašom atnešti dar vieną įrankių komplektą.

Can I order half of the dish?
Ar galiu užsisakyti pusę porcijos?

We need extra glasses.
Mums dar reikia stiklinių.

Can you bring salt and pepper (an ashtray), please?
Prašom atnešti druskos ir pipirų (peleninę).

Please wipe the table.
Prašom nuvalyti stalą.

If you are invited to somebody's house— Jei jus pakvies į svečius

If you are invited to visit somebody in their house for lunch/ dinner/coffee, it is customary to bring a bottle of wine and/or a box of chocolates for the hosts. Lithuanians love flowers, so a bouquet of flowers for the hostess will be a nice gesture on your part as well.

It is likely that you will be invited to visit somebody for a cup of coffee/tea in between lunch and dinner. Expect British-style socializing with coffee/tea, some liquor, biscuits (possibly home-made), and other sweets. Sometimes little sandwiches or salad is also served, but you will never get stuffed as this is not a full meal. Coffee/tea visits usually last two to three hours.

If you are invited to a friend's house for dinner/lunch, dress nicely and do not be overly casual. Overall, Lithuanians tend to be more formal than Americans in their dress. Most people will entertain in nice clothes. For special occasions such as Christmas Eve dinner or a birthday party, men are likely to wear shirts with a tie or even suits.

If you are served a national dish, ask how to eat it or observe the locals. If you start first without knowing exactly how to eat something, you risk an embarrassment.

If you need water, and it is not served with the meal, do not be shy and ask for mineral water. Drinking water from the faucet is safe in Lithuania, yet it might not taste very good.

Entertainment

Sightseeing—Turistiniai objektai

If you do not have a local guide and know nothing about the city, buy some postcards and try to see whatever is on the postcards. You can be almost certain that no interesting object will be left out from the postcards. The postcard will have the name of the building in both Lithuanian and English on the other side. That way, you can even point out the card to a passer by on the street and ask him or her to tell you how to get to that object.

Where is the Tourist Information Center?
Kur Turizmo informacijos centras?

I would like to get the tourist information about the city.
Norėčiau gauti turistinės informacijos apie miestą.

Is the museum open on Monday?
Ar muziejus dirba pirmadienį?

What is the admission fee?
Kiek kainuoja bilietas?

Do you have any student (children) discounts?
Ar taikote nuolaidas studentams (vaikams)?

Do I need to leave my coat (backpack) at the coat check?
Ar turiu palikti savo paltą (kuprinę) rūbinėje?

What time does the museum close (open)?
Kada muziejus uždaromas (atidaromas)?

Can we go to the top?
Ar galime užlipti į viršų?

Can I take photos?
Ar galiu fotografuoti?

I would like a guided tour.
Pageidaučiau ekskursijos su vadovu.

How long will the tour take?
Kiek laiko užtruks ekskursija?

Where can a buy a book about Lithuania (Vilnius)?
Kur galėčiau nusipirkti knygą apie Lietuvą (Vilnių)?

What building is this?
Koks tai pastatas?

What is in this building?
Kas šiame pastate?

Can we go inside?
Ar galime įeiti į vidų?

Can you tell me more about this painter (architect, composer), please?
Gal galėtumėte man plačiau papasakoti apie šį dailininką (architektą, kompozitorių)?

Souvenirs—Suvenyrai

If you decide to buy souvenirs (e.g., amber) from a street vendor, make sure to negotiate the price. Street vendors always tell a bigger price because they expect people to bargain. Seeing that you are a foreigner, they will tell you an even higher price. Therefore, ask your Lithuanian friends to enter into negotiations on your behalf. Ask for a "volume discount" if you are purchasing a few souvenirs from the same vendor.

Some vendors might even accept foreign currency. It is unlikely, however, that they will take credit cards.

You can negotiate a few Litas in some smaller privately owned souvenir shops as well, especially if you are buying more than one item.

Please be advised that amber comes in many colors: yellow, white, blue, green, and even black.

I need some postcards.
Man reikia atvirukų.

I would like to buy some amber.
Norėčiau nusipirkti gintaro dirbinių.

Please show me this bracelet.
Prašom parodyti man šią apyrankę.

Is this amber?
Ar tai gintaras?

What's the price?
Kokia kaina?

How much does it cost?
Kiek kainuoja?

The price is on the back.
Kaina kitoje pusėje.

Is this the price?
Ar tai kaina?

Too much.
Per daug.

Too expensive.
Per brangu.

Will you give me a discount?
Ar nuleisite?

Will you sell me both of these for two hundred Litas?
Ar parduosite abu už du šimtus litų?

Do you have anything smaller (bigger/ cheaper)?
Ar turite ką nors mažesnio (didesnio/ pigesnio)?

Do you have other colors?
Ar yra kitokių spalvų?

Can I pay in Euros (dollars)?
Ar galiu mokėti eurais (doleriais)?

No, thank you.
Ne, ačiū.

Nightlife—Naktinis gyvenimas

What . . . would you recommend?
Kurį . . . jūs rekomenduotumėte?

. . . night club . . .	**. . . naktinį klubą . . .**
. . . movie theater . . .	**. . . kino teatrą . . .**
. . . theater . . .	**. . . teatrą . . .**

Are there any casinos in the city?
Ar mieste veikia kazino?

I would like to see a Lithuanian movie with English subtitles. Is it possible?
Norėčiau pamatyti lietuvišką filmą su angliškais subtitrais. Ar tai įmanoma?

Can I take my children to see this movie (play)?
Ar galiu vestis vaikus į šį filmą (spektaklį)?

Who is starring in this movie (play)?
Kas vaidina šiame filme (spektaklyje)?

I'll need a babysitter for tonight.
Šiam vakarui man reikės auklės.

Two tickets, please.
Prašau du bilietus.

How much is it?
Kiek kainuoja?

Can I pay with a credit card?
Ar galiu mokėti kredito kortele?

Where is the coat check?
Kur rūbinė?

Is this a popular play?
Ar tai populiarus spektaklis?

I want to go to a . . . concert.
Noriu nueiti į . . . koncertą.

. . . jazz . . .	**. . . džiazo . . .**
. . . folk . . .	**. . . folklorinės muzikos . . .**
. . . symphony . . .	**. . . simfoninės muzikos . . .**

What nightclub has the best music?
Kuriame naktiniame klube geriausia muzika?

What kind of music do they play?
Kokia ten muzika?

What's the cover charge?
Kiek kainuoja įėjimas?

For dinner, I want to go to a restaurant that has live music.
Noriu vakarieniauti restorane su gyva muzika.

Sport and recreation—Sportas ir rekreacija

Basketball is by far the most popular sport in Lithuania. Several Lithuanian basketball players have played and still are playing in the NBA. In 2003, Lithuanians became the European Basketball Champions.

What is your favorite sport?
Koks sportas jums labiausiai patinka?

What is your favorite team?
Už kurią komandą jūs sergate?

What team is the strongest?
Kuri komanda yra stipriausia?

Can we go to a basketball game?
Gal galime nueiti į krepšinio rungtynes?

Let's go to a sports bar and watch the game on TV.
Eime į barą pažiūrėti rungtynių per televiziją.

Where can I rent . . .?
Kur galėčiau išsinuomoti. . .?

. . . a bicycle	**. . . dviratį**
. . . rollerblades	**. . . riedučius**

I need a newspaper (the internet) to check the results of the last game.
Man reikia laikraščio (interneto), kad patikrinčiau paskutinių rungtynių rezultatus.

Where can we fish?
Kur galėtume pažvejoti?

Do we need a permit for that?
Ar tam reikia leidimo?

aerobics	**aerobika**
athletics	**atletika**
badminton	**badmintonas**
baseball	**beisbolas**
basketball	**krepšinis**
boxing	**boksas**
cycling	**dviračių sportas**
fencing	**fechtavimas**
football (American)	**amerikietiškas futbolas**
golf	**golfas**
gymnastics	**gimnastika**
hockey	**ledo ritulys**
horse riding	**jojimas**
jogging	**bėgiojimas**
judo	**dziudo**

karate	**karatė**
martial arts	**kovos menai**
rowing	**irklavimas**
rugby	**regbis**
sailing	**buriavimas**
skating	**čiuožimas**
skiing	**slidinėjimas**
soccer	**futbolas**
stadium	**stadionas**
swimming	**plaukimas**
tennis	**tenisas**
volleyball	**tinklinis**
weightlifting	**sunkumų kilnojimas**

At the Zoo—Zoologijos sode

Where are the . . . ?	**Kur . . .?**
. . . giraffes	**. . . žirafos**
. . . polar bears	**. . . baltosios meškos**
. . . hippopotamus	**. . . begemotai**
. . . lions	**. . . liūtai**
. . . tigers	**. . . tigrai**
. . . penguins	**. . . pingvinai**
. . . dolphins	**. . . delfinai**
. . . parrots	**. . . papūgos**

On the beach—Paplūdimyje/ Pliaže

Is the beach far?
Ar paplūdimys/ pliažas toli?

Is it safe to swim here?
Ar čia saugu maudytis?

Is it very deep near the shore?
Ar pakrantėje labai gilu?

Is the water clean (warm)?
Ar vanduo švarus (šiltas)?

Where are the lifeguards?
Kur gelbėtojai?

I want to rent a water bicycle (motorcycle) for one hour.
Noriu išsinuomoti vandens dviratį (motociklą) vienai valandai.

Where can I rent a rowboat?
Kur galėčiau išsinuomoti irklinę valtį?

I need a life-vest.
Man reikia gelbėjimosi liemenės.

I can't swim.
Nemoku plaukti.

Help!
Gelbėkit!

I'm drowning.
Skęstu.

Going to church—Eiti į bažnyčią

Where is the nearest. . .? **Kur artimiausia. . .?**
. . . Catholic church? **. . . katalikų bažnyčia?**
. . . Lutheran church? **. . . liuteronų bažnyčia?**
. . . Russian Ortodox church? **. . . cerkvė?**
. . . synagogue **. . . sinagoga**
. . . mosque **. . . mečetė**

When is the service (mass)?
Kada pamaldos (mišios)?

I would like to talk to . . .
Norėčiau pasikalbėti su . . .

. . . a priest.	**. . . kunigu.**
. . . a minister.	**. . . pastoriumi/ kunigu.**
. . . a rabbi.	**. . . rabinu.**

Shopping—Apsiprekinimas

General information—Bendroji informacija

Most grocery stores in Lithuania open at 8 A.M., and some open as early as 7 A.M. Some grocery stores are open 24 hours a day, yet they tend to be smaller in size. Clothing, electronics, and other stores usually open at 10 A.M. and close at 5 P.M., 6 P.M. or 7 P.M. Most of these stores either are closed on Sundays or work shorter hours. Grocery stores (supermarkets) work seven days a week. They close at 10 P.M. or midnight.

When purchasing alcoholic beverages in larger grocery stores (supermarkets), you will have to pay for them separately in the liquor department. Make sure you hold on to your receipt as you will have to show it at the general check out. There is no strictly observed drinking age in Lithuania; therefore, everyone except children under 18 can buy liquor.

Tobacco products are sold at the check-out and are several times cheaper than in the United States. Minors are carded.

Akcija and *išpardavimas* mean "sale." There is no sales tax added on top of the displayed price because an 18% value-added tax is already included in the price of most goods and services.

Some large grocery stores have children's playgrounds with a babysitter. You can trust them with your child(ren) while you are shopping at the store or the mall. Some large grocery stores have a cafeteria or a pizzeria inside. There are also public restrooms in the large stores. Some large stores have a shopping mall (*prekybos pasažas*) nearby.

Some pharmacies are open 24 hours a day. They are called *budinti vaistinė*. All other pharmacies have a list of these 24–7 pharmacies and their addresses displayed at the entrance.

Most towns have farmers' markets where you can buy fresh fruit and vegetables at lower prices than in the stores. You can sharpen your bargaining skills at the market as it is a customary practice to bargain here. The biggest selection is in the mornings. Wednesdays, Fridays, and Saturdays are known as *turgaus dienos* (market days) because they attract the largest number of sellers and buyers. Farmer's markets are closed on Mondays.

Buying groceries— Maisto produktų pirkimas

Is there a children's playground in this store?
Ar šioje parduotuvėje yra vaikų žaidimų kambarys?

I would like some of this salad, please.
Prašau šių salotų.

The smallest (largest) container, please.
Prašyčiau mažiausią (didžiausią) indelį.

Can you slice this bread, please?
Gal galėtumėte suraikyti šią duoną?

I can't find the expiration date on the package.
Nerandu galiojimo laiko ant pakuotės.

Where are canned peas, please?
Atsiprašau, kur konservuoti žirneliai?

Is this fresh?
Ar tai šviežia?

Is this product made in Lithuania?
Ar šis produktas pagamintas Lietuvoje?

Do you have a city map, please?
Ar turite miesto žemėlapių?

Do you take credit cards?
Ar galiu mokėti kortele?

Do you have any 1% milk?
Ar turite vieno procento riebumo pieno?

A pack of Marlboro's please.
Prašau pakelį Marlboro.

At the drugstore—Vaistinėje

I need something for . . . , please.
Man reikia vaistų nuo . . .

. . . a headache	**. . . galvos skausmo.**
. . . a cold	**. . . peršalimo.**
. . . a sore throat	**. . . gerklės.**
. . . a cough	**. . . kosulio.**
. . . a toothache	**. . . danties skausmo.**
. . . an upset stomach	**. . . nuo skrandžio.**
. . . diarrhea	**. . . viduriavimo.**
. . . sunburn	**. . . nudegimo saulėje.**
. . . a high blood pressure	**. . . aukšto kraujo spaudimo.**

I feel nauseaous.
Mane pykina.

I need some sunblock lotion, please.
Man reikia losjono, apsaugančio nuo saulės.

Do I need a prescription?
Ar reikia recepto?

Do I take this medication before or after the meal?
Ar šiuos vaistus gerti prieš ar po valgio?

How many and how often?
Kiek šių vaistų gerti ir kada?

I need some (childrens') vitamins.
Man reikia vitaminų (vaikams).

after-shave	**kremas po skutimosi**
aspirin	**aspirinas**
band-aid	**pleistras**
birth control pills	**kontraceptinės tabletės**
cleansing lotion	**veido valymo pienelis**
combs	**šukos**
condom	**prezervatyvas**
cotton pads	**vatelės**
deodorant	**dezodorantas**
eau de Cologne	**odekolonas**
eye shadow	**šešėliai akims**
hair spray	**plaukų lakas**
hand cream	**rankų kremas**
insect repellant	**vabzdžius baidantis kremas**
lipstick	**lūpdažis**
mascara	**blakstienų tušas**
mouthwash	**burnos skalavimo skystis**
nail file	**dildė**
nail polish	**nagų lakas**
nail polish remover	**nagų lako valiklis**
needle	**adata**
painkiller	**analgetikas, vaistai nuo skausmo**
perfume	**kvepalai**
powder	**pudra**
razorblades	**skutimosi peiliukai**
sanitary pads	**higieniniai įklotai**
self tanning lotion	**dirbtinio įdegio kremas**
shampoo	**šampūnas**
shaving cream	**skutimosi kremas**
skin moisturizer	**drėkinamasis kremas**
soap	**muilas**

tampon	**tamponas**
thread	**siūlas**
toothbrush	**dantų šepetėlis**
toothpaste	**dantų pasta**

Shopping for clothes and shoes—Drabužiai ir avalynė

Do you have a larger (smaller) size (shoes, clothing)?
Gal turite didesnio (mažesnio) dydžio (batus, drabužius)?

Do you have other colors?
Ar turite kitų spalvų?

I don't know European sizes.
Nežinau europietiškų dydžių.

No, thanks. I am just looking.
Ne, ačiū. Aš tik žiūrinėju.

It's too narrow (wide, short, long).
Per siaura (platu, trumpa, ilga).

The heels are too high (low).
Kulnai per aukšti (žemi).

I like the shoes (dress) in the window.
Man patinka batai (suknelė) vitrinoje.

Do you have that in my size?
Ar yra mano dydžio?

Where are the fitting rooms?
Kur matavimosi kabinos?

I'd like to try this on.
Norėčiau tai pasimatuoti.

It did not fit me.
Man netiko.

Is it dry clean only?
Ar tai sauso valymo drabužis?

Will it shrink after washing?
Ar po skalbimo susitrauks?

Where can I buy a hat?
Kur galėčiau nusipirkti skrybėlę?

Do you take credit cards?
Ar galiu mokėti kredito kortele?

Will I be able to return (exchange) the purchase if I save the receipt and the tag?
Ar pirkinį galėsiu grąžinti (apkeisti), jei išsaugosiu kasos kvitą ir etiketę?

bracelet **apyrankė**
beads **karoliai**
belt **diržas**
blouse **palaidinė, palaidinukė**
boots **batai**
bra **liemenėlė**
brouch **segė**
button **saga**
cardigan **megztinis**
clothes **rūbai, drabužiai**
coat **paltas**
curdoray **velvetas**
denim **džinsinis audinys**
dress **suknelė**
earrings **auskarai**
fur **kailis**
gloves **pirštinės**
hat **skrybėlė**
jacket **švarkas**

jeans **džinsai**
lace **gipiūras**
leather **oda**
linen **linas**
necklace **vėrinys**
nightgown **naktiniai marškiniai**
pajamas **pižama**
panties **apatinės kelnaitės**
pants **kelnės**
pantyhose **kojinės**
pendant **pakabukas**
purse **rankinė, rankinukas**
raincoat **lietpaltis**
sandals **basutės**
scarf **šalikas, šalikėlis, skarelė**
shirt **marškiniai** (colored)**, baltiniai** (white)
shoes **batai**
shorts **šortai, trumpos kelnės**
silk **šilkas**
skirt **sijonas**
slip **apatinukas**
slippers **šlepetės**
socks **puskojinės**
stockings **kojinės**
suede **zomša**
suit (men's) **kostiumas**
suit (women's) **kostiumėlis**
sweater **megztinis**
swimsuit **maudymosi kostiumėlis**
T-shirt **marškinėliai**
tie **kaklaraištis**
umbrella **skėtis**
underwear **apatiniai (drabužiai)**
velvet **aksomas**
wallet **piniginė**
watch **laikrodis**
wool **vilna**
zipper **užtrauktukas**

open	**atidaryta**
closed	**uždaryta**
price	**kaina**

Shopping at the market—Pirkimas turguje

At the market, you can buy anything: fruit, vegetables, chocolate, meat, fish, clothes, shoes, flowers, electronics, etc. Sellers expect you to bargain. If you are concerned about brand authenticity and product quality, it is best to buy clothes, shoes, and other goods at regular stores and boutiques. Fruit and vegetables, on the other hand, are often better at the market than they are in the stores. Besides, at the market, you can get a greater variety and lower prices. Many farmers will let you taste their fruit and vegetables before you make a purchase.

Wednesdays Fridays, and Saturdays are known as *turgaus dienos* (market days). There are more sellers, especially farmers, on those days. Markets are closed on Mondays. On other days, they are open from approximately 7 A.M. to 4 P.M.

How much (for a kilogram)?
Kiek (už kilogramą)?

One kilogram of tomatoes and two cucumbers, please.
Prašau kilogramą pomidorų ir du agurkus.

Please give me this one.
Prašau, duokit man šitą.

That is too expensive.
Per brangu.

It is cheaper over there.
Ten pigiau.

Will you sell it to me?
Ar parduosite?

Is it fresh?
Ar šviežia?

Can I try?
Ar galiu paragauti?

Buying from a street vendor—Pirkimas iš gatvės prekybininkų

On a warm summer day, you will see an ice-cream seller on almost every corner of a town. In larger cities and seaside resorts, you will also encounter amber artists, painters, and people who sell sunglasses and souvenirs. You can negotiate the price with all of these vendors, except for the ice-cream sellers.

Do you have any strawberry (vanilla, coffee, caramel, chocolate, banana) ice-cream?
Ar turite braškinių (vanilinių, kavos, karamelinių, šokoladinių, bananinių) ledų?

Which tastes the best?
Kurie skaniausi?

Is this a Lithuanian ice-cream?
Ar tai lietuviški ledai?

Two please.
Prašau dvi porcijas.

Is that your painting (work)?
Ar tai jūsų paveikslas (darbas)?

Is this amber (silver, gold)?
Ar tai gintaras (sidabras, auksas)?

What's the price?
Kokia kaina?

That is too expensive.
Per brangu.

Will you sell it for less?
Ar parduotumėte pigiau?/ Ar nuleistumėte kainą?

What if I buy both?
O jei pirksiu abu (m.)/ **abi** (f.)?

At a photo shop— Fotografijos reikmenų parduotuvėje

A 24 (36) exposure roll of film, please.
Prašau dvidešimt keturių (trisdešimt šešių) kadrų fotojuostą.

A black-and-white film, please.
Prašau nespalvotą fotojuostą.

Do you have any disposable cameras?
Ar yra vienkartinių fotoaparatų?

Can you develop this film today and make pictures, please?
Ar šiandien galėtumėte išryškinti šią juostą ir padaryti nuotraukas?

When will it be ready?
Kada galiu atsiimti?

How much will it cost?
Kiek kainuos?

Make reprints of these photos, please.
Prašau papildomai padaryti šias nuotraukas.

I would like this photo enlarged.
Norėčiau, kad išdidintumėte šią nuotrauką.

I am here to pick up my photos.
Atėjau atsiimti nuotraukų.

Do you have batteries for this camera?
Ar yra elementų/ baterijų šiam aparatui?

Camera repairs—Foto aparato taisymas

Where can I get my camera repaired?
Kur pataisytų mano fotoaparatą?

The camera broke down.
Fotoaparatas sugedo.

Something is wrong with my camera.
Kažkas atsitiko mano fotoaparatui.

The flash is not working.
Neveikia blykstė.

The film seems to be stuck.
Atrodo, užsikirto juosta.

At the hairdresser's—Kirpykloje

Unlike in the American salons, 20% tips are not required in Lithuanian salons. A 3–5 Litas tip is sufficient if your haircut/color costs between 12 and 50 Litas.

Can you recommend a good hairsalon, please?
Gal galėtumėte rekomenduoti gerą kirpyklą?

Who is the best stylist here?
Kuris (m.)/ **kuri** (f.) **stilistas** (m.)/ **stilistė** (f.) **geriausias** (m.)/ **geriausia** (f.)**?**

What are your work hours?
Kokios jūsų darbo valandos?

Can I make an appointment for today (tomorrow, Friday)?
Ar galiu užsirašyti šiai dienai (rytdienai, penktadieniui)?

I would like a haircut, please.
Norėčiau apsikirpti.

My last haircut was a month ago.
Paskutinį kartą kirpausi prieš mėnesį.

I just want a trim.
Noriu tik pakirpti plaukus.

At a beauty parlor/spa—Grožio salone

Where is the nearest (good) beauty salon?
Kur artimiausias (geras) grožio salonas?

I would like . . .
Norėčiau . . .

. . . a (French) manicure.
. . . (prancūziško) manikiūro.

. . . a (French) pedicure.
. . . (prancūziško) pedikiūro.

. . . a polish change.
. . . tik perlakuoti nagus.

. . . a massage.
. . . masažo.

. . . a (bikini, leg, underarm, upper lip) wax.
. . . kad pašalintumėte (bikinio srities, kojų, pažastų, viršutinės lūpos) plaukus vašku.

. . . a face mask.
. . . veido kaukės.

. . . a professional make-up.
. . . profesionalaus makijažo.

Is there a tanning salon near by?
Ar netoliese yra soliariumas?

I like this color.
Man patinka ši spalva.

Laundry and dry cleaning— Skalbykla ir sausas valymas

Where is the nearest laundromat?
Kur artimiausia skalbykla?

Please wash and press this.
Prašau tai išskalbti ir išlyginti.

Is there a dry cleaner near by?
Ar netoliese yra sauso valymo įmonė?

Please clean these (blood, oil, coffee, wine) stains.
Prašau išvalyti šias (kraujo, riebalų, kavos, vyno) dėmes.

When can I pick this up?
Kada galiu atsiimti?

Can you do it earlier, please?
Gal būtų galima anksčiau?

How much will I have to pay?
Kiek reikės mokėti?

At the post office—Pašte

Mailboxes in Lithuania are painted yellow. Stamps are sold at the post offices and at *Lietuvos spauda* kiosks. It costs less to send a postcard than a letter.

Where is the nearest post office?
Kur artimiausias paštas?

When is it open?
Kada jis atidarytas?

Where is a mailbox?
Kur pašto dėžutė?

I need . . .
Man reikia . . .

. . . some postcard.
. . . atvirukų.

. . . (overseas) stamps.
. . . pašto ženklų (oro paštu).

. . . some (stamped) envelopes.
. . . vokų (su pašto ženklais).

How much does it cost?
Kiek kainuoja?

How much is a postcard (letter) stamp to the United States?
Kiek kainuoja pašto ženklas atvirukui (laiškui) į Jungtines Valstijas?

I would like to send this package air mail, please.
Norėčiau išsiųsti šį siuntinį oro paštu.

I would like to register (insure) it as well.
Norėčiau jį dar ir registruoti (apdrausti).

When will it arrive?
Kada jis pasieks adresatą?

What is my total?
Kiek turiu mokėti iš viso?

Do you take credit cards?
Ar galiu mokėti kredito kortele?

At a newsstand—Spaudos kioskas

Do you have any newspapers (magazines) in English?
Ar turite laikraščių (žurnalų) anglų kalba?

A small bottle of mineral water, please.
Prašau mažą buteliuką mineralinio.

A pack of cigarettes (chewing gum), please.
Prašau pakelį cigarečių (kramtomosios gumos).

A lighter (a box of matches), please.
Prašau žiebtuvėlį (dėžutę degtukų).

Do you have any tourist publications (postcards)?
Ar turite leidinių turistams (atvirukų)?

I need a city (road) map, please.
Man reikia miesto (kelių) žemėlapio.

A phone card (a pen, some notepaper), please.
Prašau taksofono kortelę (rašiklį, popieriaus užrašams).

A bus (trolley) ticket, please.
Prašau autobuso (troleibuso) bilietą.

Communications

Using the telephone—Naudojantis telefonu

You can either call from your hotel room or a payphone. To call from a payphone, you will need to purchase a phone card at any *Lietuvos Spauda* kiosk or some large supermarkets (e.g., *Iki*). They come in various denominations (e.g., 50, 75, and 100 credits (units)). If calling abroad, buy a 100 unit card. Most payphones booths have area codes and calling instructions in English.

If you are planning to stay in Lithuania for an extended period of time, consider renting a cell phone and buying cell phone cards. Most Lithuanians, especially in cities, own a cell phone. However, it is very expensive to call a cell phone from a payphone or a regular phone. On the other hand, it is relatively cheap to make a cell phone-to-cell phone calls. Unlike in the United States, cell phone owners do not pay for incoming calls. Another piece of good news is that for overseas callers (e.g. your relatives or business partners in the United States) it usually costs the same whether they dial a regular number or a cell phone number in Lithuania.

If you call the US or Canada from Lithuania, dial 00-1 + your party's number. When calling UK dial 00-44 + the number. To reach Australia, dial 00-61 + the number.

If you have questions about phone services/cost or need dialing information, call 117, toll free. If you need somebody's phone number and/or address, call the information at 118 (you will be charged for this call).

If you want to make a collect call (*pokalbis kito sąskaita*), dial 8-191 and tell the operator your name and the number you want to call.

Please bear in mind that numbers that begin with 8-800 are toll free as are the following numbers: 01 (fire), 02 (police), 03 (medical emergency), and 04 (gas leak).

I would like a 100 credit phone card, please.
Prašau šimto kreditų taksofono kortelę.

Where is the nearest payphone?
Kur artimiausias taksofonas?

Do I need to dial anything else before I dial this number?
Ar, prieš surenkant šį numerį, reikia dar ką nors rinkti?

I would like to rent a cell phone for one month (two weeks).
Norėčiau išsinuomoti mobilųjį telefoną vienam mėnesiui (dviem savaitėms).

Hello. May I speak to Mr. Laurinaitis, please?
Laba diena. Atsiprašau, gal galėčiau pasikalbėti su ponu Laurinaičiu?

May I leave a message?
Gal galėčiau palikti žinutę?

Please tell him (her) that Mr. Smith called.
Prašau pasakyti jam (jai), kad skambino ponas Smitas.

My number is . . .
Mano numeris . . .

My name is Andrew. I want to make a collect call to this number . . .
Mano vardas Andrew. Noriu paskambinti kito sąskaita šiuo numeriu . . .

It's urgent (very important).
Tai skubu (labai svarbu).

Excuse me, how do I call the United States?
Atsiprašau, kaip paskambinti į Jungtines Valstijas?

How much does one minute to the United States cost?
Kiek kainuoja viena pokalbio į Jungtines Valstijas minutė?

E-mail—Elektroninis paštas

Where is the nearest internet café?
Kur artimiausia interneto kavinė?

How much do you charge per hour?
Kiek kainuoja valanda?

I would like to check my e-mail.
Norėčiau pasitikrinti savo elektroninį paštą.

This computer is too slow.
Šis kompiuteris per lėtas.

I need a faster one.
Man reikia greitesnio.

Can I print a couple of pages?
Ar galiu atsispausdinti porą puslapių?

What do you charge per page?
Kokia vieno puslapio kaina?

What do I have to pay?
Kiek turiu mokėti?

Health

Health problems—Sveikatos problemos

Make sure you have health insurance coverage when entering Lithuania. Lithuanian hospitals will offer only the minimal emergency assistance free of charge. You or your insurance provider will be charged for everything else.

In case of medical emergency, call 03, toll free.

ache	**skausmas**
allergy	**alergija**
ambulance	**greitoji pagalba**
antibiotics	**antibiotikai**
appendicitis	**apendicitas**
asthma	**astma**
cold	**peršalimas**
cough	**kosulys**
doctor	**gydytojas** (m.)/ **gydytoja** (f.)
drugs	**vaistai**
fracture	**lūžis**
health	**sveikata**
healthy	**sveikas** (m.)/ **sveika** (f.)
heart attack	**infarktas**
hospital	**ligoninė**
indigestion	**virškinimo sutrikimas**
infection	**infekcija**
injection	**injekcija**
medicine	**vaistai**
nurse	**seselė**
pain	**skausmas**
patient	**pacientas** (m.)/ **pacientė** (f.)
pneumonia	**plaučių uždegimas**
prescription	**receptas**
stroke	**insultas**
surgeon	**chirurgas** (m.)/ **chirurgė** (f.)
swollen	**patinęs** (m.)/ **patinusi** (f.)
temperature	**temperatūra**

thermometer	**termometras**
treatment	**gydymas**
wound	**žaizda**

Can you recommend a good doctor, please?
Gal galite rekomenduoti gerą gydytoją?

I am ill.
Sergu.

I don't feel well.
Blogai jaučiuosi.

I feel nauseous.
Mane pykina.

I have a fever.
Turiu temperatūros.

I have . . .	**Man skauda . . .**
. . . a sore throat.	**. . . gerklę.**
. . . a headache.	**. . . galvą.**

I am afraid that I broke my arm (finger, toe, leg).
Bijau, kad man lūžo ranka (pirštas, kojos pirštas, koja).

I've cut myself.
Įsipjoviau.

I have a food poisoning.
Apsinuodijau maistu.

I have an allergy.
Man alergija.

I am coughing.
Kosčiu.

I have asthma.
Sergu astma.

I have the flu.
Gripuoju.

My son (daughter) burned himself/ herself with boiling water.
Mano sūnus (dukra) apsiplikino verdančiu vandeniu.

He (she) has been badly burned in the sun.
Jis (ji) labai nudegė saulėje.

It may be a sunstroke.
Tai gali būti saulės smūgis.

He (she) has been bitten (stung) by a dog (snake, insect, bee).
Jam (jai) įkando (įgėlė) šuo (gyvatė, vabalas, bitė).

I am (he/ she is) allergic to penicillin.
Aš (jis/ ji) alergiškas (m.)/ **alergiška** (f.) **penicilinui.**

My child has diarrhea.
Mano vaikas viduriuoja.

He (she) is vomiting.
Jis (ji) vemia.

I have a rash.
Mane išbėrė.

I feel dizzy.
Man silpna. / Man svaigsta galva.

I have constipation.
Man užkietėjo viduriai.

I am diabetic.
Aš diabetikas (m.)/ **diabetikė** (f.).

I have a thyroid problem.
Man struma.

I have high blood pressure.
Mano aukštas kraujo spaudimas.

I am taking these drugs.
Vartoju šiuos vaistus.

I am running out of these drugs and need a new prescription.
Baigiasi šie vaistai. Norėčiau gauti naują receptą.

I am on the pill.
Vartoju kontraceptines tabletes.

I am pregnant.
Esu nėščia. / Laukiuosi.

I am having my period.
Sergu mėnesinėmis.

I cannot sleep (fall asleep).
Negaliu miegoti (užmigti).

It is painful to . . . **Skauda, . . .**
. . . swallow. **. . . kai riju.**
. . . breathe. **. . . kai kvėpuoju.**
. . . walk. **. . . kai vaikštau.**
. . . move. **. . . kai pajudu.**

He (she) is unconscious.
Jis (ji) be sąmonės.

He (she) fainted.
Jis (ji) apalpo.

At the hospital—Ligoninėje

What hospital is the best in town?
Kuri ligoninė geriausia mieste?

What hospital is this?
Kokia čia ligoninė?

Does anybody here speak English?
Ar kas nors čia kalba angliškai?

How long will I have to stay at the hospital?
Kiek laiko turėsiu praleisti ligoninėje?

I would like to be placed in a single room, please.
Norėčiau būti paguldytas (m.)/ **paguldyta** (f.) **į vienvietę palatą.**

What's my diagnosis?
Kokia mano diagnozė?

Will I (he, she) need a surgery?
Ar man (jam, jai) reikės operacijos?

When?
Kada?

My blood group is . . .
Mano kraujo grupė yra . . .

Will you be my doctor?
Ar jūs būsite mano gydytojas (m.)/ **gydytoja** (f.)?

What can I eat (drink)?
Ką galiu valgyti (gerti)?

Do I need antibiotics?
Ar man reikia antibiotikų?

Is everything ok with my insurance?
Ar nėra problemų dėl mano draudimo?

Parts of the body—Kūno dalys

ankle	**kulkšnis**
arm	**ranka**
back	**nugara**
bladder	**šlapimo pūslė**
blood	**kraujas**
bone	**kaulas**
brains	**smegenys**
breast	**krūtis**
cheek	**skruostas**
chest	**krūtinė**
chin	**smakras**
ear	**ausis**
eardrum	**ausies būgnelis**
elbow	**alkūnė**
eye	**akis**
eyebrows	**antakiai**
eyelashes	**blakstienos**
face	**veidas**
finger	**pirštas**
foot	**pėda**
forehead	**kakta**
gums	**dantenos**
hand	**ranka, plaštaka**
hair	**plaukai**
head	**galva**
heart	**širdis**
joint	**sąnarys**
intestines	**žarnynas**
kidney	**inkstas**
knee	**kelis**
leg	**koja**
lips	**lūpos**
liver	**kepenys**
lungs	**plaučiai**
mouth	**burna**
muscle	**raumuo**
nail	**nagas**

neck	**kaklas**
nerves	**nervai**
nose	**nosis**
rib	**šonkaulis**
shoulder	**petys**
side	**šonas**
skin	**oda**
skull	**kaukolė**
stomach	**skrandis; pilvas**
throat	**gerklė**
tongue	**liežuvis**
tooth	**dantis**
vertebra	**stuburas**
wrist	**riešas**

At the dentist's—Pas stomatologą

You may consider going to a dentist while in Lithuania to save some money. Lithuanian dentists are usually very qualified, operate with new technology, and charge several times less than their American counterparts. For example, whereas in the United States a crown costs about $500, in Lithuania it costs only about 400 Litas (e.g., less than $120).

Can you recommend a good dentist, please?
Gal galite rekomenduoti gerą dantų gydytoją?

I have a toothache.
Man skauda dantį.

My filling came out.
Iškrito plomba.

Something happened to my crown.
Kažkas atsitiko karūnėlei.

It seems to be swollen here.
Atrodo, kad čia patinę.

It hurts.
Skauda.

Will you have to drill?
Ar gręšite?

Will it hurt?
Ar skaudės?

Will you give me anesthetics?
Ar suleisite nuskausminamųjų?

Will you take this tooth out?
Ar ištrauksite šį dantį?

Will I need a crown?
Ar man reikės karūnėlės?

When can I eat?
Kada galėsiu valgyti?

How much do I have to pay?
Kiek turiu mokėti?

At a health resort/spa —Kurorte

I would like a daily massage, please.
Kasdien norėčiau masažo.

I would like a mud (mineral) bath, please.
Pageidaučiau purvo (mineralinės) vonios.

I would like some procedures that would help me loose weight, please.
Pageidaučiau procedūrų, kurios padėtų atsikratyti viršsvorio.

Will you prescribe me a diet?
Ar paskirsite dietą?

How many times a day do I have to drink mineral water?
Kiek kartų per dieną turiu gerti mineralinį vandenį?

Should I drink it before or after the meal?
Ar gerti prieš ar po valgio?

What other procedures would you recommend?
Kokias dar procedūras rekomenduotumėte?

How much does this procedure cost?
Kiek kainuoja ši procedūra?

Is there . . . in this health resort?
Ar šiame kurorte yra . . .

. . . a tanning salon . . .	**. . . soliariumas?**
. . . a golf course . . .	**. . . golfo aikštynas?**

Where can I rent a bicycle, please?
Kur galėčiau išsinuomoti dviratį?

Useful Words

Numbers—Skaičiai

0	**nulis**
1	**vienas**
2	**du**
3	**trys**
4	**keturi**
5	**penki**
6	**šeši**
7	**septyni**
8	**aštuoni**
9	**devyni**
10	**dešimt**
11	**vienuolika**
12	**dvylika**
13	**trylika**
14	**keturiolika**
15	**penkiolika**
16	**šešiolika**
17	**septyniolika**
18	**aštuoniolika**
19	**devyniolika**
20	**dvidešimt**
21	**dvidešimt vienas**
22	**dvidešimt du**
30	**trisdešimt**
40	**keturiasdešimt**
50	**penkiasdešimt**
60	**šešiasdešimt**
70	**septyniasdešimt**
80	**aštuoniasdešimt**
90	**devyniasdešimt**
100	**šimtas**
101	**šimtas vienas**
200	**du šimtai**
300	**trys šimtai**

400	**keturi šimtai**
500	**penki šimtai**
600	**šeši šimtai**
700	**septyni šimtai**
800	**aštuoni šimtai**
900	**devyni šimtai**
1000	**tūkstantis**
2000	**du tūkstančiai**
10,000	**dešimt tūkstančių**
500,000	**penki šimtai tūkstančių**
1,000,000	**milijonas**
5,000,000	**penki milijonai**
1,000,000,000	**milijardas**

Ordinal nubers—Kelintiniai skaitvardžiai

1st	**pirmas** (m.)/ **pirma** (f.)
2nd	**antras** (m.)/ **antra** (f.)
3rd	**trečias** (m.)/ **trečia** (f.)
4th	**ketvirtas** (m.)/ **ketvirta** (f.)
5th	**penktas** (m.)/ **penkta** (f.)
6th	**šeštas** (m.)/ **šešta** (f.)
7th	**septintas** (m.)/ **septinta** (f.)
8th	**aštuntas**/ **aštunta** (f.)
9th	**devintas** (m.)/ **devinta** (f.)
10th	**dešimtas** (m.)/ **dešimta** (f.)
nth	**entasis** (m.)/ **entoji** (f.)

Fractions and percentages—Trupmenos ir procentai

½	**viena antroji**
a half	**pusė**
50%	**penkiasdešimt procentų**
¼	**viena ketvirtoji**
a quarter	**ketvirtadalis**

25%	**dvidešimt penki procentai**
⅓	**viena trečioji**
a third	**trečdalis**
two thirds	**du trečdaliai**
1%	**vienas procentas**
2%	**du procentai**
10%	**dešimt procentų**
100%	**šimtas procentų**

Measures—Matavimo vienetai

1 mile = 1.609 kilometer (km)
mylia, kilometras
1 kilometer = 0.621 miles
kilometras, mylia

1 foot = 0.305 meter (m)
pėda, metras
1 meter = 39.4 inches
metras, colis

1 inch = 2.54 centimeters (cm)
colis, centimetras
1 centimeter = 0.39 inch
centimetras, colis

1 US gallon = 3.78 liters (L)
galonas, litras
1 liter = 0.26 gallon = 1.05 liquid quart
litras, galonas, kvorta

1 pound = 454 grams = 0.45 kg
svaras, gramas, kilogramas
1 kilogram = 2.2. pounds
kilogramas, svaras

Days of the Week—Savaitės dienos

In Lithuania, Monday (*Pirmadienis*) is the first day of the week.

Monday	**pirmadienis**
Tuesday	**antradienis**
Wednesday	**trečiadienis**
Thursday	**ketvirtadienis**
Friday	**penktadienis**
Saturday	**šeštadienis**
Sunday	**sekmadienis**

Months—Mėnesiai

January	**sausis**
February	**vasaris**
March	**kovas**
April	**balandis**
May	**gegužė**
June	**birželis**
July	**liepa**
August	**rugpjūtis**
September	**rugsėjis**
October	**spalis**
November	**lapkritis**
December	**gruodis**

Dates—Datos

Lithuanians first write the year, then the month, and finally the day. For example, *2002 12 31, 2002 m. gruodžio mėn. 31 d.* (i.e., December 31, 2002).

2003	**du tūkstančiai tretieji (metai)**
1978	**tūkstantis devyni šimtai septyniasdešimt aštuntieji (metai)**

16th century	**šešioliktasis amžius**
20th century	**dvidešimtasis amžius**
in 21st century	**dvidešimt pirmajame amžiuje**

Seasons—Metų laikai

Spring	**pavasaris**
In spring	**pavasarį**
Summer	**vasara**
In summer	**vasarą**
Fall/Atumn	**ruduo**
In fall/autumn	**rudenį**
Winter	**žiema**
In winter	**žiemą**

Public holidays—Šventės

January 1
New Year's Day **Naujieji Metai**

January 13
Defenders of Freedom Day **Laisvės gynėjų diena**

February 14
Valentine's Day **Valentino diena**

February 16
Independence Day **Lietuvos Valstybės Atkūrimo diena**

March 8
International Woman's Day **Tarptautinė moters diena**

March 11
Restoration of Lithuania's **Lietuvos Nepriklausomybės Atkūrimo diena**

Easter **šv. Velykos**

May 1
International Labor Day **Tarptautinė darbo diena**

1st Sunday (May)	
Mother's Day	**Motinos diena**
1st Sunday (June)	
Father's Day	**Tėvo diena**
June 14	
Day of Mourning & Hope	**Gedulo ir Vilties diena**
July 6	
Crowning of Mindaugas (Day of Statehood)	**Mindaugo karūnavimo (Valstybės diena)**
August 15	
Feast of the Assumption	**Žolinė**
November 1	
All Saints' Day	**Visų šventųjų diena**
December 24	
Christmas Eve	**Kūčios**
December 25	
Christmas	**šv. Kalėdos**

Colors—Spalvos

black	**juoda**
blue	**mėlyna**
brown	**ruda**
gold	**auksinė**
gray	**pilka**
green	**žalia**
ivory	**dramblio kaulo**
light blue	**žydra**
orange	**oranžinė**
pink	**rausva/ rožinė**
purple	**violetinė**
red	**raudona**

silver	**sidabrinė**
white	**balta**
yellow	**geltona**

Common adjectives—Būdvardžiai

bad	**blogas** (m.)/ **bloga** (f.)
beautiful	**gražus** (m.)/ **graži** (f.)
big	**didelis** (m.)/ **didelė** (f.)
cheap	**pigus** (m.)/ **pigi** (f.)
cold	**šaltas** (m.)/ **šalta** (f.)
dark	**tamsus** (m.)/ **tamsi** (f.)
difficult	**sunkus** (m.)/ **sunki** (f.)
dry	**sausas** (m.)/ **sausa** (f.)
easy	**lengvas** (m.)/ **lengva** (f.)
expensive	**brangus** (m.)/ **brangi** (f.)
fast	**greitas** (m.)/ **greita** (f.)
fat	**riebus** (m.)/ **riebi** (f.)
good	**geras** (m.)/ **gera** (f.)
guilty	**kaltas** (m.)/ **kalta** (f.)
hard	**kietas** (m.)/ **kieta** (f.)
little	**mažas** (m.)/ **maža** (f.)
long	**ilgas** (m.)/ **ilga** (f.)
new	**naujas** (m.)/ **nauja** (f.)
old	**senas** (m.)/ **sena** (f.)
sharp	**aštrus** (m.)/ **aštri** (f.)
short	**trumpas** (m.)/ **trumpa** (f.)
slow	**lėtas** (m.)/ **lėta** (f.)
small	**mažas** (m.)/ **maža** (f.)
tall	**aukštas** (m.)/ **aukšta** (f.)
ugly	**bjaurus** (m.)/ **bjauri** (f.)
wet	**šlapias** (m.)/ **šlapia** (f.)

Signs and notices—Užrašai ir perspėjimai

akcija	sale
apylanka	detour
apvažiavimas	detour

atidaryta	open
atsargiai!	careful!
atsarginis išėjimas	emergency exit
aukšta įtampa	high-tension current
dažyta	fresh paint
dėmesio!	attention!
eksponatų rankomis neliesti	do not touch (in a museum)
gaisro atveju skambinti . . .	in case of fire, dial . . .
geležinkelio pervaža	railway crossing
greitoji pagalba	emergency (ER)
įeiti draudžiama	no entry
įėjimas	entrance
informacija	information
išėjimas	exit
išnuomojama	for rent
kasa	box office
kelionių agentūra	travel agency
laisva	vacant
laukiamasis	waiting room
maudytis draudžiama	no swimming
moterų tualetas/ M	ladies' room
nerūkyti	no smoking
nuodai	poison
parduodama	for sale
pašaliniams įeiti draudžiama	no unauthorized entry
pietų pertrauka	lunch break
rezervuota	reserved
rūkyti draudžiama	no smoking
stumti	push
tylos!	silence!
traukti	pull
uždaryta	closed
už važiavimą be bilieto bauda 20Lt	for traveling without a ticket a fine 20Lt
vyrų tualetas/ V	men's room
žvejoti draudžiama	no fishing

Emergencies

Toll free numbers: **01** (fire), **02** (police), **03** (ambulance), **04** (gas leak).

Help!	**Gelbėkit!**
Fire!	**Gaisras!**
Catch the thief!	**Laikykit vagį!**
Call the ambulance (the police)	**Kvieskite greitąją (policiją)**

I got robbed.
Mane apiplėšė.

My car got stolen.
Pavogė mano mašiną.

Where is the US (Canadian, British, Australian) Embassy?
Kur Amerikos (Kanados, Didžiosios Britanijos, Australijos) ambasada?